AMERICAN CONSULS
IN THE HOLY LAND
1832–1914

RUTH KARK

AMERICAN CONSULS IN THE HOLY LAND 1832–1914

THE MAGNES PRESS, THE HEBREW UNIVERSITY, JERUSALEM
WAYNE STATE UNIVERSITY PRESS, DETROIT

Library of Congress Cataloging-in-Publication Data

Kark, Ruth.
American consuls in the Holy Land, 1832–1914 / Ruth Kark. — North American ed.
   Includes biographical references (p.354) and index.

   ISBN 0-8143-2523-8

1. Diplomatic and consular service, American — Palestine — History — 19th century. 2. Consuls — United States — History — 19th century. 3. Palestine — History — 1799–1917. 4. Turkey — Foreign relations — United States. 5. United States — Foreign relations —Turkey. I. Title.
JX1706.Z4K37 1994
956.94'03—dc20   93–49878

Printed in Israel
Typesetting: The Jerusalem Publishing House, Jerusalem

CONTENTS

Tables

Figures

Plates

Appendices

ABBREVIATION OF ARCHIVES

ABCFM	American Board of Commissioners for Foreign Missions Archives, Cambridge, Massachusetts, USA
AJ	Anglo-Jewish Archives, Southampton, England
AJHS	American Jewish Historical Society Archives, Waltham, Massachusetts, USA
CMS	Church Missionary Society Archives, Birmingham, England
IM	Israel Museum Photographic Archives, Jerusalem, Israel
ISA	Israel State Archives, Jerusalem, Israel
JNUL	Jewish National and University Library Archives, Jerusalem, Israel
LP	Lambeth Palace Library Archives, London, England
MCZ	Museum of Comparative Zoology Archive, Cambridge, Massachusetts, USA
OSJ	The Order of St. John Archives, London, England
PEF	Palestine Exploration Fund Archives, London, England
PRO	Public Record Office, London, England
NMR	N.M. Rothschild Archives, London, England
SM	Semitic Museum, Cambridge, Massachusetts, USA
TAMA	Tel Aviv Municipal Archives, Tel Aviv, Israel
USNA	United States National Archives, Washington, D.C., USA
YIBZ	Yad Izhak Ben-Zvi Archives, Jerusalem, Israel

PREFACE

This book examines the work and influence of the United States consular service in the years 1832–1914 within the framework of Ottoman Middle East policies in the specific context of the Holy Land. Writing the last chapters at the beginning of 1991 Operation Desert Storm, I was struck by the contrast between America's minimal political and economic interest in the Middle East during the 19th century, and its current overwhelming involvement in the region. A century ago, oil in the form of kerosene was being imported in five-gallon tins to Palestine from the United States, and in 1913, the Standard Oil Company of New York began prospecting for oil around the Dead Sea. A year later, SOCONY acquired seven concessions, with about sixty additional ones under negotiation in the entire region.

Over the years, changes also occurred in the diplomatic and consular representation of the United States. The small consulate in Jerusalem and the consular agencies in Jaffa and Haifa established in the 19th century – which are the subject of this book – have evolved into a large, influential embassy in Tel Aviv, and into a consulate-general with special status, not subject to the American embassy in Israel, in Jerusalem.

Many diplomatic historians have focussed on the foreign policies of the United States at world and regional levels in various periods. They have studied the character, the parts played, and examples of activities of those who formed America's policies at the core in Washington and in important political and economic centers around the globe. The diplomatic historiography of the United States from the end of the 18th century and until World War One has almost totally ignored the consuls; in the rare instances when these were mentioned, they were usually depicted negatively. In effect, however, consuls played important roles from the very inception of the American foreign service.

Some attention has been directed to Palestine and its connections with the Western powers. But here too, few researchers chose to address the relationship between the United States and the Holy Land on cultural and ideological planes or in its economic and political aspects. Other historians who examined the involvement of the European powers and their consular representatives in Palestine in the 19th century, mainly emphasized the relations of the consuls with Jews and did not deal with the consulates as such.

The objective of this study is an in-depth examination of the motivation manner of functioning of American representatives in the peripheral region rather than at the core of the Ottoman Empire or other centers of power. I have sought to understand who these persons were and how they performed their work as consuls, consular agents, and other consular staff members, how they conducted their day-to-day activities, what was the measure of their professionalism, and what was their contribution to the people and the region in which they served, and to their own country. This research takes into account the relevant organizational frameworks of the U.S. foreign service and its policies in the Ottoman Empire against the background of the capitulatory system and extraterritorial rights. It deals with religious and humanitarian considerations in connection with the involvement of the European powers in the Eastern Question and their attempts at intensifying their political and commercial influence in the Middle East.

The period under discussion, 1832–1914, begins with the signing of the Treaty of Amity, Commerce and Navigation of 1830, and the arrival in Constantinople of the first senior American diplomatic representative in 1831. From 1832 onwards, this official appointed subordinate representatives in Turkey, the Levant, Palestine, and Egypt. I have fixed on the year 1914 as the end of this study because the First World War constitutes a turning point in the history of Palestine, even though the relations between the United States and the Ottoman Empire were only broken off on 20 April 1917, after the declaration of war on Germany, Turkey's ally.

This detailed reconstruction of American consular activity in Palestine coincides with a significant period in the modern history of Palestine. During the 19th century, the Holy Land was transformed politically, demographically, socially, economically, and in its map of human settlement. At the same time, from being a region of secondary importance in the Ottoman Empire, Palestine became a focus of attraction and penetration by the European powers and of various representatives of Western civilization. It has determined the geographical limits of this study. The interest of the powers in the Holy Land was not only strategic (especially after the opening of the Suez Canal in 1869) and connected with the future status of the Ottoman Empire, but the country concerned and attracted people from various nations, among them missionaries, visitors (pilgrims, tourists, and researchers), settlers, and consuls. For this reason, this study also looks at the relations between the consuls and the consular agents of the United States and their counterparts of other nations who were active in Palestine, and draws comparisons with U.S. consular services in other parts of the world.

Such facets as the role of consuls relative to extraterritorial privileges (capitulations), the influence of European powers, Western religious and cultural penetration, judicial systems, and technological innovations are considered from American, Ottoman, and local points of view. In attempting to analyze and synthesize I have relied mainly on primary sources found in the United States National Archives, as well as in the British Public Record Office, the Israel State Archives – which include the archives of the German and British consulates in Palestine, and that of Ali Ekrem Bey, one of the Ottoman governors of the Jerusalem district – and in archives at the Universities of Birmingham, Harvard, and several archival collections in Jerusalem and London. I also gained valuable insights from the general literature about the period and from secondary historical sources.

I have made extensive use of case studies to illustrate concepts and principles governing the interaction of the West with the Ottoman Empire. The methodology employed here sheds light on the history and operation of the United States diplomatic and consular core in the Middle East, as well as on the 19th century history and historical geography of the Holy Land. I believe that this material should be of substantive interest to a varied readership – students of United States diplomatic history, Ottoman studies, Middle Eastern affairs, the Holy Land including cultural and religious aspects, and to scholars concerned with historical methods.

The division of this book into six chapters proceeds from a discussion of general background and interpower relations to detailed reconstruction and analysis of United States consular activity in Palestine. After dwelling on the cultural and ideological aspects of the relations between America and the Holy Land, the first chapter clarifies the concept of consul in earlier historical periods and in the present. It examines the growth, crystallization, and reforms in the United States foreign service from the end of the 18th century to the First World War – including the State Department and the consular service – and describes the connection between the American consuls and the capitulations of the Ottoman Empire.

The second chapter traces the development of commercial, political, and consular relations between the United States and the Ottoman Empire that led to the conclusion of agreements in the course of the 19th century, and to the establishment of diplomatic and consular representations in Constantinople and Beirut in the first half of the century. The third chapter considers the development, from 1832, of the consular hierarchial structure, the spatial jurisdiction, and the activity of the consular agencies in Palestine and of the

American consulate at Jerusalem, in relation to the timing, motivation, and sequence of the establishment of consulates by the Western powers in the Holy Land. I have included a description of the interaction and communications of the American representatives with their government, with the Ottoman authorities, and with the other consulates, as well as of the changes effected by modern communication technologies – post and telegraph.

The fourth chapter deals with the consuls themselves, as a group and individually, and examines the manner of their appointment, the conditions and compass of their work, their lifestyle, relative status, different world outlooks, and their extraneous activities in writing, research, and private business. Biographical sketches of the American consuls in Jerusalem, to the extent of available information, are appended at the end of the book. This chapter also looks at the consular employees and attempts a typology of their personalities, and of functions specific to the consulates in the Orient, such as dragomans and kavasses and the connotations inherent in these positions.

In the final and longest chapters are described the gamut of services provided by the consuls and consular agents in civil, legal, economic, and social matters by means of detailed case studies. Considered are the characters, views, and actions of the clients – American settlers belonging to various Christian sects; American Jews and Jewish protégés some of whom laid the foundations for Zionist settlement in the Land of Israel; missionaries, pilgrims, tourists, and researchers who lived in or visited the country; and American businessmen seeking markets for their manufactures in the expanding American economy of the early 20th century. From the consular reports and the voluminous correspondence with Washington, a multifaceted picture emerges of general processes in Palestine – government and politics, population, the economy and commerce, settlement. Despite their selective nature, these documents are highly important sources for the history of American consular activities in Palestine as they are for the study of the country in the 19th century.

Spelling – and transliteration in particular – follows *Webster's Third New International Dictionary*. Arabic, Hebrew, and Turkish terms, such as vali, mutasarrif, kolel, halukkah, sharia, etc. that are listed in the dictionary are not italicized. They are, however, explained in the Glossary at the end of the book. Personal names are rendered as they appear in the documentation, not always consistently or according to the generally accepted transliteration.

*   *   *

It is my privilege to express my gratitude to the many persons who helped me see this work to completion. Special thanks are due to the staffs of the various archives and libraries: to Milton O. Gustafson and Richard T. Gould of the Diplomatic Branch of the United States National Archives; to Paul A. Alsberg and Gilad Livneh at the Israel State Archives; to the late Nathan M. Kaganoff and to Bernard Wax of the American Jewish Historical Society; to Shifra Gordon, Rivka Plesser, and Rafi Weizer of the Jewish National and Hebrew University Library of Jerusalem, and to Karen Sitton of the Bloomfield Library of the Hebrew University; to Nissan Peretz of the Israel Museum; to Rupert Chapman of the Palestine Exploration Fund in London; and to Nitza Rosovsky and Carney Gavin of the Harvard University Semitic Museum. At Harvard I thank also the staffs of the Houghton and Widener Libraries and the Museum of Comparative Zoology. Thanks also, to the librarians and archivists at Birmingham University, the British Library, the Lambeth Palace Library, the Mocatta Library (the previous home of the Anglo-Jewish Archives), N.M. Rothschild, Order of St. John, and the Public Record Office in England; to the Boston Athenæum, Davis Library at the University of North Carolina at Chapel Hill, the Library of Congress and the Library of the United States National Archives in Washington, and the libraries on the UCLA campus. In Israel, I thank the Tel Aviv Municipality Archives and the Yad Izhak Ben-Zvi Library and Archives headed by Yohai Goell and Shimon Rubinstein, and the special collection initiated by Moshe Davis with the help of Rivka Demsky, Ora Zimmer, and Yohai Goell on America-Holy Land relations at the Institute of Contemporary Jewry at the Hebrew University of Jerusalem.

Valuable assistance was rendered to me during the different stages of research by Joseph Glass and by Reuven Amitai, Rhoda Cohen, the late Shimshon Eshel, Daniel Halutzi, Durkas Lapidus Lewis, Uri Palit, Ian Stanfield, Eliyahu Wager, Judy Wisch, and by Yitzhak Wittelson. The cartographer, Tamar Sofer, prepared the maps. Yossi Ben-Artzi, Gideon Hermel, the late Zev Vilnay, Academic Press, Ariel, and Yad Ben-Zvi Publications permitted reproduction of several figures and plates.

I wish to thank Moshe Davis and to Menahem Kaufman who always found the time for advice, criticism, and help; and I very much appreciate the comments and suggestions of Arnold Blumberg, Robert T. Handy, Gershon Greenberg, the late Vivian D. Lipman, Henry Mattox, Jonathan D. Sarna, and Lester Vogel. Nava and Robert D. Mitchell I thank heartily for their warm hospitality in Washington, D.C. The help of Eliyahu Honig and Marlis Roth is also much appreciated.

I am grateful to the America-Holy Land Project at the Institute of Contemporary Jewry of the Hebrew University of Jerusalem, which provided the initial impetus to realise this project through a grant from the Jakob

Blaustein Fund for American Studies. The research upon which this book is based was made possible through the generous assistance of the Kurt Grünwald Fund for the study of the economic and settlement history of Palestine. To these must be added several research grants from the faculties of Humanities and Social Sciences at the Hebrew University. Among these were grants from the James Amzalak, Eshkol, Idelman, and Schein Funds which the financial administrators, Yehudit Avraham and Yehudit Schneid, so effectively and understandingly assisted me in applying to the project. Two half-sabbaticals at Harvard University (the Center for Jewish Studies) and at the Department of Geography of the University of North Carolina at Chapel Hill enabled me to bring the study to its present book form.

Finally, I want to thank Joseph Shadur whose knowledge of the period added to his translation of the manuscript from the Hebrew.

Ruth Kark

Jerusalem, 1993

INTRODUCTION

AMERICA AND THE HOLY LAND – IDEOLOGICAL BACKGROUND

America and the Holy Land – Concepts

The Bible and America as Canaan

The notion of the Holy Land and Jerusalem current in America derived from religious and cultural sentiment. It reflected the importance of religion in American life, and particularly the Protestant tradition associating Anglo-Saxon and Western Christianity with the land of the Bible. From the first days of European settlement in the new continent, the Holy Land held special appeal and fascination. Despite the denominational fragmentation during the Colonial era, which was to intensify in the 19th century, some of the Protestant sects maintained their identity through their particular interpretation of the Scriptures.[1] The Bible greatly influenced the lives of the first American Protestant Christians. They were intimately familiar with every detail of the texts, as well as with the biblical geography of the Land of Israel and the holy places. Copies of the Bible were everywhere to be found. The first work known to be printed in the present area of the United States was the Book of Psalms. It was published in Cambridge, Massachusetts, in 1640, and was referred to as the "Bay Psalm Book" or the "New England Psalm Book," and later as the "New England Version of the Psalms."[2]

It was a utopian concept of the Holy Land, which reflected in part the Christian aspiration to separate itself from places holy to Jews in the "earthly Jerusalem" and to foster the abstract ideal of the Heavenly Jerusalem. America was regarded as the New Canaan. In discussing this tradition Tuchman quotes the early 17th century English Protestant, Samuel Purchas, to the

---

1   Handy, *The Holy Land*, pp.xi-xii.
2   Evans, *American Bibliography,* p.3.

effect that "...the best pilgrimage is the peaceable way of a good conscience to that Jerusalem which is above." Purchas regarded the sanctification of sites as Jewish and having no place in progressive Christianity.[3] Using terms coined by the geographers John Kirkland Wright, Yi Fu Tuan, David Lowenthal, and Kevin Lynch regarding a synthesized concept of the past, religious traditions, and place, Vogel stresses the ambivalence in the attitudes of Americans to the Holy Land and the transference of geo-pietistic sentiment to the new Promised Land, America. The image evoked by the Holy Land was "orientally" romantic and idealized. It tied in with another notion current among the early American settlers, the "myth of the new beginning" – the New Man in the New Eden. Some even feared actual contact with the realities of modern Palestine as threatening their image of an "unchanged Holy Land of ultimate antiquity where age was enhanced by sacredness."[4]

The transposition of such an imaginary perception of the Holy Land to Protestant America permeated much of American culture. Thus, America was the Promised Land settled by the Chosen People, who frequently applied the names Zion, Canaan, and Jerusalem to their new lands and churches.[5] The most striking example of adopting the concepts of Zion and Jerusalem, not only to evoke the past but to symbolize the world to come, is found among the Mormons who hold that there will be two "space-time" capitals of the Kingdom of God on earth: Jerusalem in Israel, and a New Jerusalem in America.[6]

Nearly one thousand of the towns and villages founded by European settlers in America bear biblical names, including those of the patriarchs and matriarchs, tribes of Israel, judges, kings, prophets, and places. The most common ones among the latter are names connected with events or famous persons: names of towns or villages, mountains, rivers, or districts. Most common was the biblical name of Jerusalem – Salem – which in various combinations was given to sixty-six settlements. Twenty-five places were named Zion. Other common names were Palestine (9), Akron or Ekron (11), Canaan (12), Carmel (13), Tabor and Sharon (16), Jordan (18), Goshen (19),

---

3   Tuchman, *Bible and Sword,* p.104.

4   Vogel, "Zion as Place," pp.383–409. The term geo-piety denotes the complex relationship between earth, land, nation, and reverence and attachment to one's family, homeland, and gods.

5   Handy, "Studies," pp.288–93; Greenberg, "America-Holy Land," pp.50–62.

6   Madsen, "The Mormon Attitude," pp.1–3; Greenberg, *Holy Land and Religious America*, pp.14–40.

Hebron (21), and Bethel (22).[7] Very many American personal names were biblical. In this context may be mentioned the popular theory in the 17th and 18th centuries that considered the American Indians as representing the ten lost tribes of Israel.[8]

The interesting research of Carlos Baker shows also the influence of the Old Testament on American fiction – mainly of the 19th and the early 20th centuries – as expressed in the work of Hawthorne, Melville, Mark Twain, and others, who in turn influenced their reading public. Many American writers used metaphors of biblical origin. The outstanding allegorical image was of settlers in Colonial America of the 17th and 18th centuries coming to the Promised Land to clear the forests, to cultivate, and to plant as a crowning act in God's providential plan.[9] During the first half of the 19th century, the painters Washington Allstone, Edward Hicks, and others drew on Old Testament passages for their subjects – the prophets Elisha and Elijah, Rebecca, Belshazzar, and the Peaceable Kingdom.

Leading political figures such as Thomas Jefferson and Benjamin Franklin were influenced by this imagery. In their search for a suitable design for the Great Seal of the United States, they chose the subject of the Children of Israel led by a cloud by day and a pillar of fire by night on their way to the Promised Land. The establishment of the American republic was equated with biblical prophecy.[10]

The post-civil war years brought about a change in American religious attitudes. It was a slow process that reflected the struggle between conservative and liberal impulses. With the growing urbanization and industrialization of the United States, the obsession with Scripture began to wane in America. Critical and naturalist approaches to biblical study along with a general decline of religious influence also affected the perceptions of the Holy Land. The idea of the land of the Bible as a geographical reality was popularized by Americans who visited Palestine and published their impressions (Plate 1).[11]

---

7 Vilnay, "Biblical Names," pp.65–69.

8 Greenberg, *The Holy Land in American Religious Thought*, pp.63–93.

9 Baker, "The Place of the Bible," pp.243–72. Baker states that Nathalia Wright located some 650 references to biblical personages, places and events in Melville's writings, with the allusions to the Old Testament outnumbering the New by two to one (p.262). See Kenny, *Herman Melville's Clarel*

10 Ibid., p.246; Vogel, "Zion as Place," pp.40–44.

11 Vogel, ibid., pp.27–29,45–46.

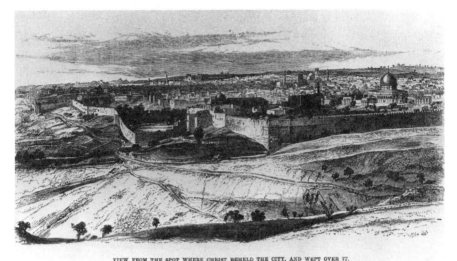

VIEW FROM THE SPOT WHERE CHRIST BEHELD THE CITY, AND WEPT OVER IT.

Plate 1. Jerusalem from the Mount of Olives
Source: MacLeod, *Eastward*

Millenarianism and the Return to Zion
The growth of religious ideas, leaders, and movements in early and mid-19th
century America was also connected with the Holy Land – in the abstract as
well as in practice. This had to do with the various interpretations of Christian
eschatology, such as the Second Coming of Jesus, the events preceding and
following it, the character of the millennium, and with the restoration of the
Jews to the Land of Israel.

In America, millenarian movements arose apparently as result of European
influence. Foremost among these were the Church of Jesus Christ of the
Latter Day Saints, founded in 1830 by Joseph Smith, and another movement
started by William Miller in 1831 with the unequivocal message that the
Second Advent of Jesus would take place in 1843. Millerism eventually
gave rise to the Adventist movement in America, known as the Seventh Day
Adventists. Gaustad characterized the religious history of mid-19th century
America: "A climate of enthusiasm (the nineteenth century sort), produced
novelty in creed and worship in personal devotion and in communal association.
Revivalists and Millenialists, communitarians and utopians, spiritualists and

prophesiers, celibates and polygamists, perfectionists and transcendentalists... were all there."[12]

The connection of the millenarian idea with the restoration of the Jews to their land occupied in particular the Millerites, who discussed it at their conventions in 1842 and 1843. The Mormons established their New Jerusalem and Zion in America, but always believed that the Children of Israel must return to their land. This belief tied in with the hope that when the Return came about, the Israelites would recognize Jesus as the Messiah, and that the return to Zion and the rebuilding of the Temple would herald the second coming of Jesus. The Mormons gave this idea emotional and ceremonial expression by dispatching their emissary, Orson Hyde, to Jerusalem in 1841, to dedicate Palestine to the Jews in festive prayer.[13]

Even before the Millerites and Mormons, and also afterwards, there were American Christians who did not relocate Zion, but interpreted biblical prophecy to predicate the eagerly anticipated millennium on the actual restoration of the Jews to the Holy Land.[14] The second president of the United States, John Adams, wrote in 1818: "I really wish the Jews again in Judea an independent nation." He also believed, however, that after establishing their independent government and no longer suffering persecution, they would gradually become liberal Unitarian Christians.[15]

Ideas relating to the return of Jews to the Land of Israel can also be found in the travel literature of the period as well as in American prose and poetry – especially in the writings of Washington Irving, William Cullen Bryant, and Herman Melville. Melville borrowed money in order to go to Palestine, where, in 1856–57, he wrote his *Journal of a Visit to Europe and the Levant.* From impressions of his journey emerged a long, spiritual poem: *Clarel: a Poem and Pilgrimage in the Holy Land.*

> ...The Hebrew seers announce in time
> The return of Judah to her prime;
> Some Christians deemed it then at hand
> Here was an object: Up and On.
> With seed and tillage help renew –
> Help reinstate the Holy Land...[16]

12   Gaustad, *The Rise of Adventism*, p.xv; Kark, "Millenarism," pp.47–50.

13   Kark, ibid.; Ariel, *On Behalf of Israel*, pp.1–23.

14   Handy, "Studies," pp.290–93.

15   Fink, *America and Palestine*, pp.20–23; Spiegel, *The Other Arab-Israeli Conflict*, p.431.

16   Melville, *Clarel* ; Bezanson, edited version of *Clarel*, p.64.

The expected restoration of the Jews to their homeland was given impetus later in the 19th century by dispensationalist doctrines which laid down a complicated time frame for the occurrence of the great event. Millenarians were much taken with modern Zionist thinking, but even earlier, a dispensationalist of Methodist origins, William E. Blackstone, initiated the presentation of a "memorial" to President Harrison and Secretary of State James G. Blane, requesting that they use their good offices and the prestige of the United States for holding an international conference "to consider the Israelite claim to Palestine as their ancient home...."[17] Christians supporting Jewish restoration regarded the Zionist movement in America as conforming to their beliefs and extended it their assistance. This stance is reflected in the writings of religious leaders, educators, and politicians, as well as in practical ways – by political involvement in the Holy Land – including the establishment and functioning of an American consulate in Jerusalem, by missionary activity, visits by pilgrims and tourists, and by actual attempts at settlement in Palestine (Plate 2).

America and the Holy Land – Presence and Contacts
During the 19th century the transcendental concept of the Holy Land began to give way to physical reality. As Handy and Vogel have shown, American exposure to the Holy Land was advanced by several key groups: missionaries, pilgrims and tourists, archeologists and biblical scholars, settlers, and consular officers. Each of these had different motives for going to Palestine, but undoubtedly, they were also influenced by the growing attention directed at that country by other Western nations, as well as by the technological advances in transport in the enhanced accessibility of that part of the world after the 1830s.[18]

17   Fink, *America and Palestine*, pp.20–23; Davis, "American Christian Devotees," pp.3–6.
18   Handy, "Studies," pp.293–98; Vogel, "Zion as Place," pp.29,384.

Plate 2. Inner Jerusalem from the north wall

American missionary activity in Palestine preceded all the other categories. In the first stages of the awakening of proselytizing fervor in the Protestant world in the 19th century, numerous missionary societies were founded. The major such organization was set up in 1810 as the American Board of Commissioners for Foreign Missions (ABCFM) at the Andover Theological Seminary in Massachusetts. This effort was mainly supported by the Congregational churches, with assistance in its initial years from other Reformed or Calvinist denominations. The ABCFM soon launched into extensive missionary work on a world scale, and in 1818 resolved to establish a mission in the Holy Land by appointing two young clergymen, Levi Parsons and Pliny Fisk, to the task. Their objectives were to work with the old Eastern churches and among Jews and Muslims.[19] Tibawi believes that this

---

19 Handy, *The Holy Land*, p.75. The extensive archives of the ABCFM containing the letters and reports of Parsons and Fisk are today kept in the Houghton Library at Harvard University.

decision was prompted by the ideology and activities of the British Church Missionary Society (CMS) and was apparently planned very thoroughly in advance.[20]

The two missionaries spent considerable time preparing themselves for their work and left for the East at the end of 1819. In his farewell sermon in Boston, Parsons expressed his faith in the implementation of prophecy regarding the restoration of the Jews to the Holy Land. From their base in Smyrna, Parsons proceeded alone to Jerusalem to ascertain the prospects there, but after a few months fell ill and died at Alexandria in 1822. Fisk, together with another missionary, Jonas King, traveled to Palestine and began missionary activities there, but he too died soon after, in 1825, in Beirut.[21] In the years 1834–1836, the Board made further attempts at renewing work in Jerusalem, with the help of the more successful mission at Beirut that had been established there in 1824. The Jerusalem station was closed in 1844 and the Board concentrated its efforts on the Levant and Turkey. The hard realities of the Holy Land proved too powerful for the myth.

In the mid-19th century, a short-lived attempt was made at establishing a mission station in Jerusalem by the Campbellites, under the medical doctor, James T. Barclay. Toward the end of the century, activities in Palestine were started by American Adventists, Baptists, Mormons, Quakers, and others – mainly in the field of education. Since Islamic religious law made proselytizing of Muslims an offense punishable by death, these missionaries restricted themselves to working among native Christians and Jews. Although their successes in attracting converts were very small, Handy believes that the missionaries played a key role in conditioning the American Protestant mind for understanding the Holy Land. For example, in 1859, William A. Thomson, who served for over a quarter of a century as a missionary of the Board in Syria and Palestine, published a work in two volumes, *The Land and the Book*, which achieved tremendous popularity, being reprinted in numerous editions well into the 20th century and selling over two hundred thousand copies.[22] American missionary activity in Palestine was of secondary importance compared with the work in other parts of the Ottoman Empire. While all writers are agreed as to the educational, cultural, and philanthropic nature of these activities, there are differences regarding the extent of

---

20   Tibawi, *American Interests*, pp.4–14.

21   Letters and diaries of Levi Parsons, Pliny Fisk, and Jonas King sent to the ABCFM in Boston, ABCFM RG16 Palestine vols.1–3.

22   Grabill, *Protestant Diplomacy*, pp.38–39; Handy, *The Holy Land*, pp.xv–xvi.

missionary influence on American policies and diplomacy in the Empire and on the mutual interaction between them.[23]

One of the large groupings that manifested a massive presence in Palestine was the swelling stream of pilgrims representing the three monotheistic religions. Many of these saw fit to publish their impressions in print, in letters, journals, and memoirs that were a mixture of fancy and reality. Among the first books by Americans on the Holy Land was S.C. Cooper's *News from Jerusalem* published in Philadelphia in 1825. A decade later, the newspaperman, John Lloyd Stephens, traveled through the region as part of an extended tour in the Old World.[24] Those who saw themselves as pilgrims rather than travelers or tourists, sought out the Holy Land of the Bible and the scenes sanctified in the New Testament. Mark Twain, who visited the country in 1867, wrote about this with his usual sharp, cynical wit:

> I am sure, from the tenor of books I have read, that many who have visited this land in years gone by, were Presbyterians, and came seeking evidences in support of their particular creed; they found a Presbyterian Palestine, and they had already made up their minds to find no other, though possibly they did not know it, being blinded by their zeal. Others were Baptists, seeking evidences and a Baptist Palestine. Others were Catholics, Methodists, Episcopalian, seeking evidences endorsing their several creeds, and a Catholic, a Methodist, an Episcopalian Palestine.[25]

Mark Twain was inclined to scoff at fundamentalist interpretations of the Bible. He marks the advent of a new kind of traveler, although even his writing on the Holy Land was not insensitive to religious sentiment (Plate 3).[26]

---

23 For a brief survey of the various approaches see: Bryson, *Middle East Diplomatic Relations*, pp.9–33.

24 Vilnay, "America's Part," p.405.

25 Twain, *Innocents Abroad*, p.511.

26 Baker, "The Place of the Bible," p.256.

FULL-DRESSED TOURIST.

Plate 3. Mark Twain's "full-dressed" American tourist
Source: Twain, *Innocents Abroad*

American political figures, ministers, and consuls – Christians and Jews –
who served in Constantinople were also caught up in strong religious emotions
which drew them to visit the Holy Land. Among these, in 1871, was former
Secretary of State William H. Seward.[27] The most notable visit was that of
former President U.S. Grant in 1877, as part of a trip around the world.
Before going ashore at Jaffa, he and his party "...had been doing a good deal
of Bible reading and revision of our Testaments, to be sure of our sacred
ground, and when after breakfast we came on deck and saw the low brown
shore of Palestine, we looked upon it with reverence..."[28] The ambivalent
feelings of the Democrat, Samuel Cox, who later became the American

27   Seward, *William H. Seward's Travels* .
28   Coolidge, *Ulysses S. Grant*, p.322.

consul-general at Constantinople and who enthusiastically supported the return of the Jews to their land, can be gleaned from his description of his visit to Jerusalem in the early 1880s:

> If at first we were disappointed at the small size and meagre aspect of the city, we are beginning already to wonder and worship. The very air, the very stones, the very dust – and especially the rocks – seem sacred. Here is the sepulchre, not of a nation merely, but of a Saviour; not of dead, buried hopes, but of living and risen glories; not of an old and honored dispensation from Jehovah, but of a new and potential Evangel.... Pilgrims from far-off America, whose geography was not known until the jewels of Spain found it – not known when these great transactions of salvation were here enacted – we could not refrain from sympathetic tears at the prospect of a city so hallowed by sacrifice, and so sanctified by time (Plate 4).[29]

A book that greatly influenced his contemporaries after it was published in 1880 was General Lew Wallace's *Ben-Hur*, which drew its inspiration from spiritual ideals of the East. Wallace wrote *Ben-Hur* ("the book of books of this age!") previous to taking up his appointment as minister of the United States to Constantinople in 1881, and before he visited Jerusalem in 1882.[30]

The first American explorers in Palestine were motivated by the desire to better understand, interpret, and analyze the Scriptures through study of the Holy Land. From the 1830s, Edward Robinson became the recognized pioneer of critical, scholarly research of the country (Figure 1). Bliss, in his survey states that "...in the scientific exploration of Palestine, America was followed

---

29 Cox, *Orient Sunbeams*, pp.284–85.

30 Wallace, *Ben-Hur* and letter of Mrs. Story, 28 October 1886, in Wallace, *Along the Bosphorus,* p.252. More recently, a movie by the same title based on Wallace's book, was awarded five Oscars, and is still frequently screened on American television.

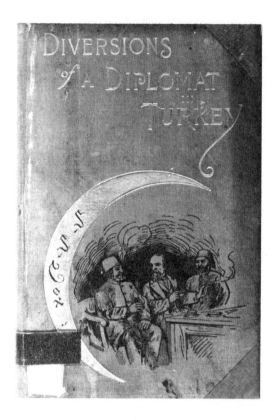

Plate 4. The cover of Cox's book
Source: Cox, *Diplomacy in Turkey*

by Germany, Germany by France, and France by England." He describes in
detail Robinson's important contribution to the physical geography of the
Holy Land and the identification of biblical sites.[31] Another important
American explorer, who came to the country after Robinson's first visit, was
the U.S. Navy Lieutenant William F. Lynch, who added significant material
to the scientific study of the Dead Sea and the surrounding region in 1847–1848
(Plate 5).[32]

---

31   Bliss, *The Development of Palestine Exploration*, pp.189–23.

32   Ben-Arieh, "William Lynch's Expedition," pp.15–21; Field, *America and the Mediterranean*,
     pp.277–79.

These represented a different type of visitor, as was noted by the American consul at Jerusalem, Rhodes, in the early sixties: "The scientific class is the most interesting. These are the men who go about with geological hammers and tape lines – the men of feet and inches, heights and depths, widths and lengths. They go to Jerusalem to work, and to work enthusiastically."[33] Some of the American consuls in Jerusalem were themselves scholars who became consuls, or consuls who took up research. The best example was undoubtedly Selah Merrill. Until they were transferred to museums in the United States, his extensive collections in Jerusalem attracted tourists and scholars. This private museum is described in a children's book on Jerusalem to which Merrill wrote the introduction. Expressing disappointment at not being able to see the collection because of the consul's return to the United States (in 1885), the author quotes a friend who "...was invited to call on Dr. and Mrs. Merrill, and was perfectly delighted with her visit. Such a wonderful collection of curiosities! Birds, animals, jars, fossils, insects, flowers, minerals, coins – everything that can be mentioned connected with the Holy Land. She said she should think there were enough to fill a museum – a Biblical one – and pictures, perfect and true to life, by the score."[34]

The development of "scientific" methods of biblical criticism and the changes in approaches in 19th century America regarding nature, the Divinity, and science are reflected in the work of Robinson and Lynch, through that of Post and Bliss, the American School of Oriental Research founded in Jerusalem in 1900, and to W.F. Albright. In the late 19th century, the older evangelical system based on inductive fact-gathering (according to the antihypothetical Baconian model of science) gave way to a new objectivity, relativism, and evolutionary theories of science and religion. The new approaches to biblical criticism engendered a more scientific outlook on the Holy Land. But they also contributed to the erosion of popular belief in the Bible and alienated many Americans from the Scriptures.[35]

33 Rhodes, "Our Consul at Jerusalem," p.439.

34 Knight, *Ned Harwood's Visit to Jerusalem,* p.262. I thank Joseph Shadur for drawing my attention to this passage.

35 Klazker, "Teaching," p.5; Vogel, "Zion as Place," p.393.

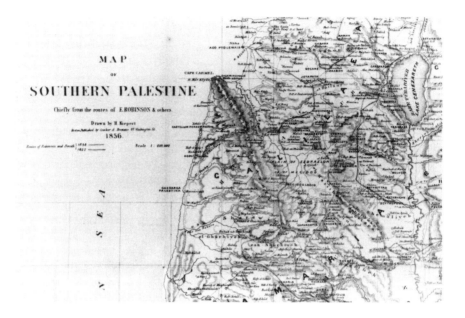

Figure 1. Edward Robinson's map of the Holy Land, 1856
Source: Robinson, *Biblical Researches*, 1856

Another category of persons whose presence in the country was continuous and in some cases lasting, were the settlers. These must be separated into Christians and Jews in urban and rural locations of Palestine most of which were inhabited by Arabs. The pioneers of modern agricultural settlement in the Holy Land were Christians. Foremost among these were several Americans who came in the 1840s, 1850s, and 1860s to settle – in disregard of warnings from local experts and from representatives of the United States government.

CARAVAN OF THE EXPEDITION.

Plate 5. The Lynch expedition caravan
Source: Lynch, *Narrative*

The leaders of such colonists were inspired by millenarist ideas and by faith in the return to Zion rife among fundamentalist Protestant sects in the early 19th century. They attempted to put their religious beliefs into practice by planning and founding agricultural settlements in Palestine. The most noteworthy among them were Warder Cresson, Clorinda Minor, and George W.J. Adams. They were followed by the German-American Templers, and later in the century, by the American Colony in Jerusalem. They also proposed establishing agricultural schools and model farms in order to teach modern farming to local settlers – Jews in particular (Figure 2).

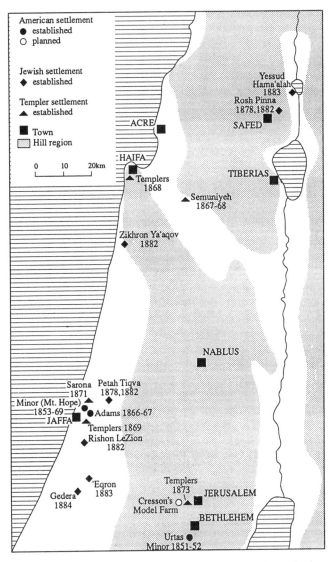

Figure 2. Location of the first American, Templer, and Jewish colonies, 1851-1884
Source: Kark, "Millenarism," p.51

The personal accounts of these visionaries provide insights into what drove them to migrate to remote and backward Palestine, and throw light on the economic concepts and practical means for implementing their schemes. Despite the failures, such attempts became important chapters in the history of agricultural settlement in 19th century Palestine. The colonists maintained a wide range of international contacts through letters, pamphlets, sermons, and press publicity in America, England, Germany, and Palestine. In addition, many people who heard indirectly about these ventures, took an interest in their ideas and experiences. Millenarist schemes influenced early preachers and founders of Jewish societies for agricultural settlement in Palestine, and indirectly affected local Arabs as well. The Jewish forerunners of the Hovevei Zion and Zionist movements promoted remarkably similar ideas. Millenarist and Jewish visionaries alike spoke of the hour being propitious for the coming of the Messiah, and favorable for settlement in the Land of Israel. Both groups established schools to teach the lore of the land and to prepare youth for agricultural pursuits. Many years after the disappearance of American settlers in Palestine, their story reverberated in Jewish polemic literature (Plates 6 and 7).[36]

Until the 1880s, American Jews settled mainly in Jerusalem and the other towns out of religious motives and the wish to be buried in the Holy City. Later, Jews came as part of the new *aliya*, aspiring to productive lives in modern urban or rural settlements. At the turn of the century, the connections between American Jewry and Jews in the Land of Israel centered mainly on providing financial assistance to Jerusalem. The American Jewish community grew from around 2,000 at the end of the 18th century to a quarter of a million in 1880. Around the mid-century, a number of Jewish newspapers began to appear which sometimes published articles on Palestine. In particular, the paper *The Occident and American Jewish Advocate* edited by Isaac Leeser supported ideas for the renewal of Jewish agriculture in the Holy Land, and in the 1850s reported on Clorinda Minor, and her attempt at Christian communal settlement in Palestine. Leeser, who was born in Germany, was among the founders and leaders of the Conservative Judaism movement in the United States and translated the Hebrew prayer book and Bible into English.[37]

---

36 Kark, "Millenarism," pp.47–62.

37 *Encyclopædia Hebraica,* 7:213. Leeser also translated from the Hebrew a book on the historical geography of Palestine by Rabbi Joseph Schwarz (*Sefer tevuot ha-aretz*), that was published in Philadelphia in 1850 under the title, *Descriptive and Brief Historical Sketch of Palestine* .

Plate 6. The village of Urtas near Bethlehem, one of the first sites
of American settlement in 19th century Palestine
Source: Photographed by Kark, 1977

Plate 7. A window in the main building of the American Colony at Jerusalem
Source: Photographed by Kark, 1978

From 1833, three Jewish organizations were founded to support their coreligionists in the Land of Israel. At the beginning, most of the help was directed to the poor, but the Board of Delegates of American Israelites – the roof organization – focussed on the advancement of agricultural education in Palestine. For this purpose, joint action was proposed in 1876 to the Anglo-Jewish Association: "A letter having been read from the President of the American Board of Delegates, asking the Association to co-operate in adopting measures for the amelioration of the condition of the Jews in Palestine."[38] In the 1880s, when the persecution of Jews in Eastern Europe drove waves of immigrants to America, this body diverted most of its means to absorption of Jews in the United States and lost its interest in Palestine. Apart from the organizations, there were in the United States also wealthy individuals who helped the Jews in Jerusalem. In the mid-century, the most important of these was Judah Touro, with whose bequest funds Moses Montefiore built

38 Efrati, "American Jewry," pp.63–88; Anglo-Jewish Association Minute Book, 17 July 1876, p.196, AJ 95/Add; Kellner, *For Zion's Sake*, pp.17, 206–210.

the first Jewish housing project outside the Old City walls. This opened the Jews of Jerusalem to the expansion of their residential areas beyond the city walls, and led to the construction of new neighborhoods in the following years.[39] Later, important ties were established between the Hovevei Zion organization in America, despite their small numbers, and the new Jewish *Yishuv* crystallizing in the Land of Israel in the years leading up to the First World War.

The last category of Americans to be permanently present in Palestine between 1832 and 1914 were the consuls and consular agents. The institutional systems they set up, their personal character, activities, and their local, regional, and international contacts are the subject of this book.

PALESTINE IN THE LAST CENTURY OF OTTOMAN RULE

During the hundred and twenty years from 1800 on, Palestine was transformed politically, demographically, socially, economically, and in its map of human settlement. From a political perspective this period in the history of the country may be divided into four phases: 1) The period of pashas and local rulers (1799–1831) – continuing the forms of government of the 18th century. 2) Syria and Palestine under Egyptian rule of Muhammad Ali through his son Ibrahim Pasha (1831–1840). In many respects this was a turning point, for despite the brevity of the period, the changes in government and other spheres were to have lasting effects. 3) The period of reforms (1841–1876) following the resumption of Ottoman rule, with attempts made at instituting new patterns of government. 4) The final decades of Ottoman rule (1877–1917). The first and greater part of this last period was marked by the highly centralized rule of Sultan Abdul Hamid II; it was followed by the advent of the Young Turks in 1908, and ended with the British occupation of Palestine in 1917–1918.[40]

During that time the population grew from about 250,000 in 1800 (mostly Muslim Arabs) to about 800,000 in 1914, including 40,000 foreign nationals.[41] The determinants of change in Palestine, and the impact on the dichotomy between tradition and modernity and on development and internal and external

---

39   Kark, "Batei-Tura," pp.157–67.

40   Kark, *Jaffa*, pp.13–52.

41   Schmelz, "The Decline in Population," p.26.

forces, are illustrated in the schematic diagram (Figure 3) of the interaction of political transformation, economic and technological change, demographic, social and cultural developments, and environmental, physical and spatial change. The schema represents a dynamic process, reflecting a hierarchical system in three different contexts, all relevant to Palestine. The international context entailed the changes in the political structure of the great powers, increased Western influence in the Ottoman Empire – also as affected by the Industrial Revolution in Europe and developments in the European economy in the 19th century (trade and international capital market and technological advances that greatly improved both marine and overland communications and enabled the opening of the Suez Canal). The second context was that of the Ottoman Empire. Strengthening links of the Empire with the West and substantial changes in the nature of Ottoman administration brought about by reforms within the Empire benefitted foreign trade, communications, urbanization, and structural social change. The third context comprised the region of Palestine. Although not a unified administrative unit in the 19th century, it was of unique character. The special attraction of the Holy Land and Jerusalem, and growing European and American political and religious interests, influenced many spheres of life in the local arena.

This was the setting in which the consuls of the foreign nations functioned – including the American consuls. As local representatives they not only reported on current developments, but intervened and became involved as part of the external forces operating in Palestine. Their actions were not necessarily compatible with the best interests of the local government and the majority of the indigenous Arab population.

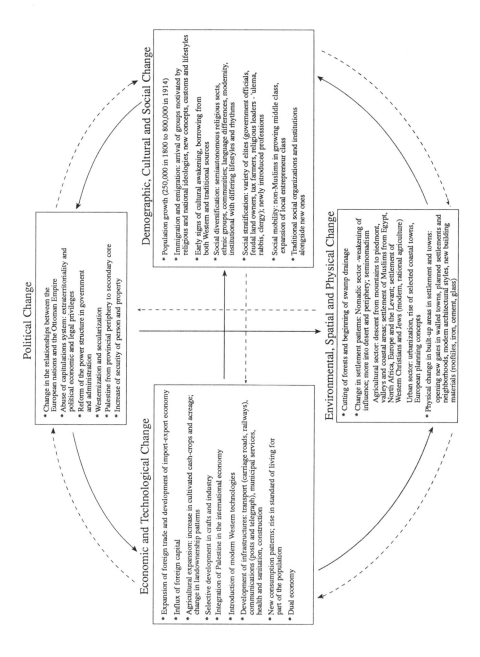

Figure 3. The interrelations between elements of change in Palestine, 1800–1914

CHAPTER ONE

CONSULS AND CAPITULATIONS

THE CONSULAR FUNCTION IN HISTORY

The Concept "Consul" in History

The term "consul" designated different types of officials in various historical periods. It was first used in ancient Rome. Two consuls, who were each elected for a one-year period of service were the highest ranking officials of the Roman Republic and continued to govern it after the Kingdom was ended. Under the Empire, the consuls lost their importance in practice but the title remained a mark of honor and was assumed also by the caesars. During the Middle Ages the classical Roman term remained in use, but had varying meanings. It was the formal title of the heads of several different independent cities in Italy and southern France, being first mentioned in Pisa in the year 1081, where, until about the 13th century, it carried administrative, judicial and military authority.[1]

According to Schuyler, the modern consular institution belongs to the history of international law, having its origins in the period following the Crusades, when Venice and other Italian city-states began to establish trading stations in the Middle East. As commercial relations developed, it became necessary to appoint agents for dealing with disputes between inhabitants of these small trading colonies in Muslim lands and in the Byzantine Empire.[2] Such agents, or "consuls" served diplomatic functions in the host country as well as governing, judging, and seeing to the interests of their countrymen. The

---

1   Grabois, Aryeh, "Supplement," in Bloch, *The Feudal Society*, p.595; *Encylopædia Hebraica*, 29:407–8; Kennedy, *The American Consul*, pp.1–4.

2   Schuyler, *American Diplomacy*, pp.42–44; Ravndal, "The Origin of the Capitulations," pp.56–89. Schuyler served in diplomatic posts in Turkey and Greece.

consuls also protected church interests and had powers of supervision over the welfare of their communities.[3]

In the towns of southern Europe this institution functioned in a juridical capacity. The merchants elected one of their fellows to adjudicate commercial disputes according to custom and usage, thus avoiding recourse to regular courts. Such arbitrators were referred to as "consul-judges". (They were the prototypes of commercial or consular courts of France, Italy, and Spain at the turn of the 19th century.) The Hanseatic towns and England saw the advantages in employing such functionaries, and began to appoint consuls to different countries.[4]

In the Middle Ages, the consuls in foreign countries were quasi-public ministers who watched over the interests of their compatriots, decided their disputes, protected their trade and enjoyed extensive juridical and commercial powers outside local law. Some of their functions were of a diplomatic nature. Lay believes that beyond dealing with the particular needs of merchants, seafarers, shipping, and merchandise they also represented national interests.[5] Thus the consular function preceded the diplomatic one. When public ministers were appointed, the consular status lost much of its diplomatic character as well as its general importance, but the growth of international trade and intensified relations between countries at the end of the 19th and the beginning of the 20th centuries, again broadened their prestige and imposed many new responsibilities on the consuls. In the mid-1930s Lay could define the consular function as follows: "Modern consular officers are commercial or business representatives of their country, stationed at foreign capitals and at important ports and trade centers, or at other points where the national interests require the support or the protection of the government."[6] In time, the commercial aspects of the consul's work took pride of place at the expense of his former diplomatic and juridical functions.

Modern diplomacy began to develop in Italy during the 13th and 14th centuries, when the Italian city-states were in frequent negotiation to form alliances or to resolve conflicts. Although much practical experience was gained in the course of several centuries, there was little order in the rules of

---

3   Sousa, *The Capitulatory Regime*, pp.17–18; Mayo, "Consular System of the U.S.," p.297; Edwards Lester, "Consular System," pp.212–14.

4   Schuyler, *American Diplomacy*, pp.42–44.

5   Lay, *The Foreign Service*, pp.124–25.

6   Lay, ibid., p.125.

diplomacy. These were shaped and defined, much in their present form, by the Congress of Vienna in 1815 and supplemented by the Congress of Aix-la-Chapelle in 1818. Four categories of diplomatic representation were defined at these congresses: Ambassadors, Envoys Extraordinary and Ministers Plenipotentiary, Ministers Resident, and Chargés d'Affaires.[7] The development of the diplomatic service brought about a change in the international status of the consuls. Jones points out that up to the beginning of the 20th century, the principles governing consular status differed in Christian nations – Europe and the United States – from those in non-Christian states. In the former, consular officers were not considered public representatives in the full sense. The wide, special powers of the consuls in representing their countries gradually devolved upon the diplomatic corps, with most of the former consular privileges and immunities preserved only where these were specifically guaranteed by treaty or custom. In non-Christian countries, including the Ottoman Empire, the consuls of the Christian powers kept their civil and criminal juridical powers along with their long-entrenched privileges which derived in part from the capitulations based on extraterritorial rights. These will be discussed in greater detail below.

However, Jones adds that along with the decline of consular status in European countries, the privileges of the consuls were gradually broadened by usage and treaties to the point where by 1906, they could in many cases claim rights not guaranteed by the law of nations.[8] These included displaying their national arms and flying their flag on offices and residences.[9] This definition of consular status has not changed much to this day, as is borne out by the relevant entry in the *Encyclopaedia Britannica*:

> Consul, public officer authorized by the state whose commission he bears to protect the interests and to foster the commercial affairs of its subjects in a foreign country and to perform such routine functions as issuing visas and renewing passports. A consul, as such, does not enjoy the status of a diplomat and cannot enter on his official duties until permission has been granted to him by the authorities of the state to which his nomination has been communicated. This permission, or exequatur, may be revoked at

7   McCamy, *American Foreign Affairs*, pp.182–83.

8   Jones, *The Consular Service*, pp.87–90.

9   Schuyler, *American Diplomacy*, pp.69–71.

any time at the discretion of the government of the country in which he resides.[10]

Today too, the consuls have no diplomatic immunity but are, to some extent, free from the jurisdiction of the host country.

The archives, for example, all other official documents and papers kept in the consulate, and all correspondence between the consul and his government are inviolable. Consuls are also often exempt from all kinds of rates and taxes and from personal taxes....Many of the modern consular privileges have been superseded by the Convention on Consular Relations (Vienna 1963).[11]

Modern Consular Bureaucracy

At the beginning of the 20th century, the consular officials of all the important commercial nations, except France, were of two classes: *consules missi* – those sent directly by the state and paid from its funds, and *consules electi* – who were residents of the country in which they were appointed and were often foreigners to the country they served. The powers of the former were similar in all the consular systems, although varying in details according to the different agreements. The rights of the latter class were more restricted. The different countries endeavored to select persons of this class from among their nationals and only if they could not do so did they appoint foreigners. The work of the *consules electi* was usually remunerated only from fees and/or from allocations for office rents, and they were permitted to engage in business in addition to their consular functions.[12] Writers on the subject point to differences between the various European powers and the United States regarding the origins of their consular services, their geographic distribution and extent, the nature of the officials, their training and employment. So, for example, prominent local merchants began to serve as British consuls in the Mediterranean already in the 15th century, their numbers increasing from 15 in 1740 to 107 in 1824 in Mediterranean towns, northern Europe, and the United States. In that year, an act of Parliament attempted to replace a group of individual state servants overseas, whose only common

10   *Encyclopaedia Britannica*, 3:576–77.

11   Ibid.

12   Jones, *The Consular Service*, pp.91–92.

denominator was the name of consul, with a single government service of full-time officials, paid and pensioned by the state.[13]

The Netherlands consular service was established at the end of the 16th and the beginning of the 17th centuries in European and Levant ports. In 1658, the States-General of the Dutch Republic proclaimed regulations regarding the duties and rights of all Dutch consuls, except for those in the Levant who enjoyed semidiplomatic status. In 1750, there were 75 serving consuls whose main responsibility was to assist Dutch merchants. Reporting on commercial developments and opportunities was at the time considered of secondary importance. This attitude changed during the 19th century after the kingdom of the Netherlands was established and Holland became a minor European commercial, maritime, and financial power and an important colonial force. In 1905 there were 542 Dutch consular representatives.[14]

In France, a regular consular service was organized as early as the mid-17th century – continuing until 1791 as a branch of the royal navy. (It is interesting to recall that from 1799 to 1804, starting with Napoleon, the highest officials of the French republic before the establishment of the First Empire bore the title of "consul".) In 1793, the French foreign office was given full authority over the consular service. The consuls were considered members of the diplomatic staff, while the vice-consuls were mainly merchants who lived from their private profits. From 1828, the consuls were requested by the foreign office to remit trimestrial reports in unified form.[15]

These are but a few examples of countries with a long-established consular service. As will be seen below, in the United States this service began, and its rules of operation crystallized, only during the last two decades of the 18th century. Japan, which was opened to the West under pressure of the powers in 1858, first established consulates in foreign countries in 1868 with the Meiji Restoration.[16]

As to the training and suitability of candidates for appointment to consular functions, a notable effort was made in European states to place the diplomatic and consular services on a sound professional footing by appropriate training, providing salaries and retirement arrangements, and by assuring the continuity

---

13   Barker, "Consular Reports," pp.266–67.

14   Tamse, "The Netherlands Consular Service," p.271.

15   Broder, "French Consular Reports," pp.279–80; *Encyclopaedia Hebraica,* 29:407.

16   Tsunoyama, "Japanese Consular Reports," p.284.

of the service. This was in marked contrast to the practice prevalent during the 19th century in the American foreign service.

Among the principles adopted in the last century in England, France, Belgium, Austria, and Germany in determining suitable qualifications for positions of "consuls of career" were education and knowledge of languages, fixed salary, a prohibition on engaging in commerce or business, and requiring consuls not to be citizens, or even natives, of the country in which they served.[17] In the course of the 19th century, reforms were introduced into the consular services of various countries, setting standards and requirements for candidacy, including written and oral examinations. Special schools were set up for this purpose in several countries, among them France, Austria-Hungary, Britain, the Netherlands, Germany, Russia, and Greece.[18] At times, such training programs – notably in Germany and Great Britain – were organized according to geographic-cultural criteria to meet the needs of the various regions of consular and diplomatic representation.[19]

In summary, it may be said that in the course of the 19th century there occurred a process of organizational establishment, professional development, numerical growth, and impressive geographical dispersion of the Western nations' consular services. Beyond reflecting internal political changes, this development may be related to the industrial and commercial revolution, to the changes in technology and transport, to imperialist policies, and to cultural and religious aspirations of the Western Christian nations for "civilizing" non-Christian peoples.

THE FOREIGN SERVICE OF THE UNITED STATES

The State Department

Early studies, as well as more recent ones, dealing with the Department of State define it as the main section of the executive branch of the government primarily occupied with external affairs. It is also the oldest of the Federal departments. The foreign affairs of the United States were administered from 1775 by a Committee which in 1789 became the Department of State.[20]

---

17   Schuyler, *American Diplomacy*, pp.71–75; Jones, *The Consular Service*, pp.93–99.

18   Jones, *The Consular Service*, pp.93–99; Mattox, *The Twilight*, pp.113–17.

19   Jones, ibid.; Cecil, *The German Diplomatic Service*, pp.11–13.

20   Hunt, *The Department of State*, pp.v-vi (1893); Department of State, *History of the Department*, pp.13–24 (1901); McCamy, *American Foreign Affairs*, pp.41–49.

From its inception, this governmental function was closer to the President than any other executive department and he was its supreme head. Early on, the State Department dealt with matters that in the course of the 19th century passed to other departments, among them the registration of patents and copyrights, and the like.[21]

Regarding the subject of concern here, it should be noted that the consular service did not immediately operate as a separate agency within the State Department. During its first years, the United States had no consular representation distinct from the diplomatic service, the same officers serving in both diplomatic and consular capacities, much as in the early European consular systems.[22] The first thorough reorganization of the State Department since its inception in 1789 took place from 1833 to 1836, under two secretaries of state, Louis McLane and John Forsyth. The new regulations stated the chief clerk's responsibilities to be administrative and supervisory – in effect making him the equivalent of an acting undersecretary of the department. He functioned as the main coordinator and director of the seven bureaus set up at that time.[23] At the beginning, there was no difference between the various branches within the State Department, each clerk having charge of a specific field. As the activities became more complex, bureaus and divisions were established with appointed officials heading the latter. Upon the reorganization of the department in 1836, and after it, some of the original functions were abolished or transferred to other sections of the government. Thus, of the seven new offices, the three most important ones were the Diplomatic Bureau, the Consular Bureau, and the Home Bureau. The Statistical Office was created in 1842.[24]

The most important of these, the Diplomatic Bureau, maintained (dispatched and received) all official communications with foreign countries, instructed American ambassadors, and provided current information to American missions abroad to keep them abreast of developments at home. At that time, the work of the State Department was also classified according to geographic regions.[25] The restructuring of the department in 1836 apparently met its practical needs, for only minor changes were instituted in it until 1870, when

21 Department of State, ibid., pp.19–37.

22 Lay, *The Foreign Service*, p.9.

23 Stuart, *The Department of State*, pp.78–79; Jones, *The Consular Service*, pp.43–44.

24 Department of State, *History of the Department*, pp.25–31.

25 McCamy, *American Foreign Affairs*, p.46.

Secretary of State Hamilton Fish introduced a rather badly-conceived reorganization scheme. Organizational problems dogged the State Department well into the mid-20th century. Instead of the six bureaus, Fish set up thirteen subunits, most of which reported directly to him without the coordinating function of the chief clerk. The only intermediaries were now the first and second assistant secretaries of state. These supervised the diplomatic and consular bureaus, which were divided into two new bureaus for each function, according to countries. The apportioning of these responsibilities to the first and second assistants was terminated in 1873, and the diplomatic and consular bureaus were placed directly under the secretary of state. Only in 1897 was a separation instituted between the economic, social, and political functions of America's foreign relations.[26]

At the beginning of the 20th century (in 1901), the Consular Bureau was responsible for conducting varied correspondence with the consular officers throughout the world, with additional executive government departments, as well as with private persons. This correspondence included directives to consuls regarding commercial matters, protection of American citizens, dealing with estates, sanitary reports, salaries and administration, etc. At the time, about 800 officials were employed by the consular service throughout the world, of whom about half corresponded directly with the State Department.

The feeling in the department at the time was that the Consular Bureau was becoming increasingly important since American enterprise was reaching out to distant lands for markets for its manufactures.

In addition, this bureau was also charged with setting and conducting examinations for candidates for the consular service. It prepared them for their positions after they were accepted, and arranged their pensions – a hard task because of the steady stream of returning and starting consuls with every change in the administration.[27] A survey of the Consular Bureau's work also points up processes of absorbing material coming in from abroad, indexing and sorting procedures, issuing of permits, and relating to correspondence at the various levels. These acts were carried out in three sections dealing with different countries: the first, Germany and Great Britain and their dependencies; the second, various countries in Europe and South America; and the third, France, the Central American nations, and the Far and Near East, including Turkey.[28]

26   Ibid., pp.41–49.

27   Department of State, *History of the Department*, pp.50–54.

28   Ibid.

The job of compiling, editing, and distributing diplomatic and consular reports on commercial and industrial topics was allotted to the Bureau of Foreign Commerce (1897) which had evolved out of the 1842 Statistical Office and the 1847 Bureau of Statistics. The bureau issued five different types of publications: Daily Consular Reports, Monthly Consular Reports, Commercial Relations (Annual Reports), Special Consular Reports, and Declared Exports. The practical value of these publications, which broadened their scope in the course of the second half of the 19th century, can be appreciated from their almost daily use in the world's leading commercial periodicals. They reflected the growing interest of the State Department in the advancement of American foreign trade, which between 1865 and 1900 transformed the United States from an importing to an exporting nation, including the export of capital. This change necessarily influenced American foreign policy and the activities of the frameworks connected with it.[29]

An additional reorganization of the State Department, during the period under review, was undertaken in 1909. In that year the entire staff of the department numbered only 210 persons, while at the same time the number of separate units became more cumbersome, having grown from 6 in 1869 to 16 in 1870 (with only 31 officers) and to 23 in 1913.[30] This situation in the State Department gave rise, in 1898, to severe (according to Stuart, "not entirely fair") criticism of it as an "...antiquated, feeble organization, enslaved by precedent and routine inherited from another century, remote from the public gaze and indifferent to it. The typewriter was viewed as a necessary evil and the telephone was an instrument of last resort."[31]

What brought on these conditions in the State Department and the foreign service? Many writers on the subject believe that the relative indifference of Americans, at the turn of the 18th and throughout the 19th centuries, to everything relating to foreign policy and to those engaged in it stemmed from the tendency to isolationism and separatism from Europe. They emphasize that the dominant issues in the United States before the last decade of the 19th century were domestic rather than foreign, expressing the preoccupation with the application of democratic principles at home. There was no inclination

29   Ibid., pp.80–82; Werking, "U.S. Consular Reports," pp.300–303; Adams, *A History of the Foreign Policy*, pp.1, 255–56; Lafeber, *The New Empire*, pp.6–10.

30   McCamy, *American Foreign Affairs*, pp.41–49; Stuart, *The Department of State*, p.219. The German foreign office at the end of the 19th century had only three divisions, see: Cecil, *The German Diplomatic Service*, pp.3–10.

31   Tyler Dennet in Stuart, *The Department of State*, p.194; Werking, *The Master Architects*, pp.15–19.

for giving high priority to foreign matters far removed from the daily life of Americans, or for directing the best talents to the foreign service. Only in times of crisis, as during the Mexican War, were America's diplomats called upon to fill important functions.[32] And there were those who thought that the political changes in the wake of the Civil War had made the foreign (diplomatic) service redundant, and that the development of transport and communications, such as the laying of the transatlantic cable, offered good alternatives to permanent diplomacy. Among these was (in 1876) Albert Rhodes, who had earlier served as U.S. consul in Jerusalem and in several consular and diplomatic positions in Europe.[33]

It was Hunt who concluded that the sources for American foreign policy concepts that crystallized in the 20th century should be sought at the end of the 18th and during the 19th centuries. They derived, he believed, from the groping of the political elite for a definition of the form the American nation was to take – what was the nation to become, and how its identity should be reflected in its international behavior. The importance of American foreign policy in the 19th century was its nationalist function in shaping, strengthening, and counterbalancing domestic trends.[34]

The U.S. Consular Service

While the consular and the diplomatic services of the United States are often treated together in discussions of their history, their periodization, and their character, this study will focus mainly on the consular service. In all attempts to trace its development, several periods have been identified that reflect the entrenchment of different criteria. These include historic changes in the foreign relations of the United States, increased numbers of officers in the service, proposals for reform, or reforms that were enacted through actual legislation or by executive order. [35] For the present purpose, three main periods based on reforms and legislation are pertinent: 1792–1855, 1856–1906, and 1906–1924.

---

32   Blancké, *The Foreign Service*, p.11; Lay, *The Foreign Service*, p.229; Mattox, *The Twilight*, pp.1–2; Steigman, *The Foreign Service*, p.16.

33   Ilchman, *Professional Diplomacy*, pp.20–23; Rhodes, "Our Diplomats," pp.169–76.

34   Hunt, *Ideology and Foreign Policy*, pp.xi-xiii, 17–18, 190–91.

35   Barnes, *The Foreign Service* ; Blancké, *The Foreign Service* ; Jones, *The Consular Service* ; Steigman, *The Foreign Service*.

As early as in the Treaty of Amity and Commerce concluded with France in 1778, the United States recognized for the first time the rights of consular representation and appointed its first consul to France in 1780 (Colonel William Palfrey, who perished at sea on his way to take up the post). During the first decade, there was no defined system of appointment or description of the consuls' responsibilities. This only came about when Thomas Jefferson became secretary of state, with the appointment, in 1790, of six consuls and four vice-consuls. The Act of Apr. 14, 1792 (I Stat.254) – Defining the Powers and Functions of Consular Officers was the first legislative attempt to this end.[36] The act empowered the consuls to deal with appeals, requests, documents, and bequests of American seamen, travelers, and merchants abroad, and to collect certain fees for their services. As to the appointees, consuls were to be American citizens receiving no salaries (except for those serving on the Barbary Coast) and were permitted to engage in business. If no suitable Americans were available, reputable foreign nationals could be appointed as vice-consuls. In 1803, the consuls' responsibilities regarding seamen and vessels were broadened. An unsuccessful attempt was made in 1816 to pay them salaries, and in 1823 they were empowered with what was to become one of their most important functions – administering oaths to exporters of merchandise upon which an ad valorem duty was collected in American ports.[37] By the 1830s, the growth of United States trade with foreign countries brought about a steady expansion of the consular service and of the powers of the consuls, and extended their geographic distribution, mainly in Western Europe (from 6 consuls in 1790 to 129 consuls and 2 consuls-general in 1830).[38]

In the appointment of merchant-consuls, the United States followed the practice of the Continent but lacked the latter's reserve of experienced commercial manpower in European port towns. Many of those appointed to American consular positions regarded their jobs primarily as a means for advancing their personal business and commercial activities at the expense of other merchants. Their activities were conducted with a minimum of guidance and supervision by the State Department and they received no fixed remuneration. Their efforts at maintaining their social standing and influence in the community led in several localities to their charging irregular and exorbitant fees, and to using the information they had access to as consuls in

---

36   Carr, "The American Consular Service," pp.891–913; Kennedy, *The American Consul*, pp.19–28.

37   Jones, *The Consular Service*, pp.1–12; Schuyler, *American Diplomacy*, pp.44–45.

38   Barnes, *The Foreign Service*, p.65.

order to gain advantages over their business rivals.[39] Examples of such cases, which will be given below, were also in evidence in the Levant and Palestine (Beirut, Ramle, Jaffa, and Jerusalem) in the mid-19th century.

Additional attempts at reorganization and reform of the consular service were made in 1833 and 1846. An important administrative change during the 1830s was the publication of a set of unified general instructions to consular officers, which was followed by the Consular Regulations of 1855, 1857, 1874, and 1896. In the 1840s, the secretary of state, James Buchanan initiated a comprehensive and systematic proposal for reform, and attempted to introduce a consular code that would define the powers and duties of consuls, their status, and salaries. Buchanan, who had a background in foreign diplomacy, understood the importance and necessity for a diplomatic and consular foreign service. He recommended the appointment of consuls-general in the more important ports of Europe and the Near East, including Alexandria, but on the other hand believed that the number of consuls should be reduced.[40]

Only in 1855 and 1856 were these proposals formalized legally, marking a new period in the consular service which continued to 1906. The act of 1856 set up an organic framework for the diplomatic and consular services, with fixed salaries for diplomatic officials. It classified consular posts according to method of compensation (salary or fees), and established regulations to govern the exercise of consular duties. Two main motivating factors lay behind this important reorganization. One was an attempt to found a regular consular corps by providing a general scheme for a large range of positions which, in effect, were independent (282 in 1860), categorizing these by a defined program, laying down guiding principles and regulations for proper behavior, and providing more appropriate compensation for service. The second factor reflected the growth of foreign trade in the three years preceding the Civil War and the realization that consuls could materially aid the expansion of American exports.[41] It may be that the appointment of the first American consul to Jerusalem in 1856 was, among other things, also connected with

---

39 Barnes, ibid., pp.33, 65; Carr, "The American Consular Service," pp.896–97; Jones, *The Consular Service*, p.10.

40 Stuart, *The Department of State*, pp.78–108. The first nomination was actually in Alexandria. Edwin De Leon, from South Carolina, was appointed consul-general as a reward for his services to the Democratic party, see: De Leon, *Thirty Years* 1:95–96. Two interesting articles criticizing the consular system were published in 1842 and 1845 in *Hunt's Merchant Magazine* by Mayo and by Edwards Lester, the U.S. consul in Genoa.

41 Barnes, *The Foreign Service*, pp.73, 158, 337, 350; Carr, "The American Consular Service," pp.901, 907.

this reform, even though most of the appointments were to shipping sites and to business centers abroad.

The act of 1856 fixed two classes of salaried officials, B and C. The former earned $1,500–$7,500 per year and were precluded from engaging in private business. Officials in the C class were paid $500–$1,000 and were free to carry on their affairs. All the consuls outside these two categories depended for their remuneration on the fees charged by their consulates. The act was also more precise in defining the consuls' duties regarding the keeping of records, reporting, absenting themselves from their posts, and other matters.[42] The reforms attempted, for the first time, to begin applying the merit system regarding new appointments, to provide formal training for the consular clerks who made up the professional staffs, and to define suitable qualifications for candidates. This was accepted only very partially in 1864.[43]

In 1860, an important act was passed, providing for the exercise of extraterritorial judicial functions by diplomatic and consular officers in certain countries (including the Ottoman Empire), and in 1874, 1895, and 1905 an act and executive orders were put into effect connected with the changes in salaries and with the attempts to expand the merit system – at the expense of the detrimental spoils system – in the appointment of consular officers. This intermediate period came to an end with the Act of 1906, which laid down new reorganizational measures in the consular service, including the reclassification of consular officers, periodic inspections of consular posts (at least once every two years by five specially appointed inspectors) and other administrative provisions. Later that year, the subject of appointments and promotions in the consular service was dealt with in executive orders in accordance with the civil service provisions of 1883, but giving due consideration to representation of all the states and territories, without regard to the political affiliation of the candidates.[44]

At the end of the first decade of the 20th century, the foreign service numbered 566 consular posts with 63 consulates-general, 241 consulates, and 262 consular agencies. This number represents a decrease compared with 1890 when there were 760 consular posts, due primarily to a reduction of the consular agencies by one half and to the abolition of the commercial

---

42   Carr, ibid.; Jones, *The Consular Service*, pp.13–26; Schuyler, *American Diplomacy*, pp.45–59.

43   Carr, ibid.; Steigman, *The Foreign Service*, pp.17–19; Blancké, *The Foreign Service*, pp.14–38.

44   Barnes, *The Foreign Service*, p.337; Carr, ibid., pp.908–12.

agencies. The number of consulates remained almost unchanged, while the number of consulates-general was nearly doubled.[45]

In 1911, the budget law provided annual allocations for purchasing, building, repairing, and furnishing diplomatic and consular establishments, of which part was used to acquire the embassy building in Constantinople. The merit system was given definitive statutory basis in 1915. The next important reform was the Rogers Act of 1924 which reflected the new demands placed on the consular and diplomatic services by the changing role of the United States in the wake of World War I. It led to the unification of the two branches in the foreign service, making it possible to transfer posts, instituting examination criteria and promotions according to capability, fixing new salary levels and tables of pension provisions, and providing allocations for ceremonial representation and residence. For the first time, the foreign service of the United States was established on sound professional foundations.[46]

The lack of professionalism that characterized the American foreign service throughout the 19th century engaged the attentions of contemporary as well as modern writers. Two thorough studies of the diplomatic level, but relating also to the consular service, summarize prevailing opinions in attempts to characterize, explain, and evaluate this phenomenon. The views presented are generally negative and dwelt on the mediocrity and the amateurism of those who were appointed mainly because of political connections – or to be rid of them. These beneficiaries of the spoils system owed their appointments to patrons or sponsors, and were frequently replaced every four years with the changes in the administration before they were able to accumulate much experience. Edwin De Leon who served as the first American consul-general in Alexandria, in 1854–1860, dwelt on the disadvantages of the system in his memoirs: "...our most defective civil service system, under which, as a general rule the Foreign Representatives of the United States are changed every four years, as well as the President and Cabinet Ministers...The American Government is always partially educating its representatives abroad, and replacing them just at the time they are beginning to understand their duties, and acquire an intimacy with the men and things around them."[47] Even so, Mattox and Kennedy conclude that in the higher echelons of the diplomatic service, and in the ranks of consul-general and consul, at least at the end of

---

45   Barnes, ibid., p.350.

46   Lay, *The Foreign Service*, pp.31, 389–428; Werking, *The Master Architects*, pp.88–120.

47   De Leon, *Thirty Years*, 1:192–93.

the last century, the United States was better served than might have been expected in view of the haphazard system of selection and the general lack of interest in foreign affairs.[48]

For lack of space, this survey cannot enter into the details and chronological development of consular functions, their rights and duties, and their connections with the administration. The chart drawn up by Lay presents an exhaustive picture of the situation during the first quarter of this century. This chart, parts of which are decidedly relevant also to the 19th century, aptly illustrates the work of the consuls and the services they provided to practically every branch of the government, to every businessman, and directly or indirectly, to every private citizen (Figure 4).

CONSULATES AND CAPITULATIONS IN THE OTTOMAN EMPIRE FROM THE GRANTING OF CAPITULATIONS TO THEIR ABROGATION

The term "capitulations" (chapters) refers to a class of commercial treaties concluded by Western powers with Asian and African states, under which Western nationals were granted extraterritorial privileges. European residents in these countries thus remained subject to the laws of their home governments and were immune from those of their host countries.[49] Capitulations were in effect in the Ottoman Empire, in all the countries of North Africa, in Persia, China, Japan, Thailand, and Ethiopia.[50]

In contrast to the modern concept which relates sovereignty to territory, earlier ideas linked it to persons. A monarch or state exercised authority over his or its own nationals and not over aliens, who were subject to the exclusive jurisdiction of their respective countries of origin from which, in case of need, they sought protection. This was particularly relevant where law was inextricably interwoven with religion, and where there existed no juridical equality between believers and nonbelievers. In Muslim countries jurisdiction

---

48   Mattox, *The Twilight*, pp.1–56, 100–112; Ilchman, *Professional Diplomacy*, pp.4–40, 69–84; Kennedy, *The American Consul*, pp.209–26. Eugene Schuyler commented in 1885 that, on the whole, the consuls functioned well despite the low salary and standard of living, and their lack of training. See: Schuyler, *American Diplomacy*, pp.95–104.

49   Hurewitz, *The Middle East*, pp.1–5; *Encyclopaedia Britannica*, 2:832.

50   *Encyclopaedia Hebraica*, 29:979–80; Sousa, *The Capitulatory Regime*, pp. 68–69.

could hardly be applied to non-Muslims and even less to aliens who were practically outlaws.[51]

In the Near East, the system developed most fully in the Ottoman Empire. As European merchants came to Ottoman commercial centers, and in encouraging trade with the West, the early sultans were not concerned with equal treatment for their own subjects.[52] Although Genoa, Venice, and Florence had obtained capitulations from the Porte at earlier dates, the French treaty of 1535 became the basis in the Ottoman Empire for the capitulatory regime under which other Western powers subsequently obtained analogous privileges. This amounted to a treaty of commerce and to a treaty allowing the establishment of Frenchmen in Turkey, and defining the jurisdiction to be exercised over them, including the right to practice their religion as individuals. The consuls in Turkey appointed by the king of France were empowered to adjudicate the civil and criminal affairs of French subjects in Turkey according to French law, and to appeal to the officers of the sultan for aid in executing the sentences they pronounced. All subsequent capitulation treaties followed this model.[53]

In treaties concluded in the 18th and 19th centuries with European powers, the sultans did include elements of reciprocity, but the corresponding benefits related to other than extraterritorial rights for Ottoman subjects. In the course of the 18th century, nearly every European power obtained capitulations, and such newly-established countries as the United States of America, Belgium, and Greece followed in the 19th century.[54] As described by Gabriel Bie Ravndal, a journalist who served many years in the American consular service – including in Beirut and Constantinople from 1898 – this had wide-ranging economic effects. Foreigners were exempt from all taxes levied by the Ottoman government except the ad valorem export and import duties of which maximums

51   Friedman, "The System of Capitulations," p.281.

52   Hurewitz, *The Middle East*, pp.1–5.

53   Hurewitz, ibid.; *Encyclopaedia Britannica*, 2:832; Sousa, *The Capitulatory Regime*, pp.43–67.

54   Hurewitz, ibid.; *Encyclopaedia Britannica*, ibid.

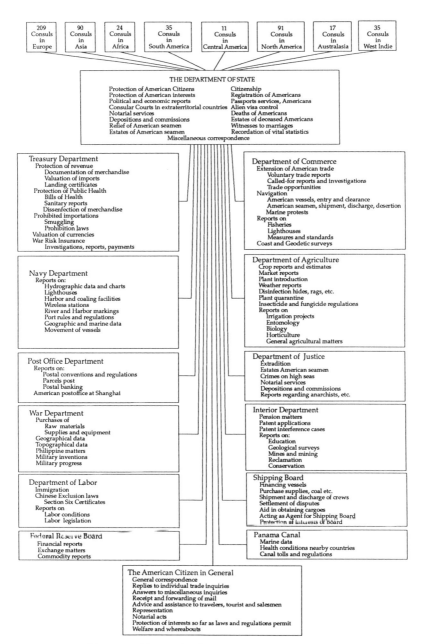

Figure 4. The work of the United States consul
Source: Lay, *The Foreign Service*, p.193

were fixed by the capitulations. Almost no internal tax could be levied on foreign goods. Any business house could establish itself in the country without the authority of the Ottoman government and could organize according to the laws of its own country.[55] According to an official United States report of 1920 which summarized the past situation, "There is no law in Turkey obliging any foreign bank, banking house, or mercantile firm, wishing to establish a branch house in Turkey to submit itself to any official or legal formality. Consequently, any bank or private firm is at liberty to establish a branch in Turkey and freely transact and conduct business."[56]

From the middle of the 19th century, the capitulatory system was increasingly abused. Extraterritorial privileges were extended by the foreign consuls to many non-Muslims, who took full advantage of these legal immunities to flout local regulations and misuse them in other ways. As the authority of the Ottoman state weakened, European banks, commercial houses and even post offices were set up in many places, while the consuls grew more insolent as their power increased. Ravndal remarked that "...the powers have abused their economic privileges in many instances to the extent of preventing Turkey from developing her own industries, while inferior European goods have been unloaded upon the country in great quantities. On the other hand, Turkey has been assisted through foreign countries providing markets for native raw products."[57]

Persons protected by foreign powers claimed extraterritorial status with partial immunity from Ottoman laws and exemption from local taxation. By the late fifties of the 19th century, the Ottoman government, increasingly aware of the encroachments upon its sovereign rights, smarted under the humiliations. In 1856, it first mooted the abrogation of capitulatory rights, regarding them as both harmful and obsolescent. What had almost disdainfully been granted by the sultans when the Empire was one of the ranking world powers, now underlined its helplessness and decline. In one important realm, that of real estate, which will be discussed below in Chapter Six, the Ottoman authorities succeeded, from the year 1867, in imposing on foreign nationals rights and obligations for administration, registry, taxation, and jurisdiction. But even when European legal codes were being introduced as part of the modernizing reforms in the Ottoman Empire after the mid-19th century, the Capitulations remained the basis for Ottoman relations with Western countries until they

---

55   Ravndal, "Capitulations," pp.431–33.

56   Eliot G. Mears' Commercial Reports, 22 May 1920, as quoted in Ravndal, ibid.

57   Ravndal, ibid.; Friedman, "The System of Capitulations," pp.281–82.

were unilaterally abrogated by the Turkish government on 1 October 1914 (Plate 8).[58]

Plate 8. Sultan Abdul Hamid II on horseback
Source: Cox, *Diplomacy in Turkey*

Consuls and Capitulations

The functions of the consuls evolved with the growth of European mercantile stations in the towns of the Empire. They had jurisdiction over their nationals and persons officially under their protection, and frequently fulfilled diplomatic functions.[59] A consulate in the Levant acted as small-scale government for its nationals and protégés. The consul, entitled by imperial

---

58 Friedman, ibid.; Sousa, *The Capitulatory Regime*, pp.93–101; Hurewitz, *The Middle East*, pp.1–5.

59 *Encylopaedia Hebraica*, 29:408.

edict *balios-bey* or *consulus-bey*, who headed this complex institution, in effect enjoyed ambassadorial status, including the honorific rights that were part of the diplomatic ceremonial, to a far greater extent than did ministers to Western states. His house was an inviolable asylum against the laws and officials of the country, he was exempt from all customs duties and he could be neither arrested nor tried in civil and criminal proceedings. His family, members of his household, his retainers, his dwellings and furnishings were considered outside the territory of the host state.[60]

His status under the capitulatory regime allowed the consul "freedom of worship" – the right to have a chapel in his house where all persons of his religion could worship. Nationals of countries having capitulatory rights could not be brought before the local courts. The consuls of the United States, Great Britain, France, Austria, Italy, and several other Western countries were empowered to try and judge criminal cases. In matters of civil law they acted as justices of the peace, tribunals of the first instance, and as tribunals of commerce with no limits on the type of case or on the sums involved. The consuls also fulfilled the functions of police magistrates and had extensive voluntary jurisdiction regarding the tutelage of minors, family counseling and advice, authorizing women to marry, adoptions, or the charge of estates and goods of those dying intestate within their district. They kept records of marriages, births and deaths; granted attestations of life; authenticated documents issued by the local authorities; performed all the functions of notaries public, both public and private; they approved last wills and testaments; had almost unlimited powers and duties in all questions regarding the masters and crews of merchant vessels; and granted, issued, or at least visaed, all passports.

The importance and the responsibilities with which the consuls were entrusted thus embraced, besides the attributes of diplomatic ministers, those of notaries, chiefs of police, mayors – in civil matters, commercial tribunals, criminal courts, justices of peace, and in general, of all powers and duties necessary for the preservation of law, order, and security in the community or colony of which they were both the judicial and administrative heads.[61] The all-encompassing powers of the consuls under the capitulations were well summed up by Arnold Blumberg:

---

60   Van Dyck, "Report on the Capitulations," pp.14–15.

61   Van Dyck, ibid.

The most important right gained in these sixteenth century capitulatory treaties, was the privilege of each consul to serve as judge and jury for the subjects of his own sovereign, residing on Turkish soil. Without spelling out the details of the consul's extraterritorial rights, a consul gained supreme power over the property, person, and even the life of his fellow nationals living within the territorial boundaries of his jurisdiction. With each consulate possessed of its own locked prison room, the French consul presided over a bit of France, and the English consul presided over a bit of England, far from home.[62] (Plate 9)

Plate 9. A model of old Jerusalem with flags over the foreign consulates
Source: Jerusalem Model in AJHS

Capitulations and Jurisdiction

The theoretical aspects of private international law were not developed in the Ottoman Empire as in Europe and therefore it must be regarded differently. "Owing to the privilege of jurisdiction accorded to Franks, very many consular

62 Blumberg, "Comments," pp.255–58.

tribunals are established upon Ottoman territory, belonging to different nations, and required to apply different laws."[63] To this confusion of legal and judicial frameworks must be added the Muslim religious legal and juridical systems, as well as those of the various Christian sects, and of the Jews, which were officially recognized in the Empire as "millets" with autonomous rights. These latter resorted to the juridical institutions of their communities, and if they were also foreign nationals, to the consular judicial systems.[64]

The key words for understanding the subject of capitulations and the consular activities of the foreign countries are extraterritoriality and extraterritorial status and the juridical authority granted in this connection.[65] One of those who wrote on these matters was Edward Van Dyck, the son of an American missionary, who served as consular clerk and vice-consul in Beirut and Cairo between the years 1873 and 1882, taught in the schools of Cairo and translated ancient works on ethics and a book on real property according to Ottoman law.[66] He defined this status in a lengthy survey and report to the Senate, in 1881, entitled, "Capitulations of the Ottoman Empire", as a "...fiction of public international law, by virtue of which, such and such a one is considered as having never quitted his own country, although he may have transferred his residence elsewhere and established his domicile in another state."

Van Dyck discussed in considerable detail the privileges bestowed by extraterritoriality in the daily life of Europeans and Americans residing in Turkey and emphasized six points:

1. Europeans in Turkey are not bound to follow the laws of the land as to the form of deeds and instruments relating to their persons and goods.
2. No action can be brought against a European before the courts of the country; the local authorities can neither proceed to arrest his person nor to sequester his goods.
3. A European resident in Turkey continues to belong to his own country and has his domicile there, for his domicile is considered to be that of the consul in authority over him.
4   Only the real property of the European situated in Turkey is subject to the laws of the land. In the matter of real estate taxes, Europeans are to pay the same as Ottoman subjects.

---

63   Van Dyck, "Report on the Capitulations," p.13.

64   Ravndal, "Capitulations," pp.430–47.

65   Jones, *The Consular Service*, pp.46–58.

66   Boyce, *American Foreign Service Authors*, p.292.

5. Even as the European is exempt from the civil jurisdiction and laws, local or territorial, of the Ottoman Empire, he is likewise exempt from all penal and criminal laws and jurisdiction.

6. A European, although not amenable to the jurisdiction of the local courts, is nevertheless bound to observe the police regulations in force throughout the country calculated for the maintenance of order and public security.[67]

The Protégé System

Many non-Muslim Ottoman subjects throughout the Empire strove to find ways of benefiting from capitulatory privileges enjoyed by nationals of Western countries. These efforts drew encouragement from the intent of the powers and their representatives in the Ottoman Empire to protect certain Christian and other Ottoman subjects. This "protection", which culminated in "nationalization" or "naturalization", was not suddenly imposed on the Sublime Porte in its entirety. The capitulations were there, or in the course of formation, and the interpretations and extensions to which they gave rise were applied as needed and were backed and strengthened by precedent. The unfolding of this phenomenon undesirable from the point of view of the Sublime Porte, from the 16th century until the promulgation of the Ottoman Law of Nationality of 1869, was described in a document of the Fifty-ninth Congress of the United States in 1907, by Schmavonian, the legal adviser to the American embassy at Constantinople.[68]

> In conformity with the capitulations of 1569 [the second French capitulations obtained on 18 October 1569], the interpreters [dragomans] of the French ambassadors were "protected" by being exempted from all "subsides et impôts". By the year 1740, this protection was practically extended not only to all employees of all the diplomatic missions, but even to those of the consulates. For certain diplomatic and consular officers this word "employés" was taken in so broad a sense that it included not only genuine employees and servants of every kind, but even friends who might be in need of "protection". In addition to real diplomatic and consular officers there was thus added a class of wealthy non-

---

67 Van Dyck, "Report on the Capitulations," pp.17–18.

68 *Senate Executive Document* No.326, 1907, pp.525–32.

Moslem subjects of the Sultan to whom were granted the titles of
Venetian, French, Dutch, or English consuls, and who were
protected by their respective diplomatic missions, and in turn
protected their own "employees" with their families. To these
were again added certain merchants called "beratlis", as well as
agents and brokers dealing with or for foreigners. So that in the
eighteenth century there was a large and increasing number of
native subjects of the Porte who, without obtaining foreign
nationality, were yet partakers of the general extraterritorial
privileges enjoyed by foreigners.

This was followed in the nineteenth century by wholesale
naturalization, granted by some representatives of certain powers
not only to protégés, but even to non-Moslem subjects of the
Porte who had never been outside the frontiers of the Empire.[69]

In this way were created categories of foreign protégés or nationals of
other foreign nations; consular – the native consuls and vice-consuls, agents,
dragomans, clerks, and guards; certain monasteries and religious communities,
and natives whose privilege of foreign protection was permanent and
hereditary. Since European consuls in Turkey had traditionally accepted Jews
and Christians as protégés even though they were not their nationals, the
practice spread to the American consulates.[70] Over the centuries, abuses of
the protégé system proliferated. Determined to remedy this offensive situation,
the Sublime Porte acted in three ways. It began diplomatic negotiations with
some of the embassies to end these practices, it granted more equality to its
non-Muslim subjects so as to mitigate the causes for their seeking foreign
protection, and it instituted strong measures against Ottoman subjects who
sought to change their nationality while residing in the Empire.

By the terms of the Treaty of Paris of 1856, which admitted Turkey to the
concert of nations, the powers could no longer persist in these blatant abuses.
This was followed in 1863 by a convention signed with Russia for the
"Regulation in Regard to Foreign Consulates in Turkey" which limited foreign
protection to Ottoman subjects actually in the employ of the consulates or to
certain monasteries and missionary establishments. The convention also fixed
the number of such protected persons. Finally, in January 1869, a Law of
Nationality was promulgated. The objections of the foreign missions to this

---

69   Ibid.

70   Sousa, *The Capitulatory Regime*, pp.93–112.

curtailment of their entrenched privileges were allayed by not making the law retroactive. The powers thus accepted the competence of the Ottoman government to regulate this as an internal administrative matter, and to establish the principle that Ottoman subjects could not change their nationality without permission of the government.[71]

After discussing the background of this law and quoting the entire text, Schmavonian analyzed its various provisions and their effect upon the civil status of United States citizens who formerly had been Ottoman subjects, and the possibilities of their owning and bequeathing real estate. Many complications beset persons who changed their nationality without the permission of the imperial Ottoman government. Schmavonian went on to say that until the year 1906, "The convention on naturalization between the United States and Turkey has not been ratified. In fact, a naturalization treaty was signed in Constantinople in 1875 setting forth conditions under which each would recognize the naturalization of the other's nationals, but a Senate amendment during the ratification debate was not acceptable to the Porte and the naturalized citizens remained a perennial problem of U.S. diplomatic relations until the first world war."[72]

Foreign Nationals and Land in the Ottoman Empire

Matters concerning real estate occupied much of the time of the representatives of the great powers in the Ottoman Empire, and particularly in Palestine. In the first half of the 19th century, foreign nationals were precluded from purchasing and registering land in their names, with the rare exception of individuals who were able to obtain a special firman (imperial decree) from the sultan. This situation was described in 1843 by William Tanner Young, the British consul in Jerusalem, in a letter to a British subject who desired to buy land for a mission in Safed. Young stressed that, "Our position in this country, in regard to landed property...the Turkish Government does not recognize the right of Europeans to become landowners."[73]

The prohibition on the sale of land to subjects of foreign powers continued officially until 1856, and, in effect, until 1867. In the 1850s, the British

---

71   Schmavonian, "Citizenship, Turkey," pp.525–32.

72   Manuel, *The Realities*, p.8.

73   Kark, "Batei-Tura," pp.157–67; William Tanner Young, British Consul, Jerusalem, to the Earl of Aberdeen, 25 May 1843, PRO FO78/540.

consul in Jerusalem, James Finn, and others expressed dismay at the waste
of a great potential for development resulting from this ban.

> It is still deplorable to see the millions of acres of fine land lying
> waste throughout Palestine, from which the Turkish government
> derives no revenue whatever – and in travelling over which, among
> deserted villages, the wish rises perpetually in the mind – "O that
> the Sultan would allow me to turn some wilderness into a fruitful
> field and make numerous people happy, even though double Miri
> [in this context, an agricultural tax] were paid for the opportunity
> of doing so" – but then it must be somewhat distant from the
> corruption and intrigues of Jerusalem.[74]

Despite the authorization in the *Khatt-i Hümayun* of 1856 for foreigners to
acquire land, and the promulgation of the Ottoman land law in 1858, final
legal permission was withheld for another decade. An imperial rescript
conceding to foreigners the right of holding real estate in the Ottoman Empire
was published on 18 January 1867 (7th of Sepher [sic] 1284).[75] This was
done with the object of developing the prosperity of the country, of ending
the difficulties, the abuses, and the uncertainties which beset the right of
foreigners to hold property in the Ottoman Empire, and of assuring in full,
according to precise regulations, the safeguards necessary to financial interests
and to sound administration. To these ends, the following important items
were included in the legislative enactments promulgated by order of the
sultan:

> *Art.1.* Foreigners are admitted, by the same privileges as Ottoman
> subjects, and without any other restriction, to enjoy the right of
> holding real estate, whether in the city or the country, throughout
> the empire, with the exception of the province of the Hédjaz
> [Hijaz], by submitting themselves to the laws and the regulations
> which govern Ottoman subjects, as is hereafter stated.
>
> This arrangement does not concern subjects of Ottoman birth
> who have changed their nationality who shall be governed in this
> matter by a special law.

---

74   James Finn, British Consul, Jerusalem, to Sir S. Canning, 14 August 1850, PRO FO78/839; a letter
     by H. Guedalla, *Jewish Chronicle*, 9 February 1866, p.6.

75   USNA RG84 Haifa Miscellaneous and Official Correspondence Received 1875–1917 Miscellaneous
     Papers 1878–1903 Green Box.

Art. 2. Foreigners, proprietors of real estate, in town or in country, are in consequence placed upon terms of equality with Ottoman subjects in all things that concern their landed property.

Art. 5. All foreigners shall enjoy the privileges of the present law, as soon as the Powers on which they depend shall agree to the arrangements proposed by the Sublime Porte for the exercise of the right to hold real estate.[76]

Thus the permission was granted on condition that foreigners accepted equality with Turkish nationals, and were subject to the jurisdiction of Turkish institutions and courts in all questions relating to property. Most of the interested governments concluded separate agreements during the years following 1869 to extend this privilege to their citizens. Although the law was drawn up and promulgated under the pressure of the powers, it aimed at removing land matters from the consuls' sphere of influence.[77]

The U.S. accepted the protocol permitting its nationals to own real estate in the Ottoman Empire, a concession which involved a quid pro quo recognition of Turkey's right to tax their property.[78] Hamilton Fish, the secretary of state, signed it in the name of President Ulysses S. Grant on 29 October 1874.[79]

That this goal was achieved to a large degree is borne out by a series of letters, dating to 1867–1907 in the files of the German consulate in Jerusalem, as well as in the archives of the U.S. consulates in Jerusalem and Beirut, and of the consular agencies at Jaffa and Haifa. At the same time, more than once, local government functionaries, or even the central Ottoman authorities, would ignore the law and involve the consuls in real estate transactions.[80]

---

76 Ibid.

77 Kark, "Changing Patterns," p.359.

78 Manuel, *The Realities*, pp.8–9.

79 USNA RG84 Haifa Miscellaneous and Official Correspondence Received 1875–1917 Miscellaneous Papers 1878–1903 Green Box.

80 USNA RG84 Haifa; USNA RG84 Jaffa Miscellaneous Letters Received 1872–1874 Box 5958; USNA RG59 T471/5 and 9; Archives of the German Consulate in Jerusalem, ISA RG67/255, 444B.

CHAPTER TWO

AMERICA AND THE OTTOMAN EMPIRE

Commercial, Political, and Consular Ties

Commercial Relations

The trade relations between the United States and the Ottoman Empire, from the end of the 18th century and until the First World War, may be divided into four phases. The first, before 1830, was one of random trade and of attempts at a permanent commercial and political arrangement; the second, characterized by relatively limited commercial activity, lasted until the signing of a new treaty of commerce and navigation between the United States and the Sublime Porte in 1862; the third phase saw a steady growth in the total volume of trade; and in the fourth phase, from the 1890s to 1914, the United States competed with the industrialized nations of the world for markets for its manufactured goods, with the Ottoman Empire one of its potential targets. During this latter period, Palestine with its growing Western population element became an important commercial objective – as will be discussed in Chapter Six, below.

In Colonial times, American merchants in the Mediterranean sailed under the British flag. After independence, when such vessels were no longer under British protection, the rulers of the Islamic states of the North African "Barbary" coast were emboldened to capture the ships and crews, since these were not covered by the customary annual tribute extorted from the European countries. Except for Morocco, the Barbary states were under the nominal sovereignty of the Ottoman Porte since the 16th century. Their attacks on American commerce raised the necessity of concluding agreements with them, and attempts to this end were made in Constantinople. However, the difficulties of the Boston and Philadelphia merchants drove the government to negotiate directly with Morocco, Algiers, Tunis, and Tripoli. It was a clear case of diplomatic measures being engendered by commercial interests. After some previous consideration, a treaty was concluded with the Sublime

Porte in 1830 permitting American navigation in the Mediterranean and through the Dardanelles and the Bosporus Straits, giving access to the Black Sea and the markets of southern Russia.[1] An official representative of the United States government came to Turkey in 1800 on board the frigate *George Washington* – the first armed vessel in the Mediterranean to fly the Stars and Stripes.[2] The first American to be officially recognized, and who later became the American consul in Smyrna, was David Offley, a native of Philadelphia. Offley arrived in that port city in the summer of 1811 and opened there the first American commercial house in the Levant. Notwithstanding the jealousy and active opposition of the British merchants of the Levant Company, he was soon able to ship consignments of Smyrna figs and raisins to the United States. American merchant ships also loaded dates and other products at ports on the Arabian coast.[3] The most-favored-nation treaty of commerce and navigation concluded in 1830 gave the United States capitulatory rights that had considerable impact on the trade relations between the two countries. The main imports to the United States from Turkey were opium, dried fruits, nuts, silver, raw wool, hides and skins; among American exports to the Ottoman Empire, cotton textiles and rum ranked foremost. In the years ending on 30 June 1829 and 30 September 1830, American exports to Turkey amounted to $27,600 and $74,263, respectively, and imports from Turkey to $293,237 and $417,392.[4]

But all in all, until 1860, although American commercial shipping was second only to England's, there was no real interest in seeking markets in the Muslim ports of the Mediterranean. Very few American merchants were attracted to the backward Ottoman towns.[5] Nevertheless, it was in those years that the foundations were laid for the establishment of consular posts in the Ottoman Empire, their main objectives being the gathering and reporting of commercially relevant information, providing services to American vessels, protecting Treasury revenues by verifying invoices of goods about to be shipped to the United States, and promoting trade.[6] As early as in the

---

1   Wright, " American Relations with Turkey," pp.1–31.

2   Ibid.; already in 1815, the British published instructions stressing the duty of the consul to promote British trade in his area, and so connected commerce with consular posts. (Middleton, *The Administration of British Foreign Policy*, pp.247–253.)

3   Gordon, *American Relations*, pp.54–55; De Novo, *American Interests in the Middle East*, pp.16–19.

4   Gordon, ibid., pp.43, 345–7.

5   Kennedy, *The American Consul*, pp.87–99.

6   Werking, *The Master Architects*, pp.1–3; Werking, " U.S. Consular Reports," p.300; see also tables of shipping traffic and export in Constantinople and on the Danube, 1859, 1860, USNA RG59 T194/7.

1840s, the consular position was considered an important one in everything connected with trade: "...A good consul, on the spot, is worth to the commerce of a country more than all the treaties in the world."[7] But the furthering of American trade by the businessmen-consuls, such as J. Hosford Smith in the 1850s in Beirut, was problematic because all too often they aimed "...to extend the commercial affairs of the officer" rather than those of the country he represented.[8]

In 1862, an additional commercial agreement was signed between the United States and the Sublime Porte. The Treaty of Commerce of February 1862 dealt with "...settlement of a tariff of custom-house duties, to be levied on export and import from and to the Ottoman Empire from and to the U.S." The agreement stipulated that, "All merchandise imported by merchants of the United States of America will pay a customs-house duty of eight per cent," but also that "The duty of eight per cent on exports is only applicable to the first year of the present tariff.... They will be reduced gradually within eight years and after to one per cent duty." To the agreement was appended a detailed table of "Tariff of Custom-House Duties, on all goods and merchandise, the produce and manufacture of the United States of America, imported into the Ottoman Empire established by the American-Ottoman Commission, February 28th, 1862." The table was accompanied by a statement that the tariffs constituted an adjustment of those fixed in January 1847 and was to be in effect for seven years.[9]

The United States was one of the interested Western powers which in the 1860s signed agreements that changed the distorted tariff structure of the 1838 commercial convention. Ottoman import duties were now raised from three to eight percent (and in 1892 to eleven percent), and reduced on exports from nine percent over several years to one percent per year. However, despite its sharpened awareness of economic considerations, the capitulatory system prevented the Ottoman government from inducing the Western powers to agree to valuation on an ad valorem basis.[10] The signing of this agreement marked a trend of American commercial expansion. A survey of Turkish imports to the United States in the period 1860–1900 shows that licorice root and rugs were the main items, while goods which had been traded before – dried fruits, nuts, raw wool, opium, skins – increased. The chief

---

7   Edwards Lester, " The Consular System," p.215.

8   Mayo, "Consular System of the U.S.," p.301.

9   Malloy, "Treaties," pp.1328–41.

10   Okyar, "Economic Growth," pp.18–28.

American exports were petroleum and petroleum derivatives, especially kerosene, and, on a smaller scale, various manufactured products.[11]

In the 1880s, the volume of trade was still modest, as is indicated in a review of American involvement in Turkey during the period 1851–1881 by Samuel S. Cox, who was later appointed United States minister to Constantinople in 1886: "Of course in all this the American nation has but a remote concern. The greatest interest we have here is our missionary enterprises, our Bible House, and Robert College. There may be in reserve for our petroleum and cotton fabrics a future market of some consequence. But as yet it is in embryo."[12] And in 1881, Edward Van Dyck, the American consular clerk in Cairo, ascribed to this attitude the low status of the American consuls in the Ottoman Empire: "Perhaps it is owing to the hitherto limited interest in foreign trade that the United States have not sufficiently appreciated the importance of consulates in non-Christian countries and the need of revising the statutory provisions in this respect."[13]

The limited activity in the Ottoman Empire in the eighties reflected the isolationist policy of the United States in all relating to foreign trade. A significant turnabout occurred in the 1890s and the early 20th century (although, according to LaFeber, the basis for this was laid already in 1850–1889.)[14] In 1885, the former diplomat, Eugene Schuyler, who in the 1870s served as the American consul-general at Constantinople, published a book on the subject based on a series of lectures he delivered at Johns Hopkins and Cornell universities: *American Diplomacy and the Furtherance of Commerce*. He expressed his dismay at this state of affairs and dwelled upon the activities of American consuls and the lack of initiative by manufacturers and businessmen in developing trade, in contrast to the vigorous activities of other nations, such as England and Belgium. He thought that the consuls could do but little to advance commerce beyond providing information, and advocated employing shipping agents as did the British, and setting up "museums" to display samples of the products of various nations, along Belgian models. Schuyler ascribed the apathy of the American business community to foreign trade to their exaggerated interest in the home market. Even when the latter contracted, after having made good beginnings abroad they abandoned these as the domestic market revived. Moreover, he accused

11   Gordon, "American Relations," pp.50–67.

12   Cox, *Orient Sunbeams*, p.132.

13   Van Dyck, "Report on the Capitulations," p.16.

14   LaFeber, *The New Empire*, pp.1–61.

Americans of assuming that whatever was good for them was good for the whole world, and deplored their lack of readiness to adapt themselves in the matter of weights and measures, styles, and in other things.[15]

Toward the end of the 19th century, and especially in the early years of the 20th, after breaking the British monopoly on shipping in 1899, American efforts were also directed to developing trade with the Ottoman Empire. Despite fluctuations, the value of American exports to Turkey rose from $442,721 in 1862 to $3,328,519 in 1914, while imports from Turkey to the U.S. increased from $959,693 in 1862 to $20,843,077 in 1914. The value of the exports to the U.S. from the consular district of Jerusalem came to $18,111 in 1876, and $17,579 in 1909 compared to imports from the U.S. of $27,472 in that year. The trade figures between the Haifa and Acre district and the U.S. in 1885/6 are: exports to the U.S. of $5,400 and imports of $12,650 – mainly petroleum. In 1912, the eight most important products in terms of their value were (in that order): cottonseed oil, oleo oil, mineral oils, cotton and wool manufactures, bronze, leather manufactures, agricultural implements, and electrical appliances. In that year, automobiles and spare parts constituted only a small proportion of the exports to Turkey. In 1928 these were to become the chief American imports into Turkey, representing an 82-fold increase of this category in the total exports and making up a third of all American exports.[16]

At the beginning of the 20th century, and particularly in 1909–1913 under President Taft and Secretary of State Knox, the implementation of "dollar diplomacy" marked an aggressive policy of extending American markets, with special emphasis on non-European countries. The Ottoman Empire now became a specific commercial objective. Turkey gained particular importance in the eyes of the leading industrial nations because these partly closed their own markets by means of tariff restrictions, and vied for new outlets for their manufactured goods.[17] It marked a climax in the changing attitude of American foreign policy regarding the promotion of economic

---

15 Schuyler, *American Diplomacy*, pp.102–4; for additional biographical notes and on Schuyler's consular and diplomatic positions see: Werking, *The Master Architects*, p.29.

16 Gordon, *American Relations*, pp.57–114. E. Hardegg, U.S. Consular Agent, Jaffa, to Third Assistant Secretary of State, Washington, D.C., 1 January 1877, USNA RG59 T471/4, and T.R. Wallace, U.S Consul, Jerusalem, to Assistant Secretary of State, Washington, D.C., 29 June 1910, ibid.; J. Schumacher, U.S. Consular Agent, Haifa, Statement showing imports and exports for Acca and Haifa for the year ending June 30, 1886, USNA RG84 Haifa Miscellaneous Papers Received 1875–1917 Miscellaneous papers 1878–1903 Green Box.

17 Werking, *The Master Architects*, pp.167–170; Gordon, ibid., pp.141–160

and commercial expansion. The State Department set objectives aiming at securing markets abroad for manufacturers and exporters, primarily for finished goods. During the 1890s, the advancement of American commerce became the main function of the consular frameworks as former restraints on consular involvement in trade were removed. Against this background should be seen also the change in the American administration regarding trade and the establishment of the Department of Commerce and Labor in 1903, which comprised the Bureau of Statistics and the Division of Consular reports – functions which until then had been filled by the Bureau of Foreign Commerce in the State Department. In 1905, the Bureau of Manufactures and the Bureau of Trade Relations were added to the new department. And at the end of the decade, the Geographical Divisions, including the Near Eastern Division, were established in the State Department.

This change was reflected also in the work of the consuls-general, the consuls, and the special agents in Turkey and the Levant. For example, detailed reports by Thomas R. Gibson, the consul at Beirut, and by Consul Edwin S. Wallace in Jerusalem, on the ocean lines, the railway, and highways of commerce in Syria and Palestine, were published in the middle of 1894 together with special consular reports from other places in a compendium of the U.S. Bureau of Foreign Commerce (as it was called until 1903) of the State Department.[18] In 1898–1906, the consul-general at Constantinople, Charles M. Dickinson, urged the consulates subordinate to him in Turkey to act energetically for increasing American trade in their districts. Despite objective difficulties due to the channeling of American shipments via England and Germany, which caused expensive delays and increased the amount of goods damaged in transit to a point of reducing profits, the results were encouraging.[19]

Dickinson was helped in his efforts by the then consul-general at Beirut, G. Bie Ravndal, who also advanced the cause of American trade in the Levant and northern Palestine. In 1903, the consular agent at Haifa wrote of "...His great endeavours to further American commercial relations in all parts of Syria, in which he has been so successful..."[20] When Oscar S. Straus (who was well-acquainted with conditions in the Ottoman Empire, having served there twice as minister) was appointed Secretary of Commerce

---

18   U.S. Bureau of Foreign Commerce, *Highways of Commerce*, pp.522–31.

19   Dickinson's personal archive in Library of Congress, quoted by Mattox, *The Twilight*, p.65.

20   Gottlieb Schumacher, U.S. Consular Agent, Haifa, to Secretary of State, Washington, D.C., 20 August 1903, USNA RG84 Haifa, Miscellaneous and Official Correspondence Received 1875–1917 Miscellaneous Papers 1875–1904 Green Box; see also: Ravndal, "Turkey."

and Labor, he commissioned the preparation of a report on Trade Conditions in Asiatic Turkey. His introduction to the fifty-page report by Charles M. Pepper of the Bureau of Manufactures, which came under Straus's department in 1907, complains about the paucity of information in the United States regarding this important potential market of 17 million consumers. Straus, who did not consider Turkey a "distant market," expressed his conviction that if American manufactures would but recognize the advantages offered by the Asiatic Turkish markets "...within a few years something in the nature of a real balance of trade may be established instead of the present lack of equilibrium, with the United States selling only $500,000 and buying $6,000,000 to $7,000,000 of products." The report related to Asia Minor and Syria and to the infrastructure of sea and land transport – especially railways, to electrical development, agricultural machinery, iron and steel products, textile imports, rubber and leather goods, as well as to the commercial activity of Britain and Germany and to possible ways for advancing the trade of the United States. Straus particularly stressed the importance of railroads for "...bringing new areas under cultivation and for the introduction of electricity. The installations that recently have been made and the additional ones that are assured, form one of the most significant chapters in the opening of old countries to new ideas, both industrial and commercial."[21]

In addition to this encouragement, in 1908–1911, a concentrated drive by American capitalists was set in motion for concessions to build a railway and engage in mining in eastern Anatolia and northern Syria. This large-scale program, known as the "Chester Project," was supported by the American administration and fitted well into Taft's and Knox's "dollar diplomacy." Even though the Chester plan did not materialize, it brought the United States for the first time into confrontations with the imperialist powers in the Ottoman Empire.[22]

Political and Consular Ties

During the first half of the 19th century, the relations between the United States and the Ottoman Empire were mainly nonpolitical. The United States presence was manifested primarily by an assorted group of missionaries, merchants, scholars and writers, philanthropists, scientists, engineers, and adventurers. American political interest in the Ottoman Empire was ambiguous

21   Pepper, "Report on Trade Conditions," p.5.
22   Gordon, *American Relations*, pp.252–266, 345.

throughout the entire century.[23] The policy of nonintervention and neutrality generally adopted by the United States was expressed in a despatch of Richard Beardsley, the American consul in Jerusalem in 1871: "The United States are not suspected of having any political design, as are all European nations. We have no direct interest in the Eastern Question."[24] At the turn of the 18th century, the American government did conduct negotiations with the Sublime Porte for privileges similar to the capitulations enjoyed by the European powers. These were granted on 7 May 1830 under the Treaty of Amity, Commerce, and Navigation.[25] The capitulatory rights of American citizens in the Ottoman Empire derived from this treaty, which was drawn up in Turkish with an official and agreed French version. The United States later came to rely wholly upon the Turkish text. Different interpretations of one of the articles (Article IV), arising from English translations, persisted until 1917, and caused strained relations especially after the 1880s. On 25 February 1862, the two governments concluded a commercial convention modeled on the British-Turkish agreement of 1861. But after the Porte repudiated this agreement in 1884, the American government based its claims to most-favored-nation treatment on the 1830 treaty.[26]

The treaty of 1830 comprised nine points to which was added a Separate and Secret Article. Most of the articles of the treaty dealt with freedom of action and remission of taxation on merchants, and on freedom of passage and the security of ships and their cargos. Some of the provisions emphasized reciprocity between Ottoman and American merchants, but in principle, the status of the latter in the Ottoman Empire was equated with that of the "most favored friendly powers". For the purpose of this study there is particular importance to Articles II and IV which provided the basis for American consular activity in the Ottoman Empire from 1831 onwards. Article II stipulated the terms for the appointment and status of consuls:

> Art. II. The Sublime Porte may establish *Shahbenders* (Consuls) in the United States of America; and the United States may appoint their citizens to be Consuls, at the commercial places in the dominions of the Sublime Porte, where it shall be found needful to superintend the affairs of commerce. These Consuls or Vice

---

23   Kark, "Annual Reports," p.129.

24   Richard Beardsley, U.S. Consul, Jerusalem, to Second Assistant Secretary of State, Washington, D.C., 30 September, 1871, USNA RG59 T471/4.

25   Hurewitz, *The Middle East*, pp.245–47.

26   Hurewitz, ibid.; Malloy, "Treaties," pp.1328–41; Sousa, *The Capitulatory Regime*, pp.128–52.

Consuls shall be furnished with *Berats* or *Firmans*; they shall enjoy suitable distinction, and shall have necessary aid and protection.

The fourth article, the formulation of which remained a source of disagreement between the parties, defined the legal status of the consul and his fellow countrymen:

Art. IV. If litigations and disputes should arise between subjects of the Sublime Porte and citizens of the United States, the parties shall not be heard, nor shall judgement be pronounced unless the American Dragoman be present. Causes in which the sum may exceed five hundred piastres shall be submitted to the Sublime Porte, to be decided according to the laws of equity and justice. Citizens of the United States, quietly pursuing their commerce, and not being charged or convicted of any crime or offense, shall not be molested; and even if they shall have committed some offense they shall not be arrested and put in prison by the local authorities, but they shall be tried by their Minister or Consul, and punished according to their offense, following in this respect, the usage observed towards other Franks.[27]

From 1831, American foreign service officials were appointed to the Ottoman Empire. The most important of these was the representative in Constantinople (Istanbul), with the consuls in Alexandria, Beirut, and Smyrna (Izmir) following, in that order.[28] In February 1862, a new treaty of commerce was signed between the United States and the Ottoman Empire, as detailed in this chapter, above.

Juridical Procedures

According to treaties concluded between the United States and China, Japan, Siam, Persia, and Turkey, certain judicial powers to be exercised through consular courts were granted to the American ministers and consuls serving in these countries. The consuls also provided notarial services and dealt with depositions and commissions, and with estates of deceased Americans.[29] In a circular issued by Lewis Cass, the secretary of state, on 1 September 1860, to the diplomatic and consular officers of the United States in China, Japan,

27   Hurewitz, ibid.
28   Kark, "Annual Reports," p.129.
29   Lay, *The Foreign Service*, pp.132–33, 193.

Siam, Persia, Turkey, Tripoli, Tunis, Morocco, and Muscat, he apprised them of the Act of Congress of 22 June 1860: "With a view to a speedy organization of the system of jurisprudence established in the Act to insure the uniformity of proceedings in each country, and to make known to the government of the U.S. and to its citizens residing abroad the manner in which the provisions of the law are to be executed." In particular, the document instructed the representatives in the countries of North Africa, Turkey, and Muscat "...to make themselves familiar with the provisions of the law, and to execute them in accordance with its spirit and intent, in order that the faith of the United States which has been solemnly pledged by treaty stipulations, may be faithfully kept, and the rights and interests of American citizens in their relations with one another, and with the subjects of foreign powers, be thereby protected." In this connection, the representatives were requested "...to prescribe the necessary forms and regulations for carrying it into effect and to arrange a tariff of fees to be charged for judicial services." The obligation of making periodic reports was stressed, the ministers and consuls being enjoined "...to transmit regularly to the department reports of all cases tried by them, agreeable to the form which is hereby transmitted."[30] In January of 1863, the secretary of state, complied with the sixth section of the Act entitled, "An act to carry into effect provisions of the treaties between the United States, China, Japan, Siam, Persia, and other countries giving certain judicial powers to ministers and consuls, etc..." which required "all regulations, orders, and decrees published in pursuance of the provisions of the said act for the government of the consular courts...to be laid before Congress for revision...", by submitting a despatch from the U.S. minister in Constantinople and the accompanying "regulations, etc..." for the American consular courts in Turkey.

In connection with these instructions, Edward Joy Morris, the minister of the U.S. at Constantinople, wrote a detailed report dealing with "Regulations, decrees, and orders for the government of the United States consular courts in Turkey." The report was submitted on 23 January 1863 by Secretary of State William H. Seward, to President Abraham Lincoln who brought it before the Senate and the House of Representatives.[31] Actually, the report was drawn up by the American consul-general in Constantinople, Charles W. Goddard, who based himself on a study of the consular judicial system as well as upon his observations and experience. There is no doubt that Goddard also drew upon the experience in this field gathered by Britain in

---

30   Goddard, "Consular Courts in Turkey," pp.1–17.

31   Ibid.

the Ottoman Empire. This is obvious from a British juridical document of
27 August 1860, entitled, "Orders of Her Majesty in Council for the Regulation
of Consular Jurisdiction in the Dominions of the Sublime Porte" found in
the archives of the American legation in Constantinople.[32] Goddard also
referred, at Seward's advice, to the "Regulations for the Consular Courts of
the United States of America in China" which were prepared according to
congressional directives of 1848 by Robert M. McLane, commissioner of
the U.S. to China, and presented by him on 24 August 1854.[33] According to
these directives, "consuls were given jurisdiction over all cases, civil and
criminal, even including capital offenses."

The detailed report prepared by Goddard in 1862 dealt mainly with ordinary
civil proceedings between American citizens residing in the Ottoman Empire
in matters of matrimonial status, marriage, divorce, births and deaths, claims,
and the registration of American citizens and protogés, and in the conduct of
criminal proceedings concerning American citizens only, with subjects of
the Sublime Porte or with citizens of any other friendly power through the
Turkish authorities or the consulates. Goddard also provided suitable directives
regarding the formulation of civil and criminal dockets and records of final
judgements. These directives formed the basis for sound bookkeeping practices
in these matters at the various levels of consular representation.

The two consular representatives mentioned above, Van Dyck and Ravndal,
who served in Beirut, and later in Cairo and Constantinople, described in
1881 and in 1921–22, the rights and judiciary duties of American consuls as
defined in the capitulatory agreements.[34] Van Dyck, whose survey was
quoted in part in the Introduction, emphasized that "The chief aim and merit
of this report ought to be to furnish that which is of practical utility and
undoubted correctness for the enlightenment of consuls of the United States
in the Levant, in the exercise of their complex and responsible functions of
judge-consuls..."[35] Despite the directives laid down by the government at
various stages, problems arose from the consuls' general lack of legal training.
This was noted by several investigators. According to Jones, "As a whole,
our administration of justice in our consular courts lacks that definiteness
which should be a characteristic of all law proceedings."[36] In the region

32   USNA RG59 T194/7 Constantinople 1850–1861.

33   Goddard, "Consular Courts in Turkey," pp.17–26; Jones, *The Consular Service*, p.51.

34   Van Dyck, "Report for 1880," and "Report on the Capitulations"; Ravndal, "The Origin of the
     Capitulations."

35   Van Dyck, "Report on the Capitulations," p.25.

36   Jones, *The Consular Service*, p.57.

which concerns us here, Jerusalem, Manuel, who studied the application of American justice by the consuls, adds that "...the whole field of consular justice was a legal limbo."[37] In the following chapters, we will return to test the aptness of this criticism.

PERIODIZATION OF U.S. CONSULAR ACTIVITY IN THE OTTOMAN EMPIRE

Foundation of the Consulate in Constantinople

Prior to the establishment of a consulate by the United States in 1832, American citizens and interests in Constantinople looked for protection to the representatives of the British Levant Trading Company. On 3 January 1832, Frederick E. Bunker of New York was appointed to the new post, but he never reached Constantinople. The consulate was sometimes headed by unpaid consuls, and at other times by the secretary of the American legation as acting consul. This situation prevailed until the Crimean War, when the consulate was closed by presidential order in 1853. Soon after reopening in 1856, the Constantinople consulate was raised to consulate-general by the act of 1857. The first American consul-general was John P. Brown (Appendix II C). As specified in the new consular regulations, the consulate-general at Constantinople was given jurisdiction over several consulates and consular agencies of the United States in the Ottoman Empire. On 27 March 1901, in addition to his existing duties, the consul-general at Constantinople was also appointed consular agent at Sofia in Bulgaria. The consulate-general and the consulate that preceded it dealt with certain criminal and civil cases involving Americans within the territory under its jurisdiction.[38] Altogether, in the period 1832–1914, twenty-two consuls and consuls-general served in Constantinople (Appendix II C). The records of the consulate and the consulate-general that were preserved from the year 1845, and documents that survived the great fire that ravaged Constantinople in June of 1870, give an idea of the consular activities. These include records of court cases, monitoring the persecution of certain minority groups in the Empire, relief work, problems of missionaries, reporting on internal acts of hostility and rebellion against the Ottoman government, and the usual consular business dealing with the protection of American persons and interests, commerce, shipping, and administration. Additional material providing information on

37   Manuel, *The Realities*, pp.24–25.

38   Stewart, "Preliminary Inventory," p.1–24

the United States consular offices in Constantinople can be found in the
records of the American legation, and in some of the consulates and consular
agencies throughout the Ottoman Empire.[39] At the end of the 19th and in
the early 20th century, there were fourteen posts under the jurisdiction of the
consulate-general at Constantinople: Aleppo, Alexandretta (Iskanderun),
Baghdad, Beirut, Candia (Crete), the Dardanelles, Erzerum, Harput, Jerusalem,
Mersin, Salonika, Sivas, Smyrna (Izmir), and Trebizond (Figure 5).[40]

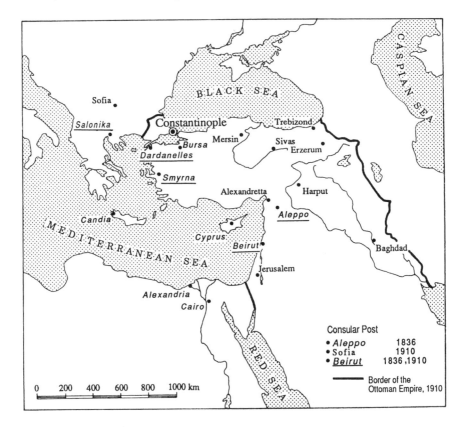

Figure 5. Consular posts under the jurisdiction of the United States
consulate-general at Constantinople, 1836 and 1910

Egypt was no longer under its jurisdiction, while the activity in eastern
Turkey was increased as a result of involvement in the Armenian Question.

39   Ibid.
40   Ibid., pp.6–7.

In accordance with the change of emphasis in the U.S. consular service, the main occupations of the consul-general in Constantinople in that period focused on the advancement of American commerce in Turkey. Nineteen consular officers assisted him in these endeavors (Plate 10).[41]

The basis for consular activity throughout the Ottoman Empire, as defined in the 1830s, was to serve American missionary and commercial interests. At the initiative of the senior diplomatic representative of the United States in Constantinople, David Porter, a network of consular agencies, which were soon elevated to consular status, were opened in various localities in the Empire. Besides the consulate in Constantinople, ten consuls were appointed in European and Asiatic Turkey (Salonika, Bursa, Smyrna, the Dardanelles), in the Levant (Aleppo, Beirut), in Egypt (Alexandria, Cairo), and in Cyprus and Crete (Figure 4). Since no other Americans were found, only the consuls in Constantinople (John P. Brown) and in Smyrna (David Offley) were citizens of the United States. The other consuls were nationals of other powers such as England and France. Porter also wanted to establish consulates in Mocha and Trebizond but did not manage to do so.[42] Since the appointments in Syria were made during the occupation by Muhammad 'Ali and the rule of Ibrahim Pasha there, it was necessary to obtain their recognition and that of the Egyptian military governor of Syria. Accordingly, at the latter's instructions, the appointment of Jasper Chasseaud as consul at Beirut was registered in the Muslim shari'a (canonical law) courts of Tripoli and Sidon.[43] Porter also appointed David Darmon, a Jew of French nationality from Ramle, to the post of American consular agent in Jaffa and Jerusalem – in the hope of eventually establishing a consulate in Jerusalem. However, in 1835, Porter dismissed Darmon for improper conduct which included selling American letters of protection to local persons and by sending ambitious proposals directly to the State Department. Without having formal authority to do so, the consuls began to appoint consular agents in the regions of their jurisdiction. These were unpaid local merchants whose services mainly consisted in accommodating and helping visiting travelers. Their remuneration was the enhanced prestige they enjoyed in the eyes of their fellows which

41   Mattox, *The Twilight*, p.65

42   Finnie, *Pioneers East*, pp.250–70; De Novo, *American Interests in the Middle East*, pp.18–19. The Welshman B.W. Llewellyn was appointed to Salonika, John Glidden to Alexandria and his son, George, to Cairo; in Aleppo served Mr. Durighello, in Cyprus Mr. Marino Mattei, and Jasper Chasseaud in Beirut.

43   Rustum, *Material for a Corpus*, 2:97–8.

Plate 10. Letterhead of passport issued by the United States
legation at Constantinople
Source: USNA RG59 T471/1

enabled them to reap certain tangible benefits.[44] Although the existence of the consulates was not a charge on the budget of the United States government, Porter was ordered by the Department of State, in 1840, to close down all the new consulates, except for the ones in Constantinople, Smyrna, and Alexandria. The reason given was that they were deemed to be of no real importance, and Porter was instructed to make it clear to the Sublime Porte that no political motives were behind this decision. Finnie raised the possibility that the actual reason for closing the consulates derived from the embarrassment of the State Department at the growing criticism of the men appointed as consuls by American travelers in the East.[45] Closing the consulate at Beirut, which also included Palestine under its jurisdiction, was especially problematical, and Porter was induced by the pressure of the resident missionaries to keep Chasseaud on as consular agent. In 1842, with the policy changes in Washington, Chasseaud was reconfirmed as consul, and Porter was requested to recommend additional places in Syria in which to establish United States consulates.[46]

Perhaps this change in attitude was connected with the retreat of Muhammad 'Ali to Egypt in 1841, and the awakening of greater interest among the European Christian powers in the fate of the Ottoman Empire and of the Holy Land. However, the American foreign service continued to manifest marked ambivalence in the opening and closing of consulates and consular agencies under the jurisdiction of the legation and the consulate in Constantinople. As in the closing of the consulates in 1840, the present minister, Dabney S. Carr, instructed the consul in Beirut in 1849, to cease the activities of the consular agencies in Damascus, Acre, Nazareth, and Ramle, as "entirely useless to any American interest..."[47] This situation prevailed until the introduction of more regularized procedures in the consular activities, consequent to the reforms in the U.S. consular service in 1856, and the end of the Crimean War.

The Consulate in Beirut

From the opening of a consular agency in Beirut, in 1832 or 1833, and its

---

44 Manuel, *The Realities*, p.9.

45 Finnie, *Pioneers East*, pp.254–5.

46 Finnie, ibid.

47 Dabney S. Carr, U.S. Minister, Constantinople, to Jasper Chasseaud, U.S. Consul, Beirut, 30 July 1849, USNA RG59 T367/2.

elevation to consulate in 1835, seventeen consuls served there up to the outbreak of World War I, in 1914. During some of that period (1867–1874, and from 1906), the consulate had the status of consulate-general, but was at all times subordinate to the legation and to the consulate, and later to the consulate-general in Constantinople. Its area of jurisdiction, until the opening of the United States consulate in Jerusalem in 1856, comprised all the sanjaks (districts) of the vilayet (province) of Beirut (Sidon), and the regions east of Mount Lebanon in the sanjaks of Damascus and Aleppo which were included in the vilayet of Damascus (Figure 6).

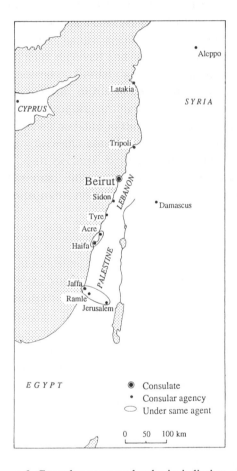

Figure 6. Consular posts under the jurisdiction of the
United States consulate at Beirut, 1832-1856

Hence, until that year, all of Palestine (the sanjaks of Acre, Nablus, and

Jerusalem) was under the jurisdiction of the consulate at Beirut. With the establishment of the Jerusalem consulate, the central and southern parts of Palestine passed under its purview, while northern Palestine remained under the jurisdiction of Beirut until after the First World War.

The opening of an American consulate in Beirut was motivated by pressure from American travelers and missionaries who, in the absence of an American representative, had to depend upon the British consul for their protection. But the personal ambitions of the consular candidate, Jasper Chasseaud, also played a role.[48] A native of Salonika, Chasseaud was a successful Beirut businessman, one of a group of local entrepreneurs who were instrumental in the growth of the city as an important commercial center of the eastern Mediterranean. Many of these merchants aspired to consular or consular agent status, or to becoming protogés or citizens of a foreign power. Consular service, although unpaid, entailed release from taxation, and gave them legal, economic, and financial privileges from which they derived considerable material and social advantages.[49] Sometimes one man served as representative of two countries at one and the same time. For at least four years (1843–1847), Chasseaud was both the American and the Prussian consul in Beirut.[50]

Chasseaud's appointment was probably helped by his family connections. His uncle, Peter Abbott, an Englishman of Levantine birth, had been in contact with the United States minister in London as early as 1797 in an attempt to convince the Americans to develop trade in colonial goods in the Ottoman Empire. Abbott was even sent on a mission to Washington in order to convince the secretary of state of the advantages of this plan, but on the way was captured by the French. After the Napoleonic wars, he became British consul in Beirut, at first (until 1825) with the Levant Company and afterwards for the Foreign Office. Abbott was reputedly most sympathetic to the Protestant missions and extended his protection over them.[51]

Chasseaud, who according to different sources was of Ottoman, French, or

48 American Missionaries in Beirut, to John Forsyth, Secretary of State, Washington, D.C., 30 November 1836, USNA RG59 T367/1; Lipman, *Americans and the Holy Land*, pp.71–77.

49 Fawaz, *Merchants and Migrants*, pp.85–92. Another family seeking consular posts was the Soursuks. In 1832, during the Egyptian occupation, Dimitri Soursuk was described as a private merchant who would become dragoman of the recently appointed American consular representative.

50 Blumberg, *Zion Before Zionism*, pp.54–57.

51 Wright, *American Relations with Turkey*, pp.10–13; Lipman, *Americans and the Holy Land*, pp.71–76. Edward Abbott van Dyck, who compiled reports from Egypt on the capitulations in the 1880s, and served as consular clerk in the American consulate at Beirut in the 70s, and later in Cairo, was Abbott's grandson. (Van Dyck, "Report for 1880," p.35.)

British – but certainly not American – nationality began to conduct regularized correspondence in the consulate from 25 March 1836. In his first letter to the secretary of state, he expressed his gratitude for: "My Comission [sic] from the Honorable President of the United States for my appointment of Consul for Beirut, Damascus, Saida" and promised to be devoted to his duties, to comply with instructions, and to establish trade with America.[52] He served in the position close to twenty years, until he was replaced by J. Hosford Smith, an American citizen, who began (salaried) service in 1850. The correspondence in the files of the Beirut consulate indicates that Chasseaud's contacts were mainly with the secretaries of state and with the ambassadors in Constantinople. His various reports seem to show that he succeeded in stimulating some direct commerce between Syria and the United States.[53] He provided accommodations and financial services to visitors and travelers – among them the scholar-explorer Edward Robinson – to Moses Montefiore (through assistance to the representative of the House of N.M. Rothschild of London, E. Kilbec Heugh & Co.), and helped the U.S. Navy expedition of William Francis Lynch who surveyed the Jordan and the Dead Sea in 1848.[54] From time to time he reported on unusual events in his consular region, such as the disastrous earthquake in Tiberias and Safed in 1837, the blood-libel accusations against the Jews of Damascus (which he believed to be true) in 1840, and the "religious madmen" coming to Jerusalem in 1843.[55] In the letter protesting his dismissal in 1850, Chasseaud expressed dismay that for only $200 per annum he provided services to U.S. naval officers, missionaries, and travelers, restored stolen goods to victims of robberies, cared for sick persons, honored the American flag on the fourth of July, and conducted negotiations with other consuls – and named one of his sons George Washington.[56] Throughout the 1840s, Chasseaud set up an extensive network of consular agencies and appointed agents on his own behalf in Syria, Lebanon, and in Palestine. In mid-century, there were such

---

52   Jasper Chasseaud, U.S. Consul, Beirut, to John Forsyth, Secretary of State, Washington, D.C., 25 March 1836, USNA RG59 T367/1.

53   Jasper Chasseaud, U.S. Consul, Beirut, to John M. Clayton, Secretary of State, Washington, D.C., 16 June 1850, USNA RG59 T367/1.

54   Several entries in USNA T367/1; E. Kilbec, Beirut, to N.M. Rothschild, London, 23 August 1840, N.M. Rothschild Archives, CACXI/120/3A.

55   Jasper Chasseaud, U.S. Consul, Beirut, to John Forsyth, Secretary of State, Washington, D.C., 15 January 1837 and 24 March 1840, and to Daniel Webster, Secretary of State, Washington, D.C., 24 March 1840, USNA RG59 T367/1.

56   Blumberg, *Zion Before Zionism*, pp.54–57; Jasper Chasseaud, U.S. Consul, Beirut, to John M. Clayton, Secretary of State, Washington, D.C., 27 April 1850, USNA RG59 T367/1.

agencies in Ramle, Jaffa (and Jerusalem), Nazareth, Acre (and Haifa), Damascus, Tyre, Sidon, Tripoli, Latakia, and probably also in Aleppo. All the agents in his service were raya (non-Muslim Ottoman subjects) – Arabs, Armenians, Greeks, and Jews (Figure 5).[57]

This plethora of local consuls and consular agents of questionable character and norms of conduct, considerably worried Dabney S. Carr, the United States minister in Constantinople. As in the case of the consular agent David Darmon in Ramle, who was rumored to have "sold the protection of the American flag for money," and was dismissed in 1835 by Carr's predecessor, Porter, in 1847, he recommended replacing Chasseaud in Beirut. In July 1849, when no suitable candidate had as yet been found, Carr issued unequivocal orders to the consul in Beirut to close several of the consular agencies in Palestine and Syria:

> Believing the consular agencies at Acre, Ramley, Nazareth and Damascus, to be entirely useless to any American interest, I have to instruct you as I hereby do to discontinue them and along with them, all the personal jurisdiction which may have been granted by you or the Agents of those places, to persons not subjects of the U.S. You will lose no time in apprising the proper authorities of the Turkish government and also the agents and protogés of these instructions and you will require in all cases the papers of protection which have been granted in consequence of these agencies returned to you.[58]

As an example Carr added: "I found 2 brothers at the consular Agent in Ramley in possession of papers of protection from you granted on a principle not acknowledged by the Government of the U.S. viz: the services of their father to citizens of the U.S."[59]

For all these irregularities Chasseaud had very convincing justification (to his mind) which he detailed in his reply to Carr ten days later. In effect, the situation remained unchanged until the introduction of the general reform in the United States consular service in 1856.[60] Chasseaud's self-image as

---

57 Dabney S. Carr, U.S. Minister, Constantinople, to Jasper Chasseaud, U.S. Consul, Beirut, 30 July 1849, USNA RG59 T367/2.

58 Ibid.

59 Ibid.

60 Jasper Chasseaud, U.S. Consul, Beirut, to Dabney S. Carr, U.S. Minister, Constantinople, 10 August 1849, USNA RG59 T367/2.

presented by him was not shared by the secretary of state and others: Among the reasons given for his dismissal and his replacement in 1850 by an American citizen was his heavy drinking, over-exploitation of his position, receiving moneys that hinted at bribery for appointing consular agents, and attempts to obtain extraterritorial privileges for the local employees of the consulate (Plate 11).[61]

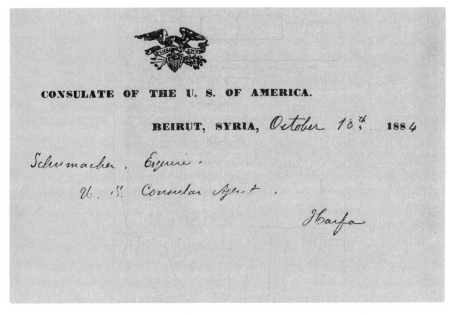

Plate 11. Letterhead of the United States consulate at Beirut
Source: USNA RG59 T367/3

Chasseaud's demise marked the end of the old working practices of the Beirut consulate and its dependent consular agencies. J. Hosford Smith's term of service may be regarded as an intermediate period during which he made desperate efforts (at least as he described it) to maintain himself and his family in a manner befitting a consul of "a great and prosperous nation" on a miserable annual salary of $500. His efforts to have the status of the consulate raised to that of consulate-general bore fruit only a decade after he completed his tour of duty, and his hopes for developing a business and trade with the United States were dashed by the outbreak of the Crimean War in 1853. These circumstances forced him to resign his post. For a short

61   Finnie, *Pioneers East*, pp.256–57.

time thereafter Smith served as consul-general in Constantinople (1861–62).[62]

In numerous letters to Washington, Smith stressed the importance of Beirut as a consular port in its own right, and also in comparison to Egypt, for there were missionaries living in Syria and Palestine, and American citizens "employed in agriculture and mechanical pursuits," as well as many travelers every year. He stated his conviction that valuable commerce would be renewed at the end of the war.[63] Smith revealed confusion in the matter of the consular agents – perhaps because he received inadequate direction – and regarding their names and titles: "The power of appointing Consular Agents who have the title of Vice Consuls, has been exercised as the prerogative of this consulate for the last 15 years..."; and in the beginning he disparaged their importance as they had little to report.[64] Later he learned that he had about ten consular agents subordinate to him, all except one being natives. He sent to the secretary of state a detailed list of the nine consular agents in Syria and Palestine holding the title of vice-consul, and expressing his reservations about Mr. Picciotto, the agent in Aleppo, a Jew, possibly of Austrian nationality, "who has and does abuse his office," but stated that he had no candidate with which to replace him.[65]

This confused and denigrating attitude on Smith's part led Secretary of State William L. Marcy to order him, in September 1853, as did Carr in 1849, to close the consular agencies in Jerusalem, Jaffa, Haifa, Acre, Tyre, Sidon, Damascus, Tripoli, Latakia, and Aleppo, and adding: "It is not believed that any inconvenience will be experienced from a compliance with this instruction." Thereupon, Smith bestirred himself and replied to Marcy with convincing arguments why the consular agencies were necessary: In six of the localities there were resident American citizens including missionaries, farmers, and merchants who, together with 250–300 travelers a year, required consular protection for their persons and property; these would have to seek British protection and would have no house of refuge from Muslim fanaticism

---

62   Smith claimed that his annual expenses came to $3,000, and see despatches of 20 and 22 January 1851, 29 July, 3 August, and 1 September 1852, and 7 July 1854, to the Secretary of State, the Treasury Department, and the Senate in: USNA RG59 T367/1 and 2.

63   J. Hosford Smith, U.S. Consul, Beirut, to Samuel H. Walley, M.C., House of Representatives, Washington, D.C., 7 July 1854, USNA RG59 T367/2.

64   J. Hosford Smith, U.S. Consul, Beirut, to Department of State, 1 September 1852, 18 January and 28 February 1853, USNA RG59 T367/1 and 2.

65   J. Hosford Smith, U.S. Consul, Beirut, to Edward Everett, Secretary of State, Washington, D.C., 18 January 1853, and Smith to William L. Marcy, Secretary of State, Washington, D.C., USNA RG59 T367/2.

in time of need. Moreover, American citizens were not willing to take on these positions, and in four of the places there were no such persons at all. He went on to point out that all but one of the agents served for many years, and that to dismiss them would be to place them at the mercy of the Turks, whom they opposed. Should the government stand by its decision, Smith requested that the agents be given time to wind up their affairs.[66]

It turned out as before: the consular agencies remained in place. This can be seen from the report of Smith's successor, Henry Wood (1854–7), who toward the end of his term (from January 1857), was paid a more appropriate salary of $2,000 per year. Wood listed ten agencies he considered essential: Aleppo, Latakia, Tripoli, Sidon, Tyre, Acre, Haifa, Jaffa and Jerusalem, Damascus, and Ramle. And he transmitted the request of the Americans residing in northern Syria for a consular agency to be established in Alexandretta.[67] In the same despatch, Wood included information on the ten agents:

> *Aleppo* – Mr. Illel de Picciotto, a native of Germany and subject of the same.
> *Lattakia* – Mr. Spiridion Nitali, a native and subject of the Ionian Republic.
> *Tripoli* – Antonio Yanni, a native and subject of the Ionian Republic.
> *Saida* or *Sidon* – Mr. Ibrahim Nachleys, a native and subject of Turkey.
> *Sour* or *Tyre* – Mr. Yacoub Akkad, a native and subject of Turkey.
> *Acre* or *St. Jean d'Acre* - Mr. George Jimmal, a native and subject of Turkey.
> *Caipha* – Mr. Gabriel Nesrella, a native and subject of Turkey.
> *Jaffa & Jerusalem* – Mr. Yacoub S. Murad, a native and subject of Turkey.

66   J. Hosford Smith, U.S. Consul, Beirut, to William L. Marcy, Secretary of State, Washington, D.C., 28 December 1853, USNA RG59 T367/2. The indecisiveness in this matter continued, and on 19 April 1883, the Assistant Secretary of State, John Davis, asked John T. Robeson, the American consul in Beirut, for his opinion regarding the closure of some of the consular agencies under his jurisdiction that Robeson in his report had accused of neglecting their duties (USNA RG84 Haifa Miscellaneous and Official Correspondence Received 1875–1917 Miscellaneous Papers 1878–1903 Green Box).

67   Henry Wood, U.S. Consul, Beirut, to [?] Abbott, Department of State, Washington, D.C., 18 February 1856, and John Appelzin, Assistant Secretary of State, Washington, D.C., to A.B. Chasseaud, New York, 1 October 1857, USNA RG59 T367/2.

> *Damascus* – Robert Wood esq., a native and subject of England.
> *Ramle* – Mr. Mattes Murkus, a native and subject of Turkey.

J. Hosford Smith, who replaced Chasseaud, may be categorized as a "merchant consul." He was an American citizen who intended to engage in commerce and believed that his position as United States consul would add to his business and social standing. Smith was born in Connecticut and lived many years in New York. In 1849 he was sent to Beirut in Syria by a private commercial firm, and was subsequently appointed consul. He wrote about himself: "I admit my chief object in going to Syria, was business – and to open a trade with the U.S." At the time of his promotion to consul-general in Constantinople, he denied accusations that he was a religious fanatic, and that he gained private benefit from having imported sewing machines for an agent of the Ottoman government.[68]

Since the limits of his jurisdiction stretched from Jerusalem to Aleppo, Smith dealt with various matters connected with Palestine, among them the American settlers in Urtas (Artas) and in Jaffa, and their disputes with British subjects and the British consul.[69] During his tenure, from 1853, Smith instituted more orderly recording and bookkeeping in the Beirut consulate, and this continued to improve in the years 1858–9 and in the 60s, under the next consul – later, consul-general – Augustus J. Johnson, who served from 1858 to 1867. The list of books kept by the consulate included financial records and correspondence, records of notarial services, vouchers of accounts and returns, and letters, beginning in Sidon in 1858, in Damascus, Haifa, and Tripoli in 1868, and in Alexandria from 1892.[70] The enactment of reforms in the United States consular service in 1856 introduced more regularized procedural norms to the Beirut consulate. Soon thereafter, in 1867, its status was elevated temporarily to consulate-general, reflecting a

68 Carr, "The American Consular Service," pp.896–97; J. Hosford Smith, U.S. Consul, Beirut, to Daniel Webster, Secretary of State, Washington, D.C., 1 September 1852, USNA RG59 T367/2; J. Hosford Smith, New York, to Henry Prescott, Department of State, Washington, D.C., 13 and 15 November 1860, and to Alexander Thompson, U.S. Vice Consul General, Constantinople, 9 November 1860, USNA RG59 T194/7. According to the letter of the missionary Dr. James T. Barclay, of 28 February 1851, Smith was "a member of a commercial house in New York." Burnet, *The Jerusalem Mission*, p.64.

69 Lipman, *Americans in the Holy Land*, pp.119–33.

70 American Legation, Beirut, to Department of O.M. (Operations Memorandum), Archives to be shipped to Department of State, 18 April 1950, USNA.

better appreciation of its importance, as mentioned above. Smith's estimation in this matter was thus proven right.

The relative failings of American policy during this period may be measured against the activity of the other powers in the Levant, particularly in Beirut whose development and economic growth was very rapid in 1830–1860. The city benefitted greatly from the Egyptian occupation. French, English, Austrian, and Sardinian consulates were active, and it became an important focus of English commerce. From 1835, Beirut was being transformed from a dreary Arab town into a bustling commercial port with a growing cosmopolitan population.[71] During the second period of the consulate, in 1856–1914, only the northern part of Palestine remained under its jurisdiction – the sanjak of Acre in the vilayet of Beirut with the Haifa consular agency. From 1872, when the American citizen, Jacob Schumacher, was appointed to head the consular agency in Haifa, he maintained an extensive correspondence with the consuls in Beirut (Appendix II D).[72]

One of the consuls in that period, whose personality stood in marked contrast to that of Chasseaud, was the Norwegian-born American journalist and politician from South Dakota, Gabriel Bie Ravndal. Ravndal began his career in the foreign service as consul in Beirut (1898–1905). From there he was posted to Dawson City in Canada, and to Constantinople (as consul-general in 1910–1914 and 1919–1925).[73] During the war years (1914–1917) he was in charge of French, British, Russian, Italian, Belgian, Serbian, Montenegrin, and Swiss consular interests at Constantinople. In the course of his service in the Levant and Turkey, Ravndal founded the American Red Cross chapters of Beirut and Constantinople, and initiated and was elected honorary president of the American Chamber of Commerce for the Levant.[74] And, he engaged in political and literary writing, including an exhaustive article and report on the capitulations and the consular institution, as well as stories of the Vikings.[75]

---

71   Issawi, "British Trade," pp.91–101.

72   USNA RG84 Haifa Copy Book 1872–1886 Box 5976.

73   Already in 1903, Ravndal applied for transfer to the State Department, mainly for financial reasons, as mentioned in a letter from George Post, Beirut, to Gottlieb Schumacher, U.S. Consular Agent, Haifa, 15 August 1903, USNA RG84 Miscellaneous and Official Correspondence Received 1875–1917.

74   Boyce, *American Foreign Service Authors*, pp.236–37; Mears, *Modern Turkey*, p.430.

75   Ravndal, "The Origin of the Capitulations," pp.1–112; Ravndal, "Capitulations," pp.430–47; Ravndal, *Stories of the East Vikings*.

CHAPTER THREE

THE UNITED STATES CONSULATE AND CONSULAR
AGENCIES IN THE HOLY LAND

ESTABLISHMENT OF CONSULATES BY THE EUROPEAN POWERS
IN THE HOLY LAND

Timing, Motivation, and Sequence of Establishment

Three political events contributed to European involvement in Palestine and bringing about basic changes in the life of the country. The first was Napoleon Bonaparte's invasion of Palestine in 1799. Despite ending in failure, it marked the beginning of a new era in the history of the country which became an object of growing interest by the European powers and a focal point of competition for influence in the Near East.[1] Nevertheless, in the years 1799–1831, under the rule of the pashas of Damascus, consular activity was very limited in Palestine. There was no foreign representation in Jerusalem. The city was under the purview of the consular officials who resided in the coastal towns of Acre and Jaffa and who extended assistance to travelers. A Russian consul, George Musteras, arrived in Jaffa in 1812 to look after Greek Orthodox pilgrims.[2] Travelers' reports of that period mention English and French consuls in Jaffa.[3] British consuls in the Near East were employed by the Levant Company until 1825, when H.M. Government caused the Levant Company to terminate its activities, and took over its consular establishments in order to develop the commerce of the British Empire.[4]

---

1   Ben-Zvi, *Eretz-Israel*, pp.320–8.

2   Spyridon, "Annals of Palestine," p.66; Hopwood, (*The Russian Presence*, p.15) says that the Russian consulate in Jaffa was opened in 1820.

3   Kark, *Jaffa*, p.20. An English consul had been appointed to Palestine as early as 1583 in the person of Richard Forster, "consul in the parts of Alepo, Damasco, Aman, Tripolis, Jerusalem..." France opened a consulate in Jerusalem in 1621 to protect the monks, but it did not last long.

4   Middleton, *The Administration of British Foreign Policy*, p.245; Platt, *The Cinderella Service*, pp.125–31.

The second event of significance was the conquest of Palestine by Muhammad 'Ali, the autonomous governor of Ottoman Egypt, and his rule over the country from 1831 to 1840. It was during this time that his son, Ibrahim Pasha, initiated steps which were without precedent in the history of Ottoman Palestine, by opening the region more widely to Western influence and modernization. Along with the establishment of a strong, centralized regime, Ibrahim Pasha abolished official discrimination against non-Muslims – both for economic reasons and out of his desire to win the sympathy of France and Britain. It was in this period that establishment of foreign consulates in Jerusalem became possible, although only Great Britain was then to set up a vice-consulate. At the same time, various missionary societies were given a relatively free hand.

The third of these historic developments, and paralleling the second, was the proclamation, in 1839, by the Sublime Porte of the *Khatt-i Sharif* of Gülhane (Rescript of the Rose Chamber). It was followed by the active support of the European powers in expelling Muhammad 'Ali's forces from Palestine by the Ottoman army in 1841. The declared purpose of the *Khatt-i Sharif* was to abolish discrimination against non-Muslim minorities in the Empire and extending their special rights. In this way, the basis was laid for strengthening the Christian element in Palestine.[5] It was from then on that most of the foreign consulates were opened in Jerusalem, with vice-consulates or consular agencies in other towns.

The idea for setting up a British consulate in Jerusalem was first mooted in 1834, despite the poverty and remoteness of the town, with no port or trade. The decision was taken at the end of 1836. In 1838, William Tanner Young was appointed as salaried vice-consul and promoted to consul in 1841. The consulate of Great Britain in Jerusalem was opened in March 1839, making Young the first official European representative in the Holy City.[6] Much has been written on the motivation behind the establishment of the British consulate in Jerusalem. Some regarded this move, along with the establishment in the 1830s of consulates in Erzerum, Aleppo, Mosul, and elsewhere, as a purely political decision, part of the British doctrine of maintaining the integrity of the Ottoman Empire to counterbalance Russian and French influence.[7] Others saw the appointment of Young as an expression of empathy among

5   Lewis, The Emergence pp.106,115; Ma'oz, Ottoman Reform, p.19.

6   Hyamson, *The British Consulate*, 1:ix.

7   Hough, "History of the British Consulate" pp.3–4; Vereté, "Why was a British Consulate Established," pp.316–345; Platt, *The Cinderella Service*, pp.125–31.

the British public and government for the idea of the Return to Zion and the restoration of the Jews to the Land of Israel. This idea was implanted in the then foreign secretary, Lord Palmerston (Henry John Temple), by his evangelist son-in-law, Lord Ashley (later, Lord Shaftesbury). And still others considered the move as reflecting a combination of religious-humanitarian considerations and Britain's commercial and political interests in the region.[8] The argument remains unresolved.

Along with the reawakening interest in the Holy Land among Christians, the powers discovered the importance of Palestine as a strategic factor in the political future of the Ottoman Empire. Within a short time, six consulates were established in Jerusalem. After Britain came Prussia in 1842, France and Sardinia in 1843, the United States (tentatively) in 1844, and Austria in 1849. Russia was the only great power that maintained only a consulate in Jaffa for another decade, before opening one in Jerusalem.9 Despite some disclaimers, German interest in the Ottoman Empire had a long history – as has been stressed by Trumpener. And indeed, the Prussian consulate in Jerusalem soon became one of the more important ones in Palestine.[10] In its early years, the Prussian consulate represented the other Protestant and Catholic states of Germany, as well as the interests of Holland and Austria, and saw to the protection of their Jewish and Templer nationals. The French consulate devoted most of its efforts to the furtherance of the Catholic presence in Palestine, and later also to economic interests. Catholic concerns were also dealt with by the Sardinian (Italian) consulate.[11]

It was during the Egyptian occupation (1831–1841), that the United States appointed a consular agent, David Darmon of Ramle, to represent it in Jaffa and Jerusalem. His tenure, however, was short-lived because of his behavior, and hopes of the American Board of Commissioners for Foreign Missions, in 1834, for the establishment of a consulate in Jerusalem were disappointed.[12] The United States was the fifth power to set up a consulate in Jerusalem – despite its remoteness from Near East affairs and its isolationist foreign policy. The main reason for opening an American consulate in Jerusalem in 1844 (which also proved abortive) was to assist American travelers.[13] The

8 Vereté, ibid.; Tennenbaum, "The British Consulate in Jerusalem," pp.83–7.

9 Eliav, *The Jews of Palestine*, p.9

10 Trumpener, "Germany" p.112.

11 Eliav, *Eretz Israel*, pp.49–61; Parfitt, "The French Consulate," pp.144–61; Fulton, "France," p.141.

12 Tibawi, *American Interests*, p.189.

13 Karp, "The Zionism of Warder Cresson," pp.3–4.

consulate resumed its existence in 1856 and from then on maintained regular activities.

Austria reorganized its consular service in Syria in the years 1841–46, after the retreat of Ibrahim Pasha to Egypt, in order to bolster its policy of safeguarding the integrity of the Ottoman Empire, and to compete with Russia, France, and Britain. In 1846 the Austrian government decided to open a vice-consulate in Jerusalem, in addition to its consular agencies in Jaffa and Acre which dated to the 18th century. Three reasons for the establishment of a consulate in Jerusalem were advanced by the Austro-Hungarian foreign minister: growing Russian-backed Greek Orthodox influence among the local population, the enhanced position of the other powers – especially of France as the chief protector of Catholic interests, and the potential future economic development of this Ottoman province. Count Josef von Pizzamano, who was appointed vice-consul in 1847, arrived in Jerusalem in 1849. The Austrian representation was raised to full consular status in 1852, and in 1857 Pizzamano became consul-general.[14]

During the Crimean War, in 1853–56, the Ottoman government again introduced important reforms that were designed to gain the goodwill of its allies in the West. These reforms, known as the *Khatt-i Hümayun* (Imperial Rescript), were published in 1856, on the eve of the peace conference in Paris. They included the granting of equal rights to Christians and other non-Muslims in the Empire, the protection of their persons and property, freedom of worship, and provision of education for children of all religious communities. Also included in the legislation was permission, at least on paper, for foreigners to acquire land.

Western involvement in Palestine reached new heights after the proclamation of the *Khatt-i Hümayun*. This was reflected in the work of the consuls and the missionaries, but also by intensified activity in commerce, transportation, banking, land acquisition, and building. Growing interest and connections with the Holy Land resulted in an upsurge of scholarly research into the geography and history of the country, the development of a lively tourist and pilgrimage traffic from Europe and America, and actual settlement by Christian and Jewish immigrants from Europe in towns and rural areas of Palestine.[15]

During the Crimean War and after it, consulates were opened in Jerusalem by Spain (1854), Persia (a consular agency, 1857), Russia (1858), Greece (1858), and Mexico (1865). Later, a Dutch consular agency and a Swedish

---

14 Eliav, *Under Imperial Austrian Protection*, pp.1–13; Bridge, "The Habsburg Monarchy," pp.31,48–49.

15 Kark, "Changing Patterns," pp.358–9.

consulate followed suit. An exhaustive table drawn up by the temporary director of the German consulate in Jerusalem in mid-1872 summed up the situation of the powers' consular representations in the country (Table I).

TABLE I Foreign Consulates in Jerusalem, 1872

Consulate	Staff	Registered citizens	Protégés	Protected institutions	In charge of
U.S.A.	Consul, dragoman, 2 kavasses	4	13	Consular agent in Jaffa; many travelers in winter	
Austria-Hungary	Consul, dragoman, vice-consul, 3 kavasses, door guard	250	920	Hospice and hospital under construction from Hungary and Galicia.	Vice-consul in Jaffa; 30 protégés - mainly Jews
Britain	Consul, dragoman, 3 kavasses	180?	700?	3 schools, 2 missionary institutions, 1 ethnic mission	Vice-consul in Jaffa; 20 protégés many travelers in winter
France	Consul, chancellor, 2 dragomans, 4 kavasses	20?	60?	Claims protection over all Catholic institutions (which these do not accept) – mainly the monastery on Mt. Zion.	Vice-consul in Jaffa; about 20 protégés
Germany	Consul, dragoman, 2 kavasses	210	470	Orphange and hospital of nuns; leper hospital; Syrian orphange; childrens' hospital; hostel in Muristan;	Vice-consul in Jaffa 237 protégés Vice-consul in Haifa-Acre with Safed, Tiberias, Nazareth, etc.; about 280 protégés.

Consulate	Staff	Registered citizens	Protégés	Protected institutions	In charge of
				mission in Bethlehem; evangelical and Templer communities; various Jewish institutions.	
Greece	Consul, dragoman, 2 kavasses	55	150		Vice-consul in Jaffa; 80 protégés.
Italy	Consul, dragoman, 2 kavasses	20?	60		
Russia	Consul, chancellor, 2 dragomans, secretary 4 kavasses, door guard	50	120	Hospice hospital mission, hospice in Beit Hakerem [Ein Karem] many pilgrims	Vice-consul in Jaffa
Spain	Consul, vice-consul, dragoman, 2 kavasses	31	100?		Many Spanish monks represented by the Latin convent.

Based on: Otto Kersten, Kanzler, German Consulate, Jerusalem, to Foreign Office, Berlin, 21 June 1872, ISA RG67 quoted by Eliav, *The Jews of Palestine,* pp. 41-3

Backed by the support of their respective governments, the consuls enjoyed great authority and were able to gain influence among the local notables. The consuls often interfered in the affairs of local government, at times acting in a manner which no diplomatic representative would have permitted himself in any other country. The position of foreign citizens and non-Muslim minorities who enjoyed the patronage of the foreign powers improved significantly in this period. To some extent, the consuls were inspired by their belief that they were contributing to the modernization of the Holy Land, but their efforts in that direction, along with their support of the religious and philanthropic work of missionaries, were certainly guided more by their perception of what best served their countries' political interests. The consuls vied for prestige and influence with their counterparts, and were often drawn into interdenominational squabbles which were so much a part of the religious life among Europeans in 19th century Palestine.

Establishment of American Consular Agencies

Chapter One discussed the background and the official, as well as the private, motivation behind the establishment of American consular agencies in the Levant, including Palestine, in the years 1832–1856. Most of these agencies were founded at the initiative and under the aegis of the consuls in Beirut, although in some instances the initiative for opening – and especially for closing – them came from the United States minister in Constantinople and from the secretary of state in Washington. This chapter will focus on the consular agencies that were opened and functioned in Palestine proper during those years, as well as in the period beginning with the definitive establishment of the American consulate in Jerusalem and until World War I (1857–1914).

Early Consular Agencies in Palestine 1832–1856

The first American consular agency in Palestine was opened in Ramle on 15 September 1832, when the chargé d'affaires of the United States legation in Constantinople, Commodore David Porter, appointed David Darmon, a Jew who was nominally a subject of France, consular agent for Jaffa and Jerusalem. Darmon had been recommended by a Jewish American traveler, Colonel Mendes Cohen of Baltimore, as a man knowledgeable on the Levant. The new consular agent, who was at the time under Porter's authority, sent a proposal directly to the State Department urging it "to take immediate possession of the island of Cyprus," and appoint him consul there. According to various sources, Darmon was dismissed in 1835 because of poor performance in accommodating American travelers, for selling American letters of protection to local persons, and perhaps, due to dissatisfaction of local Christians at the appointment of a Jew to the position.[16] Most probably, the colorful description of the American consular agent in Ramle by the traveler John Lloyd Stephens, who visited Ramle in the middle of 1836, does not relate to Darmon but to his Christian successor who told Stephens that he owed his appointment to Commodore Patterson[17] and told him his troubles:

> But a year before, he had flourished in all the pomp and pride of office. The arms of our country were blazoned over his door, and the stars and stripes had protected his dwelling; but a change

---

16 USNA RG59 M453; Manuel, *The Realities*, pp.9–10; Finnie, *Pioneers East*, p.251.

17 Commodore Daniel Patterson commanded the U.S. Mediterranean squadron. In the summer of 1834 he visited Syria and Egypt with his wife and two daughters. (See Finnie, ibid., pp.92, 199, 260.)

had come over him. The Viceroy of Syria had ordered the flags of the consuls to be taken down at Ramla, and forbidden any of his subjects to hold the office except in the seaport towns. I could not help thinking that he was perfectly right, as it was merely allowing them the benefit of a foreign protection to save them and their families, with two or three janissaries, from their duties to himself; but I listened attentively to the complaints of the poor agent. His dignity had been touched, and his pride humbled in the eyes of his townsmen, for the governor had demanded the usual duty from his sons and had sent his executive officers with the summary order, the duty or the bastinado.[18]

The agent went on to intimate that he was subject to the consul in Beirut, and that he had placed his complaints before Patterson as well as before his superior, who had forwarded the matter to Porter in Constantinople. At that time, according to Stephens, there was in Jaffa a consular agent who was also the acting Sardinian consul. This was the wealthy, childless Armenian, Murad Arutin (or Aroutin) who hosted Stephens regally for being the first American traveler to come his way since his appointment to the position. As part of his hospitality, he had the Stars and Stripes flown from his housetop, and on his guest's departure, ordered his two janissaries, "each with a large silver-headed mace in his hand," to escort him to the town gate.[19]

These agents in Jaffa and Ramle were among those appointed by Chasseaud, the U.S. Consul in Beirut, and subordinate to him. As may be gleaned from the repeated testimony of visitors, their main function was to host and assist the few American travelers who came to the Holy Land. Thus, in 1838, Edward Robinson and Eli Smith were received and subjected to the traditional washing of the feet by 'Abud Murqus, the American consular agent in Ramle – a Christian Arab of the Greek Church." [20] Similarly treated, in October 1844, were the newly-appointed American consul, Cresson, accompanied by the English writer, William Makepeace Thackeray. They were served a fine meal in Ramle by "the hospitable one-eyed Armenian, who represented the United States at Jaffa," and who saw to it that "the stars and stripes were flaunting over his terraces...." [21]

These consular agents of the United States in Palestine, who in the first

18   Stephens, *Incidents of Travel*, pp.374–78,447.

19   Ibid.

20   Robinson, *Biblical Researches*, 3:25–26.

21   Thackeray, *Notes on a Journey*, p.190.

half of the 19th century had very little to do, placed much importance upon the rules of etiquette and marks of status. In the house of Murad Arutin, the agent in Jaffa, who according to the American naval officer, Francis Schroeder, spoke no English, "The American eagle and shield were emblazoned on the wall, and prints of General Jackson and Mr. Van Buren, and a map of the United States decorated the salon..." [22]

In Acre, which during the first half of the century was the Ottoman center of government for Palestine, an American consular agent was appointed in September 1833 – Gabriel Nasralla, a native merchant subject of Turkey – who served in that capacity for many years. When Haifa began to assume greater importance as a port town and a focus for settlement by foreigners, he temporarily became the U.S. consular agent there.[23] No consular agency was opened in Nazareth, but Chasseaud gave papers of protection to certain persons so that these would show kindness to travelers visiting the town.[24]

At the end of the 1840s and the beginning of the 50s, there were other American consular agencies in Palestine besides the one in Jaffa headed by Jacob Serapion Murad, who was also responsible for Jerusalem. In Ramle the agent was Mattes Murkus, a native subject of Turkey who apparently succeeded his brother Hamsa. On the death of his father in Ramle in the mid-40s, the latter served for several years as agent (on the "all in the family" principle which was the norm in those days). The third consular agency was in Acre, with Haifa included within the jurisdiction of the veteran agent, Gabriel Nasralla. There was an attempt at setting up a separate consular agency in Haifa in the early 1850s to be headed by Nasralla, while in Acre George Jimmal was appointed, but both were later united (Figure 6).[25]

As has been seen, in the 1840s and 1850s, there were differences of opinion between the higher American foreign service echelons in Constantinople and Washington and the consuls in Beirut regarding the necessity of maintaining consular agencies in the Levant and Palestine. The former saw no value in

---

22 Schroeder in Finnie, *Pioneers East*, p.253. The map was a gift from Stephens who had stopped by in 1836.

23 Jasper Chasseaud, U.S. Consul, Beirut, to Dabney S. Carr, U.S. Minister, Constantinople, 10 August 1849, USNA RG59 T367/2. Mayer mentions that the United States maintained a consular agency at Acre at least as early as 1843, but it was, in fact, earlier. (Mayer, "Records of the United States Consular Agency at Haifa," p.1.)

24 Ibid.

25 Ibid.; J. Hosford Smith, U.S. Consul, Beirut, to William L. Marcy, Secretary of State, Washington, D.C., 9 August 1853 and Henry Wood, U.S. Consul, Beirut, to Abbott, Department of State, Washington, D.C., 18 February 1856, USNA RG59 T367/2.

most of these and thought that they should be closed since they had been given to the charge of persons who were not American citizens and who abused the privilege of protection. The consuls in Beirut, who were perhaps better attuned to local conditions, to the availability of candidates and to the general atmosphere advocated their continued existence. The main reasons advanced by the consuls for adding consular agencies was the growing trade in the coastal towns and the increasing numbers of American travelers who required their services. In Ramle, Chasseaud argued, the agency was needed because it was on the main road between Jaffa and Jerusalem, and in Acre, because it was the capital of Syria and a seaport visited by American ships of war, travelers, and missionaries. There were no hostelries in Acre, the only accommodations being in monasteries, and considering the hatred of the monks for Protestants, and especially for missionaries, it was important to provide facilities in the agent's house. Among the other reasons adduced by Chasseaud was that other nations had vice-consuls and consular agents there, and how would it appear to the authorities if after fifteen years the United States closed its agency there? [26] In retrospect, it appears that this last consideration indeed carried weight. American policy lagged behind that of the other powers by its lack of involvement, by its inferior grasp of local conditions, and in the half-hearted backing it gave its consular agents. Britain, Russia, Prussia, France, and Sardinia recognized the potential in the maintenance of consular agents, vice-consuls, and even consuls in the coastal towns of Jaffa, Acre, Haifa, and in Jerusalem.[27]

Jacob Serapion Murad – Example of a Consular Agent
A typical illustration of the men who in the first half of the 19th century served as America's consular agents in the Levant and in Palestine was Jacob Serapion Murad, a native Armenian, born to a poor Jerusalem family. His ninety-year old father, according to a description in 1852, "was known as a hawker of rosaries in Jerusalem, under one of the archways that lead to the Armenian convent."[28] Jacob Serapion's star began to rise when he was appointed secretary to Murad Arutin, a wealthy, childless Armenian merchant at Jaffa. Arutin, who was an important personality in Jaffa, served from the early 1830s as Sardinian consul there. He was also appointed Britain's vice-

---

26 Chasseaud to Carr, ibid.

27 On some of these, which were opened in Jaffa, Acre, and Haifa, see: Eliav, *Eretz Israel*, pp.41–55.

28 "Anonymous letter sent to American President," *Galignani's Messenger*, 11 September 1852. I am grateful to the Boston Athenaeum for providing me with a copy of the letter.

consul in Jerusalem at the request of J.W.P. Farren, the British consul in Syria who resided in Damascus, in order to provide services to English travelers and residents in the Holy City, and in view of the growing political importance of Jerusalem and the rivalry with Catholics and Catholic states. But the appointment of Murad Arutin was not confirmed by the Foreign Office.[29]

In 1835, Arutin began to serve as the United States consular agent in Jaffa and Jerusalem, and with the assistance of his secretary, Jacob Serapion, he continued in the position until his death at the end of 1842. Arutin cared for Jacob as for a son and even married him to his niece whom he had adopted as a daughter. On Arutin's death, Jacob Serapion inherited his position as consular agent of the United States in Jaffa and Jerusalem, and even received a commission at the same time as Prussian consular agent in Jaffa. That he fulfilled his duties with devotion until the day of his death on 30 December 1858, is attested by many reports of travelers and missionaries. Apparently at the request of Murad Arutin's widow, Heliani, Jacob Serapion added the name Murad to his own.[30]

Serapion's appointment as consular agent was confirmed by the Sultan in 1846, although from correspondence expressing thanks for his services in the archives of the consulate in Beirut, it seems that he served in the position since 1843. From that year his wealth also increased, because on the death of Arutin's widow, the greater part of her immense fortune and that of her sister and her children, of over five million Turkish piasters (about £45,500 sterling) in cash and jewelry, together with houses and gardens in Bethlehem, Jaffa, and Ramle, passed to Serapion Murad. How this happened is unclear. According to some, it was by legal process of inheritance, while others believed it to have been by robbery and subterfuge.[31] Among other things, the "Delightful suburban villa of Mr. Murad, the American Consul, which is kindly placed at our disposal," mentioned by the American missionary, Dr. James T. Barclay who lived in Jerusalem, during his visit to Jaffa in 1851, was probably part of this property. [32] As a result, Jacob Serapion Murad had become one of the richest men in the Holy Land, and according to one of his detractors, succeeded

29   Vereté, "Why was a British Consulate established," pp.316–45.

30   American Missionaries in Beirut, to J. Hosford Smith, U.S. Consul, Beirut, 1 June 1853; Theodor Weber, Prussian Consul, Beirut, to Smith, 3 August 1853 and J. Hosford Smith's Report, 27 May 1854, USNA RG59 T367/2.

31   American Missionaries, ibid.; Copies of letters regarding Murad's kindness 1842–43 in USNA RG59 T367/1 and "Anonymous Letter," 11 September 1852.

32   Burnet, *The Jerusalem Mission*, pp.145–46, for 3 February 1851.

"by the enormous power which wealth gives in the corrupt law courts of the Turkish empire" in depriving Heliani's sister, Mary Djann and her two sons, of their right to claim part of the inheritance.[33] This enabled him to maintain his position, which carried no remuneration, and to provide services to American citizens. As a rich entrepreneur, Murad also lent money at interest. This emerges from the application to Jacob and his brother Simeon by James Finn, the British consul in Jerusalem. The transaction led to a quarrel between the parties, which, Jacob complained, damaged his and his brother's good name. It appears that his duties as consular agent constituted but a part – probably a small part – of Murad's occupations.[34]

At the end of the 1840s a policy crystallized in the U.S. foreign service of abolishing some of the consular agencies in Palestine and Syria, but raising the status of the remaining ones to vice-consulates. Among the latter was also the agency headed by Murad in Jaffa and Jerusalem – despite the minister in Constantinople, Carr, being aware of Murad's abusing the right of protection. In the early 1850s there were also several Americans and Britons living in the region who were proposed for the position of vice-consul at Jerusalem. Among them were the missionary Dr. James T. Barclay, and later, the English convert from Judaism, London-born John Meshullam, who at the time lived in Urtas, a village near Bethlehem, with a group of Americans led by Clorinda Minor (Plate 6).[35] Once the decision was taken to establish a vice-consulate in Jerusalem, an American named Wigley, who had come to Syria at the beginning of 1852 "to pursue his ecclesiological investigations as an architect," proposed himself for the position. Wigley's candidature was rejected and Murad was commissioned U.S. vice-consul in Jerusalem, despite his reluctance since the position entailed expenditures on his part. Murad, who lived in Jaffa, delegated his brother, Simeon Serapion Murad, as acting vice-consul in Jerusalem, allocating $400 per annum of his own money to cover his salary and that of his janissary, and for other expenses. The appointment of Murad backed by the consul, Smith, in Beirut and by George P. Marsh, the minister in Constantinople, angered Wigley, who in September 1852 published

---

33 "Anonymous letter," ibid.

34 Burnet, *The Jerusalem Mission*, p.61 and Report of J. Hosford Smith, U.S. Consul, Beirut, 27 May 1854, USNA RG59 T367/2; Jacob Serapion Murad, U.S. Vice-Consul, Jerusalem and Jaffa to William Marcy, Secretary of State, Washington, D.C., 30 January 1857, USNA RG59 T367/3.

35 Dabney S. Carr, U.S. Minister, Constantinople, to Jasper Chasseaud, U.S. Consul, Beirut, 30 July 1849; J. Hosford Smith, U.S. Consul, Beirut, to Department of State, Washington, D.C., 28 February 1853, USNA RG59 T367/2. On Barclay's refusal, see: Smith to William Marcy, Secretary of State, 23 June 1853, USNA, ibid.

an anonymous letter to the President of the United States. Wigley argued against the preference of a man who "shames the American public," not only because he was "destitute of education and totally ignorant of English, or any other European language," but also because he was dishonest, corrupt, and had appropriated the heritage of the Arutin couple. He added that "his fellow consuls...refuse him their society..."[36] In reaction to this letter, American missionaries in Beirut and Jerusalem, the consul, Smith, in Beirut, and the Prussian consul, Weber, in Beirut whose agent Murad was as well, came to his defense, denying the allegations against him, and praising his behavior. Apparently, they preferred the experience and position of the native Ottoman subject to the American citizen who had scant, if any, knowledge of local conditions.[37]

In keeping with the norms governing the conduct of the native consular agents in that period, Jacob Serapion bestowed upon his two brothers positions in the consular agencies of the United States and Prussia in Jerusalem and Jaffa. They too adopted the name Murad. One of them, Simeon Serapion Murad, who represented Jacob in Jerusalem, continued after the arrival of the first accredited American consul in Jerusalem, Gorham, to fill the function of dragoman and deputy-consul at Jerusalem. From the year 1860 and until 1894, he served as consular agent, and from 1870 as vice-consul of Prussia and Germany in Jaffa, where he was active in land matters and owned a house in the old city with a large garden outside the walls.[38] Another brother, Lazarus Serapion Murad, who spoke seven languages, joined the Presbyterian Church in the late 1840s. He helped the missionary, Dr. Barclay, to settle in Jerusalem, and was even appointed in 1851 by the Board as assistant missionary at the Jerusalem station. When the American consul in Jerusalem, Rhodes, resigned in 1865, Lazarus was appointed vice-consul but was dismissed by Rhodes's successor, Victor Beauboucher, for his attempt to conceal the estate of Warder Cresson, an American citizen who died in Jerusalem. The sons of Jacob Murad also served in the German consulate at Jaffa.[39] In January

36 "Anonymous letter," 11 September 1852; J.S. Murad, U.S. Vice Consul, Jerusalem, to William Marcy, Secretary of State, Washington, D.C., 30 January 1857, USNA RG59 T367/3. The consul in Beirut, Smith, in his report of 27 May 1854 (ibid., T367/2) mentioned that, Wigley (first name omitted) came to Beirut in February 1852 "to solicit the appointment of U.S. Vice Consul at Jerusalem."

37 Several letters from June to December 1853 in USNA RG59 T367/2.

38 John Warren Gorham, U.S. Consul, Jerusalem, to Lewis Cass, Secretary of State, Washington, D.C., 30 June 1857, USNA RG59 T471/1; Eliav, *The Jews of Palestine*, p.323; Kark, *Jaffa*, pp.64–71,183.

39 Burnet, *The Jerusalem Mission*, pp.179–80; Albert Rhodes, U.S. Consul, Jerusalem, to William H.

1857, toward the end of his service, Jacob Serapion Murad (who died at the end of 1858) petitioned the secretary of state for financial compensation to cover the expenses he incurred as consular agent of the United States in Jaffa and Jerusalem for the "pay of the dragoman and janissary employed in the consular agency, rent of office, aid afforded to American citizens in Syria and also compensation for his services." The letters attached to the petition by the consuls in Jerusalem and Beirut, and of American citizens in Palestine and Syria, purported to show that considerable economic harm was caused to Jacob, as well as threats to his life that forced him to abandon his house in the gardens around Jaffa and to find refuge in a rented house within the walls because he helped bring to trial persons accused of rape and murder of American farmers who settled near Jaffa. Apparently, one of the reasons for sending the petition was Jacob Murad's understanding that the act passed on 18 August 1856 precluded persons who were not American citizens from serving in consular positions.[40] His petition became a kind of test case and was published as an executive document. Secretary of State Cass explained, on the basis of the newly enacted regulations, why Murad was not entitled to compensation. An excerpt of his response mentions two categories of consular officials:

> In reply to your inquiry for any information touching the same which the archives of the department may afford to the committee, I have the honor to state, that under the provisions of the act regulating the diplomatic and consular systems of the United States, approved August 18, 1856, consular officers are divided into two classes, namely, "full, principal and permanent consular officers" and "subordinates and substitutes," a distinction which, in the practice of the department was recognized substantially for a long period prior to the passage of the act. The first named class of officers is appointed by the President by and with the advice of the Senate, or by the Department of State, under the direction of the President. Officers of the second class are subordinate to the former and are appointed by "principal" consular officers subject to the approval of the President, who are held

Seward, Secretary of State, Washington, D.C., 31 March 1865, USNA RG59 T471/2; regarding this episode, see Chapter Six under "Estates" on the inept handling by Lazarus Murad of Warder Cresson's estate.

40   Jacob Serapion Murad, U.S. Vice Consul, Jerusalem, to William Marcy, Secretary of State, Washington, D.C., 30 January 1857, USNA RG59 T367/3; Cass, "J.S. Murad," pp.1–3.

responsible for the official acts of such subordinates. In this class are consular agents, who exercise powers and discharge consular duties within the limits of the consular jurisdiction of the consuls by whom they are respectively appointed and to whom they are amenable. They are appointed at seaports frequented by American vessels within any consulate, or at places where American interests are concerned, or to which American travelers resort, and where there is no "full, principal and permanent consular officer."

These offices are much sought after by individuals residing within a consulate, either for the honor which they confer, the protection they afford, or the emolument they give; and especially is this the case in the East where persons thus clothed with consular powers and also their families and dependents, although Ottoman subjects, are in a great measure withdrawn from the operation of the local laws and are subject to the jurisdiction and regulations of the government which they temporarily serve, and under whose flag they are protected.

In this subordinate class of consular officers was Mr. Murad. He doubtless assumed the responsibilities of consular office and discharged its duties with a full knowledge of the dignity and protection thereby given, and was also aware that his compensation would be derived only from the consular fees. There is abundant evidence in the files of the department to show that he discharged his consular duties in a manner agreeable to American citizens travelling or residing in Syria, and, as is believed, to the satisfaction of the government of the United States during his long period of consular service. No account has been presented to this department of his expenditures for rent of a consular office, for the pay of dragoman or janissary, nor is there any appropriation from which expenditures for this purpose by a "subordinate" consular officer could be paid. If expenses have been incurred by him for the relief of American *seamen*, they will be reimbursed by the department on the presentation of the proper vouchers. If he has "expended a large sum from his own means for the comfort and aid of United States citizens" who are not *seamen*, it lies within the discretion of Congress to afford relief...[41]

41 Lewis Cass, Secretary of State, Washington, D.C., to the Committee on Foreign Affairs, House of

Jacob Serapion Murad died in 1858 before he received a reply to his petition, and so ended his career in the foreign services of the United States and Prussia. But members of his family, his two brothers and his sons continued this type of activity along with their profitable business as local entrepreneurs in a steadily developing Palestine.

Concentration and Rationalization of the Consular Agencies 1857–1914,
New Experiments

With the establishment of the United States consulate in Jerusalem in 1856, and the beginning of its work in 1857, it was charged with jurisdiction over the territory of the Jerusalem *mutasarriflik*, and apparently also that of the sanjak of Nablus that formerly was under the consul in Beirut. Only the northern part of the country, which by the Ottoman administrative division was included in the sanjak of Acre, remained the responsibility of Beirut. Reporting in 1862 to Secretary of State William H. Seward, Franklin Olcott, the third American consul to serve in Jerusalem, described the conditions of agriculture, manufacturing, and commerce. He also expressed his aspirations for the development and enhancement of his consular district and urged the setting up of additional consular agencies:

> The District of the Consulate of Jerusalem and dependencies comprehend the whole of Palestine (with the exception of two unimportant towns Akka and Caipha which are attached to the consulate of Beirut) & the desert regions between Gasa & El Arish.
>   Consular agencies already exist at Jaffa & Ramleh & others might with equal propriety be established at Nablous & Nazareth in the North, & at Hebron and Gasa in the South, for the convenience of overland travellers from Syria & Egypt.[42]

The period 1857–1879 may be considered as an intermediate one in which attempts were made to delimit areas of jurisdiction of the consulate and to establish additional consular agencies at the initiative of the consuls in Jerusalem – in the south of Palestine (Gaza and Hebron) and in the north (Nablus, Tiberias, and Nazareth). These aspirations did not materialize, and even the old consular agency at Ramle ceased to exist from the mid-1860s

---

Representatives, 12 January 1859, Cass, "J.S. Murad," pp.1–2.

42 Franklin Olcott, U.S. Consul, Jerusalem, to William Henry Seward, Secretary of State, Washington, D.C., 30 September 1862, USNA RG59 T471/1.

after the death of the local consular agent there (of the Murqus family).[43] In 1870, applications, supported by the American consuls in Jerusalem and Beirut, of local Ottoman subjects for positions as consular agents in Ramle and Nablus were rejected by the Ottoman government.[44] Beardsley and Johnson intimated that in the absence of American residents willing to hold the office, the most suitable candidate for the position in Nablus was Hassan Ya'ish, a respected local Muslim. They believed that such an appointment would benefit American travelers, and that the agency would "prove of great moral advantage to the missionary work now going on in these parts." [45] These arguments indeed caused Ya'ish to be given the commission by the State Department, but the Sublime Porte refused to grant its firman of exequatur, on the grounds that the "...Sixth article of the 'Règlement' prohibits Turkish Subjects from becoming Vice Consuls or Consular Agents." Thus, since no foreigners resided in Nablus, it proved impossible to appoint agents there.[46]

Earlier, attempts had been made by other nations to open consular agencies in Nablus, which had an almost exclusively Muslim population. In 1856, Georg Rosen, the Prussian consul in Jerusalem tried to appoint Sa'id Kayar as Prussian consular agent, and a further attempt was made in 1869 by the Prussian consulate in Jerusalem to commission another Muslim of Nablus, Sa'id Hassan – all to no avail. The explanations of the ambassador of the North German Federation to Constantinople why these appointments failed are instructive also regarding the American attempt. The Porte was most reluctant in permitting their subjects to take on foreign consular positions. According to the agreement between the Sublime Porte and the representatives of the powers, consular agents could not be Turkish nationals. Only in exceptional cases, in places where there existed appreciable foreign commercial interests, were non-Muslim Turkish subjects allowed. Since no special North-German commercial interests were at stake in Nablus, the Ottoman disapproval was understandable.[47]

---

43 Richard Beardsley, U.S. Consul, Jerusalem, to Second Assistant Secretary of State, 12 February 1872, USNA RG59 T471/3.

44 Richard Beardsley, U.S. Consul, Jerusalem, and Lorenzo M. Johnson, U.S. Consul General, Beirut to Hamilton Fish, Secretary of State, Washington, D.C., 14 September 1870, USNA RG59 T471/3.

45 Ibid.

46 Richard Beardsley, U.S. Consul, Jerusalem, to Second Assistant Secretary of State, Washington, D.C., 1 January, 25 March, and 30 September 1871, USNA RG59 T471/3.

47 Georg Rosen, Prussian Consul, Jerusalem, to Foreign Office, Berlin, 28 March 1856, and North German Minister, Constantinople, to North German Consulate, Jerusalem, 2 June 1869, ISA RG67/73. From this it transpires that between the years 1845 and 1849, the Germans tried to establish consular

Something of the dynamics of appointing consular agents may be gleaned from the case of the Jerusalem Jew, Haim Zvi Sneersohn, who upon his return from the United States in August 1874 as an American citizen intended establishing a Jewish colony near Tiberias. Sneersohn asked Jacob Schumacher, the American consular agent in Haifa, to help in having him appointed consular agent in Tiberias, "...as there were a great many travellers passing through and it seemed to be almost necessary that an agency should be established there." Schumacher recommended this, writing: "I can give the wish of Rabbi Sneersohn my support, as his undertaking is in every respect a noble one. And as many citizens of the U.S. visit Tiberias, it would certainly be good and agreeable if a Consular Agency were established there." Various communications in this matter raised the subject of the great distance between Tiberias and Safed and the seats of the consular agents in Haifa and Beirut, as a consideration for supporting the idea. In the end however, this proposal also came to nought.[48]

During the 19th century, Safed and Tiberias were two towns in Galilee inhabited by relatively large numbers of Jews, among them foreign nationals including some Americans. An American medical missionary, Dr. Morris Julius Franklin, also lived and worked in Safed. These persons were dependent on judicial and other services of the American consular agency in Haifa and of the consulate in Beirut (see below, Chapter Six, under "Jurisdiction"). The primitive means of transport in those days, and the distance from Haifa and Beirut caused difficulties of communication and access by the consular representatives, as well as by those who required their services. One of the interim solutions to these problems seems to have been the appointment of a local person as "representative." So, for example, we find in the Haifa consular archives correspondence dated 1899–1903 between J.M. Gloshtein and Schumacher in Haifa, and with the consul in Beirut and the American chargé d'affaires in Constantinople. On the envelopes used by Gloshtein and on his letterheads appears the printed title, "Representative of the American Citizens in the District of Safed and Tiberias, in SAFED (Palestine)." [49] It is not clear

---

agencies in Nablus, Ramle, and Gaza.

48   Testimony of Mr. H.Z. Sneersohn taken at Haifa, 15–17 February 1875, ISA RG67/504; Jacob Schumacher, U.S. Consular Agent, Haifa, to Edward Van-Dyck, Vice Consul, Beirut, 18 September 1874, USNA RG84 Haifa Copy Book 1872–1886 Box 5976.

49   J.M. Gloshtein, Safed, to Gottlieb Schumacher, U.S.A. Vice Consul, Haifa, 22 July 1903; Gabriel Bie Ravndal, U.S. Consul, Beirut, to J.M. Gloshtein, Safed, 31 July 1899, 17 May 1900; Gloshtein to Ravndal, 5 May 1902 and Lloyd C. Enscon(?), Chargé d'Affaires, Constantinople, to Gloshtein, Safed; all in USNA RG84 Haifa Miscellaneous and Official Correspondence Received 1875–1917

whether the title was an official one or given to him by the population which, at least according to the correspondence, he represented.

Other nations – France, Britain, Austria, and others – maintained consular agencies in Safed. Since Jews formed the majority of the population there, these positions were usually filled by one of their number. These men served without pay but enjoyed greater personal security and prestige. One of the typical examples in Safed was the French consul (or consular agent) Shmuel 'Abu, a native of Algeria who was appointed in 1827. Upon his death in 1878, the position passed to his son, Ya'aqov Hai 'Abu. When no agents were appointed, the consuls would sometimes commission unpaid correspondents who did not deal with official matters but were required to report regularly to the consul in Jerusalem on subjects of special interest. The American consuls apparently did not adopt this system.[50] During the 1860s and 1870s, along with the attempts at setting up new consular agencies of the United States, administrative procedures were standardized and regularized in only two consular agencies – in the coastal towns which in that period began to develop rapidly: Jaffa and Haifa. The agency in Jaffa was directly subordinated to the American consul in Jerusalem, while the one in Haifa, which replaced the consular agency in Acre, was under the consul in Beirut.

The Consular Agency in Jaffa

If in the first half of the 19th century Jerusalem was under the purview of the consular agent in Jaffa, the situation was reversed from the mid-century, and Jaffa with its resident agent were subordinated to Jerusalem. Nevertheless, since in those days Jaffa was the economic and commercial center of the country, and its importance in these regards continued to surpass that of Jerusalem, the consul in Jerusalem relied for his different reports on information gathered by the consular agent in Jaffa. Until 1858, the Jaffa consular agency was run more or less as it had been during the first half of the century, with Jacob Serapion Murad continuing in office up to his death in that year. Thereafter, Gorham looked for a candidate with American citizenship for the position of vice-consul in Jaffa. The man he found was Charles Saunders of Westerly, Rhode Island, who reportedly had lived for many years in Jaffa,

---

Miscellaneous Papers 1878–1903 Green Box.

50 Blumberg, *Zion Before Zionism*, p.50; Eliav, *Eretz Israel*, p.180; Tidhar, *Encyclopaedia*, 1:310–15; Schwarzfuchs claims that Shmuel Abu was a consul, but it seems that he was a consular agent subordinate to the French consul in Beirut (Schwarzfuchs, "The Jews of Algeria.")

and was cognizant of the desires of the "people" there.[51] Saunders had come to Jaffa with his family as a Seventh Day Baptists' missionary and, in the mid-50s, had joined the American agricultural experiment led by Clorinda Minor at Mount Hope nearby. Probably, it was these residents Gorham had in mind when he referred to "the people of Jaffa." Gorham also appointed Khalil al-Turk of Jaffa to be consular agent and dragoman.[52] We know little about the length and nature of Saunders's service because the existing records of the Jaffa consular agency only date to 1866 and thereafter, and are continuous only from 1872 (Appendix II H).[53]

At any rate, in 1866, J. Hermann Loewenthal was appointed consular agent in Jaffa. Loewenthal was an apostate from Judaism who temporarily also served as the Prussian agent. An American protégé – not a citizen – he remained in the position for only two years, but these were critical ones because they coincided with the settlement in Jaffa of over 150 Americans from Maine, members of the Church of the Messiah led by George W.J. Adams. Loewenthal's relations with the colony (which ended in failure), led to accusations of tyranny and swindling on the one hand, and of praise for his humane, dedicated, and honorable attitude on the other. However, despite the backing of the United States consul in Jerusalem, Beauboucher, and others, Loewenthal decided to resign his post.[54] During his period of service, Loewenthal maintained regular contacts with, and reported to, the consul in Jerusalem, including accounts of his expenditures which in 1867 amounted to a total of $150.48 (among them $22.47 for postage, $15.77 for official telegrams, $34.66 for a flagstaff, $5.45 for the firman of exequatur, and other items).[55]

There followed two short-lived, unsuccessful attempts at again commissioning American citizens to the post in Jaffa. Lorenzo M. Johnson, of Texas, who was vice-consul in Jaffa less than a year, served for a short interval as consul at Jerusalem when Beauboucher was suspended from his

---

51 John Warren Gorham, U.S. Consul, Jerusalem, to Lewis Cass, Secretary of State, Washington, D.C., 20 March 1859, USNA RG59 T471/1.

52 Ibid.; Kark, *Jaffa*, p.175. Saunders and his wife stayed in Jaffa from 1854–1860.

53 Mayer, ("Records, Jaffa") is mistaken in writing that there is an indication of the United States maintaining a consular agency in Jaffa from 1867, and that its records begin only with the stint of Ernst Hardegg in 1871. Actually, in the Jaffa archives there is material dating from 1866. USNA RG84 Jaffa, Miscellaneous Record Book 1866–1910.

54 Different dispatches in USNA RG59 T471/2 (30 March, 13 July, 1 August 1867).

55 Hermann Loewenthal, U.S. Vice Consul, Jaffa, to Victor Beauboucher, U.S. Consul, Jerusalem, 30 June 1867, USNA RG59 T471/2.

post, and was finally appointed consul-general in Beirut, a position he filled until 1874.[56] John Baldwin Hay served in Jaffa about a year and a quarter, in 1869–1870, before beginning a three-year stint as consul-general in Beirut. Hay, who was a native of Montana, assisted his mother and his aunt, Mary Baldwin, in establishing an American mission school under Episcopalian direction in Jaffa. He was twenty-two years old when he received the appointment. Among the recommendation for the position was his mother's family connection with the late President James Madison, his excellent education, his knowledge of Greek and some French, and his pursuit of Arabic studies. Despite his youth, Hay was even proposed for the Jerusalem consulate, with the added recommendation that "He is not engaged in Commerce." [57] John Hay instituted regular reports from Jaffa on trade and shipping, customs, population statistics, and the character of the inhabitants. Thus, in his report for 1868, he states that 1,425 ships arrived at Jaffa, and 1,455 departed (30 boats were built in Jaffa), and that the total turnover of imports and exports was $96,000. The town numbered 12,000 souls, half of these Muslims, who according to him, were devoid of initiative and energy by nature.[58] With Hay's transfer to Jerusalem and to Beirut, his mother served for nearly one year in his stead as U.S. consular agent in Jaffa, as was reported by Consul Beardsley in 1871.[59] Later, Hay returned to live in Jaffa, but not in a consular capacity; his four children stayed in America. He died in 1912 and was buried in the English cemetery, leaving a house, garden, and a few old pieces of furniture.[60]

---

56   USNA M587/9, List of U.S. Consular Officers by Post 1789–1939, Vol.3 Beirut.

57   USNA M587/9. Pitman, *Mission Life*, pp.187–225; Victor Beauboucher, U.S. Consul, Jerusalem, to William H. Seward, Secretary of State, Washington, D.C., 23 February 1869 and J. Augustus Johnson, Consul General, Beirut, to Hamilton Fish, Secretary of State, Washington, D.C., 31 December 1869, USNA RG59 T471/2.

58   John B. Hay, U.S. Vice Consul, Jaffa, Statement 31 December 1869 and Report to Department of State, 30 September 1870, USNA RG59 T471/2.

59   Richard Beardsley, U.S. Consul, Jerusalem, to Second Assistant Secretary of State, 4 May 1871, USNA RG59 T471/3. Hay's aunt, Mary Baldwin, died on 20 June 1876. Hay himself suffered an attack of "mental imbecility" in Jaffa at the end of 1879 and left for Europe or America with his mother and a servant. (Joseph G. Willson, U.S. Consul, Jerusalem, to Charles Payson, Third Assistant Secretary of State, Washington, D.C., 8 May 1880, USNA RG59 T471/5.) A short time before, Hay published a newspaper article which caused a stir, on "The Colonization of Palestine," *Jewish Chronicle*, 28 November 1879, p.12.

60   Correspondence between Jacob Hardegg, U.S. Consular Agent, Jaffa and A.M. Hay, J.M. Keith and Lewis Heck, 6 April, 6 December 1912 and 22 January 1913, USNA RG84 Jaffa Correspondence Book 1912–1915 and Miscellaneous Letters 1900–1914 Box 5965.

Finally, in 1871, the position of U.S. consular agent in Jaffa devolved upon Ernst Hardegg, who held it for a long time until his resignation in 1909 at the age of 70.[61] A German by nationality, he was a member of the Jaffa German Templer colony. His father, Georg David Hardegg, was one of the two leaders of the Templers who had settled in Haifa. In 1870, Ernst Hardegg acquired the colony's hotel, apparently in the expectation that his consular appointment would help his business, as well as strengthen the position of the Jaffa German settlers.[62] His appointment was recommended by the American consul at Jerusalem, Richard Beardsley, after "long and careful consideration." He expressed his firm conviction that Hardegg was eminently suited for the position, being "...an intelligent, honest and worthy individual, and as proprietor of the only good and respectable hotel at Jaffa he is brought in direct contact with many travelers," and added that "...it will give satisfaction to our American Citizens residing at Jaffa." (Plates 12 and 13)[63]

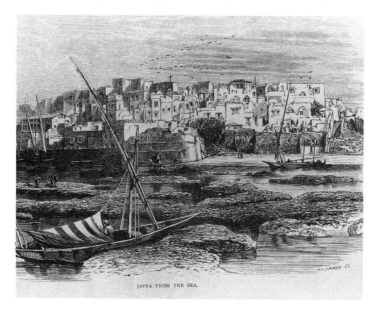

JAFFA FROM THE SEA.

Plate 12. View from the sea of the inner harbor and old city of Jaffa
Source: Manning, *Those Holy Fields*

---

61   USNA M587/9.

62   Carmel, *German Settlement*, p.28.

63   Richard Beardsley, U.S. Consul, Jerusalem, to Second Assistant Secretary of State, Washington D.C., 27 October 1871, USNA RG59 T471/3. Hardegg's hotel had the honor of accommodating former President Grant in 1877. (Young, *Around the World*, pp.322–25.)

Plate 13. Letterhead of the United States consular agency at Jaffa
Source: USNA RG84 Jaffa

From a report by Simeon S. Murad, the German vice-consul in Jaffa, when Ernst Hardegg's appointment was confirmed, there existed, or were reestablished in Jaffa the vice-consulates or consular agencies of ten nations: Germany, Austria, the United States, Spain, Great Britain, Greece, Russia, Belgium, Holland, and Persia. Most of these were subject to their respective consulates in Jerusalem, except for the Belgian one which reported to Beirut and the Persian one to Damascus. Similarly, in the same year, a Jewish businessman of Jerusalem named Haim Amzalak also received an appointment to Jaffa, which he held for a long time – until 1903.[64] Murad's report and that of the American agent in Jaffa also mentioned a French agent.[65] Most of these were Christians and Jews of foreign nationality (Table II).

---

64   Simeon S. Murad, German Vice Consul, Jaffa, to Carl Victor von Alten, German Consul, Jerusalem, 31 December 1872, ISA RG67 /451; Glass and Kark, *The Amzalak Family*, pp.115–47.

65   Murad to von Alten, ibid., Report on Consular Agents in Jaffa, January 1874, USNA RG84 Jaffa Miscellaneous Letters Received from Principal Officers in Jerusalem Miscellaneous Letters 1872–1874 Box 5958

TABLE II Foreign Vice-Consuls in Jaffa, 1874

Country	Position	Name	Nationality	Place of Origin	De-nomination
Austria-Hungary	vice-consul	Jacob Pascal	U.S.A.		Jewish
Belgium	vice-consul				
Britain	vice-consul	Haim Amzalak	English	Jerusalem	Jewish
France	vice-consul	F. Philibert			Catholic
Germany	vice-consul	Simeon S. Murad	Ottoman	Jerusalem	Armenian
Greece	consul	Constantine Cuzurelli			
Holland	vice-consul				
Persia	wakil	Scharich Bender			
Russia	consular agent	Alexander Marabuti		Odessa	Greek Ortho.
Spain	vice-consul	Joseph Moyal			Jewish
U.S.A.	consular agent	Ernst Hardegg	German	Germany	Protestant

Based on: Report on Consular Agents in Jaffa, January 1874, USNA RG84 Jaffa Miscellaneous Letters 1872-1874 Box 5958

These vice-consulates and consular agencies continued to function in Jaffa through the end of the 19th century, except for the Belgian one which was closed, and the opening of an Italian one which also represented Portugal and Romania. Some of the consular agents and vice-consuls earned $400-$2,500 per annum while others were unpaid. All these establishments retained one or two dragomans and two kavasses, about half of these without salary.[66] Throughout his thirty-eight years of service as United States consular agent in Jaffa, Hardegg kept well-organized records of official correspondence, a fee book, invoice book, etc.[67] Here and there, during the 1870s and 1880s, there was criticism of the manner in which he carried out his duties and of his being "a man with no decided character." Hardegg was accused of caring more about the development of his business than for his consular duties, of launching into new tourism ventures – including with Thomas Cook & Co. – and of abusing his position as consular agent to avoid paying taxes to the government for the goods in his hotel. But these accusations may have been the result of personal quarrels with the dragoman of the consulate in Jerusalem, Jiacomo

---

66   Selah Merrill, U.S. Consul, Jerusalem, to Thomas W. Cridler, Assistant Secretary of State, Washington, D.C., 9 September 1899, USNA RG59 T471/9.

67   Mayer, "Records, Jaffa," pp.1–13.

Panayotti, and with the veteran American settler in Jaffa and Jerusalem, Rolla Floyd (Figure 7).[68]

In his letter of resignation of 28 July 1909, Hardegg briefly described his period of service in Jaffa, and the two years as acting consul in Jerusalem, expressing his pleasure at having, to the best of his ability, served "the great Republic." [69] Thomas Wallace, the consul in Jerusalem, in forwarding the letter to Washington, wrote that he believed Hardegg's stint to have probably been "the longest period of time any person has served our government without interruption, in the Consular Service," and went on to unreservedly praise him for his "integrity, morality and charity equalled by few." Wallace cited Hardegg's respected status, his excellent work, and all that without salary:

> There are very few Americans either in public or private life who have given so much gratuitous service for the benefit of their fellow citizens as has Mr. Hardegg. The Consular Agency in question is different in character from any other Agency in our service. It is a port of entry where more than two thousand Americans, on an average, land each year to enter the Ottoman Empire. A large number of these require Consular attention for which there is no compensation. Many complications arise with

---

68 Jiacomo Panayotti (also Baniotti), U.S. Interpreter, Jerusalem, to William Hunter, Second Assistant Secretary of State, Washington, D.C., 5 August 1876, USNA RG59 T471/4; letters of Floyd, 8 June 1877, 5 October 1882, 27 January 1883, in Parsons, *Letters from Palestine*, pp.25, 65, 69.

69 Ernst Hardegg, U.S. Consular Agent, Jaffa, to Thomas R. Wallace, U.S. Consul, Jerusalem, 28 July 1909, USNA RG84 Jaffa Copy Book 1908–1912. His memory must have failed him at the age of 70, for he wrote that the consul who approved his appointment was Robert Beardsley.

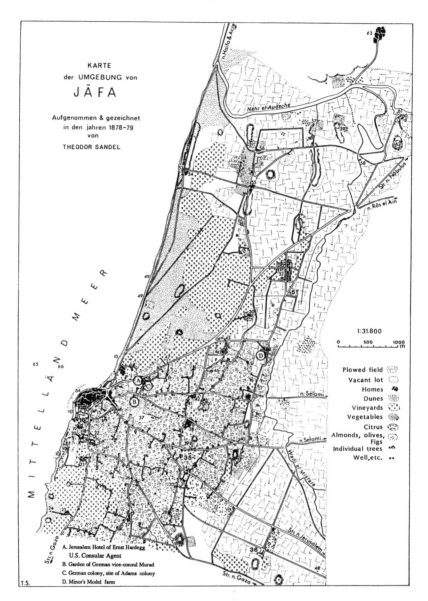

KARTE
der UMGEBUNG von
JĀFA

Aufgenommen & gezeichnet
in den jahren 1878-79
von
THEODOR SANDEL

1:31.800

0   500   1000
m

Plowed field
Vacant lot
Homes
Dunes
Vineyards
Vegetables
Citrus
Almonds, olives, Figs
Individual trees
Well,etc.

A. Jerusalem Hotel of Ernst Hardegg
   U.S. Consular Agent
B. Garden of German vice-consul Murad
C. German colony, site of Adams colony
D. Minor's Model farm

Figure 7. Jaffa and its environs, 1878-1879
Source: Kark, *Jaffa*, pp. 68–69

resident American citizens as well as non-residents requiring official interposition in their behalf. The entry of American goods, or goods shipped to Americans with other matters of official business, in cases of disputes, must be looked after by the Consular Agent, for which no compensation is allowed. No one unacquainted with the time consumed and the amount of work required in official service of this character, can form any idea of its magnitude.

The actual sum he receives in fees for official services is so small it would not pay the rent for rooms in which to transact the business.

This good old man and faithful official who has given so much time to the service of Americans free of charge, and who has devoted to our government his best efforts directed to honesty in the administration of its affairs, and ability in the execution of its official business, is deserving of high commendation.[70]

With the acceptance of Ernst Hardegg's resignation, two candidates applied for the position: Jona Kuebler and Jacob Hardegg, also a German national, who was a relative of Ernst. The latter was granted the commission, apparently, to some extent due to his predecessor's reputation, and served until 1917. Since in Jaffa, and from the founding of Tel Aviv in 1909, the number of Jews increased steadily, part of his duties consisted in assisting Jews who were American citizens.[71]

The Haifa Consular Agency

The changes in consular representation in northern Palestine, during the second half of the 19th century were similar to the ones in Jaffa. Haifa's importance grew at the expense of Acre. It became the focus of foreign settlement and of the administrative and economic endeavors of the powers that this entailed. The United States consular agency at Haifa assumed central importance, being headed by American citizens who instituted new and

---

70 Thomas R. Wallace, U.S. Consul, Jerusalem, to Assistant Secretary of State, Washington, D.C., 12 January 1910, USNA, ibid.

71 USNA M587/9; Thomas R. Wallace, U.S. Consul, Jerusalem, to Mr. Knox, Department of State, Washington, D.C., 16 May 1910, USNA RG59 T471/11 (JNUL [Fi2477/11]; William Coffin, U.S. Consul, Jerusalem, to Jacob Hardegg, U.S. Consular Agent, Jaffa, 16 March 1911, USNA RG59 Jaffa, in Bartour, "American Consular Aid," p.370 and Jacob Hardegg, to the Committee of Tel Aviv, 12 July and 30 November 1915, TAMA RG1 Box 510–11 Files 14–15. In Jaffa and Tel Aviv there were in 1914 about 10,000 Jews out of a total population of 50,000 souls (Kark, *Jaffa*, p.151).

effective administrative practices and reporting.[72] In the 1850s, there was still indecision whether to fix upon Acre or Haifa as the central agency for northern Palestine, under the consulate in Beirut. In the meantime, the consular agency which had functioned at Acre since 1833, continued to exist, but with a new consular agent, George Jimmal. The veteran agent, Gabriel Nasralla, who was an Ottoman subject, was transferred to head the United States consular agency at Haifa. Eventually, that rapidly developing town became the seat of the consular agency for the region, leaving Acre with only a dragoman subject to Haifa – although the center of Ottoman administration remained in Acre until its conquest during World War I (Appendix II I and Plate 14).[73]

Plate 14. Letterhead of the United States consular agency at Haifa
Source: USNA RG84 Haifa

The most significant change occurred in 1872, with the appointment of Jacob Schumacher as consular agent for Haifa and Acre. Schumacher served in this position until his death in 1891, when his son Gottlieb succeeded him – until 1904. Jacob Schumacher, a naturalized American citizen of German origin, was appointed at the recommendation of John Baldwin Hay, who at

---

72 On the rise of Haifa and the decline of Acre from the middle of the 19th century onward, see in: Kark, "The Rise and Decline," pp.69–89. In the period 1800–1914, Haifa grew from 1,250 inhabitants to 20,000, and from an area of 123 metric dunams to 1,201 dunams; Acre remained static with 8,000 souls and an area of 220 dunams.

73 Despatches dated 17 May and 16 June 1850, 9 August 1853 and 18 February 1856, USNA RG59 T367/1 and 2.

that time served as consul-general in Beirut. Hay proposed Schumacher partly because of the necessity to assist the American settlers from Buffalo and other places in upstate New York – members of the German-American "Temple Colony" that was founded in Haifa in 1868–9.[74] Jacob Schumacher, who had come from Buffalo and was an architect and field surveyor by profession, was a man of intellectual stature. He had settled with his family in Haifa in 1869, served as the chairman of the German-American colony, and drew up its site plan. From 1872, he began to conduct regular correspondence and records of the consular agency, compiled censuses of American citizens, reported on shipping, commerce, agriculture, and transport, and began to provide legal and civil services to American citizens in the region under his jurisdiction, which comprised Galilee and the towns of Acre, Nazareth, Safed, and Tiberias. One of his important contributions was the help he gave to the Haifa Templer colony in registering the lands they acquired.[75]

It is noteworthy that during the 1870s, three Haifa Templers served as consular agents of different powers, considerably strengthening the status of the colony. When Jacob Schumacher was commissioned to his post, the settlers saw this as highly important for their well-being and conducted a special thanksgiving service. In 1877, Friedrich Keller, who was employed by the American consular agency, was appointed German vice-consul in Haifa, and in 1879, the doctor, Johannes Schmidt, a German settler of Russian nationality became the British vice-consul in that town.[76] The most suitable candidate for the post left vacant on Schumacher's death at the age of 66, after nineteen years of devoted service, was found to be his son, Gottlieb S. Schumacher, a highly respected personality in his own right, both in and outside the community. Two copies of passport application forms Gottlieb Schumacher submitted in 1898 and in 1902 show that he was born in Zanesville, Ohio, on 21 November 1857, and arrived in Haifa from Buffalo, New York,

---

74 Mayer, "Records, Haifa," pp.1–12.

75 Ibid.; Records of Foreign Service Posts of the Department of State, RG84 Haifa, 1872–1917. On the subject of real estate see Chapter Six.

76 Carmel, *German Settlement*, pp.42–43; Carmel, *The History of Haifa*, pp.111–140. On the appointment of Keller as dragoman of the U.S. consular agency, see: Jacob Schumacher, U.S. Consular Agent, Haifa, to John B. Hay, U.S. Consul General, Beirut, 19 October 1872, USNA RG84 Haifa Copy Book 1872–1886 Box 5976.

on 28 August 1869, aged twelve. He married Mary Lange by whom he had nine sons and daughters.[77]

Gottlieb S. Schumacher, PhD. was undoubtedly the best man for the vacant consular position. He was a highly diversified engineer and architect, cartographer, and archeologist, having graduated from the Stuttgart Higher Technical Institute which he attended from 1876 to 1881. In 1885, he was appointed district engineer for Acre by the Ottoman authorities. Despite his enthusiastic German patriotism, he maintained his American citizenship, and during his service as consular agent enjoyed the economic benefits the position entailed. All that time, as well as after resigning his post in 1904, he actively engaged in researches, studies, surveys, and archeological mapping, and took part in the planning of railroads, settlements, wineries, and various buildings, and published a number of articles and books (Plate 15).[78]

One of his reports to the consul at Beirut, in 1896, in reply to a circular from the State Department, states that he allotted parts of his private home for the consular agency office, which was open for business from 9–12 in the morning and 4–6 in the afternoon. He listed his main official occupations as dealing with the export of soap, oil, and wine to the United States, and protection of the American settlers (there were 60 in Haifa, and others in Galilee) or tourists.[79] Nevertheless, Gottlieb Schumacher complained to his superiors in Beirut about the definition of his status by the Turkish authorities as a mere consular agent. To his mind, it should have been the equivalent of wakil, which was indeed the title of all the consular agents in Haifa, except for himself and the Russian consular agent who was referred to as mâmur, a lower official grade. Schumacher requested the consul at Beirut to act in order to change his rank, and listed the powers and their agents in Haifa:

---

77 Forms of application for passports, Haifa 15 January 1898 and Beirut October 1902, USNA RG84 Haifa Miscellaneous Records and Passports. In 1902, his children were listed by name and age: Alfred 18, Julia 16, Annie 14, Hedwig 12, Walter 10, Hildegard 9, Cornelia 6, and Christopher 5. When Gottlieb Schumacher died in 1924, he had 9 children and 11 grandchildren. His daughter Cornelia, who was born in 1896, died in Haifa aged 95 in February 1991. (*The Jerusalem Post*, 19 February 1991.)

78 Roth, "Gottlieb Schumacher," pp.347–50.

79 Gottlieb Schumacher, U.S. Consular Agent, Haifa, to Thomas R. Gibson, U.S. Consul, Beirut, USNA RG84 Haifa Copy Book 1886–1899 Box 5977.

Plate 15. Portrait of Consular Agent Gottlieb Schumacher
Source: Courtesy of Y. Ben-Artzi

"P. Scopinich, vice-consul and Austrian chargé d'affaires; Ronzevalle, French vice-consul; J. Schmidt, English vice-consul; Salim Khouri, Russian chargé d'affaires; Italy vacant." [80]

Schumacher's reports during his entire period of service are a valuable source for studying the mode of operations of the consular agency: applications for passports, reports of deaths and births, payments and receipts, sanitation, various events, the economic history of northern Palestine, and, of course, for the Templer colony, and for the growth of Haifa into an important port city (Figure 8).[81] After Gottlieb Schumacher's resignation at the end of October 1904, about a year-and-a-half passed before a replacement was found in 1906 – the American citizen, Theodore J. Struve. In the interval, John G. Scheerer served as acting consular agent. Struve continued in his position also during the critical first years of the World War, having been asked to deal with matters of the consular agencies of enemy countries – Russia, England, and France – and to provide intelligence reports.[82] During his stint in office, the reforms in the foreign service of the United States of 1906 were put into effect. Five inspectors of consulates, under the Secretary of State were appointed by the President. These were salaried officials who were to examine every consular office at least once in two years.[83] One of these, Alfred L.M. Gottschalk, was dispatched to the Near East in 1913, and also came to inspect the Haifa and Jaffa consular agencies. On completing his mission he sent his findings and remarks to the consul-general in Beirut.[84] It was only from 1907 onward that such control was exercised in the consular agency at Haifa which had functioned since 1833 without supervision. Struve was confronted with a number of questions regarding his methods of operation and bookkeeping, and as a result of the inspection was apparently subjected to fairly strong criticism, which the consul-general in Beirut attempted to soften somewhat after receiving Struve's reaction. But he requested of Struve:

---

80 Gottlieb Schumacher, U.S. Consular Agent, Haifa, to Thomas R. Gibson, U.S. Consul, Beirut, 31 August 1896, USNA RG84 Haifa Copy Book 1886–1899 Box 5977.

81 Part of the correspondence of the United States consular agency in Haifa during Gottlieb Schumacher's term of office was dealt with by Churkowski, "Haifa Consular Agency."

82 Theodore Struve, U.S. Consular Agent, Haifa, to W. Stanley Hollis, U.S. Consul General, Beirut, 29 October and 3 November 1914, USNA RG84 Haifa Letter Book 1910–1917.

83 Jones, *The Consular Service*, pp.119–20.

84 Alfred L.M. Gottschalk, Consul General at Large, Vienna, to the Consul General at Beirut, Syria, Turkey, 1 May 1914, Some Hints Concerning Consular Recording Compiled for the Benefit of the Consular Officers of the Middle East and Africa, USNA RG84 Haifa Miscellaneous Records and Passports.

"It (the Consulate General) expects you to report what has been done by your Agency toward carrying out the inspector's instructions." The consular agencies at Haifa and Jaffa were thus subjected to the new administrative regulations.[85]

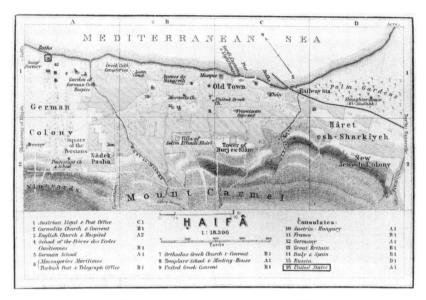

Figure 8. Haifa and its environs, 1912
Source: Baedeker, *Palestine and Syria*, p.228

ESTABLISHMENT OF THE UNITED STATES CONSULATE IN JERUSALEM

As indicated in the previous chapters, until 1844, Palestine came under the jurisdiction of the American consul in Beirut and the legation in Constantinople. On 1 May 1844, the congressman for Philadelphia, E. Joy Morris, who had recently returned from a tour in the Levant, including Palestine, wrote to Secretary of State John C. Calhoun requesting the appointment of an American consul in Jerusalem. His proposal stemmed both from the availability of a candidate from Philadelphia (Warder Cresson) and conclusions drawn from

85 Correspondence between U.S. Consulate General, Beirut and Theodore J. Struve, U.S. Consular Agent, Haifa, 10 and 21 April and 18 July 1913, USNA RG84 Haifa Miscellaneous Letters Received, Box 5991 and 17 April 1913, USNA RG84 Haifa Letter Book 1910–1917.

his travels. "Having traveled in the countries of the East," he explained, "I know the great convenience of American consulates in the interior of Syria and Palestine to the American, and the protection and comfort that is often afforded to him by official representatives of his country. Jerusalem is now much frequented by Americans. A consulate there will be of service to our citizens." As a result, Cresson was commissioned by the Senate, on 17 May 1844, as American consul at Jerusalem.[86] There are different versions of how the appointment devolved from that point, but there is no doubt about the controversial nature of the candidate. Dabney S. Carr, the American minister in Constantinople, who had not been informed of the appointment, styled Cresson a "religious maniac" and "madman". This apparently led to the refusal of the Ottoman government to grant Cresson an exequatur (*berat*, in Turkish) and to the President expressing his opinion in June 1844 that the position was not "called for by the public service" and deciding against establishing the consulate at that time. Cresson, who did not know of the cancellation, began to function as consul in Jerusalem after his arrival there on 4 October 1844. He titled himself, with flourish, "Consul-General of Syria and Jerusalem" and only "resigned" in 1846. The situation thus reverted to its former state of there being no American consulate in the Holy City (Plate 16).[87]

It was the few American missionaries residing in the city who urged the necessity of establishing a consulate in Jerusalem. American travelers who came there relied upon the services of the British consul, or of Simeon S. Murad, the brother of the U.S. consular agent in Jaffa who had been appointed by the latter to represent American interests in Jerusalem. In the early 1850s, when the proposal to open an American vice-consulate in Jerusalem was mooted, an American citizen resident in Jerusalem was sought for the post.

The only person deemed suitable by J.H. Smith, the consul in Beirut, was the medical doctor and missionary, Dr. James T. Barclay. In letters to William S. Marcy, the secretary of state, in June 1853, Smith explained why

---

86 Friedenwald, in Lipman, *Americans and the Holy Land*, pp.89–96.

87 Domestic Letters, Department of State, XXXIV, pp.255–6, in Lipman, *Americans in the Holy Land*, pp.89–96; Finnie, *Pioneers East*, p.252; Manuel, *The Realities*, p.10; Thackeray, *Notes on a Journey*, pp.189, 226.

Plate 16. Portrait of Warder Cresson
Source: Shavit, *"Land in the Deep Shadow."*

the recommendation by the State Department to appoint an American citizen resident in Jerusalem as consular agent was not implemented: "There is but one individual among them, Dr. J.T. Barclay, who would be at all competent and he has twice refused to accept it being an M.D. and a missionary." Smith also wrote that although he understood that it was important to appoint an American citizen as consul, it was unlikely that anyone would take on the position for less than $1,500 per annum. And he added this in the light of his personal experience with his low salary.[88] As has been seen above, Barclay was not the only American who could have been appointed to the position, but Wigley, the architect studying churches, who asked for the post in 1852, was considered by the consul in Beirut and by the minister in Constantinople as unsuited – perhaps because of his lack of experience and his short time in the country – and they preferred to appoint instead the agent in Jaffa, Jacob Serapion Murad (in effect, his brother Simeon).[89]

There were also at the time (1852–1853) several Americans living in the Arab village of Urtas, south of Bethlehem, who engaged in agriculture. The members of this group who came there with their leader, Clorinda Minor, were motivated by millenarian ideas, and none of them wanted to involve themselves in the consular activities of the United States in Jerusalem. Nevertheless, it seems that they appreciated the advantage of having such a representative who would see to their interests in Jerusalem, and they therefore

88   J. Hosford Smith, U.S. Consul, Beirut, to William S. Marcy, Secretary of State, Washington, D.C., 23 June 1853, USNA RG59 T367/2.

89   See "Jacob Serapion Murad – Example of a Consular Agent," above.

proposed for the position of United States vice-consul in Jerusalem the Jewish apostate missionary of British nationality, John Meshullam, who had inspired the group to come from Philadelphia to Urtas.[90]

Beginning in 1856, the United States government formally defined separate consular districts in Palestine and Syria. The central and southern parts of the country were included in the district of Palestine, while the Galilee and the consular agency in Haifa were under the jurisdiction of the consul at Beirut for most of the time. However, in many cases, especially where Jews were concerned, this separation was not rigidly maintained, and all of Palestine came under the responsibility of the Jerusalem consulate. The consuls were salaried American citizens; their primary duty was to assist tourists and pilgrims. There may well have been a connection between the timing of the appointment of the first official American consul in Jerusalem (October 1856) and the growing influence of the European powers in the Ottoman Empire after the Crimean War and the signing of the Treaty of Paris at the end of March 1856. And it certainly reflected the growing religious and historical interest in Palestine by Americans.[91]

Moreover, the establishment of a regular consulate in Jerusalem in 1856, should probably also be seen in the context of the general reform in the United States diplomatic and consular service after the passage of the act of 18 August 1856, and the attempt to set up a regular consular corps in different parts of the world.[92] On 20 October 1856, the Boston physician, John Warren Gorham, was appointed consul at Jerusalem on the recommendation of the President of the United States. The appointment was ratified by the Senate only on 30 March 1858, although Gorham took up his post in Jerusalem on 25 March 1857. Gorham was the first citizen of the United States to live in Jerusalem, officially accredited and accorded an exequatur by the Ottoman government.[93] From 1857 to 1917, sixteen American consuls and several acting consuls served in Jerusalem. Most of them filled the position for terms of one to five years. One of them, Selah Merrill served a total of sixteen years in three separate terms. Until the appointment, in 1906, of inspectors of consulates, the consuls conducted their work without orderly

---

90   J. Hosford Smith, U.S. Consul, Beirut, to Department of State, Washington, D.C., 28 February 1853, USNA RG59 T367/2.

91   Kark, "Annual Reports," p.130.

92   See in Chapter One, "The Foreign Service of the United States."

93   Blumberg, *Zion Before Zionism*, pp.128–9.

and systematic supervision. Three inspection reports on Jerusalem were filed between 1907 and 1913 (Plate 17).[94]

Plate 17. Seal of the United States consulate at Jerusalem
Source: ISA RG67 Box 459, File 504

THE CONSULAR HIERARCHY AND SPATIAL JURISDICTION

The internal hierarchal structure of the foreign consulates in Syria and Palestine, including its spatial manifestations (that is, the territorial jurisdiction at the different levels of responsibility), was affected to some extent by the Ottoman administrative organization as it evolved throughout the nineteenth century and until the World War. Other factors also contributed to changes in the rank and status of the serving consular officials and in the physical delimitation of their jurisdiction in Palestine. Among these factors were political events in the region, such as the Crimean War and the British occupation of Egypt, international developments, reforms in the foreign services of their home countries, initiatives by the Ottoman administration, as well as distance and technological developments in transport and communications. It is therefore

---

94 Gustafson, "Records in the National Archives," pp.136–37. On how the consuls were appointed, see at the beginning of Chapter Four.

interesting to examine questions such as the logic behind the geographic limits of consular spatial jurisdiction, the extent of their overlap with those of the Ottoman administrative divisions – vilayets and sanjaks – and with those between consulates of a given country. These spatial divisions determined the type and accessibility of service to which nationals of the foreign countries within these regions could have recourse.

Ottoman Administrative Divisions of Palestine and the Foreign Consulates

During the 19th century, Palestine did not constitute a separate entity of the Ottoman administration. Various districts of Western Palestine and Transjordan were part of the vilayets of Damascus and Sidon. The administrative division of 1864 fixed three sanjaks: Jerusalem, Nablus, and Acre, all under the governor of the Sidon vilayet whose center was in Beirut. The territorial continuity of the vilayet of Beirut (Sidon) was broken by the definition of Mount Lebanon as a special district. The Acre sanjak remained within the Beirut vilayet until the end of the Ottoman period. The sanjak of Nablus, which previously included all of Samaria and the Balkah region in Transjordan, lost the Balkah to the Damascus vilayet with Samaria remaining subject to Beirut.[95]

While the northern part of Palestine remained under the vilayet of Beirut, changes were instituted in the central and southern regions. Jerusalem, increasingly important, became an independent *mutasarriflik* at the beginning of the 1870s, directly responsible to Constantinople. Its northern border passed along a line from a point north of Jaffa, east to the Jordan. At first, the Jerusalem *mutasarriflik* was divided into three subdistricts – Jaffa, Hebron, and Gaza – which were the seats of kaimakams; later the area was extended to the Beer Sheba-'auja al-Hafir region in the Negev, and to the Nazareth region in the north (Figure 9).[96]

---

95   Kark, *Jaffa*, pp.30,42; Eliav, *Austrian Consulate*, p.171.

96   Ibid.; From the political report of the American consul at Jerusalem of 10 April 1871 (USNA RG59 T471/3) it appears that at that time Jerusalem became free of the paralyzing rule of the Damascus vilayet.

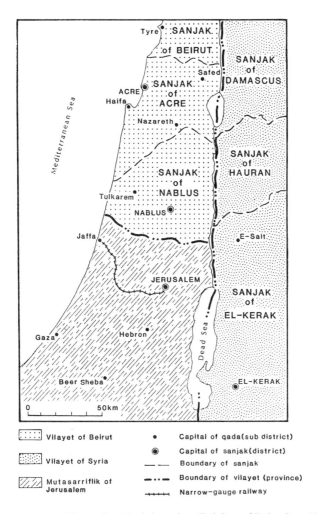

Figure 9. Administrative division of Palestine, 1900

The Ottoman decision to create an independent *mutasarriflik* of Jerusalem, and subjecting to its authority the new subdistrict (*qāda*) of Nazareth in 1906, was due to the importance of these towns to Christians and to the Western powers. This was instituted despite there being no territorial continuity between Jerusalem and Nazareth, the latter forming an enclave in the sanjak of Nablus, and in disregard of the protests by the local inhabitants whose contacts with the Ottoman authorities became more cumbersome as a result.[97] From two reports (among the most important in the Austrian consular archives in Jerusalem) sent to the foreign ministry in Vienna by the Austrian consuls at Jerusalem in 1880 and 1895, it appears that most of the consulates in Jerusalem (Austria-Hungary, France, England, Germany, Russia, Italy, Spain, the United States, and Greece) were directly subordinate to their respective embassies in Constantinople. However, the Austrian consulate found the lack of identity between the historic and geographic concept of "Palestine" and the area delimited by the autonomous *mutasarriflik* of Jerusalem problematic in its operations, for it was much smaller and did not include the sanjaks of Acre and Nablus which remained subordinate to Beirut.[98] This administrative division of the Ottoman government led those countries which adopted the new delimitations to reduce their areas of consular jurisdiction, or to extend their activities only to the sanjak of Nablus, while the sanjak of Acre remained under Beirut. Among these was the Austro-Hungarian consulate. In the early 1870s, the consulate of Germany at Jerusalem extended the area of its jurisdiction over the sanjaks of Nablus, Belkah in Transjordan, and Acre in northern Palestine, which until then had been in the district of its Beirut consulate.[99] An opposite process apparently took place regarding the consulate of Great Britain in Jerusalem. In the mid-19th century, the districts of northern, central, and southern Palestine were included in the consulate's area of jurisdiction, whereas maps of the beginning of the 20th century indicate that the consular district was coterminous with the Jerusalem *mutasarriflik* (Figure 10).

All the consulates of the powers in Jerusalem attempted to extend the areas under their jurisdiction to include also the Acre district, which comprised Galilee and the coastal strip south to Caesarea, because in that area, and especially in Safed and Tiberias, they had many Jewish protégés. But these intents were not always acceptable to the decision-makers in their respective foreign services. Some of the nations chose to conform to the Ottoman administrative divisions in fixing their consular districts, while others adopted their own particular approaches.

---

97   Great Britain F.O. Annual Series. Diplomatic and Consular Reports, Turkey. Report for the year 1907 on the Trade and Commerce of Palestine, April 1908. ISA RG67/462; Kaimakam of Nazareth Ali Selim to Mutaserrif, 1 July 1908, ISA RG83/35 (Turkish).

98   Eliav, *Austrian Consulate*, pp.171–82, 269–73

99   Eliav, *The Jews of Palestine*, p.x. This step on the part of the Germans followed the transfer of these sanjaks to the Jerusalem *mutasarriflik* by the central Ottoman administration in June 1872 who, however, canceled the order a month later.

As may be seen from the report by Willson, the American consul at Jerusalem, on the subject of "Consular Jurisdiction – Limits Between Palestine and Syria" at the end of the 70s, the United States Department of State also took an interest in this matter. In the report, which is quoted here in full, Willson explained the importance of the divisions and the delimitation:

> In reference to your despatch No.39 of July 19 1879, in regard to the boundary line between the Beirut and the Jerusalem consulates, I have the honor to report that Palestine is divided into six Turkish districts for administrative purposes, viz: Acre, Nablous, Jerusalem, Hebron, Gaza, and Jaffa; and that there seems to be no uniform rule as to the boundaries, or territorial limits of the Consulates at Jerusalem.
>
> The German Consulate imbraces [sic] *all* these Turkish districts, the English Consulate all but one, viz. Acre.
>
> I do not know that the limits of the United States Consulate at Jerusalem have ever been defined.
>
> My opinion however is that the German Consulate has the proper line of decision between Palestine and Syria, and for the following reasons, viz. Geographical position, commercial relations, the social and business habits of the people, the short distance comparatively of the several districts from Jerusalem, and the fact that *all* [sic] of Palestine, naturally falls under the supervision of the Consul at Jerusalem.
>
> I am informed by Raouf Pacha [the governor, R.K.] of Jerusalem, that a plan [exists] by which *all* these districts will be placed under the jurisdiction of the Pacha at Jerusalem.
>
> If this should be done, it will precipitate the settlement of the question; as heretofore two of the Palestine Turkish Districts have been attached to the Pachalic of Damascus; and the German Consul, and the English Consul, have of necessity, had official relations, not only with the Pacha at Jerusalem, but also, with the Pacha at Damascus. [100]

100 Joseph G. Willson, U.S. Consul, Jerusalem, to William Hunter, Second Assistant Secretary of State, Washington, D.C., 10 November 1879, USNA RG59 T471/4.

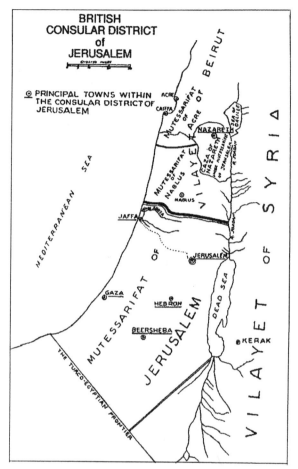

Figure 10. British consular district of Jerusalem, 1907
Source: ISA RG67/462

American Consular Hierarchy

The consular hierarchal structure of most nations, at the end of the 19th century, was graded from consul-general to consul, vice-consul, and consular agent. At least in theory, the American system was somewhat different. The consul-general had not only superiority of rank but also responsibility for the supervision of all the consulates in the country where he served. In the district of his jurisdiction, he served as consul. The only function of the vice-consul was to stand in for the consul in the latter's absence or illness. The American consular agents, like those of other countries, were appointed by the consuls and were under their direct supervision.[101]

In the Ottoman Empire, this hierarchic system of the foreign consulates differed somewhat because of the intervention of the diplomatic level in consular activities, the elevation of some of the consulates throughout the Empire to consulates-general, and by setting up a special hierarchal structure for the consulate at Jerusalem. According to Manuel, the American consular service was only loosely integrated with the diplomatic service, and the lack of clarity regarding the American administrative geographic delimitations, in relation to the Turkish ones, added to the confusion in the day-to-day relations between the United States and the Ottoman government.[102]

The correspondence of the American consuls at Beirut in the years 1836–1857, when all of Palestine was under their jurisdiction, shows that the three first consuls – Chasseaud, Smith, and Wood – sent their letters, reports, and accounts directly to the secretary of state in Washington, and not through the consulate-general or the legation in Constantinople. Circulars and queries from Washington were addressed directly to the consuls in Beirut.[103]

Even the consular agents appealed directly to the secretary of state, as did Darmon in the 1830s, and Jacob Serapion Murad in 1857. The latter, who was first appointed consular agent in Jaffa and Jerusalem by the consul at Beirut, and whose subsequent terms were commissioned by the legation in Constantinople, regarded himself upon the confirmation of his appointment in 1852 under the direction and oversight of Consul Smith in Beirut.[104] The institution of a permanent and more regularized hierarchal framework is reflected in the copy books of the correspondence beginning with the tenure of Jacob Schumacher as consular agent in Haifa for northern Palestine. From that time on, most of the correspondence was almost without exception between the consular agents at Haifa and the consulate-general at Beirut. Reports prepared at the request of the State Department regarding the functioning of the consular agency, or on special subjects such as agriculture, education, and other matters, were usually transmitted by way of Beirut.[105]

In Jerusalem, from the opening of the consulate in 1857 and until the middle of 1871, the consular reports were sent directly to the secretary of

---

101 Schuyler, *American Diplomacy*, pp.81–84.

102 Manuel, *The Realities*, p.11.

103 USNA RG59 T367/1–3.

104 Jacob Serapion Murad, U.S. Vice Consul, Jerusalem, to William Marcy, Secretary of State, Washington, D.C., 30 January 1857, USNA RG59 T367/3.

105 USNA RG84 Haifa Copy Books 1872–1899.

state in Washington, and in the following years, up to World War I, to the assistant and the second and third assistant secretaries of state.[106] This was probably connected with changes in the State Department, but in 1871–2, the hierarchic framework raised questions by the consuls. Thus, Beardsley, in a letter to the State Department, inquired "...whether by sections 45 and 47 of the New Consular Regulations for 1870, this consulate is to correspond directly with the Department or through the Consulate General at Beirut, as their meaning is not perfectly clear...considerable time [is] lost in sending despatches through Consul General at Beirut..."[107] Nevertheless, when requesting four months' leave, Beardsley forwarded his application to Washington through the legation at Constantinople for the approval of the United States minister, explaining that the mails in the Levant were slow and that "...Consular Regulations...seem to allow of...application for leave of absence being sent directly to the Department." The reply from the legation at Constantinople approving his request stated that it was being forwarded to the State Department in the hope of final approval.[108]

Reports of the Jaffa consular agency, despite its being subordinate to Jerusalem, were sometimes directly transmitted to the State Department. In most cases, however, such material was sent to the consuls in Jerusalem and was included in the latters' reports to Washington.[109] Generally, the consulate at Jerusalem had considerable autonomy. In complicated cases involving American citizens within the consulate's jurisdiction, as in the incident of murder and rape in the agricultural colony of Clorinda Minor in Jaffa in 1858, or the problems of the American settlers who came to Jaffa in 1866 under the leadership of George W. J. Adams, and Ottoman decrees affecting Jewish American citizens in the eighties, the consuls in Jerusalem had recourse to help and intervention by the consuls-general in Beirut and Alexandria, or by the consulate-general and the legation in Constantinople.[110]

---

106 USNA RG59 T471/1–11.

107 Richard Beardsley, U.S. Consul, Jerusalem, to Hamilton Fish, Secretary of State, Washington, D.C., 1 February 1871, USNA RG59 T471/3.

108 Ibid., 18 and 20 January 1872.

109 For example, 30 September 1871, USNA RG59 T471/3; October 1880, T471/5 6.

110 Thus, De Leon was summoned in 1858 from Egypt by Gorham: "...Although Jaffa was not under my jurisdiction, which only embraced Egypt and its dependencies..." (De Leon, *Thirty Years*, 1:246); and a decade later, Charles Hale from Alexandria. A notable case of such intervention took place in Galilee in the affairs of H. Sneersohn in Tiberias (*Jewish Chronicle*, 30 July 1875) and the Lubowsky brothers in Safed (see Chapters Five and Six, under "Legal Services").

Spatial Jurisdiction

The foregoing discussion dwelt on the significant changes in the regional divisions of the American consular areas of jurisdiction in Palestine, and from 1856, with the juridical area of the newly-established autonomous consulate in Jerusalem. But despite this theoretical division, there was no exact definition of boundaries between the area of jurisdiction of the consulate at Beirut and that at Jerusalem. Nor were there clear determinations of the jurisdiction of the consular agencies – which in some instances depended on the personal interpretations and initiatives of the different consuls. Thus, in 1862, Consul Olcott declared the jurisdiction of the consulate at Jerusalem to extend over the whole of Palestine, except for Acre and Haifa, which he (unjustifiably) considered unimportant.[111] The consuls who succeeded him, wanted to open consular agencies subordinate to themselves in Galilee (Tiberias and Nazareth), and in Samaria (Nablus), despite this region being regarded by the consulate-general in Beirut as under its jurisdiction. The explanation advanced by Manuel for this state of confusion was that the demarcation between the two districts was never exactly defined and that it did not conform to the Ottoman administrative divisions. He also thought that throughout the 19th century matters concerning the whole of Jewish Palestine tended to be concentrated in Jerusalem."[112]

In view of this situation, an attempt was made at the end of 1879 by the State Department and by the consulate-general in Constantinople to settle this issue. Willson and Edgar (in Jerusalem and Beirut, respectively) were requested to prepare a joint report in order "to make proper determination of these consular districts...which would assist the Department in dividing the Consular Districts of Beyraut [sic] and Jerusalem, with a due regard to the commercial and the administrative interests involved." They were to address questions such as the geographic proximity of certain towns to the consulate from the aspect of commercial travel, and consider difficulties that might arise "if one consul held jurisdiction in a vilayet or government in which the other consul was recognized by the local government."[113]

However, this attempt too did not prevent consuls appointed subsequently from adopting maximalist or minimalist attitudes regarding the area of their

---

111 Franklin Olcott, U.S. Consul, Jerusalem, to William Seward, Secretary of State, Washington, D.C., 30 September 1862, USNA RG59 T471/1.

112 Manuel, *The Realities*, p.11.

113 U.S. General Consulate, Constantinople, to U.S. Consul, Jerusalem, 25 November 1879, USNA RG59 T471/4.

jurisdiction. One of the consuls who advocated the inclusion of historic and geographic Palestine under his authority – as was the case with the consuls in Jerusalem of other powers – was Selah Merrill. On this matter, Merrill engaged in a sharp altercation with the consul-general at Beirut, Gabriel Bie Ravndal, in the years 1898–9. The dispute arose as a result of a report by Ravndal that was favorable to Jewish settlers, in which he took issue with Merrill's negative views as expressed in the latter's report on Jews and Jewish Colonies in Palestine. Merrill – who according to Ravndal "considered the whole of Palestine and its works to be his special bailiwick" – complained of Ravndal's intrusion into his territory and objected to his reporting on matters that did not regard him without having been asked to do so by the State Department. Merrill added, that just as he had no authority to go to Smyrna and Constantinople and to report on conditions there, no other American consul had the right to report on his area, something he viewed "as a breach of courtesy" and for which he demanded an apology.[114]

No such arguments arose regarding the boundaries south of the Beer Sheba-Gaza line since the region was arid and sparsely inhabited. From 1882, most of Sinai came under British control, and in 1906 the southern border of Palestine was surveyed and demarcated. At the end of the first decade of the 20th century, there appeared the first clear description, accompanied by a small map, which indicated that the juridical territory of the United States consulate at Jerusalem had been determined according to the "minimalist" conception:

> The Consular District of Jerusalem has the same limits as the Mutasarrifat of the Jerusalem [sic]. The Mediterranean bounds it on the west, the River Jordan on the east, the northern boundary is half way between Jerusalem and Nablous, and the boundary line between Egypt and Turkey is the southern limit.
>
> It is about 180 miles long in a straight line north and south, 45 miles broad from east to west on the north, and about one third of the distance south from the northern boundary, and 30 miles wide at the southern limit.

---

114 Ibid., p.74 and Selah Merrill, U.S. Consul, Jerusalem, to Thomas W. Cridler, Assistant Secretary of State, Washington, D.C., [before] 10 September 1899, USNA RG59 T471/9. Ravndal apparently hinted at Merrill's detailed, negative report of 3 October 1891 (T471/7). Merrill stated that he was in the midst of preparing a new report on this subject and had informed the State Department to that effect.

A small map is attached hereto with the boundary lines marked thereon (Figure 11). [115]

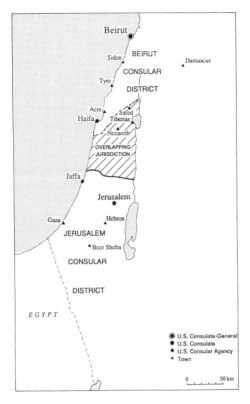

Figure 11. United States consular jurisdiction in Palestine, 1910
Source: USNA RG59 T471/11 [Fi2477] 29 June 1910, p.201

It may be that this detailed treatment of the subject derived from the changes enacted in the consular service in 1906. In that year, a similar query was addressed to Hardegg, the consular agent at Jaffa, by the consul-general at Constantinople, asking him to specify what he regarded to be the geographical limits of his jurisdiction. [116]

---

115 Statement on Consular District of Jerusalem, Thomas R. Wallace, U.S. Consul, Jerusalem, to Assistant Secretary of State, Washington, D.C., 20 June 1910, USNA RG59 T471/11 [Fi2477/11]. Already in an earlier report, of 1908, Wallace indicated that Nablus was not included in the Jerusalem consular district.

116 U.S. Consul General, Constantinople, to Jacob Hardegg, U.S. Consular Agent, Jaffa, 22 October 1910, USNA RG84 Jaffa, Miscellaneous Letters 1910–1914, Box 5965.

Before the advent of the telegraph, and later of the wheeled carriage, the
telephone, and the automobile in Palestine, greater importance was attached
to the area under consular jurisdiction because of the services and protection
it offered to its nationals and for reasons of commerce and potential markets.
In northern Palestine, within the juridical district of the Haifa consular agency
(which was subordinate to Beirut), were Safed and Tiberias – distant two
days' journey on horseback from Haifa. From the official minutes of an
agreement between the United States and the Ottoman Empire regarding the
ownership of lands, it transpires that until the turn of the century the distance
factor was a determining consideration:

> In the localities distant by less than nine hours' journey from the
> consular residence, the agents of the public force cannot enter
> the residence of a foreigner without the assistance of a consul, as
> before said....
>
> In the localities distant by nine hours or more than nine hours
> of travel from the residence of the consular agent, the agents of
> the public force may, on the request of the local authority and
> with the assistance of three members of the Council of Elders of
> the Commune, enter into the residence of a foreigner; without
> being assisted by the consular agent, but only in case of urgency,
> and for the search and the proof of the crime of murder, of
> incendiarism, of armed robbery...armed rebellion....
>
> In localities more distant than nine hours' travel from the
> residence of the consular agent, in which the law of the judicial
> organization of the vilayet may be in force, foreigners shall be
> tried without the assistance of the consular delegate by the Council
> of Elders fulfilling the function of justices of the peace and by
> the tribunal of the Canton [Qada] as well for actions not exceeding
> one thousand piasters....[117]

Concerning commercial matters, in a kind of market survey he prepared in
1895 for the Department of Agriculture, the consular agent, Gottlieb
Schumacher, cited the population numbers by area and locality in the juridical
district of the Haifa consular agency: the towns of Acre (11,000 inhabitants),
Haifa (12,000), the Safed region (25,000), Nazareth (10,500), Tiberias (4,000),
and Beisan (3,000), and a rural population totaling about 170,000 souls in an

---

117 Protocol permitting U.S. citizens to own real estate in the Ottoman Empire, signed 29 October 1874,
    USNA RG84 Haifa Miscellaneous and Official Correspondence Received 1875–1917 Miscellaneous
    Papers 1878–1903 Green Box.

area of 1,400 square miles.[118] The emphasis at the turn of the century on clearly-defined limits of jurisdiction and the gathering of more exact and reliable information within these, reflected the competition among the leading industrial nations for markets and the growing importance of Turkey's potential in this respect.[119]

INTERACTION AND COMMUNICATIONS

Relations with the Ottoman Government

The contacts of the foreign consulates in Jerusalem, and in particular that of the United States, with the Ottoman authorities were conducted at various levels – from local ones to the highest provincial instances and in Constantinople. The consuls regarded themselves as sharing the government with the Ottoman administration. Thus, Willson wrote in 1880: "There are but few Turks in Jerusalem, but they are the ruling class – the consuls divide with the Pacha the government of the inhabitants – the foreign residents being under the consulates..."[120]

The main contact of the consuls in Jerusalem was with the mutasarrif of Jerusalem, so that there was considerable importance to the character and the manner in which each of these men carried out his trust. Some governors were better-liked by the consuls and regarded as more capable; others were thought less successful. Changes of governors were often significant since they affected the relations with the consuls and the foreign nationals. So, for example, in 1871, the American consul looked forward to the appointment of 'Ali Bey as governor of the Jerusalem *mutasarriflik*: "...under the administration of 'Ali Bey we are again promised many good things..."[121] Since according to Turkish practice governors were frequently replaced, the consuls often intervened in order to prolong the tenure of a governor who was particularly esteemed by them. In 1897, Constantinople announced that

---

118 Gottlieb Schumacher, U.S. Consular Agent, Haifa, to J.S. Morton, Secretary, U.S. Department of Agriculture, Washington, D.C., 16 February 1895, USNA RG84 Haifa Copy Book 1886–1899 Box 5977. See also Churkowski, "Haifa Consular Agency," p.26.

119 Gordon, *American Relations*, pp.141–43.

120 Joseph G. Willson, U.S. Consul, Jerusalem, to John Hay, Assistant Secretary of State, Washington, D.C., 8 October 1880, USNA RG59 T471/5.

121 Richard Beardsley, U.S., Consul, Jerusalem, to Second Assistant Secretary of State, Washington, D.C., 10 April 1871, USNA RG59 T471/3.

the pasha in office, Ibrahim Hakki, was to be removed and replaced by a new governor. But the ministers of the various powers, religious heads, and government officials in Jerusalem who regarded Hakki favorably, sent many telegrams to the capital urging the government to leave him in his position; a request which was acceded to.[122]

Most of the contacts were through correspondence, some of it in French, but mainly in Arabic. And there were mutual visits and meetings, and an observance of ceremonial as on the anniversary of the inauguration and the birthday of the sultan, for Fourth of July celebrations, or to mark the death of American presidents. Such events were marked by flying the flag or bringing it down to half-mast on the citadel and over the consulate, firing gun salutes, and the like.[123] During visits of royalty, state governors, or ambassadors from Constantinople, as well as for visits of governors of vilayets, a special guard of honor was mounted at the entrance to Jerusalem, which included besides the representative of the administration, also the consuls and their kavasses in full dress uniform. Among the American visitors to Jerusalem who were honored in this manner were the former President, Ulysses S. Grant (1877), and the American ministers to Constantinople – Lewis Wallace (1883) and Henry Morgenthau (1914).

After the reform in the American consular service during the first decade of the 20th century, the consular agents in Haifa were instructed unequivocally to call upon the mutasarrif of Acre as often as necessary, even if such visits entailed hiring a carriage at their own expense and without being reimbursed for it.[124] The American consular agencies in Jaffa and Haifa maintained extensive contacts with the different Ottoman authorities at all levels. This emerges from a reading of the correspondence, in Arabic, in the "Copy Books" and the records of "Miscellaneous and Official Correspondence Received and Sent." [125] The consular agent at Jaffa corresponded with the governor of Jerusalem, with the kaimakam of Jaffa, and with various local

---

122 Yellin in Kark, "The Development," p.36.

123 Thus, for example, the mutasarrif of Acre ordered the flag flown in mourning over the fortress, and instructed the kaimakam of Haifa to attend the burial ceremony of the vice-chairman of the United States Senate who died in Haifa in January 1875 (USNA RG84 Haifa Miscellaneous and Official Correspondence Received 1875–1917 Miscellaneous Papers 1875–1904 Green Box). And in September 1881, Jacob Schumacher notified the pasha of Acre and the kaimakam of Haifa of the death of President Garfield (USNA RG84 Haifa Copy Book 1872–1886 Box 5976).

124 U.S. Consul General, Beirut, to Theodore J. Struve, U.S. Consular Agent, Haifa, 18 July 1913, USNA RG84 Haifa Miscellaneous Letters Received Box 5991.

125 SNA RG84 Haifa and Jaffa.

officials. The agent in Haifa maintained such contacts with the grand vizier in Constantinople, with the governor-general (vali) of Syria in Damascus, with the mutasarrif of Acre, the kaimakams of Haifa, Nazareth, Safed, and Koneatra (Quneitra) in the Jaulan (Golan Heights), and he was also in touch with the customs house and its officials in Beirut and Haifa, with the *ma'mur al-tabu* in Haifa, and with assorted judicial authorities – the *mahkama al-shar'iy* in Acre and Haifa, and the mixed trade tribunal.

Beyond confirming the appointments of consuls, consular agents, and consular employees by the Ottoman authorities, and bringing various decrees of the central government to the consuls' attention, these mutual contacts focussed on proper administration, municipal services, customs, health, protection of personal property and life (cases of robbery, murder, and real estate will be discussed in detail in Chapters Five and Six), and representing American citizens in the governmental administrative and legal institutions to assure their special rights.

In the period under discussion, from the mid-19th century and until the First World War, the consuls and consular agents of the United States were highly critical regarding all aspects of the Ottoman system of government, and expressed their views in numerous reports. Some of them attributed the lack of initiative, the revulsion to anything smacking of progress, the devastation of agriculture, the oppression of the population, and the relentless attempts at deriving maximal income and investing minimal efforts in the well-being of the country and the people to "...the imbecility and ineption of the local Government which has neither the inclination nor the ability to correct the abuses of its agents and factors." Others believed that no matter how good or bad the training and the competence of the pasha, he was caught up in the system and could not change anything: "The fault is with the system of provincial administration which prevails throughout the Turkish Empire – a system which practically makes the Pacha a tax-collector and the Government a machine to gather the revenue and transmit them to the Imperial Treasury."[126] Thus, in 1870, a sum equivalent to $285,170 was transmitted to the imperial treasury in Constantinople – out of a total revenue of $413,952 collected during the previous year in Jerusalem and its dependencies. The difference of $128,782 was retained for the expenses of the government. Were this difference, or even half of it, invested in various improvements

---

126 Franklin Olcott, U.S. Consul, Jerusalem, to William H. Seward, Secretary of State, Washington, D.C., 30 September 1862 and Richard Beardsley, U.S. Consul, Jerusalem, to Second Assistant Secretary of State, Washington, D.C., 30 January 1872, USNA RG59 T471/1 and 3.

such as roads, it would have contributed materially to the well-being of this impoverished district.[127]

One of the severe problems that militated against every good intention of a local administrator was the expectation of baksheesh and bribes, even in the courts of justice. This custom was so well entrenched that to obtain information for his reports, the American consul in Jerusalem complained of having to disburse "...backsheesh – a tax upon the Consul, as I know of no fund or allowance to which it may be charged. I notice in the Consular Regulations that the Consul General has a liberal allowance for this purpose."[128]

Attempts at improving the police, the courts, and education in the 1870s and the early 1880s were made by Midhat Pasha, who was appointed vali of Syria (including the sanjaks of Acre and Nablus). Raouf Pasha, the governor of Jerusalem who was described as "an accomplished man, of European culture," acted to modernize the road infrastructure of Palestine. Both men earned the praise of the American consuls in Jerusalem. Nevertheless, Selah Merrill stressed the delay of all progress: "...the government itself is only an organized system of tyranny, oppression, and robbery. It does nothing for internal improvement."[129]

There were attempts at cooperation between the foreign consuls and the Ottoman authorities to ameliorate local conditions – mainly in the municipal realm and in sanitation and health. The consuls were party to the initiative for setting up the Jerusalem municipality in the 1860s, and participated in running it. The municipality did much to improve life in the town by seeing to sanitation, lighting, cleanliness, building permits, and other matters of public concern.[130] In Haifa too, as far as is known, there was such cooperation between the kaimakam and the American consular agent regarding the activities of the town municipal council. A year before, the kaimakam of Haifa solicited the help of Schumacher in collecting taxes from the Americans residing in Haifa for installing trash containers next to houses and shops, collecting refuse from the houses, and cleaning the streets ("and dumping it in a remote

127 Beardsley to Hamilton Fish, Secretary of State, Washington, D.C., 30 September 1870, ibid

128 Joseph G. Willson, U.S. Consul, Jerusalem, to William Hunter, Acting Secretary of State, Washington, D.C., 4 October 1879, USNA RG59 T471/4; see also 23 August 1875, 4 September 1875, 28 June 1880, USNA RG84 Haifa Copy Book 1872–1886 Box 5976.

129 Ibid.; Selah Merrill, U.S. Consul, Jerusalem, to Alvey A. Adee, Third Assistant Secretary of State, Washington, D.C., 21 July 1884, USNA RG59 T471/5. During his term of office, in 1880, Midhat Pasha visited and was much impressed by the German-American colony in Haifa (28 May 1880, USNA RG84 Haifa Copy Book 1872–1886 Box 5976).

130 For more details see: Kark, "The Jerusalem Municipality."

place") which he instituted in Haifa for the first time. In the same month, Schumacher was asked to help fight the cholera epidemic that broke out in Syria and Palestine, and the need of reporting cases, maintaining cleanliness and "prohibiting the sale of unripe fruit and vegetables." [131]

Here appear the beginnings of a growing problem that was the source of serious difficulties in the proper administration of municipalities where sometimes over half of the population (as in Jerusalem in 1906) were foreign nationals who could not be taxed by the Ottoman authorities without the agreement of their consuls. This is illustrated by a memorandum submitted in 1906 by Ali Ekrem Bey, the governor of Jerusalem, to Constantinople: "In a country where more than half of the inhabitants are foreigners, it is impossible in matters relating to the municipality to consider them as though they do not exist." [132] It was but the tip of an iceberg of conflicts that arose between the Ottoman government and the local authorities on the one hand, and the consuls on the other, in matters of jurisdiction, civil rights of American citizens – including the right to own real estate, which will be discussed in greater detail below.

Relations with Other Consulates

Despite the rivalries, very close contacts were maintained between the consulate of the United States in Jerusalem and its consular agencies in Jaffa and Haifa, and their counterparts of the other powers. Ceremonial, as well as efficient administration of their offices, required cooperation and mutuality. The consulates also acted together in their contacts with the Ottoman authorities. Interconsular communications in 19th century Palestine were conducted in French, as is evident from the correspondence between the consulates of the United States, Britain, and Germany in Jerusalem. Matters of protocol included announcements of appointments, arrivals, and of new consuls taking up their posts. James Finn, the British consul in Jerusalem, entered the following notice in his journal in 1857: "Visit to the United States Consul (Mr. Gorham) on the announcement of his appointment"; and

131 Michael Shadid, Ottoman Health Officer, to Jacob Schumacher, U.S. Consular Agent, Haifa, 26 June 1875 and Mustafa Abde, Kaimakam Qada, Haifa, to Schumacher, 28 June 1875 and 22 March 1876, USNA RG84 Haifa Miscellaneous and Official Correspondence Received 1875–1917 Miscellaneous Papers 1875–1904 Green Box (Arabic).

132 Ali Ekrem Bey, Mutasarrif of Jerusalem, to Ottoman Prime Minister, Constantinople, 15 November 1906, ISA RG83/28 (Turkish).

three days later: "Visit returned by Consul of the United States."[133] In one of
the files in the archives of the German consulate in Jerusalem are notes to
the Prussian consulate from the American consulate in Jerusalem announcing
the appointments of the consuls Beardsley, Beauboucher, Rhodes, Olcott,
and DeHass.[134] In the absence of the consul, or if he had not yet arrived, the
announcements were signed by the vice-consul.[135]

It was Rhodes, when serving in Jerusalem and later in Europe, who scoffed
at these forms of protocol – the mutual visits, and the social and cultural
gatherings of the foreign consuls and their families, which reflected the
feelings shared by enlightened Europeans in the East.[136] In addition to written
announcements and meetings of this sort, there were receptions and parties
to which all the consuls were invited – and usually also the governor and
other dignitaries – for Christmas, New Year's Day, and to various national
festivities such as the Fourth of July.[137] Those attending were usually requested
to appear in their official dress uniforms, which presented a problem for the
American consuls who were not provided with clear instructions regarding
"consular outfit." [138] Dress was one of the important symbols of status in
such meetings and receptions, as was also the uniform of the kavasses – the
consular guards, including those of the Americans. Consul Thomas R. Wallace
regarded these meetings important from a diplomatic point of view: "...it
should be taken into consideration that this Consulate is rather a diplomatic
than a commercial station, and that the Consul here is constantly coming in
contact with the other foreign Consuls, and the Turkish officials, and the
ecclesiastical leaders of several Churches having headquarters here..." [139]

Reciprocal arrangements provided for colleagues of the other powers, mainly

133 Quoted in Blumberg, *A View from Jerusalem*, p.259.

134 ISA RG67/163; in the file are also announcements from other consulates.

135 Simeon S. Murad, U.S. Vice Consul, Jerusalem, to Georg Rosen, Prussian Consul for Palestine, 27
     January 1864, ISA RG67/163.

136 Rhodes, "Our Consul in Jerusalem," pp.437–47.

137 See for example, the invitation in December 1873 to the German consul for a reception at the Hotel
     Méditerrannée: Frank DeHass, U.S. Consul, Jerusalem, to O. Kersten, Chancellor, German Consulate,
     Jerusalem, 17 December 1873, ISA RG67/163.

138 Rhodes ("Our Diplomats," pp.169–70) describes the lack of clarity and of definite guidelines regarding
     uniforms of the diplomatic and the consular service of the United States, and the resulting adoption
     of the "simple garb of an American citizen of a blue coat covered with silk, gold, embroidery, and
     sword."

139 Thomas R. Wallace, U.S. Consul, Jerusalem, to Assistant Secretary of State, Washington, D.C.,
     8 August 1909, USNA RG59 T471/10 [Fi2477/10].

Britain and Germany, to stand in for the consul or consular agent when absent on leave.[140] Foreign nationals who had no consular representation could apply to the consuls of other countries. In this way, the first American missionaries who came to the Levant were represented by the British consul, and, almost until the end of the 19th century, Dutch nationals in Jerusalem were represented by the American consul. Special importance attached to such arrangements when the First World War broke out in 1914. With the departure of the Allied consular representatives (British, French, Russian, and later, Italian and Greek), their archives and the administration of their business, the protection of their institutions and nationals and their property were placed in the care of the American consulate in Jerusalem and of the Haifa consular agency. The American consular officers played a highly important role throughout the War, including in the provision of humanitarian assistance and transfers of funds (which space does not permit to describe here in detail).[141]

The American consuls joined with their counterparts in various matters connected with the Ottoman administration. This was the case in positive activities such as in municipal affairs (in Jerusalem, Haifa, Jaffa), seeing to public cleanliness, dealing with epidemics, etc. When discriminatory and restrictive regulations were imposed on foreign nationals, as in the case of prohibitions on Jews entering the country and acquisition of lands, the consular representatives of the powers acted in concert to exert pressure at both local and higher levels of the Ottoman government in Constantinople to mitigate the effects.[142]

The bulk of the contacts of the American consulate with the other consulates had to do with juridical activities and with their consular agents in Jaffa and Haifa. Since the foreign consuls were vested with legal authority, all matters dealing with claims, contracts and agreements, etc., between nationals of

---

140 See for example: Jacob Schumacher, U.S. Consular Agent, Haifa, to John T. Robeson, U.S. Consul General, Beirut, 26 May 1883, USNA RG84 Haifa Copy Book 1872–1886 Box 5976. See also: Issawi, "British Consular Views," p.105.

141 The acting British consul in Jerusalem, W. Hough, relates how on 1 November 1914 he "fled to the American Consulate for sanctuary...[having] been instructed to hand over British interests to the protection of my American colleague." ("History of the British Consulate," p.13). Similarly, there are letters from the British and French vice-consuls in Haifa to the American vice-consul there, which transfer the administration of their respective interests and properties to him (31 October 1914, USNA RG84 Haifa Miscellaneous Letters Received Box 5991). Two recent books on this period are: Eliav, *Siege and Distress*, and Efrati, *The Jewish Community.*

142 Kark, "Changing Patterns," pp.357–59.

various countries were dealt with in coordination among the consulates and consular agencies, including, at the turn of the century, the mixed trade tribunals. In cases of disputes between nationals of different countries, consuls of uninvolved countries served as arbitrators in endeavors to settle matters outside the courts. An example of such proceedings was the quarrel between the American settlers from Philadelphia of the Clorinda Minor group at Urtas in the early 1850s, and John Meshullam who was a British subject. The British consul, James Finn was directly involved, as were the American consuls in Beirut, Joseph Hosford Smith and Henry Wood, under whose jurisdiction Jerusalem was at the time. The Prussian consul, Georg Rosen, and Count Pizzamano, the consul of Austria in Jerusalem both took an active part in the attempts at arbitration.[143] Another example of such contacts was the case of the legal matters affecting the American citizens who remained in Jaffa in the 1870s after the departure of most of the settlers of the Adams colony. Among those who remained were Abigail Alley and Herbert Clark who were engaged in disputes with British subjects under the jurisdiction of the British consular agent, Haim Amzalak.[144] According to the correspondence in the archives of the Jaffa consular agency, the agent enlisted the help of the Austro-Hungarian, Greek, Spanish, French, and the German consular agents in Jaffa, and of the British, the Italian, and the Austrian consuls in Jerusalem.

Communication Networks: Post and Telegraph

The American consuls and consuls-general, like those of the other nations, relied for their communications on the postal and telegraph services. From the middle of the 19th century until the War broke out in 1914, Palestine and the other provinces in the region were served by the Ottoman postal system which was a member of the Universal Postal Union. In the last quarter of the century, Ottoman post offices in Palestine existed in Acre, Nablus, Gaza, Haifa, Nazareth, Safed, Tiberias, Jaffa, and Jerusalem. However, this service was so deficient, that Austria, France, Germany, and Russia resorted to their capitulatory rights for maintaining their own separate post offices, in parallel

---

143   Joseph Hosford Smith, U.S. Consul, Beirut, to James Finn, British Consul, Jerusalem, 8 June 1853, ISA RG123–1/9; Henry Wood, U.S. Consul, Beirut, to James Finn, British Consul, Jerusalem, 9 February 1857, ISA RG123–1/9; and see also correspondence in PRO FO78/963 for February 1853.

144   Haim Amzalak, British Consular Agent, Jaffa, to Ernest Hardegg, U.S. Consular Agent, Jaffa, 18 November 1873, 2 January 1874, 25 January and 5 February 1878, USNA RG84 Jaffa Official and Miscellaneous Letters 1872–1874 Box 5958.

with the Turkish ones. The Austrian service in particular was considered the most efficient and reliable.[145] The correspondence between the American consuls in Jerusalem and the State Department during 1884–1903, is replete with strictures regarding the Ottoman postal service for its careless handling, leaving mail exposed to the elements, pilfering, slowness of delivery, and abuse of privacy. Although instructed by their superiors to use the Ottoman post office, the American consular officials preferred to send their mail through the foreign postal services.[146] The consuls were greatly dissatisfied at these conditions and attempted to have the regulations changed. Thus, in 1884, Consul Merrill wrote that

> So far as the Consulate is concerned, I must never allow letters to go through the Turkish Post if I can possibly avoid it. Occasions frequently occur, however, when I am compelled to send a letter or letters through this channel. In such cases I have the letters sealed with wax, with the consular stamp upon them, and if the letters are important I have them registered, thus taking all possible precautions to insure their safety. All this, however, does not insure promptness of which the Turks have no idea. Other Consuls feel the same....
>
> ...Turkey is in the Postal Union and in Europe and America it is supposed that she is sufficiently civilized to deserve to be thus admitted...This is not justified.

He therefore proposed alternative ways for sending consular mail not only from, but also to, Jerusalem via Brindisi and Trieste by the Austrian post office.[147]

An almost identical despatch was sent to Washington twelve years later, in 1896, by the consul, Edwin Wallace, who lost all patience with the local postmaster. He was shocked to find that the postal workers used United States mail sacks for storing wheat and flour in their homes, and urged the State Department to use the reliable Austrian postal service by sending mail via London and Brindisi.[148] The Turkish mails were perceived as yet another symptom of Ottoman administrative ineptitude, and the Austrian services as

---

145 Kark, *Jaffa*, pp.217–20.

146 Selah Merrill and Edwin S. Wallace, U.S. Consuls, Jerusalem, to Assistant Secretary of State, Washington, D.C., 30 August 1884, 5 October 1896, 3 January 1898, 9 September 1899, 28 January 1903, USNA RG59 T471/5–9.

147 Merrill, ibid., 21 July and 30 August 1884.

148 Wallace, ibid., 5 October 1896.

a symbol of perfection.[149] It seems that this sad state of affairs, and the example of the consular services of Britain, France, Russia, and others, which avoided using the Turkish mails for their official correspondence, convinced the American administration to transmit its official mails to Syria and Palestine by way of the Austrian post office. In 1907 (to the dismay of the Austrians), a contractual agreement with a private company was made for the dispatch of official American mail through the French postal administration.[150]

The consular agents in Jaffa and Haifa also preferred and requested permission to use the foreign postal services – French and Austrian. As late as in the second decade of the 20th century, the subject of the Ottoman mails was raised in many communications in efforts to improve this vital service. One of the letters from the American consular agent in Haifa to the consul-general in Beirut in 1912, illustrates the inefficiency of the Imperial Ottoman postal services. In a letter complaining that a passport issued to an American citizen residing in Safed took thirty-five days to reach the consular agency in Haifa, he declared that he had no intention of sending it from Haifa to Safed by the Turkish post, and preferred inviting the American in question to come from Safed to Haifa in order to receive his passport.[151]

The introduction of the telegraph into the Ottoman Empire in 1854, a short time after its invention, had far-reaching effects in many realms, including government, administration, employment, economics, transport, architecture, education, culture, journalism, diplomacy, and foreign relations – as shown by Davison who traced the development of this new technology which brought about the divorce of communications from transport.[152] The telegraph caused

---

149 In 1881, 68,009 letters, post cards, and parcels arrived at the Austrian post office in Jerusalem, most of these from Europe and 4,381 from the United States; 85,392 pieces of mail were sent in this way from Jerusalem, of which 4,501 to the U.S. (Luncz, *Jerusalem Year Book*, pp.131–38).

150 Austrian Consulate, Jerusalem, to Austrian Embassy, Constantinople, 16 January and 1 April 1908, in Eliav, *Under Imperial Austrian Protection*, pp.334–37, 348. After transferring to the French post office, the consulate also received complaints about its service in Jerusalem (Thomas R. Wallace, U.S. Consul, Jerusalem, to Assistant Secretary of State, Washington, D.C., 24 December 1909, USNA RG59 T471/10 [Fi2477/10]).

151 Victor Beauboucher, U.S. Consul, Jerusalem, to Edward Joy Morris, U.S. Minister, Constantinople, 21 May 1867, USNA RG59 T471/2; correspondence in USNA RG84 Haifa Letter Book 1910–1917 including Struve to Hollis, 22 April 1912. See also: Churkowski, "Haifa Consular Agency," p.17.

152 Davison, "The Advent of the Electric Telegraph," pp.133–65. In 1844, the first telegraph connection was established between Washington and Baltimore, and in 1855 the first telegraph line was opened to commerce in England – between Paddington and Drayton. The first trans-Atlantic cable to North America was laid in 1866.

a revolution in international diplomacy, and in the diplomatic and consular services of various countries, and in their mutual relations.[153] There were some in the English and American foreign services who believed that with the expansion of railways and the telegraph, the diplomatic and consular representations, including those in the Levant and in Palestine, ought to be reduced in number; but their ideas were not adopted.[154]

The telegraph reached Syria in the 1860s. In 1861, Aleppo, Damascus, and Beirut were connected to the network, and by 1865 were added the coastal towns of Tripoli, Acre, and Jaffa, and Jerusalem. From 1866, the consuls and consular agents could maintain telegraphic contact with their superiors, with the Ottoman authorities, and even with Washington. It was only a question of urgency, cost, and where necessary, of secret codes. Unlike the postal service, the telegraph was only available in the Turkish post offices. Within the year Jaffa and Jerusalem were connected to the telegraphic network, it was resorted to by the consul in Jerusalem and by the consular agent in Jaffa in the affair of the American settlers in Jaffa and in other matters. Between July and September 1866, the Jaffa consular agent sent six telegrams to Jerusalem. These were noted in full detail – date, serial number, subject, number of words, cost – in the quarterly Register of Official Telegrams from the U.S. Vice Consulate at Jaffa. On the same subject, in 1867, the consul at Jerusalem also sent telegrams to Beirut while at the same time asking the minister in Constantinople for permission to use the telegraph.[155] The consular agency at Haifa had to use the telegraph in Acre until Haifa was also connected (Plate 18).[156]

153 Blumberg, *Zion Before Zionism*, pp.46, 137–43.

154 Platt, *The Cinderella Service*, p.129; Rhodes, "Our Diplomats," p.173; Ilchman, *Professional Diplomacy*, p.18. At about that time (1876), the minister at Constantinople used the telegraph to report to the State Department on the "fatal tumult" in Salonika, and requested an American ship for protecting citizens in Salonika and Izmir after the murder of the French and German consuls. Maynard, "Protection of American Citizens," pp.1–3.

155 Hermann Loewenthal, U.S. Vice Consul, Jaffa, 30 September 1866, USNA RG59 T471/2; Victor Beauboucher, U.S. Consul, Jerusalem, to William H. Seward, Secretary of State, Washington, D.C., ibid. It is interesting that in 1878, one of the members of the former American colony in Jaffa, Ralph Layton, wanted to give up his American citizenship and become an Ottoman subject so that he could work as a telegraph operator at which, according to him, only Turkish nationals could be employed. Ralph Layton, Jaffa, to Joseph G. Willson, U.S. Consul, Jerusalem, 30 September and 4 October 1878, USNA RG84 Jaffa Miscellaneous Letters 1874–1879 Box 5959.

156 Telegram of John T. Edgar, Consul General, Beirut, to Acre for "American Consul Haifa," 22 June 1875, USNA RG84 Haifa, Miscellaneous and Official Correspondence Received 1875–1917 Miscellaneous Papers 1875–1904 Green Box.

It seems therefore that the telegraphic network in Palestine greatly improved the effectiveness of the consular service and the speed of the services provided. But this too, suffered from malfunctioning, making it difficult for the American and other consuls: "The management of the telegraph is in a bad way, although it corresponds to everything else in Turkey. Sometimes it takes three days to send a telegram to Beirut and to get an answer, although the distance is only one hundred and twenty miles. It takes from three to five days to send a message to Egypt and to receive an answer. The Turks have never yet learned to associate promptness and speed with the idea of the telegraph.[157]

---

157 Selah Merrill, U.S. Consul, Jerusalem, to Alvey A. Adee, Third Assistant Secretary of State, Washington, D.C., 21 July 1884, USNA RG59 T471/5.

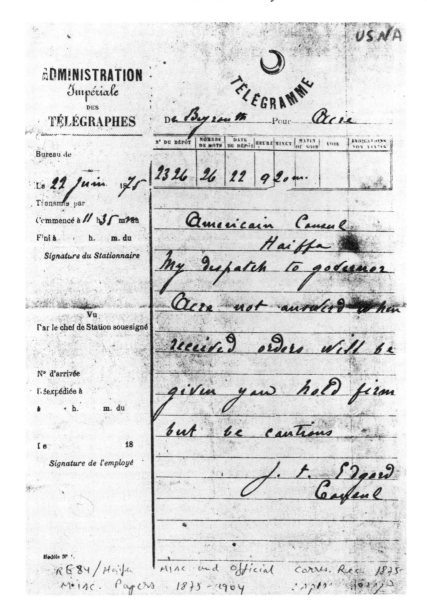

Plate 18. Telegram sent via Acre by John T. Edgar, the consul-general at Beirut,
to the United States consular agent at Haifa.
Source: USNA RG84 Haifa, Misc. and Official Corres.

CHAPTER FOUR

UNITED STATES CONSULS IN JERUSALEM

APPOINTMENTS AND CONDITIONS OF EMPLOYMENT

The Character of Appointments[1]

The way the administration appointed American diplomatic and consular representatives in the Ottoman Empire, including Turkey, Syria, Egypt, and Palestine did not differ from its accepted practice in other parts of the world. As mentioned in the Introduction, starting with the presidency of Andrew Jackson (1829–1837), appointments were made according to the spoils system, under which the party winning the elections bestowed offices upon its supporters. This practice, which corrupted the civil administration, was ended in the 1880s but persisted in the United States foreign service until the beginning of the 20th century. As we have seen, it was subjected to growing criticism at the time, and elicited negative assessments by authoritative writers on the American foreign service during the 19th century.

Besides the questionable character of such appointments, the spoils system led to frequent changes of consuls, which militated against a good understanding of local conditions by not enabling them to accumulate experience in their positions. This was especially serious in regions whose culture, religion, and language were very different from the background of the appointees. For example, compared with their British, German, Austrian, and French colleagues, the duration of service of the American consuls in Jerusalem until 1914, and in general, was the shortest. Between 1857 and 1914, 16 American consuls served 18 stints in Jerusalem (Merrill served three separate times) – an average of 3.2 years per consul. In the consulates of the other powers in Jerusalem, from their establishment until 1914, the average period of tenure was 10.4 years for the British (7 consuls between 1841 and 1914), 7.7 years for the Germans (9 consuls in 1845–1914), and 4.4 years for the

---

1   The sources for this chapter are detailed in Appendix I (Biographies).

Austrians and the French (14 consuls during 1852–1914, and 16 consuls for 1843–1914, respectively).

Motivation for Requesting Appointments

It was usually the candidates themselves who solicited their appointment. That they wished to be appointed to consular positions in Jerusalem for various different reasons emerges from the personal biographies of each one of them.[2] As noted by Mattox and others,[3] some of the reasons are similar to what caused many to seek posts at the higher levels of the diplomatic and consular foreign services. Among them were health concerns of the applicants or for members of their families (Beauboucher, Beardsley) and the desire to live in a Mediterranean climate, to conduct business, and in some cases to return to countries in which they were born or lived in previously (Page, Arbeely). However, it is noteworthy that the prevalent motivation, at least from the personal point of view, of those wishing to serve in Jerusalem was religious or scholarly and was directly connected with the Holy Land. Cresson requested the post in Jerusalem because of his belief in millenarian ideas. Willson, who besides being a newspaper editor was also a preacher, was apparently motivated by such aspirations as well. E.S. Wallace, an ordained minister, believed in the restoration of Israel, and Glazebrook, he too a minister, came to serve in Jerusalem in order to fulfill a life-long wish to live in the Holy Land.

Four of the American consuls were driven by the desire for study, research, and writing as a strong factor in seeking the position. Olcott, as his sponsor from Albany wrote in his letter of recommendation, wanted to pursue "his Oriental studies...and revel in the dust of ages, literature...." The persistent requests of DeHass for the appointment were intertwined with his religious background, his scholarly interest in biblical archeology, and his mission for the American Palestine Exploration Society. But in order to speed up the decision, he also adduced his wife's health condition. Merrill was motivated by his involvement in the study of history and archeology of Palestine, which he had begun before his appointment, and which had brought him to the region as an explorer before his period of consular service. Gillman combined political motivation with his interest in archeological and botanical research.

Until the introduction of reforms in the foreign service in 1906, it seems that the only American consul in Jerusalem who intended making a career as

---

2   See Biographies in Appendix I.

3   Mattox, *The Twilight*, p.29; Kennedy, *The American Consul*, pp.224–25.

a professional diplomat was Rhodes, who was a decided exception in this respect. Nevertheless, some of the men appointed for other reasons to Jerusalem continued in the consular service at the same status level, or as consuls-general elsewhere, after completing their stints in Jerusalem (Beardsley and Willson in Egypt, Merrill in Georgetown in British Guyana). Between 1907 and 1914, two career consuls (T.R. Wallace and Coffin) served in the Jerusalem post, but the appointment of Glazebrook in 1914 reverted to the system in force during the 19th century.

Qualifications for the Position

Judging from the known biographical details of the consuls who served in Jerusalem, it is clear that almost none of them had any previous formal preparation for this particular post. The range of occupations and professions represented was mainly in the realms of journalism, religion, law, medicine, and commerce and business – some of which could, of course, well serve the purpose, while others less so. Some of the candidates indeed claimed proficiency in European and Middle Eastern languages, and had earlier lived abroad, in Europe, Africa, or the Levant. Undoubtedly, such educational qualifications compensated to some extent for the lack of professional training for the consular position and contributed to a relatively reasonable level of performance. But to this too, there were exceptions, such as the first appointment of Warder Cresson in 1844, which did not materialize and was canceled. Cresson, a successful farmer from Philadelphia steeped in religious experiences, considered his intention to be on the spot in order to witness the millennium in three years, as sufficient preparation for the job. William Makepeace Thackeray, who on his arrival in October 1844 met Cresson in Jaffa and Jerusalem, noted: "He has no knowledge of Syria but what he derives from the prophecy; and this (as he takes his office gratis) has been considered a sufficient reason for his appointment by the United States Government." [4]

The first consul whose appointment was properly confirmed was Gorham, a medical doctor by profession, who had lived eleven years in France and Italy and who claimed to know four languages – Italian, French, German, and Spanish. Another medical man appointed to the post in Jerusalem was Arbeely, a Greek native of Damascus who became an American citizen. He was familiar with local conditions and language, but his appointment could not be confirmed. Page, the son of an American businessman who grew up in

---

4   Thackeray, *Notes on a Journey*, pp.226–7.

Constantinople and who married there, had a good knowledge of Turkish customs, law, and commerce, and knew Turkish, Greek, and Arabic. Olcott studied in a German university for several years, spoke a number of languages, and had a background in business. No information was found on Van Etten's education and training, and of the little known about Rhodes is that he spoke French.

Two of the consuls came from the world of journalism: Beauboucher wrote for Belgian liberal papers, and as is obvious from his reports, did not know English well; and Willson, a preacher, was also a newspaper editor. Two other consuls had legal training – Beardsley in international law, and T.R. Wallace, who studied law, worked as a lawyer, and had served as mayor of his city. Over one half of the fourteen serving U.S. consuls in Jerusalem until 1914, whose professional training could be ascertained, were ministers or had completed theological studies (DeHass, Merrill, E.S. Wallace, Glazebrook), or engaged in religious, educational, research, and writing activities as their main occupation, or as an important field of interest (Cresson, Olcott, Willson, Gillman). This training may explain their empathy with Jerusalem and the Holy Land, but did not necessarily meet the needs of the position they were sent to fill (Plate 19).

A number of additional conditions and inclinations, unconnected with a profession, helped the candidates obtain the appointments: previous residence or travels abroad, including study at a foreign university (Olcott and Merrill who studied in Germany), and a knowledge of foreign languages — not always relevant to the regions in which they were sent to serve (Gorham, Page, Olcott, Rhodes, Beauboucher, Arbeely). Military service in the Civil War also seemed to help in securing appointments (Beauboucher, Beardsley, Merrill) as did membership in the Masonic Order. The ages of the candidates at the time of appointment (9 out of the 16 that could be ascertained) ranged from 29 to 69; most of them from 33 to 59.

REV FRANK S. DE HASS, D.D

NEW YORK CONFERENCE

Plate 19. Portrait of Consul Frank S. DeHass
Source: DeHass, *Buried Cities*

To conclude this topic, it should be noted that the information as to the previous training of the candidates generally originated from themselves, or from their sponsors and patrons, so that a certain bias in their favor must be taken into consideration. It is also difficult to assess the effectiveness of qualifications that were not subjected to the test of formal examinations. Such matters were not considered among the criteria guiding those who made the appointments and who placed far more weight on the political allegiance and upon the demands put forth by the applicants.

Manner of Appointment

Most of the appointments of consuls in Jerusalem, like those in other parts of the world, were made according to the spoils system by whatever political party won the elections. They came about as a result of requests by the candidate himself, and of recommendations by patrons and sponsors close to the Whig, Republican, or Democratic parties. It appears that the sponsors did not always know the candidates well, and so left themselves open to criticism. This was the case regarding the appointment of Cresson, in 1844, at the recommendation of the Philadelphia congressman, E. Joy Morris to the secretary of state of the Whig administration. The appointment of Gorham, a member of a prominent Boston family, resulted from the request of the Democratic President, Franklin Pierce, to the secretary of state to appoint him as consul "...as thanks for services rendered." Page's appointment was assisted by the recommendation of James Williams of the U.S. legation in Constantinople, who apparently knew Page when he lived there. The appointment of Olcott from Albany, New York, in September 1861, resulted from a letter of solicitation of a family friend in that city, Charles Van Benthuysen, the owner of a "Printing, Binding and Paper House." Van Benthuysen channeled his recommendation by way of Thurlow Weed in Washington to "Governor Seward", who had served as governor of the state of New York in 1839–1843, and was appointed secretary of state in the Lincoln administration in 1861. Van Benthuysen proposed in the same letter that "Should the government desire any more office holders, I could readily give you a legion of names that would volunteer."[5] Van Etten, who was to replace Olcott declined the appointment by the Republican administration; instead, the position went to Rhodes. The Frenchman, Beauboucher, who was not an American citizen, received his appointment to Jerusalem at the recommendation of the Republican assistant secretary of war and former newspaper editor, Charles A. Dana, in consideration of his having volunteered for service in the Union army and being severely wounded during the Civil War, and perhaps because of his journalistic background. This was the only appointment to the post of United States consul in Jerusalem of a person who was not an American citizen.

Beardsley was helped in his appointment as consul-general in Alexandria in Egypt by the recommendation of a senator from Indiana. DeHass, on the other hand, resorted to many personal written requests to the State Department

---

5   Charles Van Benthuysen, Albany, New York, to Thurlow Weed, Washington, 9 August 1861, USNA RG59 M650.

and the President, and even appealed verbally to Grant by representing himself as a political supporter. Willson apparently was a Republican of some political standing who claimed to have been among the first to nominate Grant for the presidency (Plate 20).

R. BEARDSLEY,
U. S. Consul at Jerusalem, 1872.

Plate 20. Portrait of Consul Richard Beardsley
Source: Morris, *Freemasonry in the Holy Land*

The correlation between the administration and the candidate and the tenure of his appointment, is best exemplified in the case of the consul, Selah Merrill. Merrill was a loyal representative of the Republicans, serving three separate stints in Jerusalem that were interrupted only by the two terms of Grover Cleveland as Democratic President in the years 1885–1889 and 1893–1897. In the first interval, Arbeely was appointed by the Democrats, but was not acceptable to the Ottoman government. He was followed by

Gillman, an outspoken Democrat and enthusiastic supporter of Cleveland. Following Merrill's third period of service, T.R. Wallace was appointed consul after having served under the Republican administration in 1901 as consul in Germany. It may be that his appointment to Jerusalem, as of the succeeding consul, Coffin, both of which occurred after 1906, were motivated by professional considerations, but Glazebrook, who replaced the latter, obtained the position because he was a personal friend of the Democratic President, Woodrow Wilson.

Eligibility, Ottoman Endorsement

In the 19th century, consuls of the United States throughout the world were appointed by the President and confirmed by the Senate. Every transfer of positions required a new confirmation. In addition, on reaching his appointed post, the consul had to obtain the exequatur – recognition of his appointment – by the government of the country in which he was to serve. In some countries, among them the Ottoman Empire, the consuls had to pay a large sum for such a document of recognition, which was termed *berat* in Turkish.[6]

There were cases in which the Sublime Porte refused to grant a berat or exequatur, thus preventing the appointment from taking effect. In Jerusalem, this happened for the first time after the controversial appointment of Warder Cresson of Philadelphia. Despite his having been confirmed on 17 May 1844 as "Consul at Jerusalem" by the Senate, Cresson never received an exequatur from the Porte, and was precluded from opening an office in Jerusalem.[7] It may be that one of the reasons for the opposition of the Ottoman government to his appointment was the negative opinion of the American minister in Constantinople, Dabney S. Carr, who had apprehensions regarding Cresson's religious views. Opposition to the appointment arose also in the United States, and at the end of June 1844, the secretary of state, John C. Calhoun, wrote that the proposed establishment of a consulate in Jerusalem had been reconsidered, and that the President had decided not to proceed with it at that time.[8] Twelve years were to pass before the next appointment of a resident American consul in Jerusalem – John Warren Gorham – who was accorded a berat of exequatur by the Turks.[9] In a like manner, the Ottoman government

6   Schuyler, *American Diplomacy*, pp.95–96.

7   Manuel, *The Realities*, p.10.

8   Ibid.; Lipman, *Americans and the Holy Land*, p.89.

9   Blumberg, *Zion Before Zionism*, p.128.

refused, in the 1880s, to recognize the American consul appointed to Beirut on the grounds that he "might be too much connected with the missionaries."[10]

And several years later, the appointment of the Damascus-born doctor of Greek origin, Nageeb J. Arbeely, was declined even though he had been naturalized as an American citizen in Tennessee and had been confirmed in Washington in October 1885 as consul at Jerusalem. The Ottoman government rejected the appointment because Arbeely was a native of the Ottoman Empire, and he had to be recalled.[11]

Salaries
Conditions of Remuneration in the Consular Service
From the first appointments of consuls at the end of the 18th century until 1856, these positions carried no remuneration. Only the resident consuls on the Barbary Coast were paid annual salaries of $2,000. The act of 1792 made no provision for payments, on the assumption that the consular officers supported themselves from private business and consular fees. Several reports and proposals, put forth from the 1830s onwards, advocating payment of suitable salaries and prohibiting private business activities by consuls were not adopted.[12] As has been mentioned, the act of 1856 fixed two schedules for consular salaries: B from $1,000 to $7,500, and C from $500 to $1,000 per annum. Those officials who were not included in these grades and received no salary were authorized to engage in trade and business and to use consular fees as partial compensation. This reform too was inadequate, and still in the 1850s, as a result of complaints by many consuls – in Liverpool, Le Havre, Havana, Montevideo, and elsewhere – Secretary of State F. Lewis Cass, convinced of their financial hardships, requested an increase in compensation. Not only were the salaries low in absolute terms, but they were well below what other countries paid their consuls.[13] In 1874, Congress conducted a general review of consular salaries and classified consulates into seven grades, with salaries ranging from $1,000 to $4,000. The consular reorganization of 1906 resulted in the establishment of nine classes with a salary range of $2,000 to $8,000.[14]

10   Schuyler, *American Diplomacy*, p.86.
11   See Biographies in the Appendix.
12   Barnes, *The Foreign Service*, pp.57–58, 83–85.
13   Ibid.,pp.120–122; Rhodes, "Our Diplomats and Consuls," pp.174–5.
14   Barnes, ibid., pp.122, 164–5.

Besides the problem of low salaries, there was the matter of inadequate contingency allowances. The only provision for covering such expenses in the act of 1856 was an allocation to "non-trading" consuls for office rent to the amount of ten percent of their salary. In addition, stationery, seals, presses, bank books, flags, and coats of arms were supplied by the government, which also covered the cost of postage on official correspondence. This led to consulates being located in places and buildings of inferior condition. Even an increase in the allocation to twenty percent of the salary in 1873 proved inadequate, while the consuls of European powers enjoyed liberal local allowances that enabled them to exercise their official functions and maintain their social status in a respectable manner. The latter also had good pension rights, received special allocations for clothing and generous travel allowances which, as late as 1905, contrasted markedly with the conditions of their American counterparts.[15]

Conditions of Salaries in the Levant and Palestine 1835–1856
The salaries of American consuls in Jerusalem reflected the general policy regarding remuneration in the consular service. Prior to the official establishment of the Jerusalem consulate in 1856/7, all the American consular agents who were appointed in the various towns of Palestine (Jaffa, Ramle, Jerusalem, Haifa, and Acre) served at their own expense without any payment. The only one who received a small annual salary of $200 was Jasper Chasseaud who was appointed consul in Beirut in March 1835, and who in turn appointed unpaid consular representatives throughout Syria, Lebanon, and Palestine. Most of the expenses entailed by the consuls' official activities – providing services to American naval officers, missionaries and travelers, dealing with cases of robbery, oppression, and illness, negotiations with other consuls, and the like – were covered from the consuls' private resources.[16] Nevertheless, the consuls undoubtedly reaped decided advantages from their positions.

As early as in 1836, American missionaries in Beirut urged "the necessity of reasonable salary for Chasseaud...."[17] The American citizen who was appointed consul in Beirut to replace Chasseaud, J. Hosford Smith, deluged the State Department and the Department of the Treasury with requests to increase his dismally low salary of $500 per year, in view of the expenses

---

15   Ibid., p.122; Jones, *The Consular Service*, pp.99–103

16   Blumberg, *Zion Before Zionism*, pp.54–57.

17   George E. Whiting, John Francis, and seven other missionaries, Beirut, to John Forsyth, Secretary of State, Washington, D.C., 30 November 1836, USNA RG59 T367/1.

amounting to $3,000 incurred in fulfilling his duties. Smith, who had hoped to engage in trade and business, found his consular functions too onerous without a reasonable regular salary, especially since the general state of affairs in the region suffered with the outbreak of the Crimean War in 1853. He also adduced the importance of Beirut and the need to raise the level of the office to that of consul-general with a higher salary, as in Alexandria and the "Barbary Powers", and stressed the importance of equating the status of the consulate and consul of the United States with that of the European powers.[18] The State Department replied in January 1857 to A.B. Chasseaud's requests to the effect that the "act regulating the Diplomatic and Consular Systems of the U.S., by which the salary of the consul at Beirut was fixed at $2,000, went into operation on the 1st of January last." [19]

Dr. James T. Barclay, the American missionary who lived in Jerusalem and who, like others before him, greatly appreciated the services of the United States consular agents, saw fit, in February 1851 to raise the problem of unpaid service. He pointed out that " ...England, France, Russia, Prussia, Sardina, and various other governments pay very handsome salaries to their consuls at Jaffa and Jerusalem," while the American consular agent, who was consul in both places, "...has never received the first cent of salary from our government for his truly valuable services..." [20] Barclay referred to Jacob S. Murad, who a year later was appointed vice-consul at Jerusalem. J. Hosford Smith, who had arranged Murad's appointment despite his being a foreigner and an Armenian, did so in the belief that "there being no salary appropriated for that office, by our Government, no U.S. citizen will seek it."[21]

Salaries of Consuls in Jerusalem 1856–1914

John Warren Gorham was the first American consular representative in Jerusalem to receive a salary under the act of 1856. His post fell into schedule C, entitling him to $500-$1,000 (the records do not show the exact amount). Gorham rented an office for the consulate on "Mount Zion" (east of the citadel) for $100 per year, which was eventually increased to $150.[20] Ten years later, the consul, Victor Beauboucher, reported to the secretary of state that his salary came to $1,500 plus $150 for office rent. He complained that

---

18 Several letters dated 7 and 29 July, 3 August, 1 September 1852, and 7 July 1854, USNA RG59 T367/1.

19 A.B. Chasseaud, New York, to John Appelzin, Assistant Secretary of State, Washington, D.C., 1 October 1857, USNA RG59 T367/1.

20 John Gorham, U.S. Consul, Jerusalem, to Lewis Cass, Secretary of State, Washington, D.C., 30 June 1857, USNA RG59 T471/1.

years later, the consul, Victor Beauboucher, reported to the secretary of state that his salary came to $1,500 plus $150 for office rent. He complained that his expenses during the period from 22 September 1866 to 21 September 1867 amounted to $1,611 forcing him to spend most of his income of $1,650, so that "nothing remains for the expenses material for living which are actually at Jerusalem from 4 to 5 dollars per day..." [23] According to Beauboucher's calculations, the consul in Jerusalem needed $3,000 to cover his living expenses in Jerusalem.[24] The consuls who served after him, and even the acting consul, Lorenzo M. Johnson, voiced severe complaints about the amount of their salaries in absolute terms, as well as in relation to the salaries of American consuls elsewhere and in comparison to the consuls of other powers in Jerusalem. Johnson regarded the position in Jerusalem an important one, writing that "It is generally considered a misfortune that our government has not more liberally provided for it." [25] Richard Beardsley drew the attention of the State Department to the fact that the consulate in Jerusalem received no fees from its agencies, while other consulates collected fees in addition to the salaries. The $1,500 he was paid were insufficient to defray his living expenses. He requested an increase in his salary: "...The pay of this Consulate is totally inadequate to supply the necessities of life for myself and family."[26] For this reason, after less than three years in Jerusalem, he solicited a transfer to another post and an appointment as consul-general in Alexandria.[27]

In September 1899, Selah Merrill wrote a detailed report on the Jerusalem consulate, from which it transpired that although the consul's salary had risen to $2,500 per year, it was still low compared to the conditions and pay of most consuls and consuls-general in the city. Apart from this, only a very

---

1857, USNA RG59 T471/1.

23 Victor Beauboucher, U.S. Consul, Jerusalem, to William H. Seward, Secretary of State, Washington, D.C., 23 October 1866, USNA RG59 T471/2.

24 Beauboucher to Seward, ibid., 28 April 1867.

25 Lorenzo M. Johnson, U.S. Vice and Acting Consul, Jerusalem, to William H. Seward, Secretary of State, Washington, D.C., 30 September 1868, USNA RG59 T471/2.

26 Richard Beardsley, U.S. Consul, Jerusalem, to Assistant Secretary of State, 18 February 1871, USNA RG59 T471/3.

27 Richard Beardsley, U.S. Consul, Jerusalem, to Hamilton Fish, Secretary of State, Washington, D.C., 10 February 1872, USNA RG59 M650. For similar reasons, largely on financial grounds in order to improve their salary, two consuls who served in Beirut asked to be appointed consul-general in Constantinople. Both applications were granted: to J. Hosford Smith in 1860, and G. Bie Ravndal in 1910.

modest allocation was provided for the employees of the consulate. The vice-consul was not paid. The U.S. government covered office rent, telegrams, postage, stationery, flags, etc. and required vouchers for every expenditure. The official fees collected were reported to the government; the notarial fees were retained by the consul.[28] In 1907, on the basis of Merrill's thorough and comprehensive report, Consul Thomas R. Wallace submitted a list of the salaries earned by the various consuls and consular employees in Jerusalem.[29] These two reports also mentioned components of the consulate's finances besides the actual salary, such as allocations for accommodations and office rent, clothing, and the like. Perhaps the low salaries received by the American consuls explain their penchant for extracurricular activities to supplement their income. In 1914, the salary of the consul in Jerusalem came to $3,000 per annum. In comparison, Mattox gives figures for 1890 and 1899 of "Annual compensation of consuls in selected posts." While in Jerusalem the consul's salary in 1899 was $2,500 plus notarial fees, the salaries of American consuls-general in four important capitals (London, Paris, Havana, and Rio de Janeiro) ranged between $5,000 to $6,000 in that year, and were $2,000 in Bogota and Guatemala. The notarial fees in London and Paris amounted to more than the salary, but were not collected in Bogota and Guatemala.[30] Thus, in terms of salary levels of the consular service, the post in Jerusalem had a decidedly low rating. From the data provided in the years 1866, 1899, and 1907 by the United States consuls in Jerusalem, Beauboucher, Merrill, and Thomas Wallace, the salaries of consuls and consuls-general of the European powers in Jerusalem, and the annual budgets of the consulates for the years 1899 and 1907, may be compared (Table III).

---

28   Selah Merrill, U.S. Consul, Jerusalem, to Thomas W. Cridler, Assistant Secretary of State, Washington, D.C., 9 September 1899, USNA RG59 T471/9.

29   Thomas R. Wallace, U.S. Consul, Jerusalem, to Department of State, Washington, D.C., 22 November 1907, USNA RG59 T471/10 [JNUL Fi2477/10].

30   Mattox, *The Twilight*, p.163.

TABLE III. Salaries and Total Annual Cost of Consuls and Consuls-General in Jerusalem, in U.S. Dollars

1866

Country	Salary	Office rent	Residence rent	Total cost/yr. incl. employees
U.S.A.	1,500	150		
Austria	2,800		+	
Britain	3,500		+	
France	4,400			
Greece				
Italy				
Mexico	3,000		+	
Prussia-Germany	2,900		+	
Russia	2,800		+	
Spain				

1899

Country	Salary	Office rent	Residence rent	Total cost/yr. incl. employees
U.S.A.	2,500	+		3,600
Austria	2,500	400		4,450
Britain	4,000	+		5,848
France	4,400	+		8,040
Greece	1,600			2,450
Italy	4,095	+		5,644
Mexico			+	
Prussia-Germany	3,375	+	+	6,920
Russia	5,600	+	+	12,048
Spain	2,000	+		2,212

1907

Country	Salary	Office rent	Residence rent	Total cost/yr. incl. employees
U.S.A.				
Austria	2,500	+		5,600
Britain	4,000			7,330
France	4,400	+		8,040 + exp.
Greece				
Italy	4,095	+		
Mexico				
Prussia-Germany	3,375	+	+	6,653 + exp.
Russia	5,600	+	+	12,324
Spain				

Based on Beauboucher to Seward 23 October 1866, Merrill to Cridler 9 September 1899, and Wallace to Department of State, 22 November 1907, USNA RG59 T471/2,9,10

Status

Whatever the American consuls in Jerusalem and the consular agents in Jaffa and Haifa thought of themselves, their status can be gauged on at least three comparative levels: in relation to the other consuls of the American foreign service; as perceived by the Ottoman government and the local authorities; and in comparison with the consulates of other nations in Jerusalem. The most obvious indicators of status were the salary of the consul himself and the conditions of his service such as pension rights, housing, reimbursement of current expenditures, and travel expenses. The size and splendor of the consulate building, and whether the consul lived in it or elsewhere; the number of employees and consular officials and consular agents subordinate to him – all these determined his position in the eyes of the beholder. Entertaining and ceremonial were an important and essential part of the consul's activities, and these too affected his status. In addition there were outward symbols of national dignity involving the national flag and when and how it was shown, the use of the coat-of-arms, firing gun salutes in his and his government's honor by the Ottoman military, marking his national festivals and days of mourning, the consul's uniform, the appearance of his employees – especially of the splendidly accoutred kavasses who guarded the consulate. Great importance was placed on the effects of his nation's warships visiting the ports of the country he served in. In the port town of Haifa, one of the status symbols was a special boat, or boats, belonging to the consular agency by which important visitors were brought from their ship to the landing jetty.[31]

In almost all the matters mentioned above, the American consuls and consular agents serving in Jerusalem, Jaffa, and Haifa smarted under feelings of inferiority. In the exhaustive report he wrote in 1881 on the capitulations of the Ottoman Empire, mentioned in the Introduction, Edward Van Dyck pointed up the inferior status of the United States consulates in the Levant relative to the consular service in other parts of the world and to that of the different powers in the Levant, including Palestine:

> Of all consular institutions in non-Christian countries, those kept up by the United States are probably the worst organized and most under-manned, for a consul or consul-general (as the case may be) assisted by one paid interpreter, and one salaried clerk (and not always a clerk or an allowance for one) constitute the whole *personnel* that has to perform the multifarious official, semi-official, and extra-official labors, as well as quasi-diplomatic, judicial, and consular functions that are required of him, not only by the law and statutes, but that devolve upon him by custom and are naturally and unavoidably expected of him by his fellow-citizens in countries where the foreigner must have recourse to his consular authority in every matter, however remotely connected it may be with the government or people of the country in which he resides.
>
> Perhaps it is owing to the hitherto limited interest in foreign trade that the United States have not sufficiently appreciated the importance of consulates in non-Christian countries and the need of revising the statutory provisions in this respect.[32]

A decade earlier, Albert Rhodes, who served as United States consul in Jerusalem from 1863 to 1865, published a humorous, if no less critical, description of this aspect of his post:

> Consuls are princes in the East, except in emolument. Their constant and arduous occupation is the keeping up of consular

---

31 Jacob Schumacher, U.S. Consular Agent, Haifa, to John T. Edgar, U. S. Consul, Beirut, 6 March 1882, USNA RG84 Haifa Copy Book 1872–86 Box 5976. Schumacher requested a boat to be purchased in his name for helping disembarking and embarking guests. He added that Mr. Keller, the German vice-consul, already had two such boats.

32 Van Dyck, "Report on the Capitulations," p.16

dignity, especially in Palestine, where commerce is confined to a petty business in holy wood and blessed beads. Their headquarters are at Jerusalem, and the eyes of the Holy City are on them; some are proudly and others painfully conscious of this fact. The central figure in the tableau is the pasha, and next to him are grouped the consuls, in the order of the relative importance of the governments they represent. They are clothed with diplomatic functions – which means taking coffee with the pasha – and exercise the office of magistrate over their respective countrymen. The American consul especially is believed to be invested with great judicial powers, as there is a tradition in the Holy Land that he can hang a man without exceeding his authority.

Uneasy is the head that wears the consular crown. The responsibility of maintaining official dignity is oppressive, incompatible with mirth, and the bearing of such a burden any length of time generally develops a tendency to sadness.This is especially so with the American representative, whose quiet vegetation on Mount Zion is in such contrast to the aggressive life in America.[33]

Having illustrated the unfavorable comparison between the American consuls' salaries and service conditions in Jerusalem with those of their European and American counterparts, Table IV shows the allocation of funds and personnel of the different consulates in Jerusalem in 1899. Table V, based on Merrill's report, relates to the consular agency at Jaffa for the same year (1899).

33   Rhodes, "Our Consuls in Jerusalem," p.437.

TABLE IV. Consular Status and Number of Employees in Jerusalem, 1899

Country	Consul general	Consul	Vice-consul	Chancellor	Dragomans	Clerks	Kavasses	Total employees	Total cost in U.S. $
U.S.A.		1	1		2		2	6	3,600
Austria	1				1		2	4	4,450
Britain		1		1	2		3	7	5,848
France	1			1	3		4	9	8,040
Germany	1			1	1	1	4	8	6,920
Greece	1				1		1	3	2,450
Holland			1		1		1	3	0
Italy	1			1	1		2	5	5,644
Russia	1			1	3	2	4	11	12,048
Spain	1				1		1	3	2,212

Based on: Merrill to Cridler, 9 September 1899, USNA RG 59 T471/9.

TABLE V. Consul Status and Number of Employees in Jaffa, 1907

Country	Consul	Vice consul	Consular agent	Secretary	Dragomans	Kavasses	Total employees	Total cost in U.S. $
U.S.A.			1		2	2	5	50% of fees
Austria	1				1	1	3	1,320
Britain			1		2	2	5	50% of fees
France		1			2	2	5	2,190
Germany		1		1	1	2	5	3,670
Greece		1			1	2	4	980
Holland		1			1	1	3	none
Italy			1		2	2	5	70% of fees
Russia		1			2	2	5	3,590
Spain		1			2	2	5	400

Based on: Thomas R. Wallace, U.S. Consul, Jerusalem, to Department of State, Washington, D.C., 22 November 1907, USNA RG59 T471/10 (Fi2477/10).

These tables show that of the ten foreign consulates-general, consulates, and one consular agency in Jerusalem, the United States was in seventh place in the allocation of funds, its budget being about one third that of the Russian consulate-general. It was in fifth place in the number of workers, employing five persons to the Russians' eleven and to nine of the French. One reason for the relatively higher grading of the Americans in this respect was due to the vice-consul not receiving any salary, and the wages of the interpreter and dragoman being extremely low – much lower than was their due and far less than those of their counterparts in the other consulates. In Jaffa the comparison of consular staffs was rather more balanced, with seven of the ten consulates, vice-consulates, or consular agencies employing five persons each.

One of the important exterior manifestations was flying the national flag, which served as the symbol for communicating status between the consulate and the local authorities and the other consulates. Thus, the British consul in Jerusalem, James Finn, noted in his diary entry for 4 July 1857: "...United States flag raised in Jerusalem for the first time, being their anniversary of Independence, our new flag raised at the same time." [34] This important event was also reported by Consul Gorham to the secretary of state in Washington: "Sir, I have the honor to inform you that the flag of the United States of America was displayed, for the first time in Jerusalem, on Mount Zion, on the Fourth of July, 1857. A salute of twenty-one guns was given by the Turkish authorities, and all the flags of all the consuls were displayed on the occasion." Actually, the Turkish artillery performed only after strong pressure had been exerted on the Jerusalem local council and on the commander of the garrison, who, in the absence of the pasha "had refused to offer the United States flag a twenty-one-gun salute because the United States was governed by a mere president who did not deserve the same courtesies shown to a king." [35]

Extensive correspondence between the American consular agent in Haifa and the consul in Beirut concerning the dispatch of a new flag and the right and occasion for flying it from the consular agency and by its dragoman in Acre, is found in the books of the Haifa consular agency in the period 1872–1885. Disputes with the authorities about showing the flag and the American protests to restrictions regarding this reached the level of the vali –

34 Blumberg, *A View from Jerusalem*, pp. 260, 277.

35 Blumberg, ibid.; John Warren Gorham, U.S. Consul, Jerusalem, to Lewis Cass, Secretary of State, Washington, D.C., 12 July 1857, USNA RG59 T471/1.

the governor-general of Syria – and the secretary of state in Washington.[36] On several occasions, Jacob Schumacher mentioned the lack of respect for the government of the United States compared to other foreigners and their governments.[37] In 1881, he complained of discrimination: When the Ottoman authorities demanded that the kavasses of England and Spain be drafted into the army in 1880, the consuls in Beirut had them quickly released, while the Turks insisted on drafting the kavass of the American consular agency in Haifa. Schumacher demanded that "the U.S. should not receive less respect from the authorities than other consulates."[38] Sometimes, the informal democratic American character brought on a tendency to make light of ceremonial customs and local practices, and only the experience of the local employees of the consulate could set the American official straight. A nice example of this attitude is the description of Consul Rhodes of the pasha's visit to him:

> The half-closed eyes of the interpreter open to their utmost width, he starts to his feet, and turns out the news to his principal in a solid lump: "The pasha desires to know when he may have the honor of calling on the American consul."
>
> "Now," responds the democrat of the western hemisphere.
>
> "Gracious! you cannot think of it," is the commentary of the interpreter, with consternation on his face.
>
> "Arrange it as you see best, then," is the rejoinder, which brings peace to the soul of the Oriental.[39]

36 Of the very many such instances, the following are examples: USNA RG84 Haifa Copy Book 1872–1886 Box 5976 (19 October 1872, 1 January 1877, 9 August 1884); USNA RG84 Haifa Miscellaneous and Official Correspondence Received 1875–1917 Miscellaneous Papers 1875–1904 Green Box (5–30 June 1884).

37 Copy Book and Miscellaneous papers, ibid.; Jacob Schumacher, U.S. Consular Agent, Haifa, to John T. Robeson, U.S. Consul, Beirut, 30 June 1884.

38 Jacob Schumacher, U.S. Consular Agent, Haifa, to John T. Edgar, U.S. Consul, Beirut, 13 January 1881, USNA RG84 Haifa Copy Book 1872–1886 Box 5976.

39 Rhodes, "Our Consuls in Jerusalem," p.444.

ADMINISTRATIVE STRUCTURE AND CONSULAR STAFFS

Work Loads and Assistants

By the turn of the 19th century, the amount of business transacted and the
work carried out by the consulate in Jerusalem and by the consular agencies
in Jaffa and Haifa had increased greatly. This was at least partly due to the
enhanced professionalism of the consular service and the consequent necessity
for frequent and detailed reporting and correspondence, as well as to the
growing demand for consular services by American citizens and protégés –
mostly Jews who had settled in Palestine – and tourists. The expanding
volume of commercial activity and the quest for markets by American
companies also increased the work load of consulates and consular agencies.
In 1857, a total of nineteen despatches were sent from Jerusalem and in 1858
the number had grown to eighty (most of them to the secretary of state, and
the rest to the American consuls in Beirut and Constantinople, to the consuls
of other countries and to the Protestant bishop, Samuel Gobat, in Jerusalem).
In 1871, the consul, Richard Beardsley, reported that 248 official despatches
were sent from the consulate at Jerusalem (50 to the State Department, 25 to
the legation in Constantinople, 34 to the consul-general at Beirut, and 139
miscellaneous letters.)[40] At the end of the century, Consul Merrill wrote that
the growing number of Jews (from about 150 in 1882, to 800 in 1899)
claiming American consular protection had created a situation where "one
half of the consul, two dragomans, two cawases, and the consular agent and
his dragoman's time during the year is spent in trying to satisfy the demands
made upon them by this class of citizens." [41] It seems, therefore, that the
sense of purposelessness of the consul at Jerusalem and of his subordinates,
as described with wistful humor by Consul Albert Rhodes in the 1860s, had
changed to such a degree that the consul and his staff could no longer cope
with the many tasks imposed on them.[42] Despite working ten-hour days,
including Sundays, Thomas R. Wallace, in 1908, was unable to deal with all
the matters he was responsible for. He complained about "...the amount of
work the consul performs in attempting to attend to all of the business

---

40   John Warren Gorham, U.S. Consul, Jerusalem, to Secretary of State, Washington, D.C., 31 December
      1857 and 31 December 1858, USNA RG59 T471/1; Richard Beardsley, U.S. Consul, Jerusalem, to
      Department of State, Washington, D.C., 31 December 1871, USNA RG59 T471/3.

41   Selah Merrill, U.S. Consul, Jerusalem, to Thomas W. Cridler, Assistant Secretary of State, Washington,
      D.C., 8 March 1899, USNA RG59 T471/9.

42   Rhodes, "Our Consuls at Jerusalem," pp.437–47.

legally required of him at his post," and felt "The Department of State...to be entirely lacking in information as to the requirements of this office relative to its working force." [43]

During the 19th century and the early 20th, the consuls were assisted in their work by several functionaries, some of them unsalaried. Among these were the vice-consul, the deputy-consul, the clerk; the dragomans (interpreters) and the kavasses were specific to the Ottoman Empire. In the consular agencies, besides the agent, the staff consisted only of dragomans and kavasses. The vice-consul or the vice-consular agent were not ordinarily subject to the consul, but only filled his place when he was absent or indisposed. They had no other responsibilities and received no remuneration for their work. The deputy-consul was fully occupied in the operation of the consulate. [44] These functions were sometimes combined in one person, the consul endeavoring, whenever possible, to employ American citizens. The names of the men serving in these capacities in the Jerusalem consulate (Appendix II F), indicate that from the 1880s, all of them were American citizens – Jews or converted Jews, or sons of Christian settlers who grew up in Palestine and were well-acquainted with local conditions. For example, in August 1912, Samuel Edelman, a native of Pennsylvania, was appointed to the unpaid post of vice- and deputy-consul. But Edelman was at the same time also engaged as dragoman at an annual salary of $1,500. [45]

For a long time, salaries were determined by the consul, who also decided whether to allot payment to his replacement during his absence. Benjamin Finkelstein, who applied to the State Department regarding remuneration for his work as deputy-consul, was informed that "It is the custom...of the Department to leave the question of compensation of the subordinate officers entirely to the private agreement between the two." [46] Until the 1890s, clerks were employed intermittently for short periods (in 1867 a clerk was paid an annual salary of $365), but from 1891, such officials served regularly in the consulate at Jerusalem. [47]

---

43 Thomas R. Wallace, U.S. Consul, Jerusalem, to Assistant Secretary of State, Washington, D.C., 8 July 1908, USNA RG59 T471/10 [Fi2477/10]. In the Haifa consular agency, Gottlieb Schumacher set the office hours at 9–12 in the morning and 4–6 in the afternoon, every day (29 April 1896, USNA RG84 Haifa, Copy Book 1886–1899 Box 5977).

44 Schuyler, *American Diplomacy*, pp.81–84.

45 Consular Service of the United States, USNA M587/9, p.52.

46 J.C.B. Davis, Assistant Secretary of State, Washington, D.C., to Benjamin A. Finkelstein, Jerusalem, 30 September 1869, USNA RG59 T471/2.

47 Victor Beauboucher, U.S. Consul, Jerusalem, to Department of State, Washington, D.C., 22 October

The Dragoman

The key man at the consulate and the consular agency was the dragoman. Every consulate and consular agency, as well as convents and heads of religious communities, employed one or more dragomans (interpreters), according to their status and the languages and assistance they required in their contacts with the authorities and the local population. Usually, the dragoman was an educated native Christian or Jew, of recognized commercial and social standing, who knew some of the languages current in the region – Turkish, Arabic, French, Italian, Greek, and, particularly in Jerusalem, also Hebrew, Yiddish, and Ladino. The dragoman was indispensable to the functioning of the consuls and of the consular agents, most of whom did not know the local languages and customs. But consular dragomans were also notoriously prone to corruption and bribery.[48]

The knowledge of foreign languages was adduced by American consuls and consular agents to justify appointments of candidates they proposed for these positions. Thus, Constantine 'Azar, who was engaged as dragoman in Jaffa in December 1871, was considered the best man for the position because he knew English. Jacques (Jiacomo) Panayotti, appointed dragoman at the Jerusalem consulate in the same year, was, according to the consul, educated and proficient in Turkish, Arabic, Greek, English, and French. In Haifa, Gottlieb Schumacher sought to appoint as dragoman Theophil S. Boutagy, aged 27, an Ottoman subject native of Haifa, who was educated at the American College in Beirut, and spoke English, Arabic, Italian, and German. At the time he was offered the position, Boutagy was employed as the Haifa agent of Thomas Cook & Sons.[49]

As is apparent from their names and the periods of service mentioned in reports and records in the consular archives, most of the dragomans employed at the United States consulate in Jerusalem, and at the Jaffa and Haifa consular agencies, were Ottoman subjects (Appendix II G). The dragoman or dragomans were selected by the consuls and the consular agents, but the nominations had to be submitted to the United States legation at Constantinople and to the Sublime Porte. The latter's firman or vizierial order, approving the appointment and granting the exequatur, were then still subject to acceptance by the

1867, USNA RG59 T471/2.

48   Platt, *The Cinderella Service*, p.160; Blumberg, *Zion Before Zionism*, p.54. See also: Cecil, *German Diplomatic Service*, p.17; Kennedy, *The American Consul*, p.90.

49   19 October 1877, USNA T471/4; 5 September 1871, USNA T471/3; and 8 September 1897, USNA RG84 Haifa Copy Book 1886–1899 Box 5977.

provincial and the local Ottoman authorities – the vali and the mutasarrif. Extensive correspondence took place regarding such appointments between the consuls and the consular agents and their superiors, and with the Ottoman authorities who did not always readily grant their approval. The Turks limited the number of dragomans to two per consular agency and refused to approve additional ones.[50] Sometimes, the approval process dragged on for several years, as in the case of the nomination of Bishara Cardahi to the post of American dragoman in Acre, which was first submitted by Jacob Schumacher to the consul at Beirut in October 1872. Only in August 1875, on receipt of the imperial order, did Schumacher apply to the mutasarrif of the Acre district in the hope that he would recognize the appointment.[51]

Once the appointment of a dragoman received all the official sanctions, he came under the protection of the American consulate or consular agency, and regarded himself as entitled to the privileges enjoyed by foreign nationals and consuls. This situation frequently gave rise to confrontations between Ottoman officials and the dragoman regarding matters such as taxation, export licenses, building permits, and the like, which eventually also involved their superiors. An Ottoman survey of consuls, dated 1872, in the archives of the mutasarrif of Jerusalem, complained bitterly about the intervention of consuls and dragomans who abused their positions in matters of jurisdiction, trade, and taxation, and stressed the damage this caused to the Ottoman state and its institutions. The mutasarrif of Acre and the kaimakam and the majlis in Haifa, for example, were sensitive to this issue, and the Sublime Porte, too, recognized the problem by making the grand-vizierial approval order conditional on the limitation of privileges allowed to the dragoman.[52] Much time was devoted by the American consuls and the consular agents to correspondence with the Ottoman authorities regarding the appointments and privileges, and in dealing with the private disputes of dragomans (and kavasses) with local officials. A good part of the material in the Copy Books and the

50 USNA RG84 Jaffa Box 5959; USNA RG84 Haifa Boxes 5976, 5977; USNA RG59 Jerusalem T471/1–2.

51 Jacob Schumacher, U.S. Consular Agent, Haifa, to John Baldwin Hay, Consul General, Beirut, 19 October 1872, USNA RG84 Haifa Copy Book 1872–1886 Box 5976 and to Mutasarrif of Acca, 26 August 1875, USNA RG84 Haifa Miscellaneous and Official Correspondence Received 1875–1917 Miscellaneous Papers 1875–1904 Green Box (Arabic).

52 An Ottoman Report on the "Intervention of the Consuls in State Matters," 4 December 1872, ISA RG83 (Turkish), unsigned; Bishara Cardahi, U.S. Dragoman, Acca, to Jacob Schumacher, U.S. Consular Agent, Haifa, 8 June 1885, USNA RG84 Haifa Miscellaneous and Official Correspondence Received 1875–1917 Miscellaneous Papers 1878–1903 Green Box.

Miscellaneous Correspondence of the Haifa consular agency concerns such matters, as is illustrated in the discussion of Cardahi's case in Acre, below.

The varied functions of the dragoman may be reconstructed and summarized from material in the archives of the United States consulate in Jerusalem, and of the consular agencies in Jaffa and Haifa. In his relations with the Ottoman administrative frameworks, the dragoman assisted the consul or consular agent in transmitting and translating official documents received from the local authorities, as well as orders from the governor of Syria and the grand vizier. These included orders limiting immigration and acquisition of land by foreign nationals who were Jews, and, among other things, documents dealing with Ottoman recognition of consuls, consular agents, vice-consuls, dragomans, and kavasses, and with the exemption of the latter from military service. The dragoman translated letters from the consulate and the consular agency to the governor of the district, to the kaimakam, or to other local authorities. He conducted negotiations and meetings with Ottoman officials (including payment of baksheesh where necessary), arranged meetings of the consul with the governor, with other consuls, and with the heads of religious communities and convents. The dragoman also secured travel permits for American citizens and for various research and study missions.

Another important part of the dragoman's work was in the field of jurisdiction. He represented the consul and saw to the interests of American citizens in the Ottoman courts, and later also in the Mixed Trade Tribunals. It was thus important for the dragoman to be familiar with Ottoman law. Jacob Schumacher requested for his dragoman an Arabic book containing "all Turkish laws for use by dragomans," and Selah Merrill, in 1884, stressed this aspect of the dragoman's work: "The dragoman of the consul has to spend many hours every week in the Sirai [government house] or local Turkish court." Consul Thomas R. Wallace reported in 1908 that his dragoman spent four to five hours, almost every day, in the Turkish courts.[53]

The dragoman addressed complaints to the governor and identified suspects who had injured Americans. Sometimes he was commissioned by the consul or the consular agent to investigate charges of theft, robbery, fraud, and to clarify specific civil legal matters in remote places, entailing bothersome and

---

53 Jacob Schumacher, U.S. Consular Agent, Haifa, to John T. Edgar, U.S. Consul General, Beirut, 16 October 1875, USNA RG84 Haifa Copy Book 1872–1886 Box 5976. Selah Merrill, U.S. Consul, Jerusalem, to Alvey A. Adee, Third Assistant Secretary of State, Washington, D.C., 15 November 1884, USNA RG59 T471/5; Thomas R. Wallace, U.S. Consul, Jerusalem, to Assistant Secretary of State, Washington, D.C., 8 July 1908, USNA RG59 T471/10 [Fi2477/10].

dangerous journeys. Thus, Cardahi was despatched to Safed (to ascertain the facts regarding the complaint of the American, Dr. Franklin), to Tiberias, Nazareth, and elsewhere. Nor was the dragoman always reimbursed for the considerable expenses of such trips.

He helped resolve disputes and arrange compromises between American citizens in the consulate, especially when knowledge of a foreign language (Yiddish, for example) was required. The dragoman also assisted in matters of legal status regarding land and real estate of American citizens and protégés. For instance, the dragoman of the Jerusalem consulate helped settle the case of the plot of land of Clorinda Minor in Jaffa, which, after her death and the dispersal of her group in the mid 1850s, was occupied by the Templer community in Jaffa: "It has required great care to prevent this property from reverting to the Turks, and in this matter...had the official aid of our Consular Agent, Mr. Hardegg and of our dragoman, Mr.Gelat. Had it not been for them, this property would already have been lost and the German Government and the United States Government would be equally powerless to recover it." [54]

Another aspect of the dragoman's work was directly connected with the consulate and its administration. Besides serving as interpreter, the dragoman acted as clerk, and assisted the consul or consular agent in their daily work, in preparing reports, dealing with American ships in port, caring for travelers and tourists requiring consular assistance, or accompanying and helping investigate matters relating to citizenship, protection, and the like. Sometimes, when no other replacement was on hand, the dragoman stood in for the consul or the consular agent. The centrality of the dragoman in the conduct of consular business, caused him to be regarded as a powerful intermediary to whom all doors were open. But this also gave him many opportunities for abusing his trust by charging illegal payments for arranging citizenship, protection, and other matters, both in and out of the consulate.[55]

A good illustration of the character and mode of operation of consular dragomans was Bishara Cardahi, a businessman who in 1872 was appointed by the consular agent in Haifa as his dragoman in Acre, and served in this capacity until 1897, when he became the dragoman of the German consular agency in Haifa. Since he resided and worked in Acre, and not in Haifa

---

54 Selah Merrill, U.S. Consul, Jerusalem, to Alvey A. Adee, Assistant Secretary of State, Washington, D.C., 29 April 1899, USNA RG59 T471/9. The case was settled forty years later.

55 Rolla Floyd, in a letter from Jerusalem dated 19 October 1882, relates how the dragoman of the American consulate arranged accommodations in Jerusalem for the Spafford family at an annual rental of $300, of which he took $50 for himself. In Parsons, *Letters from Palestine*, p.66.

where the American consular agency was located, Cardahi enjoyed a considerable measure of autonomy. He represented the consular agent at the center of the Ottoman district government which was located in Acre as well, sent annual reports from Acre, noted details of the Turkish draft and military movements, received American vessels calling at Acre, and, as mentioned above, was sent to Nazareth, Safed, and Tiberias to check complaints and claims of American citizens there. In the course of his service, he studied and gained expertise in Ottoman law to the extent of being granted a diploma as an attorney, and began to practice law in the hope of making the best of both worlds.[56] The records in the archives of the United States consular agency at Haifa are full of correspondence concerning Cardahi's activities on behalf of the consulate, his reports to the agent, his representations in the courts, translations of documents received and sent to the governor at Acre, etc. But there is also much material on Cardahi's private affairs, his family, exemptions from different taxes by virtue of his status as dragoman, litigation with other citizens or with the authorities regarding his private property – a mill he sold, a shop he rented, wells he had dug in the garden of his house without permit – and other matters which the consular agents in Haifa and the consuls in Beirut had to deal with because he was under their protection.[57] To the annoyance of the Ottoman authorities, Cardahi also permitted himself to fly the Stars and Stripes from his private home in Acre on various occasions.

The Kavass

The consular staffs in Palestine also included kavasses who served as armed guards. These men were Muslims of martial appearance, either soldiers or at least men liable to be drafted into the army, who were more-or-less seconded by the Turkish authorities for service in the foreign consulates. Therefore, the procedure of engaging a kavass began with clarifying his status regarding military conscription. This not infrequently led to conflicts with Turkish governors who did not agree to the proposed candidature. In some cases, the authorities wished to induct a kavass serving for several years in the American consulate or consular agency into the army.[58] Even though the kavasses,

---

56   Jacob Schumacher, U.S. Consular Agent, Haifa, to John T. Edgar, U.S. Consul General, Beirut, 11 August 1879 and 15 November 1880, USNA RG84 Haifa Copy Book 1872–1886 Box 5976.

57   See many entries in the Copy Books 1872–1886, 1886–1899 and Miscellaneous and Official Correspondence Received, 1875–1904 and 1878–1903 in USNA RG84 Haifa.

58   John T. Edgar, U.S. Consul General, Beirut, to Jacob Schumacher, U.S. Consular Agent, Haifa,

after being confirmed in their appointment, came under the protection of the United States, the authorities considered them Ottoman subjects and occasionally claimed the right to arrest and imprison them – calling forth protests by the consular agents.[59] Occasionally, the kavasses were involved in violent incidents between Muslims and Christians outside the frame of their official position. One of the kavasses of the Haifa consular agency, Mahmud al-Zaidan, was even charged with murder and dismissed when found guilty.[60] Like the dragomans, and sometimes in concert with them, the kavasses exploited their protected status to secure privileges and private benefits, leading to the involvement of the consular agents or the consuls to back them up in their confrontations with the Ottoman authorities. A case which was much discussed in the correspondence during the year 1879, had to do with the attempt of the dragoman Yusuf Rizq and the kavass Ahmad Dik to obtain exemption from taxes which the kaimakam wanted to impose on their exports of charcoal and wood.[61]

The kavasses – two to four in each consulate, and one or two in every consular agency – were an important part of the consular staffs. They were paid low salaries, which, as Merrill noted, were particularly small in the American service. The kavasses of the United States consulate in Jerusalem earned at most $2.00 per week when the lowest wage paid for this work in the other consulates was $3.00.[62]

Besides their function as consular guards and personal bodyguards of the consuls, the kavasses were outward symbols of consular dignity. They were fitted out in picturesque uniforms, were armed, and carried a ceremonial staff: "He is the consular constable, or kawass, whose principal business is to precede his consul on visits, bear a silver-mounted mace, and thump it ringingly

---

17 November and 5 December 1877, 28 December 1880, USNA RG84 Haifa Miscellaneous and Official Correspondence Received 1874–1904 Green Box.

59 Samuel Bergheim, U.S. Vice Consul, Jerusalem, to Ernst Hardegg, U.S. Consular Agent, Jaffa, 5, 6, 7, 11, 13 August 1879, USNA RG84 Jaffa Miscellaneous Letters 1874–1879 Box 5959.

60 Jacob Schumacher, U.S. Consular Agent, Haifa, to John T. Edgar, Consul General, Beirut, 21 July and 4 August 1877, USNA RG84 Haifa Copy Book 1872–1886 Box 5976.

61 Correspondence between Bishara Cardahi, U.S. Dragoman, Acca and Jacob Schumacher, U.S. Consular Agent Haifa, March, April, May, and July 1879, USNA RG84 Haifa Miscellaneous and Official Correspondence Received 1875–1917 Miscellaneous Papers 1878–1903 Green Box.

62 In 1867 the kavass of the American consulate in Jerusalem was paid $135 per year; in 1898, each of the two kavasses earned $200. Selah Merrill, U.S. Consul, Jerusalem, to Alvey A. Adee, Third Assistant Secretary of State, Washington, D.C., 21 July 1884, USNA RG59 T471/5.

on the pavement at every step." [63] At the turn of the century, the consul, Edwin Wallace, described his feelings about this retinue in the book on his service in Jerusalem and included a photograph of the American consular kavasses (Plate 21), who compared to those of the Russian consulate, were of modest appearance: "A smile is not out of place on the face of an American as he sees [the consul's] military escort conducting him through the streets of the Holy City, and imagine what a sensation he would create were he to pass along any street of any city of his own land similarly conducted. But he is now in Turkey where nothing is done as other people do it."[64] However, such spectacles certainly impressed the local people and tourists, and enhanced the status of the consuls.

Plate 21. Consular guards at the United States consulate at Jerusalem
Source: Wallace, *Jerusalem the Holy*

---

63   Rhodes, "Our Consul at Jerusalem," p.438.

64   Wallace, *Jerusalem the Holy*, pp.152–3.

The Consulate Building

During the period under review, 1857–1914, the United States consulate in Jerusalem was lodged consecutively in three different buildings. The first of these was on the second story of a house rented by John Gorham shortly after beginning his stint in Jerusalem. He chose a central location on "Mount Zion", near the Citadel and the Jaffa Gate. From June to December 1857, the rent came to $100 per year and was raised after that to $150.[65] The consul did not live in the consulate building, even though this was the practice with part of the other consulates in Jerusalem and with the American consular agents in Jaffa and Haifa, who allocated office space for their consular work in their private homes and set times for receiving the public. In various

---

65 John Gorham, U.S. Consul, Jerusalem, to Lewis Cass, Secretary of State, Washington, D.C., 23 May, 30 June and 12 July 1857, USNA RG59 T471/1.

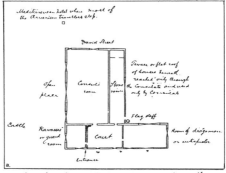

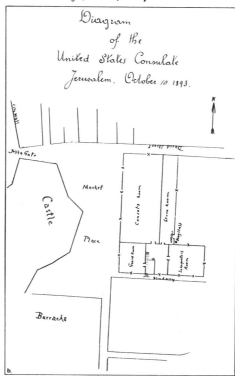

Figure 12. Building plan of the United States consulate
in Jerusalem, 1885 and 1893.
Source: USNA RG59 T471/5

books and maps of the period, the Haifa consular agency is indicated at the
house of Jacob Schumacher, which later became the home of his son, Gottlieb,
in the German-American colony. In Jaffa, the United States consular agency

was also located in the German Colony – in Ernst Hardegg's hotel. In the house rented by the American consuls in the Old City of Jerusalem, a place was set aside to serve as court room, and there was a guard room for the kavasses and a room for the dragoman. A plan of the building, dated 1885, showing the different rooms and their functions is preserved in the consular archives (Figure 12). The furnishings of the consulate were minimal. On the facade of the two-storied stone building was affixed the coat-of-arms of the United States of America and the Stars and Stripes flew from the roof, as can be seen in the picture drawn by an American traveler (Plate 22).[66]

Plate 22. The Stars and Stripes over the first building of the American
consulate in Old Jerusalem located opposite the Citadel
near the Jaffa Gate.
Source: DeHass, *Buried Cities*

In 1877, Consul DeHass allocated funds for "consular furnishings", for a court room, and for renting and "fitting up" a consulate prison. Towards the end of the 19th century, with the expansion of Jerusalem outside the walls of the Old City, many institutions and foreign consulates moved to the new neighborhoods. The American consulate also moved its premises to a new street west of the Old City near the Jaffa Road, which later became known as

66   Frank S. DeHass, U.S. Consul, Jerusalem, to A. Campbell, Third Assistant Secretary of State, Washington, D.C., 28 April 1877, USNA RG59 T471/4.

the Street of the Hospitals (today, the Street of the Prophets). In his book, Consul Edwin Sherman Wallace included a photograph of the building, which was also of stone and had two stories, with the American flag flying over it (Plate 23).[67] The building was the property of the Armenian convent. It was

Plate 23. New building of the American consulate at Jerusalem outside the
walled city.
Source: Wallace, *Jerusalem the Holy*

rented at the beginning of the 20th century to the American consul for $240 per year. The Armenians tried to raise the rent and informed the consul that they would do so on the Muslim New Year (approximately on 1 April 1902). He understood that the Armenians really wanted to rebuild this old house so that they could let it for double the rent. But despite the increased expense, the consul decided on staying in the building because of its convenient location and its suitability from all aspects. Moreover, there being only one entrance door, it facilitated control over those coming and going.[68]

Unlike the consulates of the other powers in Jerusalem, throughout the entire Ottoman period the United States consulate occupied rented premises and never acquired its own building. On the eve of the First World War, the American consulate moved to a third building, somewhat further away, but

---

67 Wallace, *Jerusalem the Holy*, p.195.

68 Selah Merrill, U.S. Consul, Jerusalem, to H.D. Pierce, Assistant Secretary of State, Washington, D.C., 28 January 1902, USNA RG59 T471/9.

of much more spacious proportions. It was the house of the German, Ferdinand Vester, near the Muslim cemetery in Mamilla. The acting British consul, who found refuge in this building when the war broke out, described its situation: "The American Consulate was already then in the building it now [1946] occupies in Mamillah Road, but it was then thought to be at the other end of nowhere. It was said at the time that the Americans had transferred their consulate to an ungettable [sic] spot half way on the road to the Convent of the Cross."[69] The building was eventually bought by the United States government, and to this day houses the consulate in West Jerusalem.

The American cemetery in Jerusalem was also under the care of the consulate. According to a report by Acting Consul Lorenzo M. Johnson, in 1868, "The consulate has in its possession a walled cemetery of about one acre. The ground was donated by an American a few years since, and may now be considered as property of the Government of the United States in Palestine. There is now but one grave therein." The key was kept in the consulate and was included in its inventory lists.[70] This cemetery, situated on Mount Zion in proximity to "David's Tomb", was mentioned earlier, in the report of the first British consul in Jerusalem to the Foreign Office in the years 1844–1845, as the cemetery of the United States surrounded by a considerable, eight-foot high wall.[71] The exact site is indicated in the map drawn up by Conrad Schick for the Palestine Exploration Fund in 1891, and in a map which was subsequently published in the *PEF Quarterly Statement* (Figure 13).[72] From a letter of the consul-general at Beirut of 1873, it appears that the American burial plot in Jerusalem was purchased years beforehand by the Presbyterian Mission, who owned it at the time of writing. In that year there were eight graves, mostly of missionaries who were active in the region, or of their children. The headstones show that the burial ground was used already in 1834/5. Later, this cemetery became the subject of an impassioned dispute

69 Hough, "History of the British Consulate," p.13.

70 Lorenzo M. Johnson, U.S. Vice and Acting Consul, Jerusalem, to William H. Seward, Secretary of State, Washington, D.C., 30 September 1868, and Richard Beardsley, U.S. Consul, Jerusalem, to Hamilton Fish, Secretary of State, Washington, D.C., USNA RG59 T471/2 and 3.

71 William Tanner Young, British Consul, Jerusalem, to Earl of Aberdeen, British Foreign Minister, London, 20 February 1844 and 1 September 1845, PRO FO78/626.

72 Plan of the American Burial Ground at Jerusalem, C. Schick, November 1891, PEF RG SCHICK/47/3. See also *PEFQS*, 1899, p.3.

between the consul, Selah Merrill, and the people of the American-Swedish Colony in Jerusalem, who were finally forced to acquire their own burial plot, which continues in use to this day on Mount Scopus.[73]

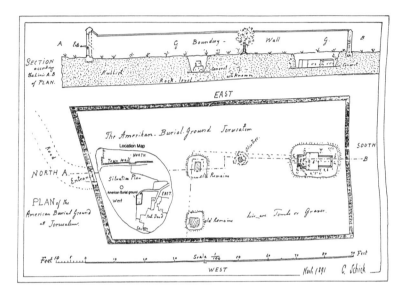

Figure 13. Plan of the American burial ground at Jerusalem, 1891
Source: PEF RG SCHICK/47/3

EXTRANEOUS ACTIVITIES

Research and Writing

It was common for foreign service officers of the powers posted in the Ottoman Empire (as also elsewhere) to engage in writing, apart from their political and other activities. Their literary efforts ranged from diplomatic and consular subjects, to personal memoirs and descriptions of travels, and to purely creative writing – or combinations of all these. Good examples are the books of memoirs by De Leon who was the American consul-general in

73 John Baldwin Hay, U.S. Consul General, Beirut, to Ernst Hardegg, U.S. Vice Consul, Jerusalem, and J. Panayotti, U.S. Dragoman, Jerusalem, to Hay, 24 September and 8 October 1873, USNA RG84 Jaffa Miscellaneous Letters 1872–1874 Box 5958.

Alexandria and Cairo in the mid-19th century,[74] by Schuyler who served as consul-general at Constantinople in the eighties, and by Ravndal in Beirut and Constantinople. The works of United States ministers to Constantinople – Lewis Wallace, the author of *Ben Hur*, Samuel S. Cox, and Oscar Straus in the 1880s and during Straus's later period of service – all include actual or imaginary motifs connected with the Holy Land.[75] Some wives of consular officials also wrote about their experiences in the region.[76] A number of the consuls who served in "Scripture Lands", took great interest in history, archeology, geography, ethnology, material culture, and in the flora and fauna of the Holy Land and of Jerusalem – in the past and the present. The rediscovery of the Bible lands by the West, and the intensification of research and exploration, also stirred the imagination of consular officials – to an extent sometimes verging on the ridiculous in the eyes of the American consul in Jerusalem, Albert Rhodes:

> Every society has its fashion, and the fashion of this Jerusalem coterie is to talk learnedly on archaeology. Hence at these entertainments (the "consular teas") it rains stones – Moresque, Byzantine, Roman, and every other kind of stone ever used in Jerusalem construction. This bombardment goes on at every tea, until those present mutually persuade themselves that they are archaeologists. Most of them have made discoveries concerning the direction of the ancient walls of the Holy City, which they explain to any victim who will listen, as they grow expansive over the tea."[77]

When writing these lines, Rhodes may have had in mind his colleague, the British Consul James Finn, and his wife Elizabeth Anne, who in the 1860s were winding up a long period of service in Jerusalem. Along with his consular duties, which also entailed the furthering of scholarly research, Finn and his wife founded the Literary Society in Jerusalem that lent itself to this

74 De Leon, *Thirty Years*.

75 Schuyler, *American Diplomacy*; Ravndal, "Capitulations;" Cox, *Diplomacy in Turkey* and *Orient Sunbeams*; and books by L. Wallace and O. Straus. The *National Geographic* magazine, which began publication in the early 20th century, devoted a special section to reports by consuls throughout the world, including the Middle East.

76 For example, Susan E. Wallace (Mrs. Lew Wallace), *Along the Bosphorus and Other Sketches*, published in 1898.

77 Rhodes. "Our Consuls at Jerusalem," p.438.

sort of social gatherings. Both published several books on the political conditions, their travels in the region, and on their observations of the life styles of the fellahin.[78]

At least some of the American consuls in Jerusalem were caught up in the fashion of research and writing – whether before their term of service, during it, or after its completion. Even Rhodes, despite his manifest cynicism, wrote a book while he served as consul, *Jerusalem As It Is*, which was published in London in 1865. Later, articles on his consular and diplomatic service experiences, and his impressions of Jerusalem and Palestine were printed in popular American and European magazines. Nevertheless, there is reason to distinguish between American consuls who served in Jerusalem and wrote personal impressions or literary or semi-literary articles on the City as did Willson in the *Jewish Chronicle* or the *Jewish Messenger*, and those consuls who themselves engaged in research or were in some other way involved in scholarly activities. Among the latter, Merrill and DeHass published articles in the *Palestine Exploration Fund Quarterly Statement* and the *Biblical World*. The focus of interest of those consuls who had a scholarly bent – DeHass, Merrill, Gillman, E. Wallace – and of others connected with the consular service who engaged in research and writing, such as the consular agent in Haifa, Gottlieb Schumacher, and the vice-consul at Jerusalem, Herbert Edgar Clark, was mainly in Biblical archeology and the historical geography of the Holy Land. One of the subjects which largely occupied their attentions was the exact site of the Crucifixion, especially after the Protestant version advanced in the eighties that sought to identify this sacred place at the "Garden Tomb," outside the Old City walls. Other subjects of interest were the Samaritans and their writings. Besides writing poetry, and a work of literary fiction inspired by Arab village life in the Jerusalem area, *Hassan: A Fellah – A Romance of Palestine*, Gillman also studied and wrote on *Wild Flowers of Palestine*, and photographed early Christian texts – although his professional background was in topographic and hydrographic surveying (Plate 24). Gottlieb Schumacher, a civil engineer by training, conducted important explorations and surveys on the Golan Heights and Transjordan as well as archeological

---

78 Among these was Finn's best-known book, *Stirring Times*, which was edited by Mrs. Finn. Their original travel journals are today kept in the Finn Archive, at the Yad Itzhak Ben-Zvi Institute in Jerusalem.

excavations. He himself drew the maps attached to his published researches, of which the best known is that of the Hauran. Clark built up an archeological collection, including an important part on the stone ages in Palestine.[79] Additional details of the research and writing of the different American consuls is given in their personal biographical sketches in Appendix I.

79 On Herbert Edgar Clark and his archeological collection, see in Kark, "Historical Sites," pp.1–17.

Hassan: a Fellah

A Romance of Palestine

By

Henry Gillman

Author of " Marked for Life," " The Ancient Men
of the Great Lakes," etc.

Boston

Little, Brown, and Company

1898

Plate 24. Title page of Consul Gillman's book
Source: Gillman, *Hassan: A Fellah*

The consul who stands out by his scholarly work, despite the criticism levelled at him, was Selah Merrill, who, in 1870, was among the founders and most active members of the American Palestine Exploration Society. Later, Merrill also helped launch the American School of Oriental Research which began its activities in Jerusalem in 1900. Already before being appointed consul at Jerusalem, Merrill had conducted surveys in Transjordan, and studied and collected specimens of birds and animals in western and eastern Palestine. He also gathered samples of plants, rocks, and objects of material culture which he sent to museum collections in the United States.[80] Subsequently, he devoted himself to the study of Jerusalem and led an archeological dig there. He summarized his research in several books, including one entitled *Ancient Jerusalem* which was published in 1908, and in numerous articles in different scholarly journals.[81] Merrill also left an interesting collection of photographs of Jerusalem and Palestine.[82]

Business Ventures

Some of the United States consuls in Jerusalem, employees of the consulate, and the consular agents in Jaffa and Haifa exploited their special extraterritorial status on the one hand, and followed their professional or commercial propensities on the other, in order to increase their income. The low salaries they were paid, or the lack of any remuneration for some of the functions they filled, forced some of the consular office holders to seek supplementary sources of income. One of the accepted practices in the consular service – and not only in that of the United States – was to engage in customs-exempt import, such as of grapes for the production of wine for non-Muslims, or of wood charcoal for heating in winter, of which surplus quantities not needed by themselves were sold profitably to their subordinates and acquaintances.[83]

---

80 Many specimens of stuffed animals and birds, with their English and Arabic names, that were hunted and collected by Merrill are kept today in the Harvard Museum of Comparative Zoology. Items of clothing, household articles, agricultural implements, seeds, builders' tools, and various objects sent by him are in the Harvard Semitic Museum. Other exhibits of the same provenance are in the Biblical Museum of the Union Theological Seminary in New York.

81 On the contribution of American researchers to the study of Palestine, between the years 1825–1939, see in Vilnay, "America's Part," pp.405–19.

82 This collection is today in the Israel Museum in Jerusalem, labelled: Merrill's Photographic Collection, Photographic Archives. I am grateful to the curator, Nissan Peretz, who kindly provided details about this collection.

83 Blumberg, *Zion Before Zionism*, p.52.

Some of the American consuls and consular employees in Jerusalem were accused of carrying on a trade in papers of protection and passports for their private benefit.[84]

One of the side occupations consuls, consular agents, vice-consuls, and dragomans tended to engage in was tourism. The numbers of tourists and organized pilgrimages to Egypt and the Holy Land, particularly of Americans, grew markedly in the second half of the 19th century and thereafter. Firms like Thomas Cook & Sons, and other tourist agencies prospered in the region and offered many profitable opportunities. There was urgent demand for Europeans, Americans, and for persons who could speak various foreign languages and who were familiar with the country and with local conditions, to take on managerial posts and develop public relations.[85] In the late 1870s and early 80s, one of the veteran American citizens resident in Jaffa and Jerusalem, who competed with Cook's in the travel business, accused the American consuls in Jerusalem of receiving certain benefits from that company. This person (Rolla Floyd) claimed that Cook's lead muleteer served five years in the American consulate, and that the American vice-consul [Samuel Bergheim, R.K.] was employed by Cook's:

> He is just the kind of thief as our Consuls like. As soon as this thief leaves, the Consul is going to appoint another thief (& one of Cook's servants) so I am told. (Of corse [sic] it is to the Consul's interest to have these thieves, Cook's servants, in office as he can then travel and ride round for nothing). The Consul and his wife go to the present vice consul for supper every two or three days. Our Consular agent in Jaffa [Ernst Hardegg, R.K.] is Cook's hotel keeper and his two official servants and Dragoman are Cook's boatmen." [86]

Selah Merrill, writing in 1884, mentioned the considerable financial inducements offered by the tourist companies during the height of the season (February, March, and April): "In general, wages paid by the large tourist companies, like that of Messrs. Thomas Cook & Son, who pay the highest

---

84 See below in Chapter Five, under Civil Services.

85 An interesting study of this tourist industry in its American aspects is the doctoral dissertation: Klatzker, *American Christian Travellers.*

86 Rolla Floyd, Jerusalem, to Aurilla Floyd Tabbutt, Columbia Falls, 13 September 1882 and 5 September 1883, in Parsons, *Letters from Palestine*, pp.65, 76–77.

salaries in order to secure the best men, are several times greater than what labouring men ordinarily receive in Palestine."[87]

More than a decade later, similar charges were levelled against Herbert Edgar Clark, the American vice-consul in Jerusalem. For many years, Clark had been the sole manager of Thomas Cook's in Palestine, and, as of 1895, was the representative and director of "Holy Land Cruises" of the Clark Tourist Company founded by his brother, Frank C. Clark, in New York. He was blamed for using his consular position to advance his private business interests. His superior, Consul Merrill, pointedly denied these allegations, but from subsequent correspondence it does appear that Herbert Clark indeed took a leave of absence coinciding with the busy months of the tourist season, when he should have devoted his time to his consular duties.[88]

In the matter of business enterprise, Merrill stands out from among all the other consuls by his character, and perhaps because of his long years of service in Jerusalem. In one of his letters, Rolla Floyd mentions a complaint a dragoman [Samuel Bergheim, R.K.] who had been dismissed by Merrill, reportedly addressed to the consul-general at Constantinople and to the State Department, accusing Merrill of: "...cheating the U.S. Government since he took charge of the office. He has mentioned some 15 items. One is charging $300 a year for office rent when it only cost him $170. Postage $15 per month when it is a little less than $4, etc. Also of the consul taking bribes from Cook to work against me [Rolla Floyd, R.K.]." [89] Although it is not certain that these charges were justified, they do indicate possible ways for consuls to supplement their income.

Correspondence in the Semitic Museum and in the Museum of Comparative Zoology at Harvard University concerning Selah Merrill and his wife clearly shows that Merrill was involved in extensive "museonic" activities and profited financially from supplying archeological, ethnographic, and natural history specimens, and especially birds, from Palestine to Andover and to Harvard.[90] In another enterprise, Merrill offered his services in 1906 to "Colonel" Clifford

87 Selah Merrill, U.S. Consul, Jerusalem, to Alvey A. Adee, Third Assistant Secretary of State, Washington, D.C., 21 July 1884, USNA RG59 T471/5.

88 Selah Merrill, U.S.Consul, Jerusalem, to Thomas W. Cridler, Assistant Secretary of State, Washington, D.C., 6 June 1898, 10 September and 23 October 1900 and Merrill to H.D. Pierce, Assistant Secretary of State, Washington, D.C., 1 February 1904, USNA RG59 T471/9.

89 Rolla Floyd, Jaffa, to Aurilla Floyd Tabbutt, Columbia Falls, 23 January 1884, in Parsons, *Letters from Palestine*, pp.78–79.

90 Archives and collections of the Semitic and Comparative Zoology Museums, Harvard University, Cambridge, Massachusetts, which I examined in 1986–7.

Nadaud of Covington, Kentucky, the president of the International River Jordan Water Company of New York for exporting freshly bottled water from the "sacred river of Judea" to the United States. Nadaud had come to Jerusalem and readied 34 tons of Jordan water for shipment. In addition to the certificates of authenticity provided by the pasha and by the Greek patriarch of Jerusalem, Merrill saw fit to also affix the consular stamp – which was later deemed improper by Washington.[91]

Finally, it should be noted that the consuls at Jerusalem were also involved in activities of various organizations and public institutions, mainly Christian and Jewish. So for example, Richard Beardsley was active in establishing a branch of the Masonic Order in Jerusalem, and Henry Gillman in founding the Ophthalmic Hospital of the Order of St. John. Consul Edwin Wallace was instrumental in setting up the "Kolel America" of Jewish-American citizens in Jerusalem.

Regarding the private residences in rented accommodations of the consuls, their life-styles and families, we have virtually no information except for an occasional mention of a consul's wife and children in connection with the consul's income, or of gossip among the consuls' wives, social gatherings, and vacation trips. Both the regular and the "extracurricular" consular activities were decidedly a "man's world."

---

91   Vogel, *Zion as Place*, pp.334–5.

CHAPTER FIVE

WORK OF THE CONSULATE AND
THE CONSULAR AGENCIES

Functions and Obligations

The first act of the new consul on assuming his position was to receive the consular archives and property from his predecessor, or from the latter's representative, and together to sign the inventory lists. One copy of this document remained in the consulate and another was sent to Washington.[1] During the first years of the American consulate at Jerusalem, its archives were minimal. The inventory drawn up by the vice-consul in 1861, listed:

> 10 volumes of the *United States Statutes at Large*, 5 reports of the sessions of the 34th, 35th, and 36th Congress in the years 1856–1860, 1 volume of the *Synoptic Index to Laws of the United States* from March 4th 1789 to March 3d 1857, and 1 volume of *Wheaton's Elements of International Law*, 1 Despatch Book, 1 Letter Book, 1 Fee Book, 1 Passport Book, 1 Invoice Book, 1 Protest Book, 1 Fees of Returns Book, 1 Register of Official Letters (sent), 1 Register of Official Letters (received), 1 United States Official Register 1855, 1 volume of *Commercial Relations (House) Part 3d.*, and 3 volumes of *Senate Commercial Relations 1857–9*. In addition to these tomes, the consulate office had 1 Press and Seal, 1 Flag of Arms of the United States, 1 Plain Moveable Bookcase, 2 Packing Boxes, and a small quantity of Cap Paper.[2]

Within another decade, the Jerusalem consular archives grew to contain many volumes of Diplomatic Correspondence, reports of the Department of

---

1 Schuyler, *American Diplomacy*, p.97
2 Simeon S. Murad, U.S. Vice Consul, Jerusalem, to William H. Seward, Secretary of State, Washington, D.C., 11 October 1861, USNA RG59 T471/1.

Agriculture, the Treasury Department, and the Bureau of Statistics, the *National Almanac* for 1864, *Rules for Consular Courts in Turkey*, a volume of the 1868 *Consular Regulations*, and two brochures with Messages of the President at the End of 1867–1869.[3] As the years went by, the expanding activities of the consulate entailed a commensurate increase of the archival material.[4] The archives were maintained and transmitted in a similar manner also in the consular agencies at Jaffa and Haifa. This may be gathered from the list of Inventory of the Office of the American Consular Agency at Haifa (Theodore J. Struve) of 1910–1912, and from a similar list from Jaffa of the second decade of the 20th century.[5] In the archives of the Haifa consular agency were listed in that year Reference Books, four volumes of *Consular Regulations*, and publications concerning customs duties, commerce, export, quarantine and immigration, as well as many catalogs of American goods and newspapers.[6]

These and other detailed inventory lists reveal the poverty of the American consular furnishings and equipment, which from the end of the 19th century also included in Jerusalem a typewriter on which despatches and reports were typed. This illustrates how, in effect, the activities of the consulate and of the consular agencies were far more limited than might be assumed from the general schema of "The Work of the Consul" (Figure 3) of 1924 as presented in Chapter One.[7] However, the work of the American consuls and consular agents in Palestine generally conformed to the obligations and duties laid down by the United States government. These were detailed by Jones in 1906 and included reporting on commercial matters, protecting customs revenue, duties concerning shipping, dealing with representatives of the government and with diplomatic and naval officers, responsibilities regarding

3   Inventory of the Consular Archives in Jerusalem, signed by John B. Hay, U.S. Acting Consul and Richard Beardsley, U.S. Consul, Jerusalem, 30 April 1870, at the date of the assumption of the Consulate by Mr. Beardsley, USNA RG59 T471/3.

4   For details of the consular archives throughout the period under discussion, see: Mayer,"Records of U.S. Consulate at Jerusalem," and"Records Haifa" and"Records Jaffa".

5   Memorandum of suggestions to the Consular Agent at Jaffa, by Alfred L.M. Gottschalk, U.S. Consul General at Large, Middle East and Africa, London, 20 March 1910, USNA RG84 Jaffa Miscellaneous Record Book 1910–1917 Box 5948 and USNA RG84, 10 June 1910, Haifa Miscellaneous and Official Correspondence Received 1875–1917 Miscellaneous Papers 1875–1904 Green Box.

6   Ibid.

7   After: Lay, *The Foreign Service*, p.193.

immigration, quarantine regulations and certificates of health, providing services to American citizens (issuing visas, protecting their private rights, administering estates of deceased persons abroad), and extraterritorial duties.[8]

In addition to their general duties, the United States consul in Jerusalem and the consular agents, were charged with functions specific to Palestine because of the makeup of its population, and because of certain processes that began there in the second half of the 19th century and the beginning of the 20th. These had to do mainly with settlers and Christian missionaries, with American visitors, and towards the end of this period, with Jewish citizens and protégés to which the consulate had to devote much of its time. The activities of the consular officials in providing civil and legal services outweighed both their political work and the advancement of their commercial functions. In this respect, the American consular establishments in Palestine had probably more in common with some of their counterparts in the country, such as the consulates of Great Britain and Austria, than with the activities of United States consulates in Europe or Latin America.[9] The combination of usual consular work and the needs dictated by the conditions peculiar to Palestine will be discussed below, along with typical situations to illustrate the various types of activities.

CIVIL SERVICES TO LOCALLY RESIDENT AMERICAN CITIZENS

Censuses
One of the important duties of the American consuls, as of the other foreign consuls in Jerusalem and elsewhere, was to maintain precise, up-to-date records of their nationals and protected persons residing within their consular jurisdiction. Besides the requirement of reporting to their superiors in the region and in Washington on citizens living abroad, the consuls relied on these mini-censuses for governing their little state within the larger one, and providing services, assistance and protection to their fellow Americans in Palestine. This became a serious responsibility when the numbers of such persons swelled appreciably, and the more so in a country where there existed

8   Jones, *The Consular Service*, pp.38–39.

9   Eliav, *Under Imperial Austrian Protection*, pp.21–33; Platt, *The Cinderella Service*, pp.152–3; Tennenbaum,"The British Consulate in Jerusalem," pp.83–108

no proper means for conducting population counts and surveys. (The first official census of all Palestine was carried out by the British Mandate government in 1922.)

The Ottoman authorities counted – mainly for taxation purposes – only their own subjects, and mostly adult males or family heads. The leadership of the Jewish and Christian millets, with their multiple sects, maintained their own records, and in every consulate there was a record book of citizens and protégés whose numbers grew steadily from the end of the 19th century (Table VI). The available statistics indicate that in the year 1872, about 770 citizens and 2,473 protégés were registered in the foreign consulates, and in 1899, 1,641 citizens and 9,245 protégés. These numbers did not include the protégés in Jaffa in 1872, who numbered some 387 persons, nor were some of the foreign citizens and protected persons in the Acre district counted.[10]

In order to obtain a sense of perspective for the data in the above table, and for the number of American citizens in Palestine, it should be noted that in 1914, on the eve of the World War and the end of the period under review here, the latest exhaustive studies by Schmelz estimate the total population of Palestine, inclusive of Bedouins, at about 800,000. This number included some 40,000 foreign nationals and protected persons, which represents a considerable rate of growth of this population element from 1899 when they were estimated at 10,900. In the lists for 1896 are included over 1,000 citizens and protégés of the United States.[11] The annual lists of Americans residing in Palestine drawn up by the consul in Jerusalem and by the consular agent in Haifa, are especially interesting because they recorded the name, age, place of birth, and date, the court of naturalization where applicable, occupation or profession, place of residence, year of arrival in Turkey, and various remarks. For each family, details of the children were listed as well. Besides their administrative value, these records are useful sources for demographic, economic, and social research.

The lists of citizens and protégés in Jaffa were included in the Jerusalem consular records, while those of Acre were drawn up separately in Haifa, and were sent to the consulate-general at Beirut. The Jerusalem lists show that in the mid-19th century very few American citizens were registered – several missionaries, some Jews who arrived from the United States, and small

---

10　Otto Kersten, Kanzler, German Consulate, Jerusalem, to Foreign Office, Berlin, 21 June 1872, ISA RG67 quoted by Eliav, *The Jews of Palestine*, pp.41–43.

11　Schmelz,"The Decline in the Population," p.26; Fishbane,"Kollel America," p.121.

TABLE VI. Registration and Number of Nationals and Protégés in Jerusalem, 1872 and 1899.

Country	Nationals 1872	Native born 1899	Protégés 1872	Jewish protégés 1899	Registration- 1899	Registration fee 1899
U.S.A.	4	50	13	800	Problematic	–
Austria	250	10	920	2,990	Annually	1.00
Britain	180?	120	700?	250	Annually	5 shillings
France	20?	250	60?	200	Annually	1-2.00
Germany	210	550	470	350	Once in 10 years	1.50
Greece	55	150	150	–		0.40-8.00
Holland	–	10	–	25	Annually	2.00
Italy	20?	300	60	10	Annually	2.00
Russia	–	200		4,000-5,000	none	–
Spain	31	1	100?	120	Annually	6.00 per family
Approximate total	770	1,641	2,473	9,245		

Based on: Otto Kersten, Kanzler, German Consulate, Jerusalem, to Foreign Office, Berlin, 21 June 1872, ISA RG67 quoted by Eliav, *The Jews of Palestine,* pp. 41-43 and Selah Merrill, U.S. Consul, Jerusalem, to Thomas W. Cridler, Assistant Secretary of State, Washington, D.C. 9 September 1899, USNA RG 59 T471/9.

groups of Christian settlers. A considerable growth in these numbers took place in 1866–1867 with the arrival in Jaffa of 157 persons (43 American families) connected with the Church of the Messiah. Some of these died within a short time, and most returned to the United States within a year.

However, a few stayed on in the Holy Land. A complete list of the names of
these settlers, who arrived on 22 September 1866, includes even the ten crew
members who manned the bark *Nellie Chapin* in which the settlers sailed
from Maine.[12] Less than a year later, the consul in Jerusalem drew up an
additional list in alphabetical order according to family names, and stating
place of birth, age on arrival, date of birth, and date of decease, and for those
who left, he registered the date of departure for the U.S. and the name of the
steamer. This list also provides information on those who remained. Until
June 1867, out of a total of 159 persons (157 who came from America and
two born in Palestine) 16 died and 55 left the country; 88 remained.[13] Most
of the families came from Maine – Jonesport, Addison, Orrington, Lebanon,
York – and a few from New Hampshire and other places. Their ages were:
45 persons 0–10 years old, 35 were 11–20 years old, 22 were 21–30 years
old, 29 were aged 31–40, 16 aged 41–50, and 10 aged 60 or more. Those
who died in the country were among the youngest of the settlers' children. A
son was born to one of the families on 27 September 1866, only a few days
after they landed on the beach of Jaffa. In any case, by the end of 1868, the
number of Americans listed with the consulate in Jerusalem had shrunk
again to 33 – 19 living in Jaffa and 14 in Jerusalem. In the following years,
1869, 1870, and 1871, the numbers were even smaller – altogether 27 persons
– and began to increase only during the 1870s.[14] In 1878, 119 persons (of
whom 15 in Jaffa) were registered in the American consulate at Jerusalem,
but according to some sources, Consul DeHass extended American protection
to about 500 Jewish families at the time of the Russo-Turkish War.[15]

Thus, in the late sixties and the early seventies, the number of American
citizens in the Jerusalem consular district was very small, and included several
individual Jews and Jewish families in Jerusalem (Lilienthal, Coppel) and
the remains of the Adams colony in Jaffa (ten persons) to which were added
a few missionaries, a merchant, and a farmer with their families. In 1879,

12 List of Americans arrived at Jaffa on the 22 September 1866, signed by Victor Beauboucher, U.S.
    Consul, Jerusalem, 22 October 1866, USNA RG59 T471/2.

13 Liste [sic] of Settlers arrived September 22nd, 1866 by bark"Nellie Chapin," signed by Victor
    Beauboucher, U.S. Consul, Jerusalem, 10 June 1867, USNA RG59 T471/2.

14 Lists of American citizens under the Jerusalem Consul 31 December 1868, 1869, 1870, 1871,
    USNA RG59 T471/2 and 3.

15 J.G. Willson, U.S. Consul, Jerusalem, to Charles Payson, Third Assistant Secretary of State,
    Washington, D.C., 2 January 1878, USNA RG59 T471/4; Bartour,"Episodes," p.121.

most of the American families in Jaffa earned their living as tourist guides for Palestine and Syria, and some of the women took in washing.[16] From the end of the 1870s, the lists of citizens and protégés in Jerusalem included mainly large numbers of Jews, most of whom were not native Americans.

In the Haifa consular agency were recorded detailed censuses of the German-American settlers of the Templer colony. The consular agent, Jacob Schumacher, who was a member of the colony, made it a point ever since taking up his appointment in 1872, to list all the families and persons of the colony in his annual reports to the consulate-general at Beirut. In 1874, for example, out of a total number of 350 souls – mostly Germans – there were 40 Americans (8 families) in the Haifa colony.[17] There were almost no other American citizens under the jurisdiction of the Haifa consular agency, except a few missionaries and Jews in Safed and Tiberias who were added to the lists in the 1880s. According to the Accurate Census of American Citizens Residing in the Consular District of Acca & Haifa, Syria for the years 1883 and 1885, it appears that the numbers remained fairly steady at 52 and 53 persons, respectively.[18] The lists were arranged alphabetically by family names, with entries for all the children in each family. Every person was given a serial number, with details of his/her name, place of birth, date of birth, last residence in the U.S., date of naturalization, date of arrival in Syria, and occupation. These lists are important sources for detailed study of the settlers and citizens in the Acre district. At times, copies of these census lists were sent to the Ottoman administration, in English or in Arabic translation.[19]

In the census of the 1890s and the first decade of the 20th century, the number of American citizens in the district of the Haifa consular agency fluctuated between 57 and 60. In the second decade of the new century the number had increased slightly, to 75. In 1913, 56 such persons were registered

16 List of United States Citizens Residing at Jaffa, 31 December 1879, E. Hardegg, U.S. Consular Agent, Jaffa, attached to report of J.G. Willson, U.S. Consul, Jerusalem, to Second Assistant Secretary of State, Washington, D.C., 2 January 1880, USNA RG59 T471/5.

17 Jacob Schumacher, U.S. Consular Agent, Haifa, to Edward Van Dyck, U.S. Vice Consul, Beirut, 19 September 1874, USNA RG84 Haifa Copy Book 1872–1886 Box 5976.

18 These census figures were entered in the Haifa Copy Books for the years 1872–1899.

19 For example: Jacob Schumacher, U.S. Consular Agent, Haifa, to the Kaimakam of Haifa, 10 June 1886, USNA RG84 Haifa Register of American Citizens and Passport Book Haifa Box 5976 and a census in Arabic of 1914.

in the Haifa German-American colony, 8 in the town of Haifa, 10 in the Jewish colony of Zikhron Ya'aqov, and one in Nazareth.[20] But despite the relatively small but steady number of American citizens permanently settled in the Acre district in 1869–1914, these greatly occupied the attentions of their consular agent and his superiors in Beirut.

Registration of Births, Marriages, and Deaths

Among the duties of the consuls and consular agents of the United States was providing services to American citizens in all matters connected with births, marriages, and deaths, and reporting these. American citizens – mainly Christians and Jews – resident in the country were obliged to register themselves and their families and to notify their consular representation of all such events. For their services in registering births and issuing marriage certificates, the consuls and consular agents charged fees which were entered in their books and reported to the State Department or to the consulate-general at Beirut. In Jerusalem and Haifa, these entries appear, after 1875, not in tabulated form at the end of the calendar year, but in the current correspondence. Therefore, unlike in the census lists of citizens and protégés, it is necessary (in Haifa, for example) to go over all the Copy Books in order to find notices of births, marriages, and deaths.[21] These documents were in turn submitted for approval to the consul-general at Beirut, who sometimes reprimanded the consular agent and returned to him improperly filled-in documents. The corrected certificates had to be sent back to the consul-general who was responsible for collating and reporting on this material.[22] Reports of births usually included the given name, sex, names of the parents, and date of birth. Sometimes the place of birth was also added. Death notices gave the name of the deceased, date, age, and the name of the spouse or the parents. Very occasionally, the cause of death was also given (heart disease, typhoid fever, drowning, etc.) as well as the place of birth and the maiden name. Cases of

---

20 Census of American Citizens Residing in the Consular District of Haifa in June 1913, ibid. A year later, in 1914, three persons are listed as residing in the new Templer colony in the Valley of Jezreel – Umm el-'Amed, or by its German name, Waldheim (today the settlement, Alonei Abba).

21 USNA RG84 Haifa Copy Book 1872–1886 and 1886–1899 Boxes 5976, 5977.

22 John T. Robeson, U.S. Consul General, Beirut, to Jacob Schumacher, U.S. Consular Agent, Haifa, 10 August 1885, USNA RG84 Haifa Miscellaneous and Official Correspondence Received 1875–1917 Miscellaneous Papers 1875–1904 Green Box.

infant mortality can be ascertained within days to a year of birth by comparing the registrations of births and deaths.[23] By the time of the World War, there were in Haifa regular birth certificates signed by the municipal midwife, and proper marriage certificates and death reports, some on printed forms. The death certificates, of which some were for young children, state among the causes of death malaria, dysentery, tuberculosis, grippe, and typhus.[24]

In the archives of the Jaffa consular agency, even towards the end of the period under review here, death reports of local American citizens and of sailors who died at sea are found dispersed in envelopes.[25] In the cases of deceased Jews, it was sometimes the community's rabbi who would make the report. The death of Joseph Eisic, a citizen of the United States, was reported to the Jaffa consular agency by Rabbi A.I. Kuck (Abraham Isaac Hacohen Kook), the rabbi of Jaffa and the Jewish settlements. Rabbi Kook was also signatory to the will, dated January 1912, of another American citizen most of whose family lived in the United States.[26]

The first notification of the decease of an American citizen in Jerusalem – the missionary, the Reverend Nathan W. Fiske – was sent together with his passport to the State Department by the American consul in Beirut.[27] With the establishment of the Jerusalem consulate, death notices of American settlers and visitors were frequently sent to the State Department, although arranging the disposal of their property often took a long time.[28] Between 1866–1875, properly composed lists of deceased Americans in Jaffa and Jerusalem were maintained, including the people of the Adams colony which were added to the annual report as Form no. 21. This form included the

---

23 See reports of deaths in the Haifa Copy Book on 26 October 1877, 26 November 1883, and 28 January 1899.

24 Small Files 1892–1916, USNA RG84 Haifa Miscellaneous Letters and Papers 1874–1904.

25 Envelopes in USNA RG84 Jaffa Miscellaneous Records 1911–1915.

26 Rabbi A. I. Kuck, Jaffa, to U.S. Consular Agent, Jaffa, 3 March 1911 and January 1912, USNA RG84 Jaffa Miscellaneous Letters 1900–1914 Box 5965.

27 Jasper Chasseaud, U.S. Consul, Beirut, to James Buchanan, Secretary of State, Washington, D.C., 16 June 1847, USNA RG59 T367/1. Fiske was buried in the American cemetery on Mount Zion.

28 Thus, for example, the property valued at $286 left by Mrs. Mary R. Williams, a member of the Clorinda Minor group who died in Jaffa at the end of 1858, was disposed of only in March 1860. And see also in the sub-chapter on Estates below. John Warren Gorham, U.S. Consul, Jerusalem, to Lewis Cass, Secretary of State, Washington, D.C., 31 March 1860, USNA RG59 T471/1.

following entries: "Date of decease, name, of what place native or citizen, where deceased, and disposition made thereof." [29]

Sometimes the report of death departed from laconic information to include personal details of the deceased and his family. Thus, in reporting of death of Olivier A. Ward, who died in 1871 aged 52 of "typhus fever", Consul Beardsley mentioned that he came from Addison, Maine in 1866 "as a member of the so-called 'American Colony'" and added that "The deceased was an honest, hard-working man...highly respected by all who knew him..."[30] And in the case of the death of Miss Mary Baldwin in Jaffa in June 1877, Consul DeHass added that she had been "...for many years connected with the mission work in Syria. Her sister Mrs. Hay will take charge of her personal effects."[31] Such added information is a useful source for reconstructing the character and activities of Americans and their families who lived in Palestine, as well as in tracing American citizens who died during visits to the country – such as Rev. Emory Gale (1815–1874) who for seventeen years served as a missionary in Minnesota and was buried in the cemetery of the Clorinda Minor group in Jaffa,[32] the tourist who in 1862 drowned in the Jordan while bathing, or the Mormons, Adolph Haag and John Alexander Clark, who died in Haifa in 1892 and 1895.[33]

In everything regarding marriages, the consuls and consular agents were responsible for formal licensing of the marriage, and for issuing the marriage certificate, and for reporting it to the State Department or to the consul in Beirut. Prior to the introduction of printed forms, the marriage certificate included a declaration in the consul's handwriting that he was present at the ceremony, the names of the couple, their ages and their places of birth, the

---

29   Names of All Deceased American Citizens, Including Seamen or Marines, December 1866, 1868, 1871, USNA RG59 T471/2 and 3 (also M453).

30   Richard Beardsley, U.S. Consul, Jerusalem, to Second Assistant Secretary of State, Washington, D.C., 23 November 1871, USNA RG59 T471/3.

31   Frank S. DeHass, U.S. Consul, Jerusalem, to J.A. Campbell, Assistant Secretary of State, Washington, D.C., 25 June 1877, USNA RG59 T471/4.

32   Inscription for Rev. Emory Gale's tombstone, Died November 25, 1874, USNA RG84 Jaffa Miscellaneous Letters Received form the Principal Officer in Jerusalem and Miscellaneous Letters 1874–1879 Box 5959.

33   Franklin Olcott, U. S. Consul, Jerusalem, to William H. Seward, Secretary of State, Washington, D.C., 30 September 1862, USNA RG59 471/1; Gottlieb Schumacher, U.S. Consular Agent, Haifa, to U.S. Consul, Beirut, 13 July 1892 and 13 February 1895, USNA RG84 Haifa Copy Book 1886–1899 Box 5977.

name of the person performing the ceremony, the place where it was conducted, the signature of the consul, and the consular seal.[34] The marriage ceremony was usually performed by a religious dignitary – priest or minister, or in the case of Jews, by a rabbi. Thus, in 1895, the wedding of Nehemia Padkorney and Jeanett Graff in Haifa was performed by the Chief Rabbi of Haifa, David Reina, in the presence of the consular agent, Gottlieb Schumacher.[35] When Jacob Schumacher served as consular agent in Haifa, he himself conducted the wedding ceremony, and to the reprimand by the consul at Beirut replied that "...he was ordained as pastor in 1863 by two American Reverends in New York State, and can thus perform marriages."[36]

Now and then, the consuls had to resolve administrative problems concerning marriages, such as questions of citizenship and the requirement for a passport in order to perform the marriage. Such problems arose regarding the second generation of resident citizens, who arrived in Palestine at a young age without a passport, or who were born in the country and for whom passports had to be issued before they could marry.[37] There were also cases where the marriage partners had different nationalities, with only one of them an American citizen. It seems that on marrying, the woman usually took on the nationality of her husband and would lose her American citizenship, or received it if marrying an American.

One of the most interesting cases connected with the marriage of an American citizen, which was also the subject of extensive consular correspondence, was that of Dr. Franklin. The affair, which is good material for a novel, provides an unusual insight into the work of the consulate and of the missions. Dr. Morris Julius Franklin, an American citizen who worked for the London Jews' Society mission in Safed fell in love with a 23-year old Jewish woman in that town, named Esther Eliahu (Mizrahi), and in September 1894 took her and her effects from her home in order to marry her. The stunned parents wrote emotional, heart-rending letters to Dr. Thomas Chaplin, the doctor of the Mission in Jerusalem, to the American consul-general in Beirut, and to

34 Marriage certificate of Frederick Kübler (28) and Catherine Briland (19), written and signed by Frank S. DeHass, U.S. Consul, Jerusalem, 11 August 1874, USNA RG59 T471/4.

35 Gottlieb Schumacher, U.S. Consular Agent, Haifa, to T.R. Gibson, U.S. Consul General, Beirut, 14 November 1895, USNA RG84 Haifa Copy Book 1886–1899 Box 5977.

36 Jacob Schumacher, U.S. Consular Agent, Haifa, to John T. Robeson, U.S. Consul General, Beirut, 7 November 1885, USNA RG84 Haifa Copy Book 1872–1886 Box 5976.

37 Schumacher to Robeson, 25 November 1884, ibid.

Jacob Schumacher, the United States consular agent in Haifa, beseeching them "to kindly induce Dr. Franklin by law or otherwise to bring our daughter and her clothes back to her parental home, and thus to avert more disgrace from our grey heads..."[38] In January 1885 Morris and Esther appeared before the American dragoman in Acre, Cardahi, and presented him with "...a contract of marriage signed by them and two witnesses requesting [him] to legalize their signature." Cardahi refused and referred them to Schumacher in Haifa. The two accordingly asked Jacob Schumacher to marry them on the spot, but the consular agent also declined the request since he had been informed that Franklin was married to a woman who lived in the United States (in New York), and requested instructions from the consul in Beirut.[39] Reports made two-and-a-half years later mention that Franklin was never officially married to Esther Eliahu, that they lived together, and had a child that was never registered in the consulate.[40] Against this background, Franklin was dismissed and left the Mission, but set up an independent mission in Safed. He quarreled with other missionaries and Jews in that town and occupied much of Jacob Schumacher's and Cardahi's time – beyond the subject of registration of marriages and births – as will be seen below, under "Jurisdiction."

Issue of Passports

At the end of the 19th century, the American passport was defined as "A document issued by the Secretary of State, or, under his authority, by a diplomatic or consular officer of the United States abroad, to a citizen of the United States, stating his citizenship, and requesting for him free passage and all the lawful aid and protection during his travel or sojourn in foreign lands." [41] The concept derived from the French *'passer porte'* – a license to pass through a city gate or through the ports of the realm.

---

38 Mr. and Mrs. Eliahu, Safed, to American Consul [sic], Haifa, September 1884, USNA RG84 Haifa Miscellaneous and Official Correspondence Received 1875–1917 Miscellaneous Papers 1878–1903 Green Box.

39 Jacob Schumacher, U.S. Consular Agent, Haifa, to John T. Robeson, U.S. Consul General, Beirut, 1 October 1884 and 27 January 1885, USNA RG84 Haifa Copy Book 1872–1886 Box 5976, and Bishara Cardahi, U. S. Dragoman, Acca, to Schumacher, 18 August 1887, Miscellaneous and Official Correspondence, ibid.

40 Jacob Schumacher, U.S. Consular Agent, Haifa, to Erhard Bissinger, U.S. Consul General, Beirut, 11 and 24 August 1887, USNA RG84 Haifa Copy Book 1886–1899 Box 5977 and Gottlieb Schumacher, U.S. Consular Agent, Haifa, to Selah Merrill, U.S. Consul, Jerusalem, 27 July 1893, ibid.

41 Hunt, *The American Passport*, pp.3–6.

In those days passports consisted of a single sheet of paper on which, from 1850, the bearer's age and height were also entered. It was only in 1905 that passport applications were printed in affidavit form (a sworn or affirmed statement of the facts), with the applicant required to swear to the correctness of the declared data before a notary public. Photographs were officially required on passports from the end of 1914, although the actual document was still in the form of a single sheet of paper. Between 1856 and 1917, passport fees of $1.00-$6.00 (in the gold coin of the United States) were levied in foreign service ports.[42] Consultation by the State Department with its Law Bureau regarding existing diplomatic instructions and consular regulations, and regarding the provisions of international law on the issuing of passports, led to the publication of revised regulations in June 1885. These laid down the conditions for the protection of United States citizens, for marriage as related to citizenship, for issuing passports in foreign countries (by the acting chief diplomatic representative, and in his absence by the consul-general, or in the latter's absence by the consul; consular agents were not allowed to issue passports), and determined the procedures, fees, entitlement (including by marriage or birth), and the granting of visas.[43] The registration and issuing of foreign passports took on special importance after the proclamation of the Ottoman Law of Nationality of 1869. One of its provisions stated that: "Every person inhabiting the Imperial Dominions is considered as an Ottoman subject and treated as an Ottoman subject. If he (or she) is a foreign subject it is necessary for him (or her) to prove it in a regular manner."[44] The Sublime Porte attempted in this way to put an end to the abuses entailed by the extension of foreign protection to non-Muslims on a vast scale, and tried to arrive at separate agreements with the different powers in this respect. Between the years 1874 and 1889. Several unsuccessful attempts were made to ratify a convention on naturalization between the United States and Turkey. The basic differences in their conceptions of citizen's rights and of citizenship were the subject of diplomatic controversy between the two powers for half a

---

42 Department of State, *The United States Passport*, pp.1–5, 207–232. This book mentions the"letters" given by the king of Persia to Nehemiah when he left for the Land of Israel in about 450 B.C.E. (Nehemiah: 2,7) as one of the earliest recorded passports.

43 USNA Department of State, Law Bureau, to Secretary of State, Washington, D.C., 4 May 1885 and Articles xii and xiii of Personal Instructions to Diplomatic Agents Relating to Passports and Marriages, Accompanying Circular of 29 June 1885.

44 Schmavonian,"Citizenship, Turkey," pp.252–232.

century. This is also evident from a document published by the 59th Congress entitled "Citizens of the U.S., Expatriation." [45] The United States continued until the early years of the 20th century to insist forcefully on the rights of its citizens, including Jews who had been naturalized, to reside in Palestine and to acquire property. Only with the introduction of "dollar diplomacy" by President Taft and Secretary of State Knox from 1909, were doubts raised regarding the fourth article of the Ottoman-United States agreement of 1830, and regarding the interpretation of the extraterritorial rights of the American consuls and the protection they could extend over foreign nationals. This was a result of the attempt by the Young Turks to induce the Americans to relinquish capitulatory rights in return for preferential economic status. The question was discussed at the time by the diplomats serving in the region with the Division of Near Eastern Affairs that was established as part of the reorganization of the State Department into geographical regions. [46]

The consuls in Jerusalem and the consular agents in Jaffa and Haifa accepted applications by American citizens for passports, extensions, and for visas. Passports were issued in Constantinople according to the following categories: 'native', 'emergency', 'naturalized', 'persons claiming citizenship by marriage or through parents' (Plate 10). [47] Passport applications to the Haifa consular agency were forwarded to the consul-general at Beirut. [48] A reading of the relevant, voluminous correspondence indicates that many of the American settlers in Haifa did not ask for or renew their passports unless they wished to travel. Thus, for example, in 1891, the consular agent, Jacob Schumacher, asked Beirut for instructions regarding Mr. and Mrs. Struve who intended going to Russia and whose passports dated to 1873 [the year they settled in Haifa, R.K.]. [49] Another question that arose was the issuing of passports to children of settlers who came to Palestine as infants, or who were born at Haifa. In 1877, Jacob Schumacher requested a proper passport for his own

---

45   Ibid.; Karpat,"The Ottoman Emigration to America," pp.189–93.

46   Phillips,"The Geographical Divisions," pp.345–366; Bartour,"Episodes," p.129; *Diplomatic Correspondence*, JNUL V810.

47   Stuart,"Consulate General Constantinople," p.13.

48   USNA RG84 Haifa, Copy Books 1872–1886, 1886–1899 Boxes 5976 and 5977, and Miscellaneous and Official Correspondence Received 1875–1904 and 1878–1903.

49   Jacob Schumacher, U.S. Consular Agent, Haifa, to Erhard Bissinger, U.S. Consul General, Beirut, 20 March 1891, USNA RG84 Haifa Copy Book 1886–1899 Box 5977.

son [Gottlieb] who wished to study in Germany for four more years. At the time Gottlieb initially left for Stuttgart, he only had a certificate to be shown to the American consul there.[50]

Regarding the American Templers in Haifa, questions arose also as to their citizenship status and their individual obligations for renewing their passports every two years, and payment of fees. The matter came up in 1885 as a result of a representation to the State Department by the Rev. Wm. F. Schwilk, pastor of the German Temple Society at Schenectady, and of Oscar Gezinner[?], elder of the Society at Buffalo, New York, to exempt the settlers of the Haifa Templer colony, like all other missionaries, from the obligation to present passports every two years and to pay a fee of ten francs. Schumacher too, argued that the American Templer settlers should be released from the passport regulations because "...the American citizens of the Temple Colony of Haifa have the character of missionaries, by having left their homes for the sole purpose of Christianizing the native population of Palestine...."[51] As far as is known from research on the Templers in Palestine, these claims had no basis in fact since these settlers did *not* engage in missionary activities.[52] The question of the civil status of the American colonists at Haifa surfaced again in 1903. Those members whose passports had expired were requested by the United States minister in Constantinople and by the consul-general at Beirut to apply for new passports and pay the fees, even though they never returned to live in the United States and there were doubts as to their qualification as missionaries.[53]

The foregoing contrasts with the discriminatory attitudes of the American diplomatic and consular representatives in the Ottoman Empire regarding citizenship and land ownership rights in favor of Christians (including American Templers), over American Jews and their offspring who lived

---

50 John T. Edgar, U.S. Consul General, Beirut, to Jacob Schumacher, U.S. Consular Agent, Haifa, 22 February 1876, USNA RG84 Haifa Miscellaneous and Official Correspondence Received 1875–1917 Miscellaneous Papers 1878–1903 and Schumacher to Edgar 14 April 1877, Copy Book, ibid.

51 Correspondence dated 19 and 27 January, 28 February, and 12 August 1885 in Copy Book, ibid., and Miscellaneous Papers 1878–1903.

52 For example: Carmel, *German Settlement*.

53 Gabriel Bie Ravndal, U.S. Consul General, Beirut, to Gottlieb Schumacher, U.S. Consular Agent, Haifa, 34 June 1903, USNA RG84 Haifa Miscellaneous and Official Correspondence Received 1875–1917 Miscellaneous Papers 1878–1903; see also bundles of papers on this subject in Miscellaneous Papers 1875–1904 ibid., and in particular, the letter from Ravndal to Schumacher of 20 September 1902.

many years outside the United States. Thus, for example, in the cases of two American Jewish settlers, Louis Lubowsky and Joseph Moses Brauner at Miron (Yessud Hama'alah), the American consul-general in Beirut refused to renew their passports and to deal with problems of land ownership because they were not missionaries and had no intention of returning to the United States.[54] On the other hand, all the dubious requests by Christians were eventually resolved in their favor.

This is the place to emphasize the importance for research purposes of this archival material. Blumberg considers the stacks of sworn affidavits by American citizens to be the most valuable part of the consular correspondence.[55] Correspondence and requests for passports are preserved also in the archives of the Jaffa consular agency.[56] The requests for passports and for renewals recorded in Haifa are an inexhaustible source of biographical and demographic information on the American citizens – Christians and Jews – in Haifa, Safed, and Tiberias. Among the most interesting items are the applications by Gottlieb Schumacher himself in the 1890s when he already served as the consular agent at Haifa.[57]

Services to American Missionaries and Christian Settlers

Assistance to Missionaries
American missionary efforts in the Ottoman Empire and the Holy Land predated regular diplomatic and consular activities, and as has been brought out by several studies, influenced the shaping of American policies in Turkey.[58] Missionary work in Palestine, of fluctuating fortunes, was initiated, as has been mentioned above, by the American Board of Commissioners for Foreign Missions by sending the Reverends Pliny Fisk and Levi Parsons to Jerusalem in 1822 and 1825, where they enjoyed the protection of the British consuls.

---

54 Gabriel Bie Ravndal, U.S. Consul General, Beirut, to Gottlieb Schumacher, U.S. Consular Agent, Haifa, 1 December 1902, ibid. Regarding the Lubowsky affair, see Services to American Jewish Settlers, below.

55 Blumberg,"Comments," p.256.

56 USNA RG84 Jaffa, Miscellaneous Record Book 1866–1910 Box 5942, Miscellaneous Records 1911–1915 and Miscellaneous Certificates 1914–1916 Box 5973.

57 For example, his application for passport sent to T.S. Doyle, U.S. Consul General, Beirut, 12 January 1898, Copy Book, ibid.

58 Tibawi, *American Interests*, pp.2–14, 188–190; Grabill, *Protestant Diplomacy*, pp.6–33, 300–305.

However, both died within a short time. In 1834, the Board made another attempt to activate a Jerusalem station, but in 1843, by agreement with the English mission which continued its activities in Palestine, the Americans adopted the painful decision to suspend their efforts at the birthplace of Christianity and to concentrate on the Levant and Turkey. Nevertheless, several individual American missionaries and small groups continued to engage in sporadic work, mainly in Jerusalem and Jaffa.[59] In the 1840s and 1850s these persons maintained close relations with the American consuls in Beirut and with the consular agents at Jaffa and Jerusalem, who helped them in matters regarding their rights and contacts with the Ottoman authorities. These "free lance" missionaries also attempted to intervene in cases of appointments and dismissals of consular representatives, and passed opinions regarding payments and salaries concerning these officials.[60] One of the missionaries who showed a particular propensity for meddling in the affairs of the consulate in Beirut, and in the Jaffa and Jerusalem consular agencies, was the physician, Dr. James T. Barclay, a Disciple of Christ who worked in Jerusalem for three-and-a-half years after his arrival there in 1851. An anonymous article, apparently written by him at the time, described missionary work in Jerusalem and noted that England and Germany "...maintain able consuls in the City for the special protection of its [missionary society] members." [61] If Barclay indeed wrote these lines, it may have been his way of expressing his disappointment at there being no American consul in Jerusalem.

Since there were but few American missionaries in Jerusalem, not counting occasional visitors for short periods, assisting them did not occupy the consulate very much. But the consuls, some of whom were clergymen themselves, maintained contacts with other missions, employed converted Jews as dragomans and in other consular capacities, and sometimes supported the missions in their struggles for Jewish souls. One of the documented incidents of this type was the involvement of Consul Beauboucher, in 1868, in the endeavor of the British mission to forcibly convert Sarah Steinberg, the

---

59 Fields, *America and the Mediterranean*, pp.92–211.

60 See above, in Chapter Three, as well as a letter signed by missionaries and settlers in Jerusalem, Jaffa, Beirut, Tripoli, Sidon, Bhamdun, and Mount Lebanon to Lewis Cass, the secretary of state in Washington of 25 September 1858 (Cass,"J.S. Murad.")

61 Handy, *The Holy Land*, pp.83–89.

young sister of the wife of the American protégé, Demetrius Golovsoff. This case which aroused strong feelings in the Jewish community eventually led to Beauboucher's dismissal.[62]

Assistance to Christian American Settlers
Unlike the limited help to missionaries, the American consuls and consular agents were deeply involved in assisting (and sometimes in quarreling with) groups and private persons who came to settle in the Holy Land out of religious and proselytizing motives. The leaders of two such American groups, Clorinda S. Minor in the 1850s and George W. J. Adams in the late 1860s, were imbued with millenarian ideas current in mid-19th century Protestant Europe and America. Their followers were influenced by them to settle in Palestine and to engage in modern agriculture – in Urtas and Jaffa, respectively – notwithstanding warnings by persons familiar with local conditions and by representatives of the United States government. Although these undertakings failed, they have become important chapters in the history of agricultural settlement in 19th-century Palestine.[63]

In the late 1860s and early 1870s, German Templers rooted in the Pietist movement came to Haifa, Jaffa, and Jerusalem with the intention of integrating rural and urban settlement as a way of implementing their religious ideology. Among them were also Germans who had been naturalized in the United States before coming to Palestine. The Templer settlements proved so successful that they continued until World War Two, when German nationals were interned and eventually left. The American Templers made many demands on the work of the American consular agency in Haifa and of the consulate-general in Beirut.[64]

Another important group of Christian settlers was the American Colony in Jerusalem. These people, who gathered around a small group of eighteen founders belonging to the Spafford family from Chicago or who were connected with it, first arrived in Jerusalem in the early 1880s and established there a religious community. In the 1890s, they were joined by dozens of religiously-motivated Swedish-Americans originating from the rural Dalarna region in

---

62 Eliav,"The Sarah Steinberg Affair," pp.78–91.

63 Kark,"Millenarism," pp.47–62.

64 Many examples of the relations between the consular officials in Haifa and Beirut and the American Templers are given throughout this book and will not be repeated here. See for example, under"Real Estate" in Chapter Six.

Sweden, and by friends and family members from that part of Sweden, as well as by a few Britons. This group was the cause of considerable anxiety to two of the American consuls in Jerusalem.[65] The work of the consular officials around these groups entailed reporting, advising against settlement, protecting persons and property, preventing them from giving up their American citizenship and taking Ottoman nationality, representing them before Ottoman and other consular officials, mediating in their internal quarrels, extending economic assistance in times of need, and quarreling with them in cases of conflicting interests (Plate 7).

Individuals who came to the Holy Land on their own also had recourse to the consulate. Jerusalem, in particular, attracted "true believers" like Miss Harriet Livermore who arrived in 1840 from New Hampshire where she had "...highly respectable connexions and a fair reputation for piety...for the purpose of participating in great religious events, believing herself to be one of the witnesses mentioned in the 11th chapter of Revelations." This lady was among those who signed a petition supporting J.S. Murad for the position of United States consular agent, sent in 1858 to the secretary of state.[66] And there were others who caused the consul in Beirut (in 1843) to ask the secretary of state for directives: "How am I to act when any crazy and distressed citizen of the U.S. comes into this country? There are several of them of late arriving with regular passport in their hands and going to Jerusalem with strange ideas in their heads that our Savior is coming this year into the world to judge the people and they are quite unprovided of the means of living, become an annoyance to the people, and place me also in an aucward [sic] position, as your honor will perceive."[67]

In 1881, Consul Willson confirmed the information that: "Mr. Hoffman the founder of the German Colonies is now in America soliciting emigrants to Palestine of German residents in the States," and added:

---

65 Dudman,"American Colony in Jerusalem," pp.168–72; Spafford-Vester, *Our Jerusalem*. On the opposing interests and the quarrels between the people of the American Colony in Jerusalem and the consuls, Selah Merrill and Edwin Wallace, see extensive correspondence in USNA RG59 T471/5–9.

66 Cass,"J.S. Murad," pp.3–4; Olin, *Travels in Egypt*, 2:318.

67 Jasper Chasseaud, U.S. Consul, Beirut, to Daniel Webster, Secretary of State, Washington, D.C., 6 September 1843, USNA RG59 T367/1.

There have been also during the last two years, three heralds, or reporters or agents, one is now here, representing a proposed American Colony from the neighborhood of Boston. The enterprise, should it be inaugurated, can only result in failure. It is not in the order of nature to move from a country where land is abundant, and wages dear to a country where land is scarce and title insecure, and wages low. Besides, the semitropical character of the climate is not adapted to outdoor work by emigrants from the Northern States.[68]

Apparently, among the religious groups which, according to the consul, ought to be discouraged from settling in a land so uncongenial, were also Mormons. This was borne out in an article published in German by Conrad Schick in 1881, to the effect that " Recently, emissaries of American sects have arrived who also have thoughts of colonization, not dissimilar to those of the Temple Society. Even several Mormons have come to buy a piece of land in order to found and build up a Mormon settlement (on the Jaffa road) about half-way between here [Jerusalem] and Jaffa. The land laws will not be able to hinder them in carrying out their intentions, as is the case in America." [69]

The special character of the Holy Land attracted a singular type of American settler. The consular officials who had to deal with the problems of such individuals and groups, whose numbers over the years never amounted to more than a few hundred, derived no gratification from these fellow-citizens. A good illustration of such a case was the relationship of the consul in Jerusalem and the consular agent in Jaffa with the people of the Adams colony in Jaffa.

The Consulate and the American Colony at Jaffa
These people – 157 Americans from Maine – led by George Washington Joshua Adams who had founded the Church of the Messiah, landed in Jaffa in September 1866. Their intention to found there an agricultural colony was short-lived; the colony lasted barely one year. Soon after arrival, the settlers,

---

68 Joseph G. Willson, U.S. Consul, Jerusalem, to Robert R. Taft, Assistant Secretary of State, Washington, D.C., 7 October 1881, USNA RG59 T471/5. A Mrs. Davis visited Jerusalem on behalf of this Boston group, and see: Gustafson,"Records in the National Archives," p.131.

69 Schick,"Studien," p.60. In 1897 and 1898, the Mormons made another attempt at acquiring land for setting up a station in Palestine.

who had believed the glowing accounts of their leader, were beset by tragic difficulties. According to the consular reports, thirteen persons, mostly young children, died during the first few months. By the middle of 1867, most of them wanted to return to the United States. Their lack of means necessitated financial help, and all but a few families eventually returned to New England. Adams and his wife left Jaffa in June 1868.[70] This is not the place to trace this attempt at settling in Palestine and to analyze the causes for its failure. But the episode illuminates the relationship, for better or worse, between the members and their leader and with the American consular officials in the region and outside it. The financial aspects of this abortive undertaking were not resolved until 1886, and the consular officials in Jerusalem and in Jaffa continued to extend civil and legal services to those settlers who remained in Palestine – and to their descendants – until the end of the Ottoman period and even afterwards (Plates 25 and 26).[71]

Extensive correspondence concerning the Adams colony is preserved in the American consular archives in Jerusalem and Jaffa. This matter occupied much of the attention of the United States diplomatic and consular officials in Palestine, Syria, Turkey, and Egypt during 1867–1868. The Representatives for the State of Maine intervened in the affair, as did Secretary of State William H. Seward. Over one hundred documents, dated between 1868 and 1886, have been found to deal with this subject, mainly relating to four central issues: contacts with the Ottoman authorities, contacts with the consular officials, matters relating to the lands of the colony, and its internal affairs. On the subject of the local administration, the minister of the United States at Constantinople, E. Joy Morris, was involved by informing the newcomers that they had been refused a firman (imperial order) permitting them to settle.[72] The pasha of Jerusalem wrote to the American consul in that city expressing his and the vali's concern at the establishment of a settlement and at the acquisition and cultivation of land by foreigners without a firman. The consul replied that there was no room for concern since it was a matter of settlement by a small number of private persons on land that was not theirs,

---

70   The story of this settlement attempt is related in full in: Holmes, *The Forerunners*.

71   Among these were the members of the Clark family (see: Kark,"Historical Sites," pp.1–17) and the Floyd family (see: Parsons, *Letters from Palestine*).

72   Declaration of Hermann J. Loewenthal, U.S. Consular Agent, Jaffa informing G.J. Adams on 22 September 1866 of E. Joy Morris's letter, 25 September 1866, USNA RG59 T471/2.

and that as American citizens they should not be discriminated against any more than were other European settlers in the Empire.[73] The Americans naively believed that by becoming Ottoman subjects they could resolve the problem of Ottoman administrative opposition to their settlement, and Adams

Plate 25. Adams's American colony which later became the
German Templer colony near Jaffa.
Source: Manning, *Those Holy Fields*

and some of his followers visited the pasha in order to apprise him of their intentions. That dignitary requested them to apply in writing. The outraged Beauboucher placed Adams under house arrest for twenty-four hours in order to drive home to him the damage he would cause, and to discuss with him internal matters and accusations against him by some of the colonists. None of the Americans changed citizenship.[74]

---

73 Correspondence between Victor Beauboucher, U.S. Consul, Jerusalem and Izzat Pasha, Ottoman Governor, Jerusalem, 19 and 21 November 1866, USNA RG59 T471/2.

74 Ibid., 28 January and 23 March 1867.

Plate 26. Prefabricated, wooden house from Maine erected
in the Adams colony in 1866-67.
Source: Photographed by Kark, 1977

This was but one of the confrontations between Adams and his followers and the consul at Jerusalem and the consular agent at Jaffa. The latter, in fact, tried to help resolve the many problems besetting the colony – the growing debts to the Ottoman government for taxes on their crops and to various private persons in Jaffa, the internal squabbles in the colony, and the like. All of this caused denigrating letters and requests for the removal of the consul and the consular agent to be sent to the State Department in Washington. As a result, the legation in Constantinople and the consulates-general at Beirut, and later at Alexandria, sent Augustus J. Johnson and Charles Hale to investigate and report on the situation in Jaffa. When they too were subjected to slanderous accusations by the unfortunate settlers, the secretary of state asked one of his friends who happened to be in the region to conduct a "neutral" investigation of the matter.[75]

As the conditions of the settlers worsened, even approaching hunger, Loewenthal, Beauboucher, and Hale took steps to obtain donations, including personal gifts by themselves, and to assist those families who wished to return to the United States. In order to meet the needs for assisting and caring for these people, Beauboucher borrowed $2,590 at 12 percent annual interest from the Jaffa banker, Antuan Bishara Tayan, in the expectation that these expenses would be reimbursed later. He never imagined that this matter

75 30 March 1867, 21, 30, 31 May 1867, 8 June 1867, USNA RG59 T471/2.

would drag on and that the capital and interest which came to $3,618.80 in gold, in 1870, would only be repaid to him (and returned to Tayan?) in March 1886 – minus the accrued interest.[76] Moreover, the consul was left with the debts incurred by Adams to private persons in Jaffa amounting to thousands of dollars, including debts owed to the kaimakam of Jaffa for government taxes on produce.[77]

The Jaffa consular agents Hermann J. Loewenthal, and after him, John B. Hay and Ernst Hardegg were much occupied with the colony's land problems from the time the land was acquired from the Greek A. Baramky with Loewenthal's help. The settlers' houses occupied the greater part of this land, which was bought at a price of 43,379 piasters ($1,735.16) but never actually paid.[78] Joint ownership of land by different settlers, registration, and final payments to the sellers compounded the difficulties regarding the legal status of these lands under the prevailing Ottoman regulations. It engendered the negative attitude of the authorities to the acquisition and registration of lands by foreigners. Moreover, until 1874, no signed agreement existed between the United States and the Sublime Porte in these matters. In 1869, the few remaining colonists on the site were joined by Templer settlers who established there their own colony. Further correspondence with A. Baramky, A.B. Tayan, and others dealing with land registration and payment of debts, and with the consular agent in Jaffa and the consul-general at Constantinople was carried on until the end of the 1870s.[79]

---

76   28 January, 30 May, 27 July 1867, 20 October and 24 December 1869, 4 and 27 January 1870 and 1 July 1870, USNA RG59 T471/2; Senate Reports, 49th Congress, 1st Session, Document No. 234, 17 March 1886. Tayan eventually became one of the biggest landowners in Palestine and sold lands to Jews at Petah Tiqvah (Melabbes) and Rehovoth (Duran). Members of his family later sold lands in Emeq Hefer (Wadi Hawareth).

77   8 October 1867 and 20 March and 31 May 1869, USNA RG59 T471/2,.

78   USNA RG84 Jaffa Miscellaneous Record Book 1866–1910 Box 5948, many entries between November 1866 and March 1873.

79   24 June, 3 July 1872, 24 April, 7 July and 5 December 1874, USNA RG84 Jaffa Official and Miscellaneous Letters Received 1872–74 Box 5958, and 7 November 1879, Miscellaneous Letters Received 1874–1879 Box 5959.

Services to American Jewish Settlers

Defending the Rights of Jewish-American Settlers in Galilee – The Lubowsky Family
The case of the Lubowsky family illustrates well three matters of principle:
the status of American citizens, American citizenship, and land and settlement
in Galilee. Their story exemplifies the operations at the level of consular
agent, consul-general, of the embassy in Constantinople, and of the State
Department in Washington in dealing with American citizens in northern
Palestine. It entailed assuring the extraterritorial rights of American citizens
vis-à-vis the Ottoman authorities, bestowing of citizenship rights, and the
extension of American protection to certain persons.

By reconstructing evidence from various documents of the 1880's, it
appears that Mordecai Yitzhak Lubowsky was a former land owner and
businessman from Sejny in Lithuania. Lubowsky and his family probably
emigrated to the United States in the 1870's and were naturalized there. In
September 1884 Lubowsky arrived in Palestine in order to join a group of
emissaries of the Hovevei Zion Society from the Polish-Lithuanian town
Suwalki, with whom he had been associated before going to America, with
the object of buying land for settlement. He toured the country with some of
the emissaries, and even tried to acquire with them lands in Meron, Gush
Halav and Arbel. Eventually he left their company and, on 12 November
1884, bought with his own money a large tract of land of 2,800 dunams at
"Maroun" (meaning, the Waters of Merom – the Hula Valley) in the district
of Safed. The land was bought from Ya'aqov Hai 'Abu, a wealthy Jew of
Safed who served as the French consular agent in that town. Lubowsky
named the place Shoshanat Hayarden ("Lily of the Jordan") because of its
situation on the bank of the Jordan River (near the Bridge of Jacob's Daughters),
and intended setting up a private estate for his family – or perhaps, as some
would have it, an American-style cattle ranch. The recently-founded Yessud
Hama'alah moshava (smallholder settlement) served as base for Lubowsky
and his two sons who arrived in Safed at the beginning of May 1885, and for
the rest of the family, the wife and two daughters, who came later that
year.[80]

The arrival of the family should be seen against the background of Ottoman
policy. From 1882, the Turks shut the gates of the country to Jewish immigration
and settlement and prohibited the acquisition of land by Jews. In particular,

---

80 For details of the purchase of land and settlement see, Aaronsohn and Kark,"Rose of the Jordan,"
   pp.55–57 and Wisch,"Simon Berman," pp.17–24.

this policy was emphasized in a proclamation on 8 April 1884 forbidding the immigration of Jews of any nationality, except for pilgrims who were restricted to a stay of thirty days. The ambassadors of the foreign powers in Constantinople, and the consuls and consular agents in Jerusalem, Jaffa, and Haifa acted on instructions from their foreign offices in Austria, Germany, Britain, and the United States. In accordance with the terms of their respective capitulatory agreements with the Ottoman Empire, they insisted emphatically on the abrogation of the discriminatory policy against the Jews.[81] How these decrees affected the Lubowskys emerges from correspondence of the second half of 1885 preserved in the files of the United States consular agency in Haifa,[82] and in a compendium of documents collected by Oscar Solomon Straus, who in the years 1887–89 and 1898–99 served as minister, and in 1909–10 as U.S. ambassador in Constantinople.[83]

In May 1885, Lubowsky's two sons, Louis and Jacob, arrived in Safed in order to help their father establish themselves on the land he had acquired in Galilee. In a letter of complaint to Jacob Schumacher, the American vice-consul in Haifa, Louis related the attempt to extort from them, despite their being American citizens, money for *"tascorey"* (travel permits), the intention to arrest his brother Jacob, and the announcement of the kaimakam of Safed that they must leave the country within ten days and hand over 400 Turkish pounds as security for their departure.[84] Louis asked the vice-consul to protect their rights as American citizens and Schumacher, with the help of his dragoman in Acre, B. Cardahi, immediately addressed a protest to Ziwar Pasha, the mutasarrif of the Acre district, against the action of the kaimakam in Safed regarding the Lubowsky brothers: "This act being in opposition to the regulations & treaties existing..." [85] The mutasarrif replied to Schumacher that the kaimakam of Safed acted "...according to the instructions he has to prevent the Jews coming from all countries to establish themselves in Palestine, that this is a political measure taken by the Sublime Porte." The mutasarrif

---

81 Eliav,"Diplomatic Intervention," pp.117–32.

82 USNA RG84 Haifa Miscellaneous and Official Correspondence Received 1875–1917 Miscellaneous Papers 1878–1903 Green Box.

83 "Foreign Relations: Diplomatic Correspondence of the U.S. with Turkey, Having Reference to the Jews, 1840–1901," *JNUL* MS V810.

84 Louis Lubowsky, Safed, to Jacob Schumacher, U.S. Vice-Consul, Haifa, 27 May 1885, Miscellaneous and Official Correspondence Received, ibid.

85 Jacob Schumacher, U.S. Vice-Consul, Haifa, to the mutasarrif of Acca, 29 May 1885 (Arabic), ibid.

rejected the dragoman's arguments that the prohibition applied only to Russian and Romanian Jews. Accordingly, Cardahi anticipated the refusal of the mutasarrif to annul the expulsion order against the Lubowskys, "...considering the fanaticism of the mutasarrif and his ill disposition to the foreigners..." and suggested that Schumacher report the matter to the American consul-general in Beirut.[86] Jacob Schumacher telegraphed to the consul-general and at the same time again tried to approach Ziwar Pasha with the argument that "I beg to state that a Jew, if once a citizen of the United States, enjoys the same rights as the believer in any other religion, and I therefore energetically protest against any such action... which is a violation of the treaty between the Sublime Porte and the United States of America, which treaty allows citizens of both respective powers to reside untroubled in either of the countries, and I leave the execution of the order you mention to the entire responsibility of your excellency." [87] When the telegram reached the consul-general in Beirut, John T. Robeson, he sent a protest against exile, on 1 August 1885, to the governor-general of Syria.[88] From the beginning of August until November 1885, correspondence regarding the principle raised by the Lubowsky brothers' case was exchanged between the consul-general in Beirut, the consul-general in Constantinople, G.H. Heap, the U.S. chargé d'affaires at Constantinople, W.C. Emmet, the U.S. minister of the legation at Constantinople, Samuel S. Cox, and Secretary of State Thomas F. Bayard.[89] All these officials backed one another, and the documents underlined their determined position in two matters: One, that people cannot be expelled without legal procedures: "Their expulsion would be without the process of law and conviction of crime or misdemeanor would be illegal and in violation of international comity, treaties, and capitulations." The second point was that American citizens could not be discriminated against only because they belonged to a certain religion, as

86   Ahmed Ziwar Pasha, Mutasarrif of Acca, to Jacob Schumacher, U.S. Vice-Consul, Haifa, [29] May 1885 and Bishara Cardahi, U.S. Dragoman, Acre to Schumacher, 30 May 1885, ibid. (Arabic).

87   Jacob Schumacher, U.S. Consular Agent, Haifa, to Ziwar Pasha, Mutasarrif of Acca, 31 July 1885 (Arabic), ibid.

88   John T. Robeson, U.S. Consul-General, Beirut, to Governor-General, 1 August 1885, ibid.

89   G.H. Heap, U.S. Consul-General, Constantinople, to John T. Robeson, U.S. Consul, Beirut, 6 and 19 August and 1 September 1885; Robeson to Heap, 6, 7, 14 August 1885; Thomas F. Bayard, Secretary of State, Washington D.C., to Samuel S. Cox, U.S. Minister, Constantinople, 29 August and 15 October 1885; Cox to Bayard, 24 September and 3 November 1885; Heap to Cox, 21 September 1885,"Foreign Relations," ibid.

stated by the secretary of state in a letter of August, to the effect that the U.S. asks and expects "that no race or class distinction shall be made as regards American citizens abroad", and in his letter in October that: "This Government cannot assent to any religious test being applied to the citizens of the United States by any power whatever." The Lubowsky (or as it appears in some of the correspondence "Lubrowsky") brothers were advised not to give in to the Turkish authorities and to oppose the expulsion. Despite this unequivocal support, one of the brothers, Jacob, returned to America in August "owing to ill-treatment and sickness." But Louis remained in Safed and the authorities did not expel him. The determined American action brought positive results in this case, and, as was hoped, would serve as a precedent in other cases.[90]

Despite the delays in transferring the land of Shoshanat Hayarden and in obtaining building permits, and with all the difficulties faced by private individuals settling in hostile surroundings, Mordecai and Louis began their work which continued for about two years. According to some sources, a well was dug at Shoshanat Hayarden, stables for horses were erected and a small house was built. One of the Lubowsky sons (probably Louis; see below) lived there for an unknown period. It is not clear what Lubowsky and his son did besides watching over part of the land that was farmed out to Arab sharecroppers in return for the usual one-fifth of the crop. At one point, perhaps when they came to realize that they would not be able to carry out their plans for a cattle ranch, they considered other uses for their settlement, which was situated on the important road crossing the Jordan. They raised money in Europe and apparently rented the khan at the nearby Bridge of Jacob's Daughters, intending to rehabilitate it as a hotel. However, all the plans failed, and the private entrepreneurs were forced in 1888 to leave the Shoshanat Hayarden lands and move to Yessud Hama'alah. In 1890, Mordecai sold part of his land to David Shub, one of the founders of the Jewish settlement, Rosh Pinna. Shub divided the land he bought into eighteen tracts of one hundred dunams each, and rented these to agricultural workers of Safed who established there the moshava Mishmar Hayarden ("Guard of the Jordan").[91]

---

90 Heap to Robeson, 19 August 1885 and Cox to Bayard, 3 November 1885, ibid. It is interesting to note that even two and a half months after Jacob left, the correspondence keeps dealing with the two brothers, probably because of the important principles raised by the case.

91 The descendants of Louis's family live to this day in Yessud Hamaalah; Aaronsohn,"Stages in the Development," pp.38–39, 54.

Another collection of documents, in the U.S. National Archives in Washington, entitled "Case Lubowsky Safed" shows that at the end of 1902, new problems arose with the Ottoman administration regarding the lands that remained in the hands of Mordecai Yitzhak Lubowsky (the former Shoshanat Hayarden).[92] Mordecai empowered his son Louis, who had remained in Galilee (at Kafr "Zubeir" [probably Zbeid] in the Safed district), to represent him in all administrative and legal matters, including this one. This was witnessed by two persons and apparently was later ratified by the consular agent in Haifa, where Mordecai was living at the time.[93] From Louis's appeal to the American consular agent in Haifa, Gottlieb Schumacher, in November 1902, it transpires that the kaimakam of Safed issued an order at the behest of the vali of Beirut for Mordecai Lubowsky "...to give over, within ten days, the land which he holds many years, and the houses built upon it a few years ago to Mr. Abraham Elstein, an Ottoman subject of Beirut." Regarding this order, which according to Lubowsky, "is contrary to the treaties of the Powers," he requested the consular agent, Gottlieb Schumacher, "to take steps for its cancellation and to assure his rights as an American citizen and to turn to the relevant court of justice in such matters for protest and action." [94] The paucity of documentation leaves unclear the background to the order and what happened. At any rate, it seems that this time, the American consular authorities did not respond with the same alacrity and sympathy as in 1885. When Max (Mordecai)[95] and Louis Lubowsky applied in December 1902 to Schumacher for American protection, the latter refused – and this with the backing of the mission in Constantinople and of the consul-general in Beirut, G. Bie Ravndal. The reason given for the refusal was that Lubowsky lived in Palestine since 2 May 1885: "Not being a missionary nor a merchant engaged in trade with the United States his continued sojourn abroad without any apparent intention of returning to the United

---

92 The correspondence is in an envelope entitled,"Case Lubowsky Safed," USNA RG84 Haifa Miscellaneous and Official Correspondence Received 1875–1917 Miscellaneous Papers 1873–1903 Green Box.

93 M.I. Lubowsky, Haifa, Power of Attorney to Lewis Lubowsky, 12 November 1902, (Arabic) and another version (English), ibid.; Zbeid (or as given in the letter,"Zubeir") was an Arab village near the Jewish settlement, Yessud Hamaalah.

94 M.I. Lubowsky, Haifa, to U.S. Consular Agent, Haifa, 12 November 1902, (Arabic), ibid.

95 According to Bartour, ("American Consular Aid," pp.302–3) Mordechai Yitzhak was also called Max, but no other evidence was found to that effect.

States, deprived him of any right to claim protection of the United States Government." Behind this official reason, there was another consideration, which seems to have been connected with the new Ottoman regulations regarding Jewish immigration and ownership of real estate in Palestine that came into effect in January 1902. This transpires from Ravndal's letter to Schumacher: "Pending telegraphic advice from Constantinople as to how to treat Mr. Louis Lubowsky I gave it out that the present case was one affecting real estate in which matters Ottoman jurisdiction is exclusive. I am now prepared to give the real reason for my reluctance to intervene. Your views as to foreign intervention even in real estate affairs are shared in this office." [96]

Thus it appears that in the case of settlement attempts by a private family, the difficulties placed in its way eventually brought on a retreat from its original intent. However, it is important to point out that the members of the family remained as settlers in Yessud Hama'alah and Haifa, and that the lands acquired by them formed the basis of a Jewish settlement, Mishmar Hayarden, in 1890.

The Jerusalem Community and Kolel America
The small numbers of American citizens of Jewish faith who until the mid 1870s lived in Jerusalem, Safed, and Tiberias received the same civil, legal, and other services as did all other American citizens. Except for Warder Cresson, the unconfirmed first American consul who converted to Judaism and established a family in Jerusalem, most of the American Jews were naturalized, European-born immigrants to the United States who subsequently settled with their families in the Holy Land.

One of the outstanding personalities among the Jewish Americans in Jerusalem, in the years 1846 until his death in 1874, was Benjamin Lilienthal. Born in Bavaria in 1805, a merchant by occupation, Lilienthal came to New York in 1841 and five years thereafter was naturalized as an American citizen. He then moved to Jerusalem and fathered there seven children who according to the 1868 census of American citizens registered at the consulate ranged

---

96 Gabriel Bie Ravndal, U.S. Consul, Beirut, to Gottlieb Schumacher, U.S. Consular Agent, Haifa,
    1 December 1902, Correspondence Received from the Consulate, Beirut, USNA RG84 Haifa Green
    Box 1873–1903, ibid.

from three months to twenty years of age.[97] Since none of his family returned to live in the United States, the confirmation of their citizenship raised a problem of principle regarding persons who never lived or stayed in America, despite having been registered on birth as American citizens at the consulate as stipulated by law. In the early years of the 20th century, the State Department refused to confirm Lilienthal's son as a citizen born to an American citizen. This approach derived from the changed attitudes of consuls and consular agents at the turn of the century in all matters relating to the services extended to American-Jewish citizens. [98] Besides the personal services provided to the American Jewish citizens by the Jerusalem consulate, the consuls also helped in Jewish public and communal affairs deriving from their separate identity, with the collection and distribution of funds, their productive employment, and settlement. The involvement of the foreign consuls generally, and of the American consuls in particular, in such parochial activities should be seen in the light of the peculiar Jewish communal structure in 19th century Palestine. The Jewish community consisted of a number of self-contained, close-knit groupings intimately connected with the various Diaspora communities from which they originated. These communal groupings were known as "kolels" (the plural Hebrew form is *kolelim*) comprising families and individuals from a particular town or district in the Diaspora who received a distribution of funds (*halukkah*) contributed there for the support of their people in the Holy Land. The funds were apportioned, and the internal affairs of the kolel administered, by head men for each kolel. This fragmented organizational structure was compatible with, and was reinforced by the capitulatory system and the consequent rights of protection exercised by the foreign consuls. And, except for a general roof organization, it effectively prevented any unifying process within the Jewish community as a whole. In 1868, the American acting consul, Lorenzo M. Johnson, was a member of the committee set up for distributing funds collected in America: "Two intelligent American Jews visited Jerusalem with a view of distributing considerable money...This plan (to settle Jews on lands adjoining the city) met with their approval, and in leaving the city, they appointed a banker, a physician, and myself to act as a committee, for the distribution of such funds as might be hereafter sent from America."[99]

---

97 List of All American Citizens Under the Jerusalem Consul, 31 December 1868, USNA RG59 T471/2.

98 Bartour,"Episodes," pp.121–28.

99 Lorenzo M. Johnson, U.S. Acting Consul, Jerusalem, to William H. Seward, Secretary of State,

In the 1860s and 1870s, with the intensified emigration of Jews from Eastern Europe to America, the United States became a major source of funds for the support of institutions and private persons in the Holy Land. Among the beneficiaries of this new resource were the Va'ad Ha-Kelali – the general committee of all the kolels, founded in 1866. However, those Jews in Palestine who were American citizens felt slighted by their low status and their share of the distribution which did not reflect the amounts sent from America (which they considered as their country of origin in the Diaspora). They enlisted the help (in 1879) of the U.S. consul in Jerusalem, J.G. Willson, in an attempt to form an independent American kolel, and prepared a book of by-laws which was sanctioned by him. The new kolel, named "Shelom Yerushalayim – Community of Peace" competed with the Va'ad Ha-Kelali for funds raised in America. But the attempt failed when the State Department rejected their petition to intercede on their behalf with the American Jewish community.[100]

The failure to establish an American kolel exacerbated the discrimination against the American Jews in Jerusalem, and they received none of the funds collected in the United States. In 1882, in the name of thirty American families, Simon Bermann presented the United States minister in Constantinople, Lewis Wallace, during the latter's visit to Jerusalem, with the request that the thousands of dollars transmitted through the consulate be remitted to them rather than to the rabbis and other irresponsible officials who "first help themselves and their relatives." Bermann also applied to Consul Selah Merrill to "...erect an American house of Industry [that] may serve to instruct the young in some useful trade to enable them to work and make an honest living, the profits of such institution will serve to assist the poor, sick, and old men...."[101] Lew Wallace tried to help the applicants and sent a letter to the secretary of state in which he suggested bringing the

---

Washington, D.C., 30 September 1868, USNA RG59 T471/2. For a detailed study on the Jewish community between the years 1800 and 1882, see: Gat, *The Jewish Yishuv in Eretz-Israel* and Parfitt, *The Jews in Palestine*.

100 Heads of the American Kolel in Jerusalem (4 signatures) to Third Assistant Secretary of State, Washington, D.C., 22 Iyar 5639 (1879), USNA RG59 T471 in Bartour,"American Consular Aid," pp.305–6 and Fishbane,"Kolel America," pp.120–136.

101 Simon Bermann, Jerusalem, to General [Lew] Wallace, Ambassador of the U.S. to the Sublime Porte in Constantinople, 13 November 1882, AJHS RG Solomons Box 2 Miscellaneous File P-28. Simon Bermann was known at the time for his (failed) attempts at establishing a Jewish agricultural colony in Galilee.

matter to the knowledge of "influential Israelites" in New York or Philadelphia, to "shrewd Jewish businessmen" in America, and to the press. The concluding remarks in his letter are interesting: "Now I know very well this is not a matter in which the President can officially interest himself; neither is it in any degree a Governmental matter; yet I presume to trouble you with it, thinking it of interest to the thousands of Israelites who, while good citizens of our country, very naturally remember the land of their fathers, and care greatly that justice may be done there as well as elsewhere."[102] The State Department indeed tried to act along Wallace's recommendations, and brought the contents of his and Simon Bermann's correspondence to the attention of at least one of the American Jewish communal and welfare leaders, Adolphus S. Solomons, in whose archives it has remained.[103]

In 1896, the leaders of the American and Canadian Jewish community in Jerusalem, which had grown to about one thousand souls, made another attempt at establishing their own kolel, this time naming it "Colel America Tiphereth Jeruscholaim" (The American Congregation—the Pride of Jerusalem). This kolel eventually became an important factor in the demise of the entire halukkah system and brought the conflicts within the Old Yishuv to a head. In the renewed – this time successful – struggle for setting up an American kolel, and allocating the great amounts of money contributed in the United States to its members, Consul Edwin S. Wallace played an important role. Although Rabbi Joshua Diskin, who was chosen to head the new kolel, was of Russian nationality, Wallace extended American consular protection to him. The agreement reached with the Va'ad Ha-Kelali stipulated that two-thirds of the American halukkah funds would go to the Va'ad, and the remaining third to be distributed by the American kolel. In view of the smaller numbers of people in the new kolel relative to the many European and other Jews, the former's share of the American funds was proportionately greater.[104] During the first decade of the 20th century, the American kolel built a housing

102 Lew Wallace, U.S. Minister, Constantinople, to Frederick T. Frelinghuysen, Secretary of State, Washington, D.C., 12 January 1883, ibid.

103 John Davis, Department of State, Washington, D.C., to A.S. Solomons, Washington, D.C., 12 February 1883, ibid.

104 Fishbane,"Kolel America," pp.120–136; Bartour,"American Consular Aid," p.299. Bartour believes that the total amount of assistance from America to the Jews of Palestine between 1880 and 1890 amounted to about one-half million dollars. This seems too high. According to one source, in 1913, Kolel America numbered 485 souls. (See Freiman, *Jerusalem Memory Book*, p.60.)

project for its members in Jerusalem – the "Ahvah" neighborhood – and established a separate burial plot on the Mount of Olives by the "Agudat Achim Anshe America" (American Brotherhood).

The United States consul in Jerusalem, Thomas Wallace, also helped a group of the Old Yishuv of persons from Hungary – not Americans – after becoming convinced of their constructive objectives. This was the "Kehillat Jacob Society for Agriculture Interest in the Holy Land," which he regarded as a philanthropic enterprise worthy of his endorsement, since it enhanced opportunities for self-support by self-labor instead of dispensing charity. Wallace urged helping this society because as a result of its activities on behalf of the Jews of Jerusalem, "The economic, social, and sanitary conditions of their lives would be greatly improved if changed from the present conditions in which they live, to the farm, the gardens, and the orchards."[105]

At the beginning of the 20th century, many Jews settled also in Jaffa and Tel Aviv, and under the aegis of the American consular agent, Jacob Hardegg, who became an honorary member, the American Club of Jaffa was formed by American citizens. The objectives of the Club were to unite and assist citizens, and to aid and encourage commercial relations between the U.S. and Palestine. The heads of this club who appear on its letterhead, were all Jews (judging from their names), apparently businessmen of Jaffa and Tel Aviv. Their declared aims reflected the growth of Jaffa into an important port town of the eastern Mediterranean (Plate 27).[106]

In conclusion, it appears that the services provided by the American consuls in Jerusalem to Jewish-American citizens went at times beyond the limits of the usual consular activities, and passed into the realm of political and social involvement in the internal affairs of the Jerusalem Jewish community.

---

105 Thomas R. Wallace in Bartour, ibid., pp.308, 369 (27 May 1909) and same in YIBZ RG4/2/50/01.

106 USNA RG84 Jaffa Miscellaneous Records 1911–1915 Miscellaneous Correspondence from the American Club Jaffa 1914–1915.

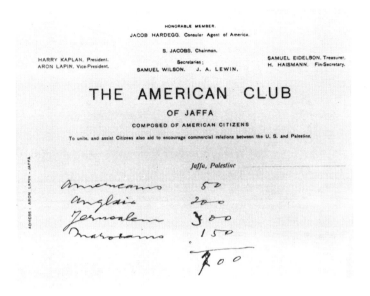

Plate 27. Letterhead of the American Club at Jaffa
Source: USNA RG84 Jaffa

SERVICES TO LOCAL JEWISH PROTÉGÉS

It was common practice during the 19th century for the various consulates in the Levant and in Palestine to extend consular protection over Christians – and especially Jews – without looking too closely at the documents attesting to the origins of such persons. Thus was created in the consulates of the foreign powers a distinction between actual citizens and protégés who were de facto citizens. The latter included persons who were stateless or who had relinquished their former nationality. Protégés were registered at the consulates and were issued special certificates entitling them to consular protection in everything relating to their personal security and in juridical and administrative matters, as though they were citizens. The benefits extended also to economic privileges.[107] This practice was usually endorsed by the governments of Great Britain, France, Austria, and Prussia, all of which had an interest in claiming maximal numbers of protégés to justify broadening their influence in Palestine.

107 Eliav, *Eretz Israel*, pp.104–109; Fawaz, *Merchants and Migrants*, pp.85–92.

In addition to such political considerations were also religious (and perhaps missionary) and humanitarian motives, causing Russian Jews in Jerusalem to become English, Austrian, and Prussian protégés. In 1839, Lord Palmerston instructed the first British consul in Jerusalem "to afford protection to the Jews generally," and extending it, by 1848, to cover certain Polish Jews who had been Russian subjects, as well as to Europeans who, having no other consular protection, had asked the British consul to take them under his wing.[108] But even admitting initially laudable motives, this practice soon led to blatant abuses as corrupt and ambitious foreign consuls sought to bring in as many local persons as possible under their protection.[109] The Ottoman authorities frequently expressed their dissatisfaction (to say the least), protested against the harm to the Empire, and complained about "some consuls without conscience who invite such persons in order to keep them under their protection."[110]

During the first years of its existence, the American consulate at Jerusalem had very limited contacts with the Jews there. There were but few Christian and Jewish protected persons, and these made no particular demands upon the attention of the consuls and of the consular agents. In view of the traditional American policy of non-intervention, and the known interests of the Ottoman administration in minimizing the practice, Washington and its diplomatic representatives in the Levant followed no clearly formulated policy on the granting of consular protection to individuals and groups. The subject sometimes gave rise to differences between the consuls in Jerusalem and the higher diplomatic echelons in Constantinople and Washington. When, in the 1860s, Consul Page granted letters of protection to Jews in Jerusalem at his own initiative, the minister at Constantinople forced him to resign, in 1861, after only one year in office.[111] Consul Beauboucher, himself an American protégé, granted de facto protection to Jews in Jerusalem and Jaffa and to their families who came from Poland, Germany, Serbia, and Morocco. His report to the State Department, states that the ten families in question met the American consular conditions for qualification as protected persons: "They are scrupulously honest and in every respect worthy of the protection of the

---

108 Eliav, ibid.; Platt, *The Cinderella Service*, pp.138–9.

109 Platt, ibid. Platt adduces statistics for tens of thousands of persons protected by Britain throughout the Levant during the first decades of the 19th century.

110 Ottoman Report on the Consuls, 4 December 1872 (unsigned), ISA RG83 (Turkish).

111 Bartour,"Episodes," pp.111–13.

Consulate which is renewable at the discretion of the Consul." However, the consul-general at Beirut thought differently, and after several months rescinded the protection granted to these persons, since he did not consider it compatible with the instructions of the Department of State.[112]

The cases of Jews – in part, converts to Christianity – who during the 1860s applied to the United States consulate at Jerusalem for protection, multiplied markedly in the 1870s and included mainly European Ashkenazim. In 1877, Consul DeHass issued certificates of protection and passports to about five hundred Jewish families who, impelled by the hardships they suffered as a result of the Balkan wars, offered to pay large sums (according to one version) for American consular protection and security over their persons and property.[113] The Ottoman Imperial Ministry of Foreign Affairs protested this move on 28 February 1878, claiming that in his list of American citizens, DeHass also included many Jews who were Ottoman subjects. Accordingly, the American legation at Constantinople requested DeHass to resign and ordered the new consul, Willson, to cancel the certificates of nationality his predecessor had granted to persons who were not American citizens. Nevertheless, both Willson and Merrill after him, had to deal with the DeHass protégés and their descendants for many years.[114] These Jews, who despite having paid good money were denied American protection, accused their former benefactor. DeHass rejected their contentions, declaring that he had acted out of humanitarian motives to help the Jews who were liable to arrest and mistreatment by the Turkish authorities, and only collected the regular fee fixed by Congress. Moreover, he denied deducting any commission on funds transmitted through the consulate for the relief of poor Jews in Jerusalem. In consequence, the consuls were warned by the State Department not to engage in such activities at their own initiative, and in the 1880s, supervisory measures over them were tightened:

112 Victor Beauboucher, U.S. Consul, Jerusalem, to Department of State, Washington, D.C., 31 December 1868 and Johnson's comment, 1 August (1869?), USNA RG59 T471/2.

113 Bartour,"American Consular Aid," pp.284–304. Bartour adduces a name list of such protected persons from the consular archives and from newspaper clippings of 1877. See also several articles in *The Jewish Chronicle*: 29 June, 2 November, 28 December 1877, and 11 January 1878.

114 Manuel, *The Realities*, pp.42–43; at the end of 1877, an 8-page list by Consul J.G. Willson with a random number (not consecutive numbers), names, and ages of the protégés. Joseph G. Willson, U.S. Consul, Jerusalem, to William Hunter, Second Assistant Secretary of State, Washington, D.C., 28 December 1877, USNA RG59 T471/4.

Abuses which have heretofore occurred in granting protection from the local authority in eastern countries, and especially in the Turkish dominions, to persons who, in the opinion of this Department, have no claim thereto, render it advisable that the Legation and Consulates there should, once in six months, report the number, names, and occupations of all persons to whom, during the six months preceding, such protection may have been given, or by whom it may have been claimed.[115]

In the 1890s and during the first decade of the 20th century, Jews in Jerusalem sought ways – legal and illegal – to obtain American consular protection by naturalization. In 1898, the consulate had to provide services to several hundred naturalized Americans, most of them Jews. Merrill took a dim view of the latter "...some of whom" he understood to have "obtained their naturalization papers by perjury and fraud and many...were naturalized merely to obtain American protection." He shared these views with Dickinson, the consul-general in Constantinople, who visited Jerusalem in April 1898, showing him "...that they were increasing rapidly in numbers, that their many demands and frequent quarrels laid a great burden upon this Consulate, and that a considerable number of them appeared to hold passports to which they were not legally entitled." In Merrill's eyes, these Jews could not be considered "real Americans."[116]

The attitude of the American consul in Jerusalem, who, on the one hand, fought for the rights of his fellow citizens to free entry and passage in Palestine despite the Ottoman decrees, and, on the other, tried to reduce their numbers, was at best ambivalent. In 1906, the Turkish governor of Jerusalem, 'Ali Ekrem Bey, mentioned in his memorandum on Jews and the consuls that the efforts of the Ottoman authorities to prevent the entry of Jews into Palestine and the concentration of property in their hands, did not achieve desirable results, but that on the contrary, "They propel the Jews towards foreign nationality, and especially American, which is easily obtained."[117]

---

115 Personal Instructions to Diplomatic Agents, Articles xii and xiii of Personal Instructions to Diplomatic Agents Relating to Passports and Marriages, Accompanying Circular of June 29, 1885.

116 Charles Dickinson Archive, Library of Congress, 16 June 1898 in Bartour,"American Consular Aid," p.347; Selah Merrill, U.S.Consul, Jerusalem, to Thomas W. Cridler, Assistant Secretary of State, Washington, D.C., 5 March 1898, USNA RG59 T471/9 and Merrill to Ernst Hardegg, U.S. Consular Agent, Jaffa, 14 December 1906, USNA RG84 Jaffa Box 5963 in Bartour, ibid., p.338.

117 Ali Ekrem Bey, Ottoman Governor, Jerusalem, to Grand Vizier, Constantinople, 15 November 1906, ISA RG83/28 (Turkish).

Services to Transient Americans

Pilgrims and Tourists

In the course of the 19th century, Palestine became a "must" in the itineraries of many Americans traveling abroad. The country which had attracted pilgrims since ancient times, was now also a major tourist objective. As Handy and Vogel have noted, although Protestant Christians placed less emphasis on pilgrimage in the traditional sense, many sought out the scenes of Jesus's ministry and other sites with biblical associations as an act of faith. Others, who came mainly as travelers and observers of exotic lifestyles, were nevertheless affected by the cultural and spiritual connotations of the Holy Land – as was even Mark Twain, who undoubtedly was one of the most cynical.[118] This movement of travelers intensified with the founding of the large travel agencies, such as Thomas Cook & Sons, and a company established in New York by Frank C. Clark (one of the children of the Adams colonists at Jaffa), who provided relatively comfortable travel under generally primitive conditions. Frank Clark was represented in Jerusalem by his brother Herbert, who had remained in Palestine and who served as the American vice-consul in Jerusalem (and is described as such in the company's brochures). "Clark's Cruises to the Orient" in large, chartered steamships, carried 600–800 passengers every year around the world, from 1895 to 1925. Their major advertised attractions were tours of Egypt and the Holy Land.[119] The growth of tourism was, among other things, connected with the development of modern means of transport, with cultural changes and fashions, and with social and economic status.

The number of pilgrims, travelers, and tourists from the United States increased steadily from a few dozen in the 1830s and 1840s to about 250 (2 percent of a total of 12,500 pilgrims) in 1867–8, to 500–555 in 1879–81, and to 1,625 tourists (28 percent of a total of 5,759 tourists, not including some 20,000 pilgrims) in 1910–11.[120] The growth was not only in the absolute

---

118 Handy, *The Holy Land*, pp.xvi-xvii; Vogel,"Zion as Place," pp.85, 336.

119 Klatzker,"American Christian Travelers," p.29.

120 The tourist "year" generally went from June through the following May. L.M. Johnson, Jerusalem, to W.H. Seward, Washington, D.C., 30 September 1868; and J.G. Willson, Jerusalem, to R.R. Taft, Washington, D.C., 7 October 1881, USNA RG59 T471/2,4,5; Kark, *Jaffa*, pp.285-88.

numbers of American travelers, but also in relation to tourists of other nations which increased as well. So, for example, the American consul in Jerusalem, Henry Gillman, reported in 1890 that "The number of visitors to the Holy City this year largely exceeded that of any previous year. This may also be said of American visitors who greatly preponderated over those of any other nationality. The English were the next largest in number. In this statement are not considered the large bodies of pilgrims who come to worship at the sacred shrines, in thousands."[121]

An important responsibility of American consuls throughout the world was to assist American travelers. "In the 1840s," writes Mayo, "...there has been no American traveler in foreign countries who has not been indebted to consuls, if not for services, at least for useful and gratifying civilities."[122] Beyond this, according to the American consul in Genoa (in 1845), "The consul is expected to entertain his countryman, not only with hospitality, but with a considerable degree of luxury."[123]

In Palestine, providing consular services to pilgrims and tourists was one of the consuls' primary duties, particularly in view of the deficient conditions of personal security, the undeveloped infrastructure of tourist facilities – at least in the earlier years of the 19th century, and because of the special juridical status of the consuls and of the visiting foreign nationals. The annual consular report for 1868 illustrates this:

> The unusual topics considered herein have been suggested by
> the exceptional character of Palestine and duties of its Consulate.
> It is not a post of much commercial importance, but of great
> interest to the travelling public, of which comparatively little is
> known, while great curiosity exists. It is often in the power of
> Consular officers to be of great service to those who would
> understand its history, geography, and political status. The
> performance of such duties generally entails its own reward in
> the appreciation of strangers, who often spend weeks within the
> ancient walls of Jerusalem. If such duties are superfluous and

121 Henry Gillman, U.S.Consul, Jerusalem, to Department of State, Washington, D.C., 30 September 1890, USNA RG59 T471/7.

122 Mayo,"Consular System of the U.S.," p.298.

123 Edwards Lester,"The Consular System," p.216.

unofficial elsewhere, they are not so here, else the Consulate has much less importance...."[124]

According to Willson, the Jerusalem consulate had become the "Head Quarters for Americans sojourning at Jerusalem; nearly or quite five hundred names are recorded annually in our Register." And indeed, since October 1877 (except for the period from October 1914 to February 1917, during the First World War), a Register of Visitors was maintained at the consulate at Jerusalem, with Cook's First Party entered at the beginning of the first volume.[125] The consuls and consular agents assisted travelers with advice regarding the security of their persons and their effects – although not always successfully, considering the conditions prevailing in Palestine, the insecurity of the roads, and the complex relations with the Ottoman authorities. They obtained for them travel permits (*teskeras* [sic]) and saw to the engagement, where required, of armed guards to accompany them on their travels.[126]

In the mid-1860s, the American consul expressed confidence that with the help of the local government and the consulate, travelers could feel safe and protected: "It is thus that reliance may be placed upon the efficacy of the protection granted to travellers by the Local Government on the demand of the Consulate, and in consequences of the responsibility which must incessantly and invariably be imposed upon the said authorities *by the consul* and it is equally allowable to state that a trip through Palestine can be accomplished with the utmost safety and tranquility relative to brigandage!" But he himself noted that an American traveler was robbed that same year by Arabs near Nablus, although as a result of the dedicated actions of the consul the evildoers were apprehended, punished, and were even compelled to pay compensation to the victim.[127]

It was too optimistic an assessment. Robberies of Americans (and of other foreigners and local people) continued until the demise of Ottoman rule over Palestine. Such incidents occupied the American consular officials who

124 Lorenzo M. Johnson, U.S. acting Consul, Jerusaelm, to William H. Seward, Secretary of State, Washington, D.C., 30 September 1868, USNA RG59T471/2.

125 Joseph G. Willson, U.S. Consul, Jerusalem, to Robert R. Taft, Assistant Secretary of State, Washington, D.C., 7 October 1881, USNA RG59 T471/5; Register of Visitors, Vol.I (October 1877 to December 1894), USNA RG84 Jerusalem 1877–1894 [Fi8ı29]

126 Willson to Taft, ibid.

127 Victor Beauboucher, U.S. Consul, Jerusalem, to William H. Seward, Secretary of State, Washington, D.C., 24 July 1867, USNA RG59 T471/2.

represented the victims in the Turkish courts and conducted extensive correspondence with their superiors in matters relating to the protection of citizens temporarily present in the country, as will be discussed below. Cases of robbery occurred in various places in the country – outside Jerusalem, on the road between Jerusalem and Jaffa, in Jaffa, near Nazareth, in the Jordan valley, and elsewhere.[128] There were also instances when the consuls were obliged to deal with improper behavior of visiting fellow citizens, as in the case of property damaged by drunken American sailors from the U.S. sloop of war, *Alaska*, who rampaged through the streets of Jaffa in 1874.[129]

Another matter in which the consuls assisted tourists was in the drawing up of complicated contracts with local tour guides (dragomans), and specifying exact payment rates, or in dealing with complaints against tour dragomans for breach of such contracts. The consuls at Jerusalem also exerted themselves in maintaining good relations with Bedouin sheiks and village mukhtars (headmen) along the tourist routes, and even with carriage drivers – and with pickpockets and thieves – in order to keep their visiting compatriots from being victimized and annoyed.[130] The consular officials also tried to help in health matters. Intestinal infections, such as diarrhea and dysentery were commonplace, and sometimes caused the death of travelers. In outbreaks of contagious diseases, such as the severe cholera epidemic of 1902, and in helping American visitors quarantined by the authorities, the consular staffs did important work.[131]

128 See under Legal Services, below; Richard Beardsley, U.S. Consul, Jerusalem, to Hamilton Fish, Secretary of State, Washington, D.C., 30 September 1870, USNA RG59 T471/3 and correspondence between Theodore Struve, U.S. Consular Agent, Haifa and G. Bie Ravndal, U.S. Consul General, Beirut, Re – Robbery of 4 American Tourists at Haifa, April, May, and August 1910, USNA RG84 Haifa Copy Book.

129 Vogel,"Zion as Place," pp.327–8.

130 Blumberg, *Zion Before Zionism*, pp.51–52; Klatzker,"American Christian Travelers," pp.58–62; Vogel,"Zion as Place," pp.296–329. In 1903, Gottlieb Schumacher, the consular agent at Haifa, was requested by the representative of the Clark company to pay two weeks in advance for the *teskeres* out of his own pocket on the understanding that the money would be refunded to him. G. Karram, F.C. Clark Tourist Agency, Jerusalem, to Gottlieb Schumacher, U.S. Consular Agent, Haifa, 25 February 1903, USNA RG84 Haifa Miscellaneous and Official Correspondence Received 1875–1917 Miscellaneous Papers 1878–1903 Green Box.

131 G. Bie Ravndal, U.S. Consul General, Beirut, to Gottlieb Schumacher, U.S. Consular Agent, Haifa, 12 November 1902, USNA RG84 Haifa, ibid.

Jewish Visitors

Towards the end of the period under review, the consuls and consular agents had to deal with Jewish American tourists who suffered from the restrictions imposed by the Ottoman administration on the immigration of Jews to Palestine. From the early 1880s, with the growing influx of Jewish immigrants into Palestine and the extension of Jewish settlement, the Ottoman authorities took steps to stem this movement by enacting various regulations. But limitations on the entry of Jews to the country also affected Jewish American tourists and visitors who had no intention of remaining in the country. The American consular officials reacted aggressively in their attempts to protect the rights of these citizens. In 1898–1899, the minister of the United States at Constantinople reached an agreement with the Ottoman minister of foreign affairs which stipulated that "American citizens should not be obstructed in visiting any part of the Ottoman Empire as was their right under our treaties. The object of the restrictive regulations was to prevent the entrance of Jews who come en masse for purposes of colonization in Palestine, as distinguished from individuals who come to live, to visit, or to travel."[132] This created a situation whereby all the American Jews who arrived in Jaffa declared that they were tourists, despite Merrill's conviction that ninety-five percent of them intended remaining in the country as settlers. To the anger of bona fide visitors, the Turks, who suspected every Jew coming to the country of being a colonist, forced all who came to provide guarantees for their departure within three months.[133]

At the beginning of 1901, due to their lack of success in stemming the entry of Jews – in part, because of the uncompromising stance of the United States and the other powers in this matter – the Ottoman minister of the interior issued a new order affecting all Jews who came to Palestine from other countries as pilgrims or visitors. According to this decree, which was also sent to the consul of the United States at Jerusalem, every visitor was obliged to deposit his passport with the Jaffa port authorities for a period of up to three months. At the end of this period, he had to leave the country and

---

132 O. Straus in Selah Merrill, U.S. Consul, Jerusalem, to Thomas W. Cridler, Assistant Secretary of State, Washington, D.C., 5 March 1899, USNA RG59 T471/9.

133 Merrill to Cridler, ibid.

surrender his Turkish permit in order to retrieve his passport. The Ottoman government requested the consuls to enforce this ruling regarding their Jewish nationals.

In a report to the State Department, the American consul described the difficulties and problems raised by this decree, and requested clear directives as to his course of action. The secretary of state replied that the United States agreed to the regulation limiting visits to three months but rejected any discrimination on religious or racial grounds affecting Jews "...in view of our constitutional inhibition against any disability founded on creed," and went on to state that no consul of the United States should "...intervene to constrain the departure of an American citizen from Turkish jurisdiction. Neither can the consul be called upon to forego the performance of his duty in case an American citizen should be harshly dealt with in contravention of treaty or law."[134] The effect of this unequivocal American stance helped advance the settlement effort of Jews in Palestine, but aroused suspicions at all levels of the Ottoman administration regarding American intentions, as also those of the other powers, for intervening in their internal affairs.[135]

Researchers

The "rediscovery" of the Holy Land and systematic research in its history and geography gained great impetus in the 19th century. The first Americans to engage in scholarly study of Palestine and the Bible lands were clergymen striving for a better understanding of the Scriptures. Among the best-known and most important of early American explorers were Edward Robinson, in 1838 and 1852, and the Lynch Expedition of the U.S. Navy in 1848. At that time, there was as yet no developed framework of American consulates and consular agencies in Palestine. Even after an American consulate had been established in Jerusalem, and the number of Americans of the "...scientific class" had increased, "the road of the antiquary...[was] not fringed with flowers." [136]

134 Selah Merrill, U.S. Consul, Jerusalem, to Lloyd C. Griscom, Department of State, Washington, D.C., 14 January 1901, Griscom to John Hay, Secretary of State, 31 January 1901 and Hay to Griscom, 28 February 1901, Diplomatic Correspondence JNUL MS V810. See also: Bartour,"American Consular Aid," p.307.

135 On detailed treatment of this subject in the two decades preceding the First World War, see: Landau & Öke,"Ottoman Perspective," pp.261–302.

136 Rhodes,"Our Consul at Jerusalem," pp.439–40.

In the writings and published works of American students of Palestine there is little reference to the consulates, and the subject received but scant attention in articles and books about the work of the researchers. Nevertheless, the support and assistance provided by the consuls, the consular agents, and by the diplomatic representatives to explorers and travelers well exceeded the call of duty – even if these were less prestigious than the United States Navy expedition to the Jordan and the Dead Sea under Lt. William Francis Lynch in 1848. In this particular case, the American seamen went by boat and on shore from the Sea of Galilee down the Jordan and to the Dead Sea, mapping and conducting geological, astronomical, meteorological, natural history, and other surveys (Plate 28).[137] The expedition, which left the United States in November 1847, was assisted by the American minister at Constantinople in obtaining a firman permitting exploration in the sultan's domain and ordering the governors at Sidon and Jerusalem to extend it full assistance. Correspondence in the United States consulate at Beirut, including letters from Consul Jasper Chasseaud to the State Department, a letter written by Lynch to Chasseaud during his work in the field, and from the American consular agent at Acre, G. Nasralla, to Chasseaud, between 31 March and the end of June 1848, as well as from the records of the Lynch expedition, it appears that much help was provided them. Besides the aid he received from Minister D.S. Carr in Constantinople, Lynch had recourse to Chasseaud in depositing and transferring all the money he brought with him, in arranging accommodations for the expedition on its return to Beirut, and in transmitting directives to the consular agents in Jaffa and Acre. The expedition was presented to the governor of Acre, and Murad, the consular agent at Jaffa also made himself useful. Lynch enjoyed the support of the British consul-general in Syria who ordered the consular agents subordinate to him to extend every possible assistance to the American expedition.[138] In Jerusalem, Lynch was most gratified by the cooperation of the British consul: "...There being no U.S. Consul, or Consular Agent in Jerusalem, I was under the necessity of availing myself of the friendly offices of Mr. Finn, H.B.M. Consul at that place...Mr. Finn kindly became our banker and refusing all remuneration, accepted my drafts upon him in payment for the services of

137 Ben-Arieh,"William F. Lynch's Expedition," pp.15–21.

138 Expedition to the Dead Sea by Lt. Lynch, December 1847 to February 1849, USNA T829/438 and USNA RG59 T367/1.

RUINED BRIDGE OF SEMAKH

Plate 28. Camp of the Lynch expedition near a ruined bridge over the
Jordan river at Semakh, south of the Sea of Galilee.
Source: Lynch, *Narrative*

the Arabs, thereby enabling us to move about among predatory and lawless
tribes...." His indebtedness to Finn prompted Lynch to ask Secretary of the
Navy J.Y. Mason to exercise his influence on the President for expressing
official thanks to H.M. Government.[139]

---

139 William Francis Lynch, Washington, D.C., to John Y. Mason, Secretary of the Navy, Washington,
     D.C., 30 January 1849, Lynch, Expedition, ibid.

CHAPTER SIX

LEGAL AND ECONOMIC AID
AND CONSULAR REPORTING

LEGAL SERVICES

Civil and Criminal Courts

Already in 1830, when the treaty giving extraterritorial rights to American citizens was signed between the United States and Turkey, there was a lack of clarity regarding the jurisdiction, and particularly criminal jurisdiction, over cases involving Ottoman and American nationals. Jones, in his book on the United States consular service published in 1906, points out that, "The fourth article of the treaty of 1830 reads as follows: 'If disputes should arise between the subjects of the Sublime Porte and citizens of the United States, the parties shall not be heard nor shall judgement be pronounced unless the American Dragoman be present'. He remarked that this was one of the points in the agreement that was not challenged: "The part of the treaty which is undisputed provides that the American dragoman shall be present at all trials of our citizens." But in practice, there arose also on this point differing interpretations and versions by the Ottoman government and the American representatives.[1]

Judgement by the Ottoman Judicial System of Ottoman Subjects who Injured Americans
Beyond the differences over the principles involved in the interpretation of this item in the law, the consuls and consular agents who tried to protect American settlers and travelers in Palestine met with many difficulties in appealing to the local judicial system. This was especially so with the many incidents of Americans being robbed by local people. One of the more extreme cases that required the intervention of the consul in Jerusalem John Warren Gorham, of his Prussian colleague Dr. Georg Rosen, of the American consul-general in Alexandria Edwin de Leon, and of the U.S. consul at Beirut

---

[1]   Jones, Consular Service, pp.48–49; J.G. Willson, U.S. Consul, Jerusalem, to Ernst Hardegg, U.S. Consular Agent, Jaffa, 15 September 1880, USNA RG59 T471/5.

Augustus J. Johnson, was the violent attack on families at the American agricultural mission in Jaffa on the night of 11 January 1858. The women were raped, Walter Dickson was beaten unconscious, and his son-in-law, Frederick Steinbeck was fatally shot. The memoirs of Edwin de Leon, translations of official despatches sent by Grand-Vizier 'Ali in Constantinople to Suraya Pasha, the governor of Jerusalem, and communications sent by Gorham to the American embassy in Constantinople, show that diplomatic pressure had to be applied at the highest levels in order to apprehend and punish the perpetrators of these serious crimes. As a result of the incident, the mission in Jaffa was abandoned in September 1858, and the Dickson family returned to its place of origin, Groton, Massachusetts.[2]

Despite the improvement in government and of security conditions in Palestine between 1858 and 1880–81, robberies of American citizens visiting the country continued, as did the difficulties in arresting the culprits, bringing them to justice and punishing them. This is illustrated by three cases of robbery and theft, described by the American consul in Jerusalem as the Latrone case, the Singel case, and the Hebron case. Willson sent many despatches about these to Raouf Pasha, the governor-general of Palestine, to the consul-general of the United States in Constantinople, and to the State Department in Washington. In all of these he complained of "...delay and irregular proceedings so as to conform to the treaty stipulations on Consular Regulation...." Moreover, the dragoman had to be present in the Turkish courthouse during many weeks for "hearing testimony and arguing law points." At the end, the verdicts in the two first cases were one-half to one year of imprisonment and payment of damages to the value of the thefts.[3]

Quarrels between Templer Settlers and Local Arabs (1874–1879)
From the year 1873, the German Templers began talking of a decided "spirit of enmity" that spread against them among the population of the country. From then on, the dangers from local inhabitants to the German enterprise had to be given serious consideration in planning the expansion of the colonies and in the acquisition of additional lands. This was apparently a result of the experience of the Haifa settlers whose women were molested and the tombstones of their dead systematically hacked to pieces in the burial ground

2   De Leon, *Thirty Years*, 1, pp.246–90; Augustus J. Johnson, U.S. Consul, Beirut, to Lewis Cass, Secretary of State, Washington,D.C., 12 January 1859, USNA RG59 T367/3; Vogel, "Zion as Place and Past," pp. 244–48.

3   J.G. Willson, U.S. Consul, Jerusalem, to Charles Payson, Third Assistant Secretary of State, Washington, D.C., 10 September 1880 and 19 January 1881, USNA RG59 T471/5.

the Templers shared with the local Arabs (until the settlers set up their own cemetery).

Real threats to the lives of the German settlers in Palestine resulted from the crises and wars in the Balkans in the years 1875–78. The struggles of the Christians there to rid themselves of the sultan's yoke, and the Russian designs on Constantinople, were relayed to the Muslim population throughout the Empire as a sign of yet another Christian onslaught against Islam. The intensified draft of soldiers into the ranks of the Turkish army and the pressure of added taxation to pay for the wars, carried out with great cruelty, caused the population to blame all the Christians, including Christian Arabs, for their suffering. The tension with the German and American settlers in Haifa led to violent confrontation in a few cases when blows were exchanged.[4] In 1879, the Haifa Templer, Fr. Keller, who was also the German consular agent in Haifa, wrote that the many settlers occupied him mainly because their constructive undertakings were regarded by the Turkish government not, as he would have wished, with appreciation and encouragement but as an intrusion, and that the population consequently felt the same, to the injury of the German settlers' rights. As much as possible, he tried to resolve conflicts by compromises, in a peaceful manner.[5]

Oldorf (1874–1876)

Since some of the settlers were American citizens, the consular agent in Haifa and the consul in Beirut had to see to their rights and frequently to intervene with the vali of Damascus. Generally, this was done jointly with the German consular representative in Haifa, whose nationals were also involved in the various confrontations. Two incidents in 1875 illustrate this. The first was connected with the complaint of an American citizen named Ch. Oldorf, and the second with complaints of German-American settlers, among whom were American citizens, regarding trespasses upon their properties. These occurrences were reconstructed from excerpts of relevant correspondence. In the first case, which happened before June 1875, Oldorf, who was an American settler in the Haifa Templer colony, was attacked by shepherds who entered his courtyard with their flocks and caused damage. Oldorf was beaten and injured by sticks and stones, and when he summoned the kavasses of the American consular agency to his aid, one of the attackers,

---

4   Carmel, *German Settlement*, pp.183–84.

5   Report of Fr. Keller, German Consular Agent, Haifa, 20 January 1879, ISA RG67/454 (German).

Qasim al-Aswad, wounded one of them with an axe.[6] The second confrontation happened in similar circumstances, at the end of August 1875. When some of the German-American settlers were harvesting maize in their field, shepherds from Haifa came up, and when the settlers tried to keep them away, the Arabs cursed them, beat them with staves and stones inflicting bloody wounds. In this connection another attack was carried out on *Khawadja* [Mr.] Keller, an employee of the German consular agency in Haifa.[7] Among those attacked were several settlers [probably five, the names in the Arabic document are garbled, R.K.], and among the attackers were mentioned later the names of Hassan 'Amiriya, Muhammad Abu Salem, Muhammad al-Dar'a, and the sons of al-Aswad.[8] In all these incidents, sharp representations were made by the American and German consulates. The American consular agent, Schumacher, wrote in Arabic to the kaimakam of the Haifa district that "The attacks on American citizens prove the unstable security situation and that the government is unable to assure the safety and lives of the settlers from wild attacks."[9] He demanded emphatically that the culprits be punished rigorously with at least three months in prison and a fine of ten pounds in the case of Oldorf and the others.[10] The Turkish officials who investigated the matter did not evince enthusiastic support for the American and the German claims. They arrested the suspects but hurriedly released them pending trial. Finally, after delays on legal pretexts, and after the intervention of the American consul in Beirut with the vali of Damascus in the Oldorf case, light sentences were handed down, invoking Item 176 of the Sultan's Legislation. Oldorf's attackers were fined two Turkish pounds (and fifteen days in jail, according to one American source), and the attackers of the other settlers were given ten days in prison. The consul in Beirut expressed disappointment at this lenient treatment.[11]

6   Jacob Schumacher, U.S. Consular Agent, Haifa, to Sedek Bey, Kaimakam of Haifa District, 1 June
    and 31 August 1875, USNA RG84 Haifa Miscellaneous and Official Correspondence Received
    1875–1917, Miscellaneous Papers 1875–1904 Green Box (Arabic).

7   Ibid., Schumacher to Sedek Bey, 27 and 28 August 1875 (Arabic). At the time, Keller was the
    dragoman of the German consular agency at Haifa.

8   Ibid., Sedek Bey to Schumacher, 5 October 1875 (Arabic). According to one theory, the attacks
    were connected with a dispute over land between the Templers and the Carmelite monastery in
    Haifa.

9   Ibid., Schumacher to Sedek Bey, 31 October 1875 (Arabic).

10 Ibid., Schumacher to Sedek Bey, 9 June and 27 August (Arabic).

11 Ibid., Schumacher to Kaimakam, Haifa, 28,29,30 August and 5 October 1875 (Arabic); John T.
    Edgar, U.S. Consul, Beirut, to Jacob Schumacher, U.S. Consular Agent, Haifa, 7 October 1875,

Consular Action in the Robbery of Americans in Nazareth (1875)

Among the important responsibilities of the consuls and the consular agents was the protection of American pilgrims and travelers visiting the Holy Land. Not infrequently, foreign travelers of American and other nationality were attacked and robbed in the course of their travels, or had their equipment stolen. When such things happened, the victims could only complain to their consular representatives, who in turn appealed to the local authorities so that these would see to the apprehension, trial, and punishment of the culprits, and to the indemnification of the injured foreigners. Sometimes, travelers tried to prevent such predicaments by hiring private guards, or an escort of soldiers appointed by the kaimakam at the request of the consular dragoman. That even such measures did not always help can be seen from the deposition made by an American traveler named Benjamin F. Robb in the Beirut consulate and from the ensuing correspondence between the kaimakam of the Nazareth district and Jacob Schumacher, the consular agent in Haifa in 1875. It appears that five American travelers, accompanied by an escort of Turkish soldiers fell prey to robbery in Nazareth on the night of 13 April 1875. Robb himself had clothes and effects valued at least at \$47-\$50 taken from him.[12] When the complaint was lodged, the kaimakam of the Nazareth district and the mutasarrif of Acre undertook an investigation. Four out of five suspects were arrested and detained. The stolen property was recovered and the dragoman of the consulate was summoned to receive it. The demand of the American consul in Beirut for damages to goods amounting to \$250 was rejected. Edgar asked Schumacher to pack the restored effects compactly in a box and to forward this to him by Austrian steamer to Beirut. The procedures and the trial of the suspects were speeded up in this case by the consul in Beirut appealing to the vali, who intervened with the mutasarrif of Acre.[13]

ibid., Miscellaneous Papers 1878–1903, and 18 November 1875, 22 February 1876, ibid., Miscellaneous Papers 1875–1904.

12   Affidavit of Benjamin F. Robb before George S. Fisher, U.S. Consul, Beirut, 20 April 1875, including list of belongings stolen, USNA RG84 Haifa Miscellaneous Papers and Official Correspondence Received 1875–1917 Miscellaneous Papers 1875–1904 Green Box; Correspondence between the kaimakam of Nazareth, the mutasarrif of Acca and Jacob Schumacher, U.S. Consular Agent, Haifa, 5,6 July and 18,25,30 August (Arabic), ibid.

13   John T. Edgar, U.S. Consul, Beirut, to Jacob Schumacher, U.S. Consular Agent, Haifa, 7 October 1875, ibid. 1878–1903 and 18 November 1875, ibid. 1875–1904.

The Robbing of an American Citizen in Safed and the Trial of the Accused Ottoman Subjects by the Authorities (1885–1886)

Another example of the dispute concerning Article 4 of the treaty with the United States, can be gleaned from the English and Arabic correspondence found in the files of the American consular agency in Haifa dating to January–June 1886.[14] The case is presented here in detail to illustrate the complexities of dealing with such matters and interpreting even the simplest of legal issues. It deals with the theft of silver objects from Morris Julius Franklin, MD, the Christian American physician mentioned above, who lived in Safed at the end of 1885. The parties involved in the exchanges of letters were Dr. Franklin in Safed, Jacob Schumacher, and two consuls-general, Erhard Bissinger and John T. Robeson, in Beirut. At the end of January 1886, Dr. Franklin appealed to two of his acquaintances in Safed for their help in identifying the thieves and their loot. Muhammad Namek Effendi replied to Franklin that he remembered the silver objects – forks, teaspoons, and bracelets – and pointed to Bishara ibn Musa al-Basha, a youth who frequently prowled around Franklin's house. According to the reply by Yitzhak Pessah, the theft was from Franklin's shop. Pessah recalled that he assisted as a translator in presenting the complaint to the police in the office of the kaimakam in Safed. Among the suspects were the sons of two Christian family heads, Musa al-Basha and Salim ibn Yusuf Nadaf. Two of them were taken for interrogation to the court house and imprisoned.[15]

The trial of the accused took place without the presence of the American dragoman, and it appears that they were released without punishment. Schumacher sent a protest to the mutasarrif and also reported to Robeson, his superior in Beirut, in December 1885, that the mutasarrif "...neglected to conform to the treaty stipulations." Robeson instructed Schumacher, with the help of the American consular agent in Acre, Mr. Cardahi, to write a second note to the mutasarrif, giving details of the case, protesting sharply against the illegal proceedings of the Safed authorities, and requesting "...that the accused be arrested and tried according to the rights guaranteed American citizens by our treaty with Turkey in such cases." Robeson promised him to transmit a copy of this request to "the U.S. Legation at Constantinople with

---

14   USNA RG84 Haifa Miscellaneous and Official Correspondence Received 1875–1917 Miscellaneous Papers 1875–1904 Green Box.

15   Morris Julius Franklin to Yitzhak Pessah and Muhammed Namek and answers of both, 20 January 1886 (Arabic), ibid.

the hope that it may take up the matter."[16] In March 1886, Schumacher sent his protest against this violation of the treaty between the Sublime Porte and the United States of America by the Safed authorities. The infringement related to "Article 4 of the Treaty of May 7, 1830, which was reinforced by Art.1 of the Treaty of Feb. 13–25, 1862." These items stated that: "No investigation in each case as that of Dr. Franklin can be held unless a Representative of the consulate be present...." Since this article was violated, Schumacher asked "his excellency" to renew the investigation in the presence of the consular representative and to retry the accused.[17] The answer sent by the mutasarrif, Yusuf Muhammad, to Schumacher in May 1886 expressed his belief that the investigation and the trial were conducted in a legal manner by the district vice-prosecutor-general, and that the American dragoman was not invited because of the great distance between Safed and Haifa (nine hours or more) and the absence of an American consulate there.[18] On receipt of this reply, Schumacher passed on the entire correspondence to his superior, Erhard Bissinger, the consul-general in Beirut. Bissinger delved into the tomes of the Législation Ottomane and found contradictory provisions in this matter. According to him, in the second volume (page 426, 9°),[19]

> The Capitulations prescribe that in the trial of foreigners for crime or misdemeanor, Ottoman judges can not proceed but in the presence of the Ambassador, consul or their substitute. The latter are not judges in these cases; their presence is only requested so that they may be able to see that no irregularity has been committed. *The presence of the Consul, or Dragoman is not required by the Capitulations in the trial of an Ottoman subject for crime or misdemeanor committed against a foreigner.*

While on the other hand,

> In our own Treaty with Turkey, of May 7,1830, Art.IV, page 157, Volume IV of the Législation Ottomane and page 313,

---

16   John T. Robeson, U.S. Consul, Beirut, to Jacob Schumacher, U.S. Consular Agent, Haifa, 8 January 1886, ibid.

17   Jacob Schumacher, U.S. Consular Agent, Haifa, to Mutasarif [sic] of Acca, 3 March 1886, ibid. (Arabic and English).

18   Yusuf Muhammad, the Mutasarif of Acca, to American Republic Consul in Acca and Haifa, 5 May 1886 (Arabic) ibid.

19   Erhard Bissinger, U.S. Consul, Beirut, to Jacob Schumacher, U.S. Consular Agent, Haifa, 8 June 1886, ibid.

paragraph 941 of the Consular Regulation occurs the following passage: "If litigations and disputes should arise between subjects of the Sublime Porte and citizens of the U.S. *the parties shall not be heard, nor shall judgement be pronounced, unless the American Dragoman be present. Cases in which the sum may exceed five hundred piasters shall be submitted to the Sublime Porte, to be decided according to the laws of equity and justice.*"

In view of these opposing legal statements, and with the Turkish authorities refusing to conduct a new trial, Bissinger felt that he was insufficiently qualified to take action in a matter connected with "international principles" without seeking advice from the legation in Constantinople. However, he totally rejected the relevance of the allusion by the Ottoman authorities to the distance between Safed and Haifa. No further material has turned up to inform us of the juridical conclusion of the case.

Adjudication Involving Nationals of Several Foreign Powers in the Ottoman Empire (1884)

The principles laid down in the capitulations specified that the extraterritorial rights of foreign states in the Ottoman Empire carried with them the right of jurisdiction over the foreign nationals by their respective consular representatives. Accordingly, court cases between foreigners from different countries were to be tried by the consul of the accused: "Trial in the consular court of the defendant of questions between foreigners of different nationalities." [20]

Two letters of October 1884, from the consul-general in Beirut, John T. Robeson – one to Dr. Morris Julius Franklin in Safed, and the other to the U.S. consular agent in Haifa – illustrate some of these proceedings and their effectiveness.[21] These documents related to the complaint of Dr. Franklin against Leon Oczeret and Joseph Miklasiewiez who were Austrian subjects, and against Mordechay Segal who claimed British nationality. The complaint dealt with the supply of medicines which Franklin had paid for. In conformance with the consular proceedings as detailed by Robeson, the case should have been tried in Beirut before the Austrian and British consuls-general and with

---

20   Jones, *Consular Service*, p.50.

21   John T. Robeson, U.S. Consul, Beirut, to Morris J. Franklin, M.D., Safed, 17 October 1884 and to Jacob Schumacher, Haifa, 18 October 1884, USNA RG84 Haifa Miscellaneous Correspondence Received 1875–1917 Miscellaneous Papers 1875–1904 Green Box.

the assistance of the American consul. It is interesting that the matter did not go before the consular agents in Haifa who had jurisdiction over Safed. Although Robeson was prepared to help and give full backing to his fellow citizen in Safed, he urged him to reach a pretrial compromise. Robeson adduced a number of reasons that shed considerable light upon the many difficulties which the system of consular courts entailed, among them:

> Courts in this country are conducted slowly and decisions uncertain, and I understand that Consular Courts are not "exceptional to the rule." Any damages you might obtain against said gentlemen before the Consular Courts here would not likely be very satisfactory; the trouble and expense is [sic] having the case tried at Beirut would be very considerable.

And further,

> The British Consul-General here does not recognize, in any way, Mr. Mordechay Segal, as British Representative at Safed (Safed is in Mr. Eldridge's Consular district.)

And there was still the need to prove, before the trial, that Segal was a British subject. In the light of all these, Robeson recommended to Dr. Franklin to reach with the defendants an "amicable and honorable understanding" which would be "generous and wise". Of Schumacher he asked "to use your best efforts to have the matters settled without bringing it before the consular Court at Beirut." All of this points up the slowness and inefficiency of the interconsular judicial system, and the many problems it entailed. There was thus an incentive to arrange out-of-court settlements.

Management of Estates

Another defined area of the American consul's juridical responsibilities was the settlement of estates of Americans who died abroad. The reports by United States consuls in Jerusalem and the consular agents in Jaffa and Haifa contain information on dealing with estates of transients such as seamen or travelers, and of American citizens who were locally resident. According to the directives from Washington, the correspondence in these, as in other, matters was conducted with the Consular Bureau of the State Department.[22] The accepted procedure was that "In case of death, where no legal representative is present, the consul takes possession of the estate for delivery to the legal

---

22   Department of State, *History of the Department of State*, pp.50–54.

heirs. He notifies the relatives or friends of the deceased, reports the circumstances to the Department of State, and in many instances arranges for the disposal of the remains either by burial or cremation abroad, or shipment to the United States for interment."[23] In every case of death of an American citizen within the region under the jurisdiction of the consul or consular agent, subject to the State Department, he was obligated to arrange the estate for the heirs. If there were no heirs, or if these could not be located, he had to act in the interest of the United States government. This transpires from the correspondence regarding the possessions of Clorinda Minor of Philadelphia, who settled in Urtas and Jaffa at the beginning of the 1850s, and died and was buried at her Jaffa property, "Mount Hope" in 1855. The consul, Selah Merrill, was appointed to settle her estate in 1898–99.[24]

After reporting the death of an American citizen, the consul or consular agent proceeded to draw up a detailed inventory of the estate in the presence of witnesses: personal effects and property (clothing, bedding, books, etc.); cash; real estate (dwelling house, cultivated land); mortgages on property; debts; credits; and even livestock. The announcement of death and an accounting of the property held by the consul were transmitted to the heirs. After deducting a consular fee, the balance was remitted to them. In cases where executors were appointed to the estate, the consul delivered to them all the articles belonging to the deceased. On completing the inventory, the objects were stamped with the seal of the government and deposited in the consular archives until they could be lawfully claimed, or to be disposed of as prescribed by the State Department rules.

Every two or three months, the consul had to send a report to the State Department which listed – as can be seen from a document dated 31 March 1866 in the archive of the consul, Victor Beauboucher – the names of all deceased American citizens, including seamen or mariners, together with the value of the personal effects belonging to them that were taken into custody and deposited with the consul. The list comprised the following items: "Date of death, name of the person, of what place a native or resident, where deceased, value of effects, disposition made thereof."[25]

Beyond the necessity of drawing up lists of property of the deceased from a civil and legal point of view, such information is of considerable importance

---

23　Lay, *The Foreign Service*, pp.143,193.

24　Correspondence dated 25 May 1898, 18 November 1898, and 8 March 1899, USNA RG59 T471/9.

25　Victor Beauboucher, U.S. Consul, Jerusalem, to William H. Seward, Secretary of State, Washington, D.C., concerning the Cresson family case, 31 March 1866, RG59 T471/2.

as primary source material for the economic history of the Middle East and Palestine in the period under discussion. Thus, for example, there is a complete inventory of all the real estate and other property, such as household goods, credits, and personal effects left by Gottlieb Deininger "deceased at Haifa, Syria, Turkey, September 2d 1891." [26] Deininger, who came to Haifa from Philadelphia in 1873, was one of the first to settle in the Haifa Templer colony. The inventory drawn up in the presence of witnesses at the request of his widow, Marie Deininger, "Administratrix of the Real Estate and the Property by Andrew Struve and George Scheerer." On the day of the inventory, 5 November 1891, Struve and Scheerer signed it in the office of Gottlieb Schumacher, the acting United States consular agent in Haifa, who countersigned it and imposed the consular seal. Appended to the document was a statement giving the value of the entire estate in current market piasters (50,488) and the equivalent in Turkish piasters (40,820), and in U.S. dollars ($1,796). An interesting and important item in the list is the one entitled "Real Estate", which describes in detail the house of the deceased and the cultivated lands, their location and monetary value. The dwelling house "...is built of stone, containing 3 rooms and a kitchen in the first story and a cellar and cistern below and small stables built to its eastern side, situate on the eastern extremity of 'wine' road in the 'colony' near Haifa, surrounded by a kitchen garden of the area of one half (1/2) acre english; total value 29,837 Market Piasters." In addition, the deceased owned an acre-and-a-half of cultivated land and two-and-a-half acres of vineyards valued at 8,356 market piasters in total.

This was the estate of a well-to-do settler in Palestine, but there were also cases of visitors to the country – pilgrims or tourists – who died there. The consul or consular agent had to make his report and see to the burial and to the estate. Thus, for example, the consul in Jerusalem, Frank S. DeHass arranged the estate of the reverend Emory Gale, an American citizen who died in Jaffa on 24 November 1874, and sent the "Cash balance of $20.72 with other effects to his widow." [27] A photograph of Gale's tombstone taken around 1930 in the burial plot of the Mount Hope agricultural colony in Jaffa, shows that he came from Minneapolis, Minnesota and was fifty years old when he died. The stone is decorated with a wreath. [28] Sometimes the

---

26   In USNA RG84 Haifa Consular Agency, Miscellaneous Records [no date]. Authorization of the Deininger's estate on 5 November 1891.

27   Frank S. DeHass, U.S. Consul, Jerusalem, to William Hunter, Second Assistant Secretary of State, Washington, D.C., 14 July 1876, USNA RG59 T471/4.

28   Ilan, "The Hope," *Davar* (19 March 1985).

cause of death and details of the deceased are given, as in the case of the American tourist, Adolph Haag from Utah, who died of typhoid fever after illness on 3 October 1892. Haag, aged twenty-six, was described as "...watchmaker, elder of the Mormon Church of Salt Lake City. Born in Stuttgart, Germany." The consular agent made all the arrangements for transmitting his effects to his wife Eliza and to Mr. Musser, the executor appointed in Utah.[29] To the report of the death of another young Mormon, John Alexander Clark, aged twenty-three, who came as a tourist and died in Haifa in 1895, the consular agent enclosed Clark's passport issued in Washington, a full list of personal effects and property and the value in market piasters. (After deducting expenses, debts, and fees, the dollar equivalent of the balance came to $31.33.) The inventory gives an idea of the effects carried by tourists in the Holy Land, which included "1 Arabic bible, 1 English bible...."[30]

Frequently, the consul had to cope with complicated legal questions or to solve problems encountered by the consular agents in the division of property of the deceased between his or her spouse and children. The decisions had to conform to Federal law and to the laws of the state in which "...the decedent had his domicile in the United States, which was generally one-third to the widow and two-thirds to the children. In such a case, consuls in the Ottoman Empire, by virtue of extraterritorial privileges, are made administrators and are vested with the right to appoint guardians for the children." In the case of the wife's death, "her property goes to her husband who, however, is legally bound to support the children."[31] There were also estates that entailed debts, or which were disputed, and were difficult for the consuls to resolve. In Jerusalem, during the terms of service of Selah Merrill and Edwin S. Wallace, in the years 1893–1898, many problems arose concerning the estates of Shalom Kanstoroom and Meyer Nachtigal, causing the consuls to be accused of ineptitude. From the relevant consular report it appears that Kanstoroom

---

29   Gottlieb Schumacher, U.S. Consular Agent, Haifa, to Erhard Bissinger, U.S. Consul, Beirut, 5 and
     26 October 1892, 7 and 13 March 1893, USNA RG84 Haifa Copy Book 1886–1899 Box 5977.

30   Complete list of all the personal property and effects left by J.A. Clark, American Citizen, deceased
     at Haifa, Syria, Turkey on the 8th day of February 1895, which was drawn up on 18 April 1895,
     USNA RG84 Haifa Miscellaneous and Official Correspondence Received 1875–1917 Miscellaneous
     Papers 1878–1903 Green Box.

31   Gerhard Bissinger, U.S. Consul, Beirut, to Jacob Schumacher, U.S. Consular Agent, Haifa,
     31 January 18[?], USNA RG84 Haifa ibid. Bissinger justified the decision of the U.S. consul in
     Jerusalem. The letter must have been written between January 1886 and January 1891 since Bissinger
     started his term of office during 1885 and Jacob Schumacher died in 1891.

"...left no money; nothing for his family to live upon; except three pieces of real estate heavily mortgaged." The report mentions the dispute between Kanstoroom's heirs and the banker, [Johannes] Frutiger, of which the deceased "was his agent for buying and selling land, for several years previous to his death," but the United States consuls had no documentation regarding this.[32] No doubt this had to do with the flourishing speculation in land in Jerusalem and the ensuing collapse that led to the bankruptcy of Frutiger's and other banks.[33]

A good part of the consul's time was taken up by post factum searches in the United States for relatives of citizens who died in Palestine, in connection with the disposal of their property – sometimes many years after the event. In 1909, James P. Meshullam of Newark, New Jersey, whose parents of British nationality lived in Jerusalem and Urtas in the mid-19th century, applied to the State Department in Washington to find out what happened to "the alleged property owned by his parents." The consul in Jerusalem, Thomas R. Wallace, undertook a thorough investigation and wrote that no property was found. His reply, incidentally, sheds light on an important episode in the development of modern agriculture in Palestine: The relations between the petitioner's father, John Meshullam, and the wife of the British consul in Jerusalem, Elizabeth Anne Finn, regarding the lands of Urtas village, south of Bethlehem (Plate 6). It turned out that Meshullam died penniless in 1877, and that the property was eventually sold at a loss to a resident of Bethlehem in 1906.[34] Similarly, there is the correspondence between the United States consular agent in Jaffa, Ernst Hardegg and the members of the "Committee of the Colony Rehobot" regarding information about the land left by Mrs. Malke Yaffe.[35]

The consul or the consular agent could not always go to every corner of the area within their jurisdiction in order to deal with estates of deceased nationals, or other matters. Thus, in 1907, the consul-general in Beirut, G. Bie Ravndal, rebuked the consular agent in Haifa for the way he handled estates of Jews in

---

32   Selah Merrill, U.S. Consul, Jerusalem, to Thomas W. Cridler, Assistant Secretary of State, Washington, D.C., 19 and 20 September 1898, and Edwin S. Wallace, U.S. Consul, Jerusalem, to Cridler, 31 May 1899, USNA RG59 T471/9.

33   Kark, "Land Acquisition," pp.179–94.

34   Thomas R. Wallace, U.S. Consul, Jerusalem, to James P. Meshullam, Newark, New Jersey, 29 September 1909, USNA RG59 T471/10 [Fi2477/10].

35   Correspondence between the Committee of the Colony Rehobot [sic] and Ernst Hardegg, U.S. Consular Agent, Jaffa, 23 June, 19, 24 and 25 July, and 13 September 1910, USNA RG84 Jaffa Miscellaneous Letters 1900–1914 Box 5965.

Safed: "I do not quite understand how estates are being administered amongst the American citizens of Safed. It is, as you know, a consular function which cannot be delegated to others." [36]

Abuses of Consular Status - The Estate of Warder Cresson
Matters did not always conform with the consular regulations or with sound administrative standards. One example hints at improper behavior by Lazarus I. Murad, the vice-and-acting consul in Jerusalem at the end of 1865. It had to do with the estate of Warder Cresson, who in 1844 was nearly appointed to be the first American consul in Jerusalem. Warder Cresson, a Christian who converted to Judaism, settled in Jerusalem in the late 1840s. He married and raised a family under the name of Michael Boaz Israel (Plate 16). Warder Cresson died in Jerusalem in 1860, leaving as only heirs, a daughter, Abigail Ruth Israel, and a son, David Ben-Zion Israel, according to a will deposited with the consulate. As executors on behalf of Abigail were appointed the American citizen, B. Lilienthal and the Syrian "citizen" Joseph Taineyan and all of Cresson's effects were given over to them. David had died three years before, and Abigail died in the cholera epidemic of November 1865. The consul, Beauboucher, who arrived on 31 January 1866, assumed that Warder Cresson was divorced and a father of children from a previous marriage, and that these were most probably living in America. Since no heirs remained to Cresson in Palestine, Lazarus Murad, on the authority vested in him, ordered the executors of the estate, under threat of arrest, to hand over to him all the effects listed and described in the inventory. Although he told the executors that he would report the proceedings to the State Department, he did not do so – claiming to have received a letter from Abraham Hart, a friend of Cresson's from Philadelphia, entrusting him to "dispose of the inheritance of...Mr. Cresson." Murad kept the property and did not, as required, deposit it in the archives of the consulate. Beauboucher formed the impression that Murad intended to appropriate the effects and to keep all knowledge of the subject from him. The details of the case were related by Lilienthal and Taineyan to Beauboucher who forced Murad, at the end of 1866, to return the estate forthwith. In view of Murad's improper behavior, Beauboucher, who had kept him on as a dragoman, decided to dismiss him: "I dishonorably discharged him of the service of the consulate and gave notice of it to the consular officers of each government residing in Jerusalem..." He also informed

---

36   Gabriel B. Ravndal, U.S. Consul-General, Beirut, to Theodore J. Struve, U.S. Consular Agent, Haifa, 26 March 1901, in Bartour, "American Consular Aid," p.374.

Murad that a copy of the report to Seward was being sent to the minister and American consul-general in Constantinople, and that his salary would be withheld until the State Department reached a decision regarding the matter. Cresson's effects, which had been returned, were stamped with the governmental seal in the presence of two witnesses and placed for safe-keeping in the consulate's archives until "they will be lawfully reclaimed." To these was joined the list of articles deposited by Benjamin Lilienthal in the consulate on 30 November 1865.[37]

Contacts with the Ottoman Authorities
In all matters connected with reporting and administration of estates, the consul was generally autonomous within the framework of the agreements with the Sublime Porte and the extraterritorial privileges bestowed upon him. Nevertheless, after 1867, complications arose as a result of the proclamation of the Imperial Rescript (Khatt-i Hümayun) which permitted foreign citizens to hold real estate, subject to the jurisdiction of Turkish institutions and courts in all questions relating to landed property.[38] In those cases where the estate of the deceased included real estate or mortgages, conflicts arose between the consul and the Ottoman authorities in carrying out their respective duties. This emerges clearly from the correspondence of the consul, Selah Merrill, with the State Department regarding the estate of one Levi Sadler, originally from Sharon, Pennsylvania who died in Jerusalem on 8 August 1884.[39] Sadler's estate, valued at $5,105, consisted mainly of five one-year mortgages upon the properties of Abd al-Latif Effendi, Salem Hussain Effendi, Raghib ibn Alhasi, Saleh ibn 'Omar, and Mendel Katz. For five months, Merrill busied himself with the necessary and regular steps for the settlement of the estate, with payments being made upon the mortgages. At that point, the Turkish authorities noticed that by the terms of the treaty a consul could not discharge mortgages since they had to do with land matters. As Sadler's heirs were living in America, the local officials in Jerusalem requested that they provide the consul with a power of attorney and that this be certified by the Turkish ambassador at Washington. On presenting the power of attorney at the court in Jerusalem, the consul would be allowed to discharge the mortgage in question. Accordingly, Merrill notified the

---

37   Victor Beauboucher, U.S. Consul, Jerusalem, to William H. Seward, Secretary of State, Washington, D.C., 27 March 1866 and appendixes dated 27,29,31 March 1866, USNA RG59 T471/2.

38   See Real Estate, below.

39   Selah Merrill, U.S. Consul, Jerusalem, to Alvey A. Adee, Third Assistant Secretary of State, Washington, D.C., 2 January 1885, USNA RG59 T471/5.

deceased's son, A.N. Sadler in Kansas City, Missouri, and the latter sent the power of attorney to Washington where it was held up in the State Department or in the Turkish embassy so that no rapid action was forthcoming. This case too should be regarded as part of the trials of strength between the Ottoman officials and the foreign consuls. The Turkish authorities attempted to implement their newly proclaimed rights, while the consul made efforts to bypass them by stressing the legitimacy of his actions: "One who knows the spirit of the Turks need not be told they are sore put respecting the terms of the treaty and they will take advantage of the smallest technicality if thereby they can annoy foreigners or hinder them in carrying out their legitimate duties."

Contacts with other Consulates
At times, because of the complexities of the affiliation of foreign nationals in Jerusalem with various countries, and with different religious communities, it was necessary to cooperate with other consulates in settling estates. One such episode was the "courtyard dispute" which shook the Jewish Old Yishuv of Jerusalem in the 1870s. ("Old Yishuv" refers to the traditional Jewish communities of the 19th and early 20th centuries in Palestine, as distinct from "New Yishuv" which represents the beginnings of modern Zionist settlement from the turn of the century.) This quarrel was connected with Rabbi Shaul Benjamin Cohen of Radoshkovichi, who came from Russia but became an American protégé. With money borrowed in his name and in that of the Prushim sect (followers of the Gaon of Vilna) in Jerusalem, Cohen acquired a large courtyard with partly ruined buildings in the Old City. In 1873, in order to secure his position and the repayment of the funds, he registered the property in his wife's name and transferred his support to the rival Hassidim sect in Jerusalem. This sparked a prolonged conflict between the two religious communities. The courtyard property was mortgaged by Cohen's wife to Yehudah David, who was an Austrian subject, as security for a financial loan. As required by law, the mortgage was registered in the local court of justice. Part of the story became the subject of correspondence between the Foreign Ministry in Vienna and the Austrian consul in Jerusalem in the years 1875 and 1877.[40] Yehudah David apparently died at the beginning of 1877, and in order to settle his estate, his brother-in-law and executor, Nissan Bek, acting under the protection of the Austrian consul, had to pay the debts of the deceased. With the help of the Austrian, German and American

---

40   Eliav, *Under Imperial Austrian Protection*, pp.161–65; Malachi, *Chapters*, pp.272–79.

consuls, Bek managed to reach compromise agreements with all the claimants, while the son of the deceased appealed to the Turkish authorities to cancel Bek's power of attorney and the compromise agreement. Eventually, with the backing of the Austrian consulate, Bek was able to sell the courtyard and to pay off the debtors.

Real Estate (Land and Property)

Before the 1860s, few Europeans succeeded in purchasing land in Palestine – usually by some subterfuge or nonlegal means, such as registering the land in the name of fictitious owners or by disbursing large bribes. But with the promulgation of the law of 1867 by the Ottoman government, the way was opened for land purchases on an ever-increasing scale by groups and private persons – mainly European Christians and Jews. The liberalization of Ottoman land acquisition policies spurred the spread of European settlement in Palestine.

The constantly increasing influx of European Christians and, from the mid-1850s, the growth of the Jewish minority reflected the change in Ottoman land laws and the strengthened European influence in the Empire, as well as the more liberal policy of the government towards immigration and settlement generally. This policy was adopted for a number of demographic, economic, political, and psychological reasons.[41] In the years 1859–1880, two million Muslim refugees from Russia and the Balkans were resettled throughout the Empire, small numbers of these also in Palestine and Transjordan. Along with this massive relocation, the Ottoman government widely publicized its liberal policy in the European press, offering all sorts of inducements to foreigners who would settle in the Empire – on condition that they would accept Ottoman nationality. At the same time, however, the Ottomans regarded those European settlers who refused to give up their foreign nationality, such as the German Templers in Palestine, as barely-tolerated intruders, and often actively opposed them on these grounds. Although they understood that the European settlements would help improve the weak economy of the Empire, the Ottoman authorities were increasingly apprehensive about the growing foreign presence. They feared that it would serve as yet another pretext for the powers to interfere in the Empire's internal affairs, or worse, for gaining control over parts of it.[42]

---

41   Karpat, "Ottoman Immigration Policies," pp.58–72.

42   Ibid.; Carmel, *German Settlement*, pp.62–79.

In 1881, on the eve of the First *Aliya* (wave of Jewish immigration), changes were introduced in the declared Ottoman immigration policies, particularly regarding the influx of European Jews and acquisition of land by Jews in Palestine. These changes were motivated by the fear of creating yet another nationality problem backed by foreign political interests that might threaten the multiethnic and multinational structure of the Empire. The Turks also intended stemming the presence of foreign nationals in the Empire, and particularly in Palestine where a large number had already settled.[43] The policy changes found expression in laws and regulations limiting immigration and land acquisition. In November 1882, Palestine was virtually closed to Jewish immigration; in March 1883, an attempt was made to limit the sale of real estate to Jews of foreign nationality; and in April 1884, Jewish immigration was prohibited altogether. These restrictions were eased in the years 1887–88 at the intercession of the local consuls and the foreign ambassadors in Constantinople, and by the home governments of the powers. However, with the coming of the second wave of Jewish immigrants, a total prohibition on the immigration of Jews was again enacted in 1891. A year later (1892), came an absolute ban on land purchases by European and other foreign Jews. This time again, by 1893, representations by the powers brought about a modification of these regulations.[44]

The stringent laws limiting Jewish immigration and the prohibition on the buying of land were once again renewed, this time in the aftermath of Theodor Herzl's attempt to obtain a charter for settling Jews in Palestine and the founding of the World Zionist Organization in 1897. In this connection, the Ottoman ambassador in Washington wrote to the sultan in 1898, urging that he revoke the permission previously granted by his predecessors to various communities – Catholic, Russian Orthodox, Protestant, and Jewish – to settle in Palestine, which had only served to advance the political and religious ambitions of the powers.[45]

In the first decade of the 20th century, Ottoman policy towards foreigners hardened again. A number of consuls wrote of the hostility of the authorities to land transfers to foreigners and to foreign settlements, especially those engaged in agriculture. Local and central Ottoman authorities were attempting to stem the intensified land purchases by Jews in any way possible, and were

43 Karpat, ibid.; Eliav, "Diplomatic Intervention," pp.117–32.

44 Eliav, ibid.; Friedman, "The System of Capitulations," pp.280–93.

45 Öke, "Ottoman Empire and Zionism," pp.329–41.

even willing to transgress their own laws to achieve this goal.[46] This time, the Ottoman government resisted the pressures applied by the consuls. According to the consular reports of the period, the objectives of the Ottoman position were: "Prevention of Jewish settlement in Palestine, preventing foreigners from purchasing land near the Hedjaz railway, a desire to deny Europeans all possibility of existence in the region, and their expulsion from the area holy to the Muslims." [47]

In a more optimistic vein, the United States consul in Jerusalem, Thomas R. Wallace, replied, in 1910, to M. Lazarus, an American citizen from Syracuse who had bought land near Jaffa and who had requested to be informed: "What rights and privileges a United States citizen has in Turkish dominion such as Palestine in regard to buying land in the past ten years?" Wallace wrote that

> An American citizen is allowed to buy property in Palestine, provided the land is freehold property [*mulk*, R.K.]. Crown land (moiri) [*miri*, R.K.] is not sold to foreigners in large quantities, so as not to deprive the native villagers of their source of livelihood. Foreign Jews are not permitted to buy freehold property unless they have resided in the country for five years. Since the adoption of the Constitution [of the Young Turks, R.K.], the authorities have not been so strict in the enforcement of rules covering such matters, and it is believed that it will eventually cease.[48]

This optimism did not prove justified, and in 1913, the new consul in Jerusalem, William Coffin, wrote to E.P. Ross of Dukedom, Tennessee: "With respect to the purchase and ownership of real estate in Palestine, the Turkish government is inclined to make it difficult for newly arrived Jews to buy and hold property in their own names." [49]

---

46 Archives of Ali Ekrem Bey, Ottoman Governor of the Jerusalem District, 1 July 1907, ISA RG83/28 (Turkish); Landau & Öke, "Ottoman Perspective," pp.261–302.

47 F. Keller, German Vice-Consul, Haifa, to A. Schroeder, German Consul, Beirut, 20 August 1907, ISA RG67/1748; E.C. Blech, British Consul, Jerusalem, to Sir N.R. O'Connor, British Ambassador, Constantinople, 1 November 1908, PRO, FO 195/2287.

48 Correspondence between Department of State, Washington D.C., M. Lazarus, Syracuse, N.Y., Thomas R. Wallace, U.S. Consul, Jerusalem and E. Hardegg, Jaffa, 5, 15 January and 29 April 1910, USNA RG59 T471/11 [Fi2477/11]; A.T. Saad, Jerusalem, to U.S. Consulate and A. Slor, Petach Tikvah, to E. Hardegg, Jaffa, 23 February and 2 May 1910, USNA RG84 Jaffa Miscellaneous Letters 1900–1914 Box 5965.

49 William Coffin, U.S. Consul, Jerusalem, to E.P. Ross, Dukedom, Tennessee, 7 February 1913, in Bartour, "American Consular Aid," pp.282–83.

Actually, these stringent measures, which remained in effect until World War I, had only limited impact in preventing the growth of Christian and Jewish communities in Palestine.[50] One of the major factors in the failure of Ottoman policy in this respect was the vigorous intervention by diplomatic representatives of the foreign powers. To this should be added the wide disparity between Ottoman law and its application in practice. The central authorities were ambivalent and inconsistent in their attitudes to land acquisition by foreigners, the formulation of the laws were unclear and open to various interpretations, and corruption and openness to bribery were widespread at all levels of the Ottoman bureaucracy.[51]

The foregoing, rather detailed account of the historical background is necessary for understanding how foreign nationals were able to purchase and develop lands in Palestine. All in all, during the 19th and early 20th centuries, the Ottoman Empire underwent a gradual process of transition from xenophobia and a relative imperviousness to Western influence to an increasing acceptance of these forces. This openness was to bring in its wake fundamental internal political changes throughout the Empire in general, and to Palestine in particular, resulting in improvements of the administrative system and enhanced security of life and property. Yet, paradoxically, in the final years of Ottoman rule, these trends also led to a more successful repetition of earlier attempts for closing the Empire to foreign settlement.

The acquisition of real estate, and securing the rights of American citizens and protégés in Palestine in these matters was central to the work of the United States consuls in Beirut and Jerusalem and of the consular agents in Jaffa and Haifa. Often, because they entailed issues of principle and international agreements, these matters had to be referred to the American diplomatic legation in Constantinople and to the State Department in Washington – as can be seen from the relevant voluminous correspondence in the National Archives in Washington. From the middle of the 19th century, such exchanges of correspondence were especially intensive regarding American Christian and Jewish settlers who came to Palestine individually and in groups, and tried to acquire agricultural land on which to establish communities or farms.

Foreign settlement attempts usually aroused the opposition of the Sublime

---

50   *Ha-Poel Ha-Tzair* 6, 15 November 1912, pp.2,18 (Hebrew).

51   Karpat, "Ottoman Immigration Policies," pp.58–72; Öke, "Ottoman Empire and Zionism," pp.329–41; Archives of Ali Ekrem Bey, Ottoman Governor of the Jerusalem District, 1 July 1907, ISA RG83/28 (Turkish); Eliav, "Diplomatic Intervention," pp.117–32; Pinnes, *Building the Country*, 2:51.

Porte and/or of the local Ottoman authorities who, as will be seen below, made many efforts to prevent the registration of real estate in the name of the foreign nationals. Revealing examples illustrating the procedures and struggles around these attempts were the Christian settlement projects of Clorinda Minor and her group in Urtas and Jaffa, of the Church of the Messiah believers in Jaffa led by G.W.J. Adams, of the Templers in Haifa, and of private attempts at developing the Holy Land such as that of Herbert E. Clark in the Arab village of Media [Modin] in Samaria, and of Jews like Mordecai Lubowsky in Galilee.[52] Of these, the vicissitudes of the German-American Templer colony in Haifa can serve as an example of Christian group settlement. This case emphasizes the crucial nature of the land tenure problem as the basis for success or failure of settlement in the Holy Land under Ottoman rule.

Lands of American Templers in their Haifa Colony (1869–1895)
American diplomatic and consular activity, at various levels, for assuring the rights of American citizens who settled in Palestine to obtain title deeds to property in their names, can be followed in the case of the German-American Templers in Haifa. It illustrates the contributory role of the United States consular representatives in the process of land acquisition and settlement. These consular activities reveal the hostility of the Ottoman government to what in effect was an endeavor for establishing an extraterritorial foothold by foreign nationals in the heart of the Ottoman Empire. In order to deter the Templers from developing their colony in Haifa, the Ottoman officials for many years evaded granting them title deeds for the lands they had purchased. The local authorities, being far from the center of the Empire and the influence of the powers, evinced an even more hostile attitude than the Sublime Porte. Nevertheless, it is noteworthy that in the early 1870s, the governor of the Damascus province was willing to rent, or give outright to the Templers, twelve thousand dunams of unexploited state lands on Mount Carmel. This however never materialized.[53]

Most of the Pietist Templers who founded the colony in Haifa came from Württemberg in South Germany. They were joined by kindred families of German origin from southern Russia, and by some who had emigrated to America and became citizens, mainly from New York State. In 1874, there

---

52   Kark, "Millenarism," pp.47–62; Kark, "Historical Sites," pp.1–17.

53   Carmel, *German Settlement,* pp.62–65, 80–83, 90; Carmel based his research on the Templers's periodical, *Die Warte,* and on German diplomatic and consular documents.

were in the colony eight families of American citizenship (40 persons out of 350). The entire colony owned at the time fifty-five houses, thirty acres of vineyards, and five hundred acres of cultivated land.[54] Even before starting their settlement, the group's leaders tried, in 1868, to obtain a firman in Constantinople allowing them to buy land in Palestine and to settle there, but their efforts failed. Nevertheless, and despite warnings by the American consul in Jerusalem, Victor Beauboucher, the Templers purchased, early in 1869, the first of their lands in Haifa. They began building their colony in the clear understanding that their acquisitions were contrary to Ottoman law. As reported by one of the leaders of the colony, Georg David Hardegg, to the committee of the Templer Society in January 1869, in order to get around the prohibition still in effect for foreigners, including German and American nationals, on buying real estate in the Empire, the settlers carried out the transactions through a local Ottoman subject, who bought the lands in his name. The kadi of Haifa was quick to detect the deception and informed the local buyer that the deal was invalid.[55]

The dispute over the registration of the Templers' lands in their names was for long years the main source of strained relations between them and the Ottoman authorities. When the Templers were setting up their colony in Haifa and were acquiring land, the Imperial Rescript of January 1867 conceding to foreigners the right of holding real estate in the Ottoman Empire had been proclaimed, and may have influenced the timing of their arrival in Haifa and Palestine. But each of the powers had still to sign a separate protocol with the Porte. The settlers were thus in principle precluded from registering the lands in their names until the North German Confederation signed the protocol later in the year; the American citizens had to await the signature of the United States in 1874. In practice, the Turks raised difficulties in issuing the title deeds even several years after the ratification. This restrained the impetus of the settlers in Haifa who feared to buy additional land or to erect structures on plots for which they could not obtain legal rights of possession.

In all the negotiations and the preparation of the agreement between the United States and the Sublime Porte regarding real estate, and also after the treaty was signed, Jacob Schumacher was extremely active in dealing with this crucial matter for the colony. Schumacher, one of the founders of the Templer colony, was an American citizen and served as the American consular

---

54   Jacob Schumacher, U.S. Consular Agent, Haifa, to Edward Van Dyck, U.S. Consular Clerk, Beirut, 19 September 1874, USNA RG84 Haifa Copy Book 1872–1886 Box 5976.

55   Carmel, *German Settlement*, pp.18–20, 173–76.

agent in Haifa from 1872 to 1891. He approached this issue both as a matter of principle and as the representative of the American families. As a settler who himself had bought land in Haifa, he had a decided personal interest in all aspects of the problem. In August 1873, Schumacher reported to John B. Hay, the United States consul in Beirut who was his superior, that not only did the settlers, being foreigners, pay high prices for land the boundaries of which were not respected by the Muslims, but that until then no real estate had been registered in their names. He mentioned that the German Empire had already signed the treaty with Turkey, but that the kadi of Haifa claimed not to have received any instructions for issuing title deeds, so that the settlers resorted to roundabout ways in purchasing land for the colony with the help of G.D. Hardegg, one of their leaders. "The land bought by negotiation in his name, and transferred privately by witnesses to the Germans." And he adds in an additional letter, "Trustees purchased the land but no titles could be given to colonists." [56]

In the joint struggle of the German and American colonists, petitions were sent to C. Weber, the German consul-general in Beirut and to George H. Boker, the U.S. minister-resident at Constantinople, requesting "that all lands purchased by them should be transferred to their names." The appeal to the minister in Constantinople was made after the new American consul in Beirut, John T. Edgar, applied to the vali who opposed the granting of title deeds to the settlers without specific instructions from Constantinople.[57] Jacob Schumacher continued at the end of 1874 and throughout 1875 to carry on ramified correspondence concerning real estate and the title deeds to the lands of American citizens in the colony. He transmitted to George S. Fisher, the consul in Beirut, information regarding real estate, including what he learned from Sadiq Bey, the kaimakam of Haifa. Regarding the affairs of American citizens, the interpretation of the kaimakam was that these should become Ottoman nationals if they wished to register the land in their names.[58] The protocol with Turkey was ratified by the United States on 29 October

---

56   Jacob Schumacher, U.S. Consular Agent, Haifa, to John Baldwin Hay, U.S. Consul, Beirut, 23 August 1873 and George S. Fisher, U.S. Consul, Beirut, 27 January 1875, USNA RG84 Haifa Copy Book 1872–1886 Box 5976.

57   Schumacher to Hay, ibid. John T. Edgar, U.S. Consul, Beirut, to Jacob Schumacher, U.S. Consular Agent, Haifa, 28 January 1874, USNA RG84 Haifa Miscellaneous Papers Received 1875–1917 Miscellaneous Papers 1878–1903 Green Box.

58   Jacob Schumacher, U.S. Consular Agent, Haifa, to George S. Fisher, U.S. Consul, Beirut, 4 October 1874, 6, 9 November 1874 and Sedek Bey, Kaimakam, Haifa, to Schumacher, 15 November 1874 (Arabic), USNA RG84 Haifa Copy Book 1872–1886 Box 5976.

1874, and on 16 December of that year the consulate in Beirut issued its Notification No.5, in print, which gave the contents of the proclamation of the President of the U.S. for the information of "Consular Agents of this Consulate and the citizens of the U.S. resident in Syria for their information and attention." [59] Fisher even met with the vali of Damascus in order to clarify the status of American citizens regarding real estate, including the people of the German-American colony in Haifa who acquired land and did not receive the title deeds. He also tried to help the Americans in Haifa in their struggle against the ruling of the mutasarrif that American citizens could not buy lands and main sites from Germans, which limited the possibilities of internal transactions between arriving and departing colonists.

As an aid in dealing with these matters, Fisher asked Schumacher to send him the map he had made which showed the "local inhabitants and boundary of each tract of land belonging to our citizens which has to be transferred from one or other persons." [60] Schumacher was indeed the right man for the job, for by profession he was an architect and field surveyor. Already in 1873, he sent the consul in Beirut the map he drew of the colony. As requested by Fisher, he sent him an identical or new map in 1875, which included the plots and buildings of all the settlers in the colony, streets, public structures and additional land purchase and expansion plans. The plots of the American citizens (six families) were marked with American flags. Apparently, part of this map which today is kept in the Israel State Archives was printed in five colors in Buffalo, New York in that year. It is one of the earliest modern cadastral maps drawn in Palestine in the last century. Later, in 1877, Schumacher made a remarkably accurate drawing of the Templer colony, looking from the Carmel to Haifa Bay. Much can be learned from this drawing about the houses, farm structures, the plots around the houses, cultivated areas, and other land uses (Figure 14 and Plate 29).[61]

---

59   In USNA RG84 Haifa, Miscellaneous and Official Correspondence Received 1875–1917 Miscellaneous Papers 1875–1904 Green Box. It seems that Schumacher received the document several days before 16 December because he acknowledged its arrival in a despatch to Fisher on 12 December 1874, see USNA RG84 Haifa Copy Book, ibid.

60   Jacob Schumacher, U.S. Consular Agent, Haifa, to George S. Fisher, U.S. Consul, Beirut, 27 January 1875, Copy Book, ibid., and Fisher to Schumacher, 2 February 1875, Miscellaneous and Official Correspondence, ibid.

61   Jacob Schumacher, U.S. Consular Agent, Haifa to John B. Hay and George S. Fisher, U.S. Consuls, Beirut, 28 June 1873 and 20 February 1875, Copy Book, ibid., Jacob Schumacher, Sketch of the German-American Colony and Mission Station of "The Temple Society," near Caifa, at the foot of Mount Carmel, Palestine, Clay, Cosack & Co., Buffalo, N.Y., U.S.A. (n.d.), ISA RG690/681; the drawing: "Temple Colony Near Haifa at the Foot of Mount Carmel, Syria" is reproduced in

Beyond the efforts of the consul in Beirut, and after the United States signed the protocol, Schumacher himself tried to arrange the registration of lands, bought by the Americans from local persons, with Sidqi al-Sharif, the mutasarrif of the Acre district and with the kaimakam of Haifa. It turned out that the local authorities had made no great effort to acquaint themselves with the details of the agreement and raised demands against the colonists for retroactive payments of various taxes,[62] including *"vergi* of real estate" on the lands they had bought. In mid-1875, the kaimakam of Haifa also transmitted to the German consular agent the claims of the tithe tax farmers who were to have collected the tax on crops, to the effect that the settlers were not paying land taxes, and for many years had not paid produce taxes.[63]

The dispute affected others concerned with settlement in Palestine. Already at the end of 1874, the editor of the Jerusalem Hebrew newspaper, *Havatzeleth*, Yisrael Dov Frumkin, wrote about the heavy obstacle imposed on the Jewish and Templer settlements in the form of taxation on produce which amounted to 12.5 percent. He cited the example of the "Württembergers who settled in the colony on Mount Carmel" who tried to develop the region and to pave roads, but who were severely handicapped by the yoke of taxes. Frumkin proposed obtaining from the sultan a full exemption from taxes and customs duties for all the new colonies to be founded in the Holy Land, at least for a few years after their inception, to allow for their establishment.[64]

At the end of 1876 and the beginning of 1877, the settlers were informed of the decision of the mutasarrif of Acre, of the kaimakam of Haifa, and of the provincial administrative council (*meclis-i 'umumi*) recommending the appointment of a committee for investigating and valuing the property and lands of the Germans (and the Americans) in the Haifa colony, in order to register these. According to the decision as transmitted to Schumacher in his capacity of United States consular agent in Haifa, the committee was to include, as representative of the settlers, one of their members, Friedrich Keller, who was also an official of the German consular agency in Haifa.

Carmel's *German Settlement,* last page.

62   Correspondence in Arabic between Jacob Schumacher, U.S. Consular Agent, Haifa, and Sedek Bey, the Kaimakam of Haifa, 26 November 1874, 8, 11, 20 February 1875, 24 June 1875, 10, 26 July 1875 and 15 March 1876, Copy Book, ibid.

63   The Kaimakam of Haifa to E. Ziffos, German Vice-Consul, Haifa, 12 July 1875, ISA RG67/439.

64   Frumkin, "On Working the Land," pp.54–55.

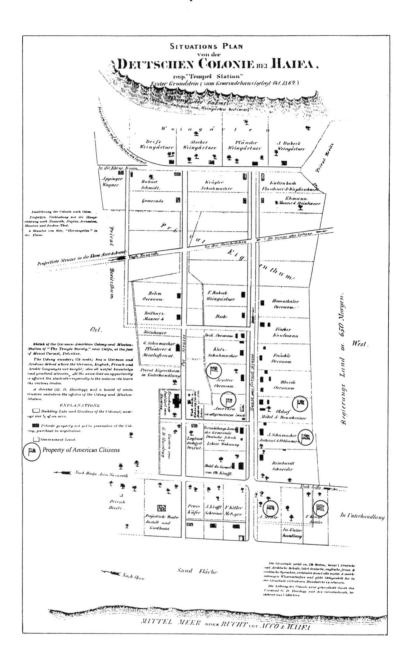

Figure 14. Plan of the German-American Templer colony at Haifa, 1875
Source: ISA RG690/681

Plate 29. German-American Templer colony near Haifa
Source: Courtesy of Y. Ben Artzi

The committee was charged with examining the legal status of the government lands (*miri*) and of the abandoned lands (*mawat*) at the foot of Mount Carmel which formed part of the colony's holdings, to prepare a list of sellers and buyers, and a list of the lands. The real purpose behind the formation of the committee was mainly to determine the taxes due to the authorities for vacant lands.[65]

According to Alex Carmel, a change in the approach of the Ottoman authorities came about only in 1877 because the German government revised its negative attitude towards the Templers who had been regarded as nonconformists (and not because of American pressures). This change led to diplomatic pressures being exerted by the German foreign ministry and embassy in Constantinople on the Sublime Porte and on the Ottoman ambassador in Berlin, with the Porte finally acceding to the requests for registering the Haifa lands at the end of 1877. It seems that it was also due to the pressures by the German consul in Jerusalem, Thankmar von Münchhausen, on the governor of Acre, to the demonstrative presence of a fleet of five German warships along the coasts of Palestine in mid-1877 (which was to deter the local population and the authorities from attacking German nationals in the Orient), and to Turkey's humiliating defeats in the war with Russia

65   Document of the Kaimakam of Haifa sent to Jacob Schumacher, U.S. Consular Agent, Haifa, 13 February 1878, USNA RG84 Haifa Miscellaneous and Official Correspondence Received 1875–1917 Miscellaneous Papers 1875–1904 Green Box (Arabic).

which was going on at the time.[66] This may have been true regarding the German citizens of the colony, but from the American consular correspondence it appears that already at the end of 1876 and the beginning of 1877, the authorities in Acre arrived at a decision, at least ostensibly, to take preliminary steps for the registration of the lands. At the end of 1877, ten American settlers of the colony addressed yet another petition to the American secretary of state (the German settlers similarly applied to their government asking for help in settling the land registration issue). They pointed out that the continued holding of the title deeds by the previous owners enabled them to exploit the settlers' position to "Extort more money than actual tax payment, reclaim the land and also move boundaries." [67]

From the congratulatory letters of the American consulate in Beirut to Schumacher, in March 1878, on the success of his efforts, it appears that as a result of the State Department's intervention, vizierial orders were issued from Constantinople to the authorities in Damascus to give "title deeds to the lands of the Americans at Haifa." The consulate in Beirut asked the vali in Damascus to forward these orders to the mutasarrif of Acre.[68] Additional delay in registering the properties was caused, as discovered by John T. Edgar, the American consul in Beirut, by the old claim that in order to carry out the transfer and registration of titles, the settlers must pay the fees for the procedure, as well as taxes on crops, retroactively, despite the lands not having been registered in their names. As to the amount of the fees: "If the farmer owners of the lands were the absolute owners this is, if their titles were *mulk* [freehold] **not** *taboo* [or *miri* state lands, R.K.] the fee charged should be one percent; but, if the titles were *taboo*, not *mulk* the fee should be five percent...." Edgar added his opinion regarding the legal status of the lands: "I suspect that all the titles were *taboo*." [69] The congratulations were thus premature, and at the end of May 1878, the registry of titles of the German and American nationals had not been implemented, despite the work

66   Carmel, *German Settlement,* pp.94–99, 176. According to Schumacher's report to John T. Edgar, U.S. Consul, Beirut on 15 September 1878, ten men-of-war anchored in the bay of Haifa, including English, German, and French vessels, USNA RG84 Haifa Copy Book 1872–1886 Box 5976.

67   Ten settlers in Haifa to William M. Evarts, U.S. Secretary of State, Washington D.C., 26 October 1877, Copy Book, ibid.; Carmel, ibid., pp.64–65, 98–99.

68   John T. Edgar, U.S. Consul, Beirut, to Jacob Schumacher, U.S. Consular Agent, Haifa, 7 March 1878, ibid.

69   John T. Edgar, U.S. Consul, Beirut to Jacob Schumacher, U.S. Consular Agent, Haifa, 12 March 1878, USNA RG84 Haifa Miscellaneous Papers Received 1875–1917 Miscellaneous Papers 1878–1903 Green Box.

of several committees appointed to study the subject. According to Schumacher, only the direct intervention of the United States minister with the Sublime Porte, and unequivocal orders by the governor of Syria would force the local authorities to comply.[70] Only on 12 February 1879 were the title deeds finally given to the American settlers in Haifa. Schumacher believed that this was due in no small measure to the new, capable kaimakam of Haifa, Ahsan Bey. It only remained to decide the question of the place and manner of the registration – whether in the consular agency in Haifa or the consulate in Beirut, "if there is a particular form for recording real estate titles." According to a private report, in German, from Schumacher to the consul in Beirut, the settlers received *tapu* title deeds issued by the local administration and "Hadschies" [*hujjet,* or registration certificates from a Muslim court, R.K.] from Constantinople. The gardens attached to the houses, the planted vegetation and the vineyards were registered as *mulk sarf* (lands categorized as liable only to *vergi* taxes).[71]

This episode served as one of the sources for an important report written in 1881 for the United States Congress, on the Capitulations and land in the Ottoman Empire (see above, Chapter I). In March of 1880, Edward A. Van Dyck, the U.S. consular clerk in Cairo, requested Schumacher, who had gained considerable experience regarding land matters, to brief him on the registration of the Templer lands in Haifa:

> I remember that up to the year 1876 you & the other members of the Haifa Colony [sic] had not yet got the title-deeds (*Hodjets*) of your lands, & that the *mahkameh* of Haifa had not up to that time any official knowledge of the Law & Protocol granting to foreigners the right to hold real property in Turkey.
>
> Please tell me if you have at last succeeded in getting the *hodjets*; & if not, please tell me briefly the main points in the history of the difficulties you have had to encounter & the opposition you have met with.
>
> I want this information to insert in my official report to the U.S. government & will therefore be obliged to you for all the facts and observations you may see fit to give me on the subject

---

70 Edgar to Schumacher 25 April and 30 May 1878, ibid., and Schumacher to Edgar 2 May 1878, Copy Book, ibid.

71 Jacob Schumacher, U.S. Consular Agent, Haifa, to Erhard Bissinger, U.S. Consul, Beirut, 28 December 1887, USNA RG84 Haifa Copy Book 1886–1899 Box 5977 (German).

of the Law and Protocol & its workings & results up to the
present time.[72]

However, the tribulations of the German and American settlers in Haifa
did not end even then. During the eighties, with the beginning of the wave of
Jewish immigration to Palestine known as the First *Aliya*, and the establishment
of Jewish agricultural settlements in 1882, the fears of the Ottoman government
flared up again. Despite the potential contribution to the development of the
country and its economy by American and European settlers in the Empire,
there were growing apprehensions that these would become pretexts for
intervention by the powers in the internal affairs of Turkey and would stimulate
the nationalistic aspirations of minority groups. Accordingly, a number of
decrees were issued in 1884, 1887, and 1888 restricting immigration and
land purchases by foreign nationals.[73] These decrees were aimed mainly
against Jews, but affected also Americans citizens, and probably also Germans.
Several Americans who, in 1887, bought agricultural lands near the Haifa
colony applied to the Ottoman authorities to have these registered. The
authorities refused to transfer land to American citizens according to a new
order issued by the vilayet of Syria, a copy of which could not be obtained.
Jacob Schumacher, who still served as the American consular agent in Haifa,
stated that the Ottoman government made every effort in Haifa to keep
foreigners from acquiring land. The orders from the Sublime Porte in these
matters were secret, and imposed severe punishment on any official who
dared to register lands in the names of foreigners. Schumacher requested the
consul in Beirut to intervene with the vali for the abrogation of this policy
and the instructions which were contrary to the existing agreements with the
United States. Bissinger, the consul in Beirut, discovered with certainty that
for about one year the vali had indeed "instructions emanating from the
Sublime Porte to prohibit only the transfer of lands to Jewish immigrants,"
and that he had issued the orders in this matter.[74]

---

72   Edward A. Van Dyck, U.S. Consular Clerk, Cairo, to Jacob Schumacher, U.S. Consular Agent,
      Haifa, 29 March 1880 USNA RG84 Haifa Miscellaneous and Official Correspondence Received
      1875–1917 Miscellaneous Papers 1875–1904 Green Box.

73   Karpat, "Ottoman Immigration Policies."

74   Jacob Schumacher, U.S. Consular Agent, Haifa, to Bishara Cardahi, U.S. Dragoman, Acre,
      28 December 1887, and Schumacher to Erhard Bissinger, U.S. Consul, Beirut, 7 February,
      10 March and 30 June 1888, USNA RG84 Copy Book 1886–1899 Box 5977; Nasif Meshake, U.S.
      Consular Agent, Damascus to Bissinger, Beirut 25 February 1888 and Bissinger to Schumacher
      27 February 1888, Miscellaneous and Official Correspondence Received, ibid.

Moreover, a decade later, in 1887, new differences arose regarding the definition of the legal status of the lands of the German-American colony. Following directives of an imperial firman, the kaimakam of Haifa ordered the settlers to pay a tithe of their crops, which was the normal tax on *miri* lands but not on *mulk* lands. Schumacher wrote an angry private letter – in German, as opposed to the usual correspondence in English – to Bissinger, the American consul in Beirut. He protested vehemently against the attempt of the government "to go against Article 2 of the agreement with the United States [see above] and to change the absolute property status of American citizens [meaning *mulk*, R.K.] to *ard miri* (*miri* land) which is worth less and those who held it were subjected to the exploitation of officials and to losses, as proven by the case of Arab fellahin."[75]

And again almost ten years later, in 1895, Gottlieb Schumacher, who had succeeded his father as the American consular agent in Haifa, mentions disputes in the matter of land ownership by him, together with other American citizens, over land they bought from Elias Haddad. It may be that the lands referred to were those acquired by the settlers more than twenty years earlier, when they first settled in the colony. In any case, here too, Schumacher interpreted the verdict of the *mahkama* in Haifa against the Americans as a pretext aimed at foreigners. He asked Gibson, the consul in Beirut, to conduct an investigation to prove American ownership of the land and to demand the dismissal of the judge of the *mahkama*.[76]

This tedious process of registering the American Templers' lands in the Haifa German colony illustrates, on the one hand, the negative attitude of the Ottoman administration to the settlement of foreigners in Palestine, and, on the other, the ceaseless efforts on behalf of the settlers by the consular agents in Haifa and their superiors in Beirut, as well as by the ministers and ambassadors of the United States in Constantinople, and the State Department in Washington. The interested American citizens tried every possible legal loophole and pressure to achieve their objectives. This they sometimes did in a decidedly one-sided, manipulative manner, bypassing accepted protocol and the Ottoman bureaucracy, not less than did the local authorities and

---

75 Schumacher to Bissinger, 28 December 1887, Copy Book, ibid.

76 Already in the despatch of the kaimakam of the Haifa district of 8 February 1875 to Jacob Schumacher in Haifa, he indicates having received the latter's notification regarding the purchase of a tract of land from Messrs. Ayyub el Gadda' and Ilyas Haddad which the Templers wanted to register in their names. And see, Miscellaneous and Official Correspondence Received, ibid.; Gottlieb Schumacher, U.S. Consular Agent, Haifa, to T.R. Gibson, U.S. Consul, Beirut, 29 June and 5 May 1895, Copy Book, ibid.

judges. This is fully borne out by the success of the settlers in registering their lands as *mulk* which were freehold, while almost certainly, before the settlement of the Templers, these lands were *miri*, of which the rights to full ownership (*raqabah*) were vested in the State, and only the rights of usage (*tasarruf*) by the holders – and hence also their liability to higher taxation. This explains the long "tribulations" imposed by the authorities on the settlers, and the continuous disputes regarding the legal status of the lands and the taxes due on them. In summary, it may be said that it was the doggedness of the settlers and the backing they received from the diplomatic representatives of the powers that enabled them to succeed and to build up the thriving German-American colony in Haifa.

SERVING AMERICAN BUSINESS AND PRIVATE INTERESTS ABROAD

The Business Community

From the mid-19th century and until World War I, the advancement of American business interests in Palestine by the United States consular representatives was mainly conditioned by the overall relationship between the powers and the Ottoman Empire rather than by any local factors. As suggested at the beginning of this book, the trade relations between the United States and the Ottoman Empire should be seen against the background of the industrial revolution in Europe and America, the competition for markets between the industrialized nations, and the move of American economic policy from a domestic-centered one to full participation in the international imperialist scramble. All the powers shared a decided interest in the perpetuation of the capitulatory system. At the time of the Young Turk Revolution in 1908, American commercial enterprise in the Ottoman Empire expanded considerably and began to bear fruit, but came to a halt at the outbreak of the War in 1914.[77] Although it was but a small corner of the Ottoman Empire, Palestine was a potentially important market in the region because of its growing European population. The consuls of the European powers and of the United States in Jerusalem, and the consular agents in Haifa – and especially in Jaffa, which was becoming an important port city of the eastern Mediterranean – made efforts to foster their nations' economic interests by collecting information and reporting to their governments on

---

77   Gordon, *American Relations*, pp.70,141; De Novo, *American Interests*, p.48.

commercial activities. But there were also direct contacts between companies, commercial houses, and industrial establishments and their respective consular representatives in Palestine, for names and referrals to reliable local businessmen who might qualify as commercial agents, and who could be entrusted to accept consignments of goods and merchandise on credit.[78]

During the second half of the 19th century, the American consuls in Jerusalem and Beirut usually restricted themselves to reporting to the Department of State and to other governmental departments. With the help of the consular agents at Jaffa and Haifa, they gathered statistics on imports and exports of various types of goods in their districts, on the nationality of the shipping companies, the extent of trade with the United States and other countries, details of the firms engaged in this trade, local banking facilities, assessments of American trade potentials, and on other types of foreign enterprise in industrial production, mining, insurance, finance, and agriculture.[79] Remarkable events connected with international commerce received special attention, such as the Russian Floating Exposition at Jaffa which displayed the products of 134 Russian manufacturing firms on board the S.S. *Empereur Nicolas II* visiting ports of the Black Sea, the Aegean, and the eastern Mediterranean at the end of 1909 and the beginning of 1910.[80]

Some of these reports appeared in official publications, as will be seen below, and were available to American business and manufacturing firms. Nevertheless, direct contacts between the latter and the American consular officials in Palestine were few. Here and there, the official correspondence mentioned requests from "American Merchants", as for example, regarding the import of cotton textiles to Palestine in 1889.[81] A real turn of interest in the American business community regarding Palestine as a potential market for its products, and ensuing contacts with the consular officials in Jerusalem and Haifa, but especially with the Jaffa consular agent, came about in 1909–1914. It was probably no coincidence that it occurred with the inception of "dollar diplomacy" during the Taft administration.

---

78   Such a request was addressed to the German consul in Jerusalem as early as in 1873: H. Rothenberger, Damascus, to German Consul, Jerusalem, 27 June 1873, ISA 67/451. And see several examples in: Eliav, *Under Imperial Austrian Protection*, pp.284–90,338,382,413–15.

79   Gustafson, "Records in the National Archives," pp.136–37.

80   Thomas R. Wallace, U.S. Consul, Jerusalem, to Department of State, Washington, D.C., 5 February 1910, USNA RG59 T471/11 [Fi2477/11].

81   Henry Gillman, U.S. Consul, Jerusalem, to William F. Wharton, Assistant Secretary of State, Washington, D.C., 17 December 1889, USNA RG59 T471/6.

This appears from a detailed analysis of a large amount of relevant material in the archives of the United States consulate in Jerusalem and in the Haifa and Jaffa consular agencies.[82] In these repositories are found hundreds of letters from American firms, including catalogs, descriptions, and price lists of various products manufactured or handled by them, questions regarding local market conditions, supply and demand, and marketing possibilities in different fields, as well as queries about local businessmen and commercial houses that could represent American firms, and about their reputations and the scope of their activities. To these should be added requests from the chambers of commerce of Boston, New York, and other places. The letterheads of the business and manufacturing firms that applied to the consular officers are of considerable interest in themselves, for they provide information on their location, their branch offices, the names of the businessmen involved, etc. Their standard format indicates that such letters and material were sent to many consuls in different parts of the world, and not only to those in Palestine.[83] This archival material is important not only for a better understanding of the frameworks for developing foreign trade in the American economy and of the functions and contribution of the consuls to this end, but also for illustrating the penetration and diffusion of new products and technologies to underdeveloped parts of the world, and how it influenced changes in economic activity of these regions. Here, the discussion is limited to Palestine on the eve of World War One, where the beginning of this process can be detected. However, Smout adduced examples of similar activity in Scotland, as early as in the seventies of the last century.[84]

A nice example of such letters is one dated 12 August 1912 from the Campbell Horse Shoe Company Export Department in Philadelphia to "The American Consul, Haifa, Syria":

> As the representative of our government, you are in a favorable
> position to know some concern in your district that could handle
> our product to advantage. Its nature is concisely described in the
> advertising part of this letterhead. Would you have the kindness
> to recommend such a firm to us, of financial responsibility? It

82   U.S. Consulate, Jerusalem, Indexes of Despatches to and from the Department of State 1908–1912, USNA RG59 T471/10–13 [Fi2477/11–12, Fi7582/3–4]; U.S. Consular Agency, Jaffa, USNA RG84 Jaffa Miscellaneous Letters 1900–1914 Box 5965; USNA RG84 Haifa U.S. Consular Agency, Haifa, Miscellaneous Letters Received.

83   Ibid.

84   Smout, "American Consular Reports on Scotland," pp.304–8.

would aid us materially in establishing a trade which would mean a great deal to our country as well as to our enterprise. The Campbell horseshoe is already being extensively used by the larger express companies in this country, and by manufacturing concerns that make use of large numbers of horses. The shoes are packed for shipment in 100-pound kegs, and sold F.O.B. Philadelphia, Baltimore, or Boston at $10 per keg..." [85]

Sometimes there was a whole series of questions. On 24 December 1913, the Export Department of the Motor Car Equipment Co., Wholesalers of Importers and Manufacturers of Automobile Accessories, New York, requested the following information from the "American Consular Service" wherever it may be, and in this case, at Haifa: [86]

FIRST. A complete list of the dealers and jobbers in automobiles and automobile supplies in your territory.

SECOND. A list of general commission houses and merchants.

THIRD. A list of manufacturers' agents.

FOURTH. A list of hardware dealers and jobbers.

FIFTH. Can you give us the names of such houses who represent the various American car manufacturers as well as European car manufacturers? We are particularly interested to know who are representing in your territory the following automobile manufacturers:

FORD MOTOR CO.	Mitchell-Lewis Motor Co.
Cole Motor Car Co.	Oldsmobile Co.
F-I-A-T Co.	Packard Motor Car Co.
Haynes Automobile Co.	Peerless Motor Car Co.
Hudson Motor Car Co.	Pierce -Arrow Motor Car Co.
Knox Automobile Co.	Pope Mfg. Co.
Locomobile Co. of America.	Regal Motor Car Co.
Maxwell Motor Car Co.	Studebaker Corporation.

SIXTH. Would you be interested to receive our catalogue, and will you keep our name in your reference file as manufacturers, jobbers and importers of automobile supplies? This is the only house that does an extensive wholesale business...

85 USNA, Haifa, ibid.

86 USNA, Haifa, ibid.

P.S. How many automobiles are at the present time in use in
your territory?

It might be mentioned here that the first motor car in the Holy Land was
brought by an American, Charles J. Glidden, who covered 750 miles in 1908
and raised the possibility that cars with high road clearance held the promise
of a lucrative export trade. But at the time of the New York firm's letter,
there were only a very few cars in the country.[87]

Clearly, for the consular agent to provide such a wealth of information
demanded many hours of work, even though he had a ready stock of standard
data on file. In Jaffa, for example, there were few local businessmen who
met the requirements as possible commercial representatives.[88] From over
two hundred letters in the archives of the Jaffa consular agency for the years
1909–1914, and over one hundred and fifty such requests in the Jerusalem
consular archives for 1908–1914, a picture emerges regarding the types of
products and the places from which marketing outlets were sought (Figure
15).[89]

The main categories were: agriculture (farm machinery, engines, pumps, as
well as agricultural produce and animals, and/or means for processing and
marketing, such as mill machinery, packing paper and boxes for citrus fruits,
incubators, etc.); industry (machinery and tools); raw materials, minerals,
and construction (lead, cement, coal, steel); energy, transport, and
communications (petroleum, electrical equipment, locomotives, electric
vehicles, bicycles, boats, telegraph lines, wireless equipment); insurance and
manpower services; pharmaceuticals and medical services; music,
entertainment and culture (musical instruments, moving pictures, books);
office equipment (writing supplies, typewriters); food products (canned
preserves, powdered foods); household (furniture, ice boxes, cutlery); footwear,
clothing, and personal equipment (wigs, razors, watches); and miscellaneous.

The letters came from different states and cities in and outside the United
States. Many of them were from New York City and the state of New York,

87   Report of 15 April 1908 quoted by Gustafson ("Records in the National Archives," pp.133–34)
     USNA RG59/13653.

88   See, for example, one of many responses by the consular agent at Jaffa to the questions from a
     company dated 10 August 1913, in which he lists the hardware dealers in Jaffa. USNA RG84 Jaffa,
     ibid.

89   Miscellaneous Letters 1900–1914, USNA RG84 Jaffa Box 5965 and Indexes of Despatches and
     Despatches to and from Department of State, U.S. Consulate, Jerusalem 1908–1912, USNA RG59
     T471/10–13 [Fi2477/11–12, Fi7852/3–4].

others were from Ohio, Wisconsin, Michigan, Illinois, Indiana, Pennsylvania, Massachusetts, and California. The American consular representatives in Palestine also received requests for commercial information from London, Marseilles, Geneva, Naples, Constantinople, Smyrna, Beirut, Tripoli, Cairo, and the Philippine Islands.

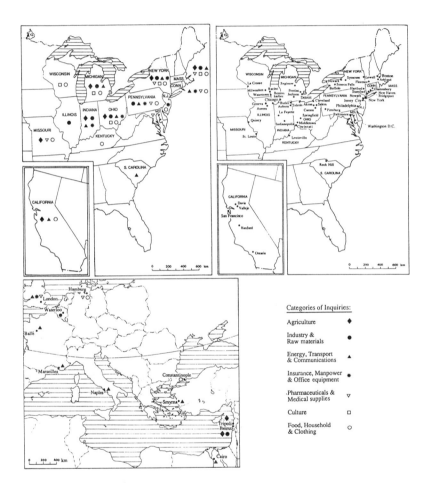

Figure 15. United States marketing inquiries in Palestine, 1908–1914

Other Services

In addition to providing services in the realms of trade and business, the American consular officials in Palestine were charged with assisting private persons, and American agencies and institutions who requested such help. This may be classified into two broad categories: information and legal matters. A few examples will serve to give an idea of what these services entailed. Requests for information were extremely varied and sometimes even rather peculiar. Thus, in 1875, a man named A. Blohapman from Los Angeles wrote to Ernst Hardegg, the consular agent in Jaffa, asking for oranges.[90] Other questions touched upon churches or religious groups in the country. Bishop G.J. Bedel from Cleveland, Ohio asked Hardegg to write to him "...about the Armenian Church in Jerusalem and others (German)..." [91]

Sometimes the requests were forwarded to the consular agents from Jerusalem or Beirut. Even though the questions were not always understood, or some requests appeared strange, they were always treated in all seriousness. One of the most interesting of such letters and the manner in which it was dealt with was a request received by the American consul at Beirut, Thomas S. Doyle. It was sent from Chicago in 1898 and related to the beginnings of the Bahai faith in Acre. Doyle, who was totally ignorant of the matter, asked his agent in Haifa, Gottlieb Schumacher, to prepare for him

> an account of this sect [so] that I may reply intelligently to my correspondent. This lady in the U.S. wants to know of a certain sect whose headquarters are at Acca – they call themselves "Babists" – so my correspondent writes the word; she may have meant "Baptists" – you will know. She wants to know where these "Babists" come from, what their teaching is and about how many of them "reside at the so-called household."
>
> She says, further, the gentleman teacher that is here (in "Chicago") is said to be a prophet of God and giving not very **"quietly** what he claims is the only truth for this world and the Headquarters is at Acca. He is master of 7 languages "and a learned man...He claims that "the same Jesus Christ that was here 2000 years ago is "reincarnated and lives there. Is such a

---

90   A. Blohapman, Los Angeles, to Ernst Hardegg, U.S. Consular Agent, Jaffa, 10 April 1875, USNA
      RG84 Jaffa Miscellaneous Letters Received from the Principal Officer in Jerusalem and Miscellaneous
      Letters 1874–1879 Box 5959.

91   Ibid., 28 October 1876.

thing known there" (in Acca) and what name does He go under now [sic]."

And Doyle added: "I have quoted from the letter – It looks to me as if the writer is being duped by some impostor or is a person herself whose intellect is just a little weak." [92]

With the imposition, at the turn of the century, of severe restrictions on Jews in Palestine by the Ottoman government, there were also letters from Jews in America asking the State Department for information, such as on "...the question What [sic] rights and privileges a United States citizen has in Turkish dominions such as Palestine in regard to buying land in the past ten years..." This letter was referred to the consul at Jerusalem, as was the request "to be afforded the good offices of the consular Agent at Jaffa in protecting certain property in that vicinity..." The replies were sent directly from Jerusalem to the writer.[93] Some applicants asked for help in locating relatives in Palestine.

The consuls filled an important legal function which included dealing with claims from the United States against American citizens residing in Jerusalem, and with the arranging of burial, estates, and bequests of persons deceased in Palestine whose heirs (or some of whose heirs) lived in the United States.[94] Occasionally, the consul had to deal with property in the United States, as in the case of the young girl who applied to the American consul at Jerusalem, Thomas R. Wallace, in 1908 "...with an original notice for the sale of real estate in which she had an interest and which had been returned to her because of defective service." She hoped to receive a small sum of money that was due to her. Wallace wrote that the girl lived in California, that her father was a "religious enthusiast, away over in Arabia, working in the vineyard" and that the property to be sold was claimed to be in Iowa, and added that he prepared for her the return of the "service" as stipulated by law.[95]

---

92   Thomas S. Doyle, U.S. Consul, Beirut, to Gottlieb Schumacher, U.S. Consular Agent, Haifa, 29 March 1898, USNA RG84 Haifa Miscellaneous and Official Correspondence Received 1875–1917 Miscellaneous Papers 1878–1903 Green Box.

93   M. Lazarus, Syracuse, to Department of State, Washington, D.C., 5 January 1910, W. Barr, Department of State, to Thomas R. Wallace, U.S. Consul, Jerusalem, 15 January and 6 June 1910 and Wallace to Lazarus, 29 April 1910, USNA RG59 T471/11 [Fi2477/11]. See also under "Real Estate," in this chapter.

94   See under: Management of Estates, above, and the report by Consul Willson on his work: Joseph G. Willson, U.S. Consul, Jerusalem, to Robert R. Taft, Assistant Secretary of State, Washington, D.C., 7 October 1881, USNA RG59 T471/5.

95   Thomas R. Wallace, U.S. Consul, Jerusalem, to Assistant Secretary of State, Washington, D.C.,

One of many requests dating to 1910 in the archives of the Jaffa consular agency, was accompanied by a description, photograph, and offer of a reward of $100 by the Headquarters of the Metropolitan Police Detective Bureau of Washington, D.C., asked for assistance in locating and arresting one Horton Sympson, aged 43, a public school principal convicted by the Grand Jury of the District of Columbia for participating, with two physicians, in a criminal operation for abortion on a teacher in his school.[96] And the Pinkerton detective agency also hoped for help from American consuls and consular agents in various countries. In July 1910, a printed announcement with photograph was sent to the Jaffa consular agency from the Boston branch of the Pinkerton National Detective Agency, with the request to help locate a 21 year-old student, Albion Davis Pike of Lubec, Maine, who disappeared on 15 March 1907. And there is a request from their New York branch office, with a reward offer of $1,000 for help in apprehending the escaped prisoners, the gambler Timothy A. Sheedy, and his associate James Cornell.[97]

REPORTING TO REGIONAL AND STATE DEPARTMENT SUPERIORS

Annual and Special Reports

Various sources dealing with the operations of United States consuls throughout the world, from 1778 to the end of the second decade of the 20th century, emphasize the increasing importance of suitable reporting to the different government departments in Washington.[98] Several writers have dwelt on the development and expansion of such reports and on the improvements in their levels of competence since the introduction of reforms in the consular service in 1856, 1906, and in 1924.[99] At the end of the 18th and the beginning of the 19th centuries, consuls occasionally reported on American vessels entering or clearing from a particular port, and from time

---

8 July 1908, USNA RG59 T471/10 [Fi2477/10].

96   Major & Superintendent of Metropolitan Police Department, Washington, D.C., to Ernst Hardegg,
     U.S. Consular Agent, Jaffa, 10 May 1910, USNA RG84 Jaffa Miscellaneous Records 1911–1915.

97   Pinkerton National Detective Agency, Boston, 1 July 1910 and New York, 13 August 1910, to Jaffa
     Consular Agency, ibid.

98   References to many articles and reports discussing the subject appear in Griffin, *List of References.*

99   Carr, "The American Consular Service," pp.891–913; Jones, *The Consular Service*, pp.60–86;
     Schuyler, *American Diplomacy*, pp.47–59; Lay, *The Foreign Service*, pp.124–151,193.

to time supplied political and commercial information of interest to the United States.[100]

From the year 1856, the State Department was required to transmit annually all the commercial information sent to it by the consuls. This resulted in the yearly publication of the *Commercial Relations of the United States*, from 1856 to 1914. These reports, of uneven value, which in the 1890s grew into two heavy tomes, described the economic and social conditions in the countries in which the consuls functioned, including the state of business, export and import, and improvements in transport. The growing interest of the State Department in advancing foreign trade led to the publication, from 1880 to 1910, of monthly and annual consular reports. Shortly thereafter began to appear the *Reports on Special Commissioned Topics*, at first as part of the monthly series, and from 1890 in separate series of volumes. By the end of the 1890s, the promotion of American exports occupied most of the consuls' time. In 1898, the State Department began to publish consular reports on a daily basis, which, in 1921 became weekly reports. From 1903, the newly established Department of Commerce and Trade became responsible for the publication of the reports, and for employing special agents to provide information on general commercial conditions and on special products in the various places, such as the *Report on Trade Conditions in Asiatic Turkey (1907)*.[101] The consular reports served mainly smaller and medium-size manufacturing firms that did not have large export departments or agents overseas. As the quality of the reports improved at the end of the last century, they became an invaluable tool in the development of American export trade. Nevertheless, many Americans regarded these publications as inferior and requiring improvement compared with parallel reports of the leading commercial nations.[102]

Because the Ottoman Empire generally, and Palestine in particular, were not very important commercially in the first half of the 19th century, no consuls were appointed there, and only consular agents, under the consul at Beirut, were sporadically active in central Palestine in the period between 1836 and 1856. The reports of the consul in Beirut, Jasper Chasseaud, in all concerning Palestine in 1836–1850, of J. Hosford Smith in 1851–1855, and

100 Carr, ibid., p.895.

101 Werking, "U.S. Consular Reports," pp.300–303.

102 Werking, ibid.; see also an issue of *Business History* (23, 1981) devoted to consular reports, and Jones, *The Consular Service*, pp.85–86.

of Henry Wood in 1855–1857 were sporadic and depended more on the occasional incident in this marginal region, from their points of view. Thus Chasseaud reported in January 1837 on the severe earthquake that destroyed Tiberias and Safed.[103] Besides relating to the areas of their jurisdiction in the consular region of Beirut and in that of the consular agents serving there, the reports dealt with the visit in Palestine of the William F. Lynch expedition to the Dead Sea in 1847–1848, and with the episode concerning the settlement and property of the religious group led by Clorinda Minor in Urtas.[104] The reforms introduced in the consular service of the United States in 1856, indeed found expression in the reports of the consul in Beirut, Wood, to the secretary of state. In September 1856, Wood dispatched a "Report Describing the Consular District, the Ports of Jaffa, Cesarro, Caipha, Acre, Soar, Saida, Beirut, Tripoly, Latakia and Alexandretta."[105] In October 1856, he sent a report which included a description of agriculture in the district and mentioned possible trade activities.[106] This was followed in April 1857 by a report on agricultural and industrial products and on the commerce of northern Syria.[107]

More regular reporting from Palestine began to come in after the United States government formally established a separate consular district there. In compliance with their instructions from Washington, the consuls in Jerusalem managed to file annual reports nearly every year. During the 1860s and 1870s these reports were prepared at the end of September; during the 1880s and 1890s they were written in October, November, and even in December. The consular agents in Jaffa frequently wrote supplements and special reports, and enclosed them with the annual reports. The early annual reports were relatively brief and gave a current overview of many topics. From 1877 to 1891, when J.G. Willson, Selah Merrill, and Henry Gillman served as consuls, the reports became longer and more encompassing. Besides their annual reports, the consuls wrote special papers on such matters as "Turkish Financing", "Business and Commerce in Palestine", "Irrigation as Practiced in Palestine", and "Jews and Jewish Colonies in Palestine."[108] Some of the

---

103   Jasper Chasseaud, U.S. Consul, Beirut, to John Forsyth, Secretary of State, Washington, D.C., 1 January 1837, USNA RG59 T367/1.

104   USNA RG59 T367/1 and 2.

105   Henry Wood, U.S. Consul, Beirut, to William L. Marcy, Secretary of State, Washington, D.C., 15 September 1856, USNA RG59 T367/2.

106   Wood to Marcy, 1 October 1856, ibid.

107   Wood to Marcy, 4 April 1857, ibid.

108   Kark, "Annual Reports," p.132.

reports were drawn up for the use of various departments of the government – especially the Treasury Department and the Department of Agriculture. The reports dealing with the north of the country began to come in regularly from 1872, with the appointment of Jacob Schumacher as consular agent in Haifa, under the consul-general in Beirut.[109]

Contents of the Reports
The contents of the annual and special reports are reviewed here according to subject matter, rather than by discussing the activities of each consul separately as is the general practice in studies dealing with this period.[110] Four principal areas of interest may be discerned:

Government and Politics: This may be broken down into three subtopics. The first deals with Ottoman governors, army and police, security, administration, municipal administration, courts, taxes and revenues from the districts, the Turkish mail and telegraphs, the weakness and corruption of the Turkish authorities, and development plans and reforms. The second pertains to the American consulate and the other foreign consulates. The reports discussed the performance of the American consulate, the consul's salary, rights, and obligations, other positions within the consulate, the consulate building, American citizens, protection offered to Jews, and the activities of the consuls of the other powers. The third area relates to international events, wars, the Great Powers, the "Eastern Question", Britain, the Berlin Convention, the Paris Exhibition, the visit of the Prussian crown prince to Palestine, and so on.[111]

Population: This subject was dealt with in reports on different sectors of the population – urban dwellers, fellahin, and Bedouins – and characteristics of various religious and ethnic groups, including the Christian and Jewish communities, and the relations among them (Regarding the Jews, information was provided on the size of the community, immigration, pertinent government edicts, their economic condition, charities, and education). Quantitative data were supplied about population and occupations, and in accounts of immigration and population distribution. The character of the various segments of the population and their life styles were also described, and topics such as

---

109 In USNA RG84 Haifa Copy Book 1872–1886 Box 5976.

110 Based mainly on despatches from the U.S. consuls in Jerusalem, Palestine, 1856–1906, USNA RG59 T471, and documents in USNA RG84 Haifa and Jaffa.

111 Kark, "Annual Reports,", p.132.

education and health (epidemics, famine, sanitation, hospitals, infirmaries, and drugs) were touched upon.

Settlement: The geographic information on Palestine is reviewed, including climatic conditions (rain, temperature, and so on). Settlement of Palestine, both past and contemporary, was described with emphasis on the neglect and abandonment of villages and lands. A topic of great interest to the consuls was foreign settlement in Palestine. Understandably, they paid special attention to American colonization attempts. Detailed correspondence exists about the Adams colony in Jaffa in the 1860s and about the American Colony in Jerusalem from the 1880s on. The reports also mentioned German colonies (Templers), Jewish agricultural settlements, the colony at Urtas, and Laurence Oliphant's proposal. In connection with urban development (information was provided mainly on Jerusalem, Jaffa, and Haifa), the role played by local and foreign Christians was emphasized, including that of the monasteries and missionaries. The consuls also thought it important to report on the scholarly research and archeological digs being conducted in the country (as for example, by the American Palestine Exploration Society and Conder's discoveries).

The Economy: The reports were particularly detailed in this field. A central theme was agriculture: its potential in Palestine; yields and prices; natural adversities such as locusts and drought; water availability and irrigation; the status of the fellah and his living expenses; the types of farms and agricultural methods – for instance, animal husbandry (sheep and wool, cattle, manure), irrigated crops (watered gardens, citrus fruits, cotton, rice, and sugar) and unirrigated crops (wheat, barley, sorghum, tobacco, licorice, olives, figs, and grapes). Regarding manufacturing and crafts, the reports described the production and use of sesame oil, soap, wool, and cloth, religious artifacts, shoes, leather, and ice. An attempt was also made to investigate certain natural resources, such as land (land ownership in villages; its availability for purchase; initiative and capital; and mortgaging), coal, charcoal, salt, lead, and zinc.

Commerce was another important topic treated in the reports. Foreign trade was dealt with in even greater detail than local trade. Under foreign trade, the following subjects were broached: imports and exports, customs, shipping lines, trading possibilities with the United States (including the transportation of American petroleum), and investment in Palestine. In addition, the reports mentioned technological innovations (agricultural equipment, carriages, carriage roads, and railroads) and the profitability of bringing in American farm machinery, grinding mills, sawing machines, stones, wood, and other commodities.

A large amount of material is also found on miscellaneous related subjects: monetary affairs (exchange rates, devaluation of Turkish currency, interest rates, middlemen and moneylenders, mortgaging and investment of capital); transportation (camels, roads, railroads, ports, canals, concessions, and development); mail and telegraph; construction (building permits, paving and sewers – especially in Jerusalem); pilgrims and tourists (quantitative data with emphasis on U.S. citizens, income generated from tourists and accommodations; insurance; the cost of living (commodities and housing). A most interesting document is "Report on Condition of Labor and the Laboring Class in Palestine."[112]

Examples of Reports and the Promotion of Trade
Two annual reports, prepared by different individuals in the late 1860s, are illuminating. The first, by Victor Beauboucher, is dated 24 July 1867. Beauboucher, who served as consul from December 1865 to October 1869, temporarily left his position between 27 February and 1 October 1868. During this period he was replaced by the acting consul, Lorenzo M. Johnson, who normally served as American vice-consul in Jaffa. Johnson filed his report on 30 September 1868.[113]

Johnson's report is twice as long as Beauboucher's. The writing of both consuls seems spontaneous rather than systematic; both touch on a wide range of subjects, including tourism and pilgrimage; the heavy taxation imposed by the Ottoman administration; the consulate in Jerusalem; the Jaffa-Jerusalem road; the American colony in Jaffa; agriculture in Palestine; repair of the Church of the Holy Sepulchre in Jerusalem. Johnson tends to provide more details about some of these topics.

Certain subjects were treated only by Beauboucher: improving security in Palestine; Ottoman government relations with foreigners and foreign consulates; the non-Muslim communities; the port of Jaffa; control of trade by local Christian Arabs and Greeks; the cost of living; the exchange rate of foreign currencies in Jerusalem. Johnson alone wrote about the political situation; the Bedouins; the import of petroleum; the export of agricultural

---

112 Selah Merrill, U.S. Consul, Jerusalem, to Alvey A. Adee, Third Assistant Secretary of State, Washington, D.C., 5 July 1884, USNA RG59 T471/5. A detailed discussion of this document is in preparation.

113 Victor Beauboucher, U.S. Consul, and Lorenzo M. Johnson, U.S. Vice-and Acting Consul, Jerusalem, to William H. Seward, Secretary of State, Washington, D.C., 24 July 1867 and 30 September 1868, USNA RG59 T471/2. On the dismissal of Consul Beauboucher and related matters, see Eliav, "The Sarah Steinberg Affair," pp.78–79.

products, first-time travels of a European in Transjordan without an escort. About Jerusalem, he had information on the construction of the Russian Compound; private construction outside the city walls; archeological excavations; the city's general population and the Jews in particular; and the American cemetery.[114]

Most of the consuls were concerned about trading possibilities with the United States, though the discussion of this issue remained for the most part purely theoretical.[115] Sometimes they attempted to explain why trading relations between America and Palestine were not closer. In their view, the main deterrents were distance and the lack of direct shipping lines, both of which greatly inflated the price of products. Victor Beauboucher, writing in 1867, thought that "...no American vessel has yet touched at Jaffa, neither would it be an advantage in the present state of things."[116] This situation remained relatively unchanged in the following decades, despite the absolute growth in foreign trade in those years and the increase in regular shipping lines between Europe and Palestine: "With the United States there is but little trade. The distance is too great, shipment is not direct, and the cost of transfer at Liverpool and Alexandria too onerous..."[117] Even as late as 1894, the consular agent in Haifa wrote that the lack of a direct commercial line between the United States and the coast of Syria accounted for the fact that the price of American products was not competitive.[118]

Among the goods the consuls recommended as imports from the United States to Palestine were cutlery, garden tools, light farming implements, ironware, petroleum, zinc, lead, kitchen stoves, sewing machines, lumber, furniture, drugs (cod liver oil, quinine), cotton textiles, shoes, flour, bacon,

---

114   For a brief assessment of the Johnson report, see, Manuel, *The Realities*, pp.13–14. Compare British Consul Temple Moore's treatment of the same topics in his report for 1866 published in *The Jewish Chronicle*, 26 April 1867 (Kark, "Annual Reports," pp.167–69).

115   Henry Gillman, U.S. Consul, Jerusalem, Lead and Mining Report, to William Wharton, Assistant Secretary of State, Washington, D.C., 3 October 1890, USNA RG59 T471/7; Gottlieb Schumacher, U.S. Vice-Consul, Haifa, Commercial Report on the Import of Flour, to State Department, Washington, D.C., 20 January 1894, USNA RG84 Haifa Copy Book 1886–1899 Box 5977.

116   Victor Beauboucher, U.S. Consul, Jerusalem, to William H. Seward, Secretary of State, Washington, D.C., 24 July 1867, USNA RG59 T471/2.

117   Joseph G. Willson, U.S. Consul, Jerusalem, to Robert R. Taft, Assistant Secretary of State, Washington, D.C., 7 October 1881, USNA RG59 T471/5. See also, Kark, "The Rise and Decline," pp.69–89.

118   Gottlieb Schumacher, U.S. Consular Agent, Haifa, to State Department, Washington, D.C., 20 January 1894, USNA RG84 Haifa Copy Book 1886–1899 Box 5977.

corned beef, potatoes, apples, and canned fruit.[119] In his annual report for 1889, Consul Gillman seemed somewhat optimistic about the chances for some of these items:

> It would seem from judicious management and intelligent agencies a larger demand for various goods manufactured in the United States might here be stimulated, while a market for some articles which have not yet been introduced might be created. The superiority of our cotton textiles is unquestionable, and is generally recognized. There is no reason why, with proper representation, they should not secure a good share of the trade. Cotton textiles are imported into this district from England to the amount of $120,000 per annum. I constantly receive many inquiries on the subject from our American merchants, to which I give prompt and careful attention doing what lies in my power to fasten the introduction of this class of our goods as well as others into this market. My report upon cotton textiles imported into this district, under the date of July 18th, last, gives full particulars; and renders unnecessary I should say further upon this subject. Among other of our manufactures which should find a ready market here are sewing machines, drive-pumps, agricultural implements, carpenters' and other tools, stoves and ranges, cooking utensils, cutlery, hardware of various kinds, labor saving machines, improved lamps, novelty manufactures, engines and boilers.[120]

But the trade potential envisioned by the consuls was not realized in the second half of the 19th century. Imports from America were limited to a few commodities brought into Palestine at the initiative of private individuals, mainly Europeans or Americans, for their business or private use. These items were both of an "advanced" technological nature and luxury

---

119   Joseph G. Willson, U.S. Consul, Jerusalem, Turkish Reforms and Facilities between Palestine and the United States, to F.W. Seward, Assistant Secretary of State, 10 May 1879, USNA RG59 T471/4; Selah Merrill, U.S. Consul, Jerusalem, to Alvey A. Adee, Third Assistant Secretary of State, Washington, D.C., 15 November 1884; Henry Gillman, U.S. Consul, Jerusalem, to James D. Porter, Assistant Secretary of State, Washington, D.C., 16 December 1886 and 21 November 1887, USNA RG59 T471/6; Gillman to William F. Wharton, Assistant Secretary of State, Washington, D.C., 3 October 1890, USNA RG59 T471/7; Gottlieb Schumacher, U.S. Consular Agent, Haifa, to State Department, Washington, D.C., 20 January 1894, USNA RG84 Haifa Copy Book 1886–1899 Box 5977.

120   Gillman to Wharton, 17 December 1889, USNA RG59 T471/6.

commodities: agricultural machinery, mills for grinding wheat and sawing olive wood, steam engines, sewing machines, ironware, guns, and food articles such as flour, bacon, corned beef and dried fruit.[121]

In the 1870s, Duisberg & Co., a German firm based in Jerusalem, with branches in Haifa and Jaffa, made an attempt at importing American products via Liverpool. However, Mr. Duisberg was reported as saying that shipping expenses were so prohibitive that no further thought could be given to any additional order, at least until a direct shipping line was established between the United States and Alexandria and Beirut. The reporting consul also mentioned other trade limitations such as poverty of the local population, the lack of adequate retail stores, the need to hand out baksheesh to the local authorities, and the fact that imported goods were damaged as they lay in the harbor and customhouse.[122] An agent of the New York Life Insurance Company who visited Palestine in the 1880s and succeeded in selling many expensive policies, expressed surprise at the number of transactions he had completed.[123]

Strange as it may seem today, there was one commodity that was regularly imported to Palestine from America over more than four decades. This was kerosene, introduced to Palestine for home consumption, primarily for lighting, in 1865–66.[124] Until the late 1870s kerosene was brought only from America, being shipped in ever increasing quantities via Beirut and Alexandria. It was marketed in five-gallon tins, which were packaged in wooden crates holding two cans. A wide variety of uses was found for the empty crates and tins.[125]

121   Joseph G. Willson, U.S. Consul, Jerusalem, to Frederick W. Seward, Assistant Secretary of State, Washington, D.C., 10 May 1879; Willson to John Hay, Assistant Secretary of State, Washington, D.C., 8 October 1880, USNA RG59 T471/5; Selah Merrill, U.S. Consul, Jerusalem, to Alvey A. Adee, Third Assistant Secretary of State, Washington, D.C., 10 October 1882, ibid.; Gottlieb Schumacher, U.S. Consular Agent, Haifa, to U.S. Consul, Beirut, 17 August 1898, Copy Book, ibid.

122   Willson to Robert R. Taft, Assistant Secretary of State, Washington, D.C., 10 May 1879, USNA RG59 T471/4.

123   Henry Gillman, U.S. Consul, Jerusalem, to James D. Porter, Assistant Secretary of State, Washington, D.C., 21 November 1887, USNA RG59 T471/6.

124   Avitzur, *The Port of Jaffa*, pp.50–52.

125   Lorenzo M. Johnson, Vice-and Acting Consul, Jerusalem, to William H. Seward, Secretary of State, Washington, D.C., 30 September 1868, USNA RG59 T471/2; Joseph G. Willson, U.S. Consul, Jerusalem, to W. Hunter, Second Assistant Secretary of State, Washington, D.C., 5 October 1878, and Acting Secretary, 4 October 1879, ibid. T471/4; Willson to John Hay, Assistant Secretary of State, Washington, D.C., 8 October 1880, ibid. T471/5; Selah Merrill, U.S. Consul, Jerusalem, to Porter, 10 November 1885, ibid.

After the Russo-Turkish war of 1877–78 and the annexation of the Black Sea port city of Batumi by the Russians, Russian kerosene began to compete with the American product in Palestine – despite the American consuls' claim that the quality of Russian petroleum was greatly inferior. This competition and the eventual reduction of the import of American kerosene to Palestine is treated in a number of consular reports written at the end of the 1880's:

> *Petroleum*
> A deplorable feature in the commercial results of the year presents itself in the fact that American Petroleum has been almost eclipsed by the Russian oil. The rapid increase in the demand for the American oil, as shown in my last annual report, when sales amounted to $36,400 as compared with $22,000 worth the previous year, was a hopeful sign which has not been sustained. As shown in the annexed Return of Imports, the sales this year have fallen to $1,560, the import of Russian oil advancing to $38,376. This result cannot be altogether attributed to the want of care in forwarding only the best article from the United States, and keeping the price as low as possible, by selling at a fair remuneration, as recommended in my former report. The advantages of Russia in such a competition are manifest. Her greater proximity to this market would alone give her advantages not easily overcome. Added to this, the quality of Russian petroleum has been greatly improved, while it is sold at from 12 to 15 percent cheaper than the American oil. In short our former lead in this import was due altogether to the natural objection had [sic] to the poor character of the oil sent here by the Russian forwarders, which objection they have now taken care to remove.[126]

According to these consular sources, the value of American kerosene imports in the Jerusalem consular district fell from $40,000 in the mid-1880s to less than $2,000 by the end of the decade. In the Haifa consular agency's district it amounted in June 1884 to $76,250, out of a total import value of $81,502 from the United States. Yet the total quantity and value of imported kerosene

---

126   Henry Gillman, U.S. Consul, Jerusalem, to James D. Porter, Assistant Secretary of State, Washington, D.C., 21 November 1887, ibid. T471/6. See also Gillman to Porter, 16 December 1881; Gillman to William F. Wharton, Assistant Secretary of State, Washington, D.C., 17 December 1889 and 21 October 1890, ibid. T471/6 and 7.

and other petroleum products continued to rise until the beginning of World War I. Besides its domestic applications, petroleum began to be used as fuel for motors, pumps, and flour mills. In 1913, the value of kerosene imports reaching the country by way of the port of Jaffa was $400,000, but American kerosene had long since ceased to play a role in this trade (Plate 30).[127]

Plate 30. Advertisement for American oil imported to Palestine
Source: *The Truth,* 1912

The consuls also reported on the few products exported from Palestine to the United States, mainly items that had religious or sentimental value and were manufactured in Bethlehem or Jerusalem. Their sale rose in proportion to the growing interest in the Holy Land. Among such goods were objects made of olive wood, mother-of-pearl, Dead Sea stone, and native wood, as well as specimens of minerals and sacramental wine. An attempt was also made to export oranges from Jaffa to New York. The limited extent of this trade is evident in the report for the year 1884–85, when the total value of

---

127 Despatches, ibid.; Jacob Schumacher, U.S. Consular Agent, Haifa, Annual Report of Import and Export, 30 June 1884, USNA RG84 Haifa Miscellaneous and Official Correspondence Received 1875–1917 Miscellaneous Papers 1878–1903 Green Box; Avitzur, *The Port of Jaffa,* pp.50–52.

oranges sent from the Jerusalem consular region to the United States amounted to no more than $4,500.[128]

The consular documents dealing with trade, both real and potential, between Palestine and the United States represent a most interesting chapter in the economic history of both countries. They show that while Britain, Germany and Russia increased their volume of trade with Palestine in the last decades of Ottoman rule, the United States did very little in this field.[129] This policy reflects the lack of a consistent political and economic interest by the American government and business community in the Ottoman Empire in general, and in Palestine in particular before the 20th century.[130]

128   Joseph G. Willson, U.S. Consul, Jerusalem, 7 October 1881; Selah Merrill, U.S. Consul, Jerusalem, to Alvey A. Adee, Third Assistant Secretary of State, Washington, D.C., 17 July 1884; Merrill to James D. Porter, Assistant Secretary of State, Washington, D.C., 10 November 1885, USNA RG59 T471/5.1

129   For comparative data, see Avitzur, *The Port of Jaffa*, pp.62- 63 and tables 2 and 14. On the interest of the U.S. State Department and the Department of Agriculture in examining possibilities for marketing American goods in Syria and Palestine, see the reports of Gottlieb Schumacher, U.S. Consular Agent, Haifa, 20 January 1894 and 16 February 1895, Copy Book, ibid.

130   Ma'oz, "America and the Holy Land," pp.66–67; Davison, "The Search for Sources," pp.96–97; Kaganoff, "Observations," pp.79- 82.

CONCLUSIONS

The Importance of Documents as a Source for Research on Nineteenth Century Palestine

Systematic attempts at comparative evaluations of consular reports of different nations, such as the United Kingdom, Belgium, Holland, Denmark, France, Germany, Japan, Russia, and the United States in the years 1978–1981, proved these documents to be a rich but unjustifiably neglected historical source.[1] Consular surveys of economic conditions in the more backward countries were of particular importance where local source material on their economic history was usually hard to come by. Thus, for example, Russian consular reports, some of them of exceptional value, reflected intimate knowledge and protracted systematic observations, including notes of oral information, on the countries in question.[2] Similarly, Werking regards reports by American consular officials as providing valuable historical source material and useful information on economic and social conditions, while giving insights into the perceptions of consuls and their foreign offices.[3] Most of the writers agree that each consul's work requires careful evaluation and that the levels of information provided differed considerably from one town to the other, or even with successive consuls in the same locality, as did the quality levels of data obtainable locally and the abilities of the consuls in analyzing such material.[4] This is supported by Smout, a business historian, who in his research made use of American consular reports for Scotland in the years 1899–1912. He stresses that these reports are important mainly as a source for certain studies of British economic and commercial activity, technological advance, engineering products, modern mechanization, and for

---

1　See papers by Barker, Broder, Bovykin et al, Gehling, Kurgan, Moller, Smout, Tamşe, Tsunoyama, and Werking in *Business History* 23 (1981):265–308.

2　Bovykin, "Russian Consular Reports," pp.291–93.

3　Werking, "U.S. Consular Reports," pp.300–304.

4　Barker, "Consular Reports," p.265; Broder, "French Consular Reports," p.280.

labor and wages. Smout notes that the quality of the reports varied with the energy and character of each consul.[5]

The consular reports and documents by American representatives in the part of the world of concern here, bear out the above evaluations regarding the importance of this material as a valuable research tool and for appraising the personal influence of individual consuls on its quality.

The Influence of the Consuls' Personalities

How can the value of the American consular reports be assessed? Should one agree with Manuel, who writes that "...from time to time these agents of a young democracy at the other end of the world sent objective intelligence of the land?" Or should one perhaps be more cautious and refrain from searching for objective historical truth: "Since all historical judgements involve persons and points of view, one is as good as another and there is no 'objective' historical truth?" [6] Whatever one's opinion on these questions, all historical research that makes use of these reports must take into consideration the personalities of the consuls who composed them, their preconceived notions, their personal inclinations, and the biased American world view regarding the "Orient" that frequently emerge from the texts. For example, Lorenzo Johnson styled the Bedouins "oriental savages," [7] while John Hay mentioned "...a noted fact throughout the East, that the Mahometans are gradually decreasing in number and lack that energy of character and enterprise which the native Christian population possesses in marked degree...." [8] Even Willson adopted the view of the "immovable East" and its negative influence: "Meanwhile all things continue as they were," he argued. "The Orient is unchanged and apparently unchangeable.... The European residents become orientalized, enfeebled, and sooner or later yield to the dominant Arab influences and tendencies." [9] Henry Gillman noticed the "fatalism of the East", explaining the miserable and poverty-stricken condition of the fellahin

---

5   Smout, "American Consular Reports on Scotland," pp.304–308.

6   Manuel, *The Realities*, p.12; G. Clarke, cited in Carr, *What is History*, p.8.

7   Lorenzo M. Johnson, Vice-and Acting Consul, Jerusalem, to William H. Seward, Secretary of State, Washington, D.C., 30 September 1868, USNA RG59 T471/2; Gustafson, "Records in the National Archives," pp.135–37.

8   John B. Hay, U.S. Vice-Consul, Jaffa, Annual Report – Jaffa, to State Department, Washington, D.C., 30 September 1870, USNA RG59 T471/3.

9   Joseph G. Willson, U.S. Consul, Jerusalem, to Robert R. Taft, Assistant Secretary of State, Washington, D.C., 7 July 1881, ibid. T471/5.

in Palestine by "...an almost sublime reliance upon Providence, attributing everything that befalls them, whether good or evil to 'the will of God,' and doing little or nothing to arrest the consequences of adverse circumstances."[10]

The consuls' personal backgrounds also influenced their decisions and reports on other topics, as Bartour and Dudman have shown to be the case regarding their attitude to the Jews and to colonization attempts by Americans.[11] Consul Selah Merrill was a notable example of such bias. Having completed his doctorate in theology and serving as chaplain in the Union forces during the Civil War, Merrill taught Hebrew at the Andover Theological Seminary, and published an essay titled *The Galilee in the Time of Christ*.[12] In 1874 he was appointed archeologist of the American Palestine Exploration Society, which sent him to the Near East the following year. Merrill was appointed American consul to Jerusalem in 1882, and remained there for two years. In 1891 he returned to that post, serving almost continuously until 1906. Beginning in the 1870s, he wrote a number of books and studies on Palestine's past and present. Despite being a graduate of a theological seminary, he declined using the title "minister", preferring to emphasize that he was a scholar, geographer, and explorer. He considered himself an authority on both ancient and modern topics relating to Palestine and the Near East.

From the start of his first term as consul, which paralleled the beginning of the First *Aliya* in 1882–83, Merrill expressed his misgivings about the new Jewish settlers. Another wave of Jewish immigration, beginning in 1890, known as the Tyomkin *Aliya*, preceded his second tenure in Jerusalem. It was a time of intense activity, with the immigration of thousands of Jews and concentrated Jewish attempts to acquire large tracts of land for dozens of new, independent settlements. These projects were mainly initiated by the Hovevei Zion (Lovers of Zion) organization active among Russian Jewry. It enjoyed the support of both Jewish and Christian circles in Europe and America who enthusiastically favored the return of the Jews to their ancestral homeland.[13] An important instance of such support was the *"Blackstone Memorial"*, a petition initiated by William E. Blackstone and signed by 413 eminent Americans on 5 March 1891 that was presented to President Benjamin Harrison. The memorial urged the United States government to help the

---

10   Henry Gillman, U.S. Consul, Jerusalem, to William F. Wharton, Assistant Secretary of State, Washington, D.C., 21 October 1890, ibid. T471/7.

11   Bartour, "Episodes," pp.129–31; Dudman, "American Colony in Jerusalem," pp.168–77.

12   Merrill, *The Galilee*. For additional biographical details, see Appendix I.

13   Kark, "Land Acquisition," pp.179–94.

Jewish restoration to Palestine by establishing a Jewish state and transferring millions of Jews there.

Merrill's doubts in the face of this widespread encouragement prompted him to write a report on 3 October 1891, describing the situation in a "realistic" manner and focusing on the "real characteristics of the Jews", which, he contended, had been ignored by their supporters. The result was a compilation of information on such topics as the reasons for the Jews' arrival in, and exodus from, Palestine; their numbers in the urban and rural settlements; the booming land market; the position of the Ottoman government on land acquisition; and Jewish immigration. On the basis of his so-called objective information and revealing his anti-Semitic prejudices, Merrill analyzed the deficiencies of the Jewish personality and Jewish culture, especially as these affected the Jews' settlement in agricultural colonies.[14]

Steeped in Puritan traditions and imbued with missionary zeal, Merrill also exhibited an extreme antipathy toward those American Christians belonging to "obscure sects", who along with their "ignorant" leaders had landed in Palestine believing that "...their coming is connected with some crude religious notions which they expect will be realized the moment they have planted their feet upon the soil of the Holy Land."[15] This was the background for Merrill's ongoing conflict – which continued throughout his years of service – with the people who founded the American Colony in Jerusalem in 1881. He accused them of apostasy, "communism", and sexual perversion. This antagonism between the consul and the members of the American Colony apparently led to Merrill's eventual removal from his post.[16]

Critical Assessment of the Reports

Despite their subjectivity, it seems that the consuls tried to exercise a measure of self-criticism regarding the information they forwarded. Some of them, conscious of this problem, reported on how difficult it was to obtain reliable statistics on population numbers, the extent of commerce, the cost-of-living expenses of the fellah, and other questions. Moreover, some of them were

---

14   Selah Merrill, U.S. Consul, Jerusalem, to William F. Wharton, Assistant Secretary of State, Washington, D.C., 3 October 1891, USNA RG59 T471/7. On the Blackstone Petition see Ariel, "An American Initiative," pp.87–102.

15   Selah Merrill, U.S. Consul, Jerusalem, to Alvey A. Adee, Third Assistant Secretary of State, Washington, D.C., 5 July 1884, ibid. T471/5.

16   Dudman, "American Colony in Jerusalem," pp.168–77; Gustafson, "Records in the National Archives," p.134.

aware – as we are today – of the low credibility of the literature, newspapers, and periodicals dealing with Palestine. The consuls thus advised their superiors in the State Department to read the reports with a healthy measure of caution and skepticism.[17] Gillman wrote about the inhabitants of Jerusalem in this manner: "As to the population of the city of Jerusalem, there has been more or less doubt, owing to the difficulty of obtaining statistics of any and every kind in this country, and the absence of any properly taken census. My exertions to be exact in this matter have not been as successful as I hoped and expected. I have been obliged to fall back on the official returns of the government, which usually would be considered sufficient...."[18]

However, these limitations did not hamper the consuls in presenting information as well as various statistical data. Lorenzo Johnson wrote in his annual report that the total population of Jerusalem in 1868 was 18,000.[19] These figures were identical, or quite close, to those provided by other sources: 18,000 by the British consul, Noel Temple Moore, in 1866; 20,000 by the German consul, G. Rosen, in 1867; 20,850 by Father Liévin de Hamme's guidebook in 1869. While all these statistics were in the same range, and may well have derived from the same source, there was a discrepancy between Johnson's figures and those of Moses Montefiore. The latter found only 5,650 Jews in Jerusalem, not the 9,000 Johnson had counted.[20]

The position taken by Justin McCarthy, who studied population data for the Ottoman Empire, is relevant here. He contends that "...no population statistics other than Ottoman government statistics were in any way reliable...no journalist, consul, or traveler, however astute, could have known enough of any large geographic area to be able to estimate population accurately." He admits that data on the population of the Arab provinces of the Empire were not published or readily available before 1878, and that he was unable to

---

17   Richard Beardsley, U.S. Consul, Jerusalem, Annual Report to Second Assistant Secretary of State, Washington, D.C., and Commercial Report, 22 November 1871, USNA RG59 T471/3; Joseph G. Willson, U.S. Consul, Jerusalem, to Robert R. Taft, Assistant Secretary of State, Washington, D.C., 4 and 7 October 1881, ibid. T471/5; Selah Merrill, U.S. Consul, Jerusalem, to Alvey A. Adee, Third Assistant Secretary of State, Washington, D.C., 10 October 1882, ibid.

18   Henry Gillman, U.S. Consul, Jerusalem, to James D. Porter, Assistant Secretary of State, Washington, D.C., 21 November 1887, ibid. T471/6.

19   Lorenzo M. Johnson, U.S. Vice-and Acting Consul, Jerusalem, to William H. Seward, Secretary of State, Washington, D.C., 30 September 1868, USNA RG59 T471/2.

20   For data on the population of Jerusalem, see Kark, "The Development," pp.109–13. It is worth noting that Montefiore possessed detailed information on Jerusalem's Jewish population. Consul Moore's estimate appeared in the *Jewish Chronicle* (26 April 1867), p.3.

locate printed Ottoman population statistics for Jerusalem. In the end he found it necessary to resort to statistics culled by Yehoshua Ben-Arieh from Western sources.[21]

It is possible to cite many examples of inexact information and statistics, late, inadequate, and superficial reports, and contradictions between different sources. A good illustration is the widely divergent estimates of the American and British consuls of the volume of petroleum imported in 1889 – the first spoke of a total of 53,000 crates, while the other quoted a figure of 35,000 in his report for the same year.[22] In addition to the problems stemming from the consuls' personal prejudices and their objective difficulties in obtaining information, the reliability of their reports was further limited by their ignorance of the local languages.[23] Although some consuls regarded themselves as experts on the region and even published books and articles on Jerusalem and Palestine, for the most part they were not intimately acquainted with the many ethnic and religious groups comprising the local population.[24]

Should modern students of 19th-century Palestine reject these consular reports out of hand because of their drawbacks? No such suggestion is advanced, of course. It is important to view the annual and special reports of the American consuls and consular agents who served in Palestine in the 19th and early 20th centuries in the wider context of the memorandums and reports dispatched by their counterparts to their governments in Great Britain, Germany, Austria, France, Russia, and elsewhere.[25] As Eliav indicates, the consuls generally observed events as they transpired, and in their surveys and reports reflected the political, religious, economic, and social situation of various sectors of the population – or, rather, their own interpretation of events and processes. Thus they are a first-rate historical source for the study

21   McCarthy, "The Population," pp.4,25–29.

22   Henry Gillman, U.S. Consul, Jerusalem, to William F. Wharton, Assistant Secretary of State, Washington, D.C., 17 December 1889, USNA RG59 T471/6; Avitzur, *The Port of Jaffa*, pp.50–52.

23   Ma'oz, "America and the Holy Land," pp.70–72.

24   Merrill, *East of Jordan* and *The Galilee*; Gillman, *Hassan– A Fellah*; Wallace, *Jerusalem the Holy*; Schumacher, *Across the Jordan,* and *The Jaulan.* See also articles in the *Jewish Chronicle* by J.B. Hay (28 November 1879), p.12; J.G. Willson (17 September 1880), p.11. G. Schumacher published numerous papers in the *Palestine Exploration Fund Quarterly Statement* and *Zeitschrift des Deutschen Palästina Vereins.*

25   Eliav, "Austrian Consulate," pp.73–110 and *The Jews of Palestine*, pp.7–36; Carmel, "Historical Sources," pp.148–57; Parfitt, "The French Consulate," pp.146–61.

of life in Palestine and the development of the country.[26] Moreover, even though the reports of the American consuls were quite modest in comparison with the reports (and activities) of the officials and agents of the other powers, they remain an important source for the historian.

Obviously, it is not possible to reconstruct from these reports alone a complete and accurate picture of Palestine, and of the trends and processes at work in that part of the world at the end of the Ottoman period. But their contribution is invaluable in piecing together the completed mosaic made up of information from many different types of sources. Besides the use of these reports as critical and comparative tools for verifying different kinds of sources, American consular reports also shed light on subjects about which no other information exists. Often they are the only source for a given situation or development. Good examples of this are the reports containing information about work and laborers, and irrigation.

Unique evidence is also provided by the American consuls – not in their reports so much as in their correspondence with the State Department – about American settlement attempts in Artas, Jaffa and Jerusalem. While the consuls and consular agents had their own views of the American settlers and their leaders, their life style and the chances for the success of their projects, there is no doubt that the whole picture could not be reconstructed without the consular reports and correspondence. One may attempt to balance these materials by delving into other sources – which are usually one-sided as well. The same applies to what consular sources had to say about Jewish settlement.[27]

E.H. Carr describes the role of the historian in integrating sources as follows:

> No document can tell us more than what the author of the document thought – what he thought had happened, what he thought ought to happen or would happen, or perhaps only what he wanted others to think he thought, or even what he himself thought he thought. None of this means anything until the historian has got to work on it and deciphered it. The facts, whether found in the documents or not, have still to be processed by the historian before he can make any use of them: the use he makes of them is, if I may put it that way, the processing process.[28]

26   Eliav, "Austrian Consulate," p.74.

27   Spafford-Vester, *Our Jerusalem.* See also Kark, "Millenarism," pp.1–19.

28   Carr, *What is History?,* p.16.

In the case of American consular reports and correspondence, the documents must be "processed" within the context of Palestine in the last decades of Ottoman rule, a time when the region was emerging from a quarter-millennium of decline. Around 1800, Palestine was still a remote province of the Ottoman Empire, for the most part rural and sparsely populated, with an economy that was both traditional and poor. Half a century later, a process of change began that led the country to marked resurgence and development.

An important feature of the American consular reports is their pragmatic approach and their attempt at quantification. They provide valuable information on such topics as agriculture, manufacturing and industry, and the introduction of new technologies in Palestine. The consular correspondence and reports in general, and those of the Americans in particular, constitute important raw material for the modern scholar eager to assess the characteristics and determinants of the transformation of the country, because they were recorded by men present when the events occurred. Until recently, such primary sources were utilized mainly by scholars of political and administrative history, or of the history of the Jews in Palestine. The time may have come to make fuller use of them to write the economic and social history of Palestine, and describe the settlement patterns and trends of all its inhabitants, Muslims, Christians, and Jews alike.

APPRAISAL OF U.S. CONSULAR ACTIVITY IN THE HOLY LAND

Having scrutinized the work of the consuls and consular agents as reflected in the archives and other sources, we can now assess American consular activity in the Holy Land. From the viewpoint of the core, this entails an evaluation of its involvement, functioning, and degrees of professionalism. At the periphery, we will consider the impact on those with whom it came in contact – "clients" of the consular officers, other local people, and the Ottoman authorities at various levels.

American involvement in the Ottoman Empire and in Palestine unfolded in the general context of the growing Western influence in that part of the world during the 19th century. The European powers were motivated by political, strategic, military, commercial, cultural, and religious interests and financed from various sources.[29] They seized upon every possible means of

---

29 Kent, *The Great Powers*, pp.1–4.

penetration in keeping with the old principle of "quintuple" representation –
missionaries, commercial agents, scholars, military advisors, and consuls.
Although sometimes this order was altered and one of these factors performed
multiple roles, the five can always be identified. Of these, the consuls of the
powers were the most influential, spreading their hierarchical networks
throughout the Empire. The consuls acted in ways no representative of a
foreign country would have dared in another state. They exploited the weakness
of the Ottoman Empire and made full use of the special privileges that had
been granted them, their nationals, and their protégés under the capitulatory
system.[30]

On a global plane, the entry of the United States into the Ottoman Empire
occurred relatively late and was far less pervasive than that of the European
powers. In the 19th century, American political interest in the Ottoman Empire
was conditioned by its policy of non-intervention and neutrality. American
economic activities in terms of exports and imports were limited. Only at the
beginning of the 20th century did a change come about in American economic
and political objectives in the Ottoman Empire. Until then, as one writer put
it, it was "...the missionaries who had been on the frontier of United States
cultural internationalism in the Empire and who influenced American policy
in the area. They had first gone to proselytize Muslims and Jews and to
revive Near East Christians." [31]

It is therefore not relevant to measure the relations of the United States
with the Ottoman Empire and Palestine in terms of tons of cargo, numbers of
American citizens, or the numbers and sizes of the American consulates that
functioned there; nor even by their political status or the influence they
wielded with the Ottoman authorities. American activity in the Ottoman
Empire and in the Holy Land should be viewed from humanitarian and
philanthropic perspectives, with the consular officers providing support,
protection, and their personal involvement.[32] In the early 1880s, Samuel Cox
wrote about American intentions in Turkey: "...The greatest interest we have
here is in our enterprises, our Bible House, and Robert College..."[33] On the
eve of the First World War, hundreds of American educational and
philanthropic institutions were active – mainly in Anatolia, and fewer in the
Levant and in Palestine. Among them was the American University at Beirut

---

30   Eliav, *Eretz Israel*, p.50.
31   Grabill, *Protestant Diplomacy*, p.4–34.
32   Ma'oz, "America and the Holy Land," pp.65–69.
33   Cox, *Oriental Sunbeams*, p.132.

which became the cradle of the Arab national movement in the Middle East. Concurrently, American commercial activity developed and intensified.

Many writers have pointed out that American interest in the Holy Land tended to be personal and unofficial. The policy of the United States and of its representatives in Palestine, as in the Ottoman Empire generally, was concerned with humanitarian protection of minority groups and insistence on the constitutional principles of non-discrimination because of class, race, or religion, and against subjection to unjust laws which affected American citizens and American protected persons – particularly Christian sects and Jews.[34]

The motivation behind the establishment of the consulate in Jerusalem and the consular agencies in Jaffa and Haifa should be sought in the peculiar perceptions of the Holy Land myth in the American Protestant world view. In line with the chronological pattern of "quintuple" penetration, the first Americans to arrive in the Holy Land in the 1820s were missionaries devoid of any governmental backing. They were followed by the explorers, the pilgrims, and the tourists, and by a particularly important group, the settlers – at first messianic Christians, and later, Jews impelled by love of Zion and ideological Zionism. Most of the settlers came in disregard of the warnings by their diplomatic and consular representatives in the region. Trade and commercial interests were negligible. The establishment of the consulate at Jerusalem was affected to some extent also by considerations of prestige, since every other important nation had consular representation in the Holy City in the 19th century. Thus, the American consulate in Jerusalem was not set up for the reasons that governed the establishment of other American consulates throughout the world – assisting American merchants and seamen. The ideological impact of missionaries and scholars, the growth in the number of American pilgrims and tourists, and the needs of individuals and groups of religiously-motivated settlers – all converged to involve and give direction to American consular activity in Palestine. Political and commercial factors came much later and on a small scale. In this, the American consular presence in the Holy Land was unique in relation to that of the other powers. At least until the turn of the century, the United States was "...not suspected of having any political design, as are all European nations,...[and having] no direct interest in the Eastern Question."[35]

---

34 Davis, in Kaganoff, *Guide*, 2:xvi; Davison, "The Search for Sources," pp.88–89; Kaganoff, "Observations," p.81. See for example the case study of the Lubowsky family in Chapter Five.

35 Richard Beardsley, U.S. Consul, Jerusalem, to Second assistant Secretary of State, Washington, D.C., 30 September 1871, USNA RG59 T471/3.

Despite the difference in motivation between the American and other consular representations – French, British, Russian, Austrian, German – in Palestine, the American consular officers adopted similar modes of operation. Under the capitulatory agreements, they exercised considerable influence, forcing the Ottoman governors and the local inhabitants to relate to them and to their citizens with respect and to avoid injuring them. In conflicts with the Ottoman administration, they frequently asserted their privileged status to intervene in internal affairs of the Empire, particularly in matters relating to land ownership, taxation, and restrictions on immigration, in ways which sometimes contravened Ottoman law and the spirit of the agreements between the powers. Such instances left deep scars of resentment on the Ottoman psyche.[36]

The beneficiaries of this preferred status were the citizens and protected persons in the "state within the state" provided by the consulate and the consular agencies. These made available to their clients a wide gamut of civil, legal, and business services, assisted them in safeguarding the security of their persons and property, and establishing themselves in Palestine as a Western implant that contributed to the modernization of the country. Among those having recourse to the consular officers were the Christian settlers of the Adams colony in Jaffa who remained in the country, the Americans in the German-American Templer colony in Haifa, and the members of the American Colony in Jerusalem. American consular assistance and protection also benefitted the Jews in Palestine – until the eighties, the Old *Yishuv*, and from the turn of the century, the New *Yishuv* and the Zionist movement.

Some of the consuls were impelled to extend protection and help to both American and non-American Jews by their Protestant belief in the messianic implications of the return of the Jews to Zion. Other consuls manifested the American abhorrence of a despotic, xenophobic Oriental regime. The consuls acted to undo Ottoman restrictions on the immigration and settlement of Jews in Palestine, helped them to acquire land, and assisted them in their internal communal organization and with economic problems. In some cases, American intervention on behalf of the Jews in Palestine strained relations with Ottoman officials in Jerusalem and Constantinople. The latter were apprehensive of such American involvement since they regarded the Zionist movement as yet another troublesome national minority group that endangered the hegemony of the Empire by striving for separate Jewish statehood. Several of the American consuls in Jerusalem, Beirut, and Constantinople, as well as some of the senior State Departmment officials in Washington, were critical

---

36   See above, in Chapters Five and Six.

of this sort of local American political activity. This reaction led, at the beginning of the 20th century, to a decline in American official sympathy and to ambivalence towards the Jewish cause, and to discrimination between Christians and Jews in favor of the former. But during the presidency of Woodrow Wilson, there was a revival in the support for "restoring the Holy Land to the People of Israel" and for establishing a democratic, Zionist state in place of Ottoman despotism as a refuge for Jews. The Wilson administration materially helped the Jewish *Yishuv* in Palestine during the First World War, and the President eventually supported the Balfour Declaration in 1918.[37]

The consuls and consular agents of the United States in Jerusalem and the Holy Land, in the period 1832–1914, were part of the budding American consular service whose objectives, methods, and organization only took on definitive form in the course of the 19th century and at the beginning of the 20th – unlike the long tradition of the main European powers. American consular officials were appointed at a time when the spoils system reigned supreme with no consideration for merit. They were generally assessed by 19th century writers as failures and unsympathetic bureaucrats, who were "...incompetent, corrupt, unregenerate alcoholics, or, at best, political hacks" – a view that has recently been challenged.[38]

Although the consuls in Jerusalem were appointed under the norms governing the consular service of the United States, it is only fair to note their special motivation for seeking the appointment and for carrying out their consular and diplomatic work in the Holy Land – a place they considered of great religious, cultural, and historical importance. Their activities were more a reaction to how the realities of the Holy Land affected Americans who had gone there, than a result of considered political or diplomatic initiatives. They operated under the fairly difficult conditions of their working environment and communications, and at times labored under unclear and indeterminate criteria of territorial jurisdiction.

The consuls filled extremely varied and complicated functions at the periphery of the American foreign service. Sometimes they acted with considerable autonomy and contrary to the policy and directives from the

---

37 Bartour devotes his doctoral dissertation (Bartour, "American Consular Aid") to the close connections of the United States with the Jews in Palestine under Ottoman rule. For discussions of the attitude of the American administration and the consuls to the Jews of Palestine see also: Landau & Öke, "Ottoman Perspective"; Manuel, *The Realities*, pp.88–116; Ma'oz, "America and the Holy Land," pp.65–69; Spiegel, *The Other Arab-Israeli Conflict*, pp.10- 12.

38 Kennedy, *The American Consul*, p.viii.

center, without being able to take counsel due to the slow communications and the lack of clear directives. They maintained contacts with officials of the Ottoman administration and the governors, with other consulates, with the heads of religious communities, and with different sectors of the local population. They were busy gathering data, adjudicating, registering births, marriages, and deaths, conducting censuses, and promoting American trade. They provided a multitude of services to their fellow citizens in the Holy Land and to Americans in the United States with interests in Palestine. As a rule, the consuls performed their work conscientiously. Their personal lives were conducted in the subculture of the diplomatic corps and of the Western clergy and religious laymen who lived and worked in the Holy Land. Some of them also engaged in extraneous activities such as research, writing, hunting, and business, according to their individual predilections. This study has refrained from idealization of the American consular figure in the Holy Land. Nevertheless, considering that the men who served there had no advance training, no previous experience in consular affairs, and were not professionals, the overall picture that emerges is one of reasonable adequacy.

Close examination of American consuls and their activities in Ottoman Palestine has opened a window onto historic themes, trends, and contexts at broad levels of significance. Analysis of the motivations and functioning of these officials gives new insights into the transformation of perceptions and of the political, social, and economic conditions in Palestine. The study illuminates yet another facet of the involvement of the Western nations in the Ottoman Empire and in Palestine, and helps understand the lives of the inhabitants and modern settlement in the Holy Land.

APPENDIX I

Biographies of the American Consuls in Jerusalem, 1844–1919

Warder Cresson — 1844[1]

Warder Cresson was born on 13 July 1798 to Mary Warder and John Eliot Cresson, a wealthy Philadelphia Quaker descended from Pierre Cresson of Picardy in France who had immigrated to Holland and to the New World in 1657. The family became successful merchants in Philadelphia; Warder Cresson's uncle, Eliot Cresson, was a leading citizen of that city, renowned for his philanthropy.[2]

Warder Cresson married Elizabeth Townsend and they had eight children. A 49-acre farm he purchased near Philadelphia prospered under his management, as did a second farm he acquired subsequently. Cresson's farming methods applied the latest scientific and technological advances, known then as "scientific farming", in the promotion of an ideology current at the time for the development of the "modern village," which would serve as alternative to the city, the center of sin. Such an exodus to rural areas had aspects of romanticism and mysticism, but without a return to primitive ways of life.[3]

Although raised as a Quaker, Warder Cresson was reputed, despite his denials, to have adopted at various times the Shaker, Mormon, Millerite, and Campbellite persuasions. In 1827, he entered into religious disputes with Quakers, attacking their wealth, social snobbishness, and extravagance.[4]

Under the influence of a distinguished Philadelphia rabbi, Isaac Leeser, and of the renowned Jewish leader Mordechai Emanuel Noah, Cresson had

1   Warder Cresson was commissioned on 17 May 1844. A month later, on 22 June, the commission was rescinded for reasons of "insufficient business in Jerusalem". See: Mayer, "Records of U.S. Consulate at Jerusalem."

2   Johnson, *Dictionary of American Biography*, 4:540-541; Kark, "Millenarism," pp.50-53; Manuel, *The Realities*, pp.16-17.

3   Johnson, ibid.; Bar Yosef, "Warder Cresson," pp.1-3; Shavit, "Land in the Deep Shadow," p.99; Chiel, "An Inquisition," pp.16-17.

4   Karp, "The Zionism of Warder Cresson," pp.1-20; Fields, *America in the Mediterranean*, pp.276-277; Bar Yosef, ibid.

been confirmed in the belief that "salvation was of the Jews" and of the need for their return to Zion. Moved by these views he decided, in 1844, to settle in Palestine and devote himself to assisting the poor oppressed Jews there. In that year he also wrote *Jerusalem the Centre of Joy of the Whole Earth* in which he expressed his view of the Jew as the instrument of redemption.[5]

The Philadelphia congressman, Edward Joy Morris, after returning from a voyage to the Levant, introduced Warder Cresson to Secretary of State John C. Calhoun whom Cresson asked for an appointment as American consul at Jerusalem. The application was successful. Before embarking for his overseas post, Cresson divorced his wife, and leaving his family behind, set sail for Palestine taking his favorite dove with him. William Makepeace Thackeray, who met Cresson in Palestine, wrote that he had "no other knowledge of Syria but what he derives from the prophecy; and this (as he takes the office gratis) has been considered a sufficient reason for his appointment by the United States Government." The appointment was canceled a month later when protests reached the State Department.[6]

Pending the confirmation of his position as consul in Jerusalem by the American legation in Constantinople, Cresson established himself in the Holy City and launched into consular activities, even though diplomatic protocol required that he await full accreditation. He began issuing protection papers to Jews and others who were not United States citizens – to the consternation of both the American consul at Beirut and of Dabney S. Carr, the minister at Constantinople. Carr disavowed Cresson to the Sublime Porte and warned Cresson that he would be expelled if he persisted in calling himself consul (Plate 16).[7]

Nevertheless, Cresson roamed the country with his consular entourage. It was during one of these jaunts that Thackeray came upon him and recorded the meeting in his book, *Journey from Cornhill to Cairo*, "...another party of armed and glittering horsemen appeared. They, too, were led by an Arab, who was followed by two Janissaries, with silver maces shining in the sun. 'Twas the party of the new American Consul-General of Syria and Jerusalem,

5   See: Shavit, "Land in the Deep Shadow," pp.100-110 for a discussion of the relationships between Cresson and Leeser and between Cresson and Noah. Included in this article is a copy of a letter sent from Cresson to Noah in 1847; Cresson, "Jerusalem"; Bar Yosef, ibid., pp.4-5; Karp, ibid.; Fields, ibid.

6   Thackeray, *Notes on a Journey*, pp.188-89; Bar Yosef, ibid., pp.5-7; Karp, ibid.; Fields, ibid.

7   Wm. T. Young, British Consul, Jerusalem, to The Earl of Aberdeen, London, October 9, 1844, PRO FO78/581 in Lipman, *Americans and the Holy Land*, p.91; Bar Yosef, ibid.; Karp, ibid.; Fields, ibid.

hastening to that city, with the inferior consuls of Ramleh and Jaffah to escort him. He expects to see the millennium in three years, and has accepted the office of consul at Jerusalem, so as to be on the spot in readiness." [8]

Thackeray further elaborated on Cresson's playful behavior upon encountering a warlike Arab on the plains of Jaffa. The horseman charged toward Cresson and the following scene ensued. "The American replied in a similar playful ferocity – the two warriors made a little tournament for us there...in the which diachylon, being a little worsted, challenged his adversary to a race, and fled away on his grey, the American following on his bay. Here poor sticking-plaister was again worsted, the yankee contemptuously riding round him, and then declining further exercise." [9]

Cresson continued to reside in Jerusalem, in the expectation of beholding the restoration of the Jews to their ancestral homeland and attempted to help the destitute Jews of the Holy City. Increasingly identifying with them, by 1848, Cresson was attacking the English Episcopal mission in Jerusalem. In several articles, he criticized missionary labors in Palestine and eventually came to voice doubts about Christianity. He regarded Judaism as the true religion. On 28 March 1848 he became a Jew, was circumcised, and assumed the name of Michael C. Boaz Israel.

Cresson returned to America in September 1848 to settle his affairs. While in Philadelphia, his former wife and one of his sons obtained an inquisition of lunacy against him, which however failed and he was found sane. The trial was a sensation at the time, becoming a test case for the principles of civil and religious liberty. Cresson's winning the case was considered in 1851 as a "landmark in American growth to religious equality." He published a booklet, *The Key of David. David the True Messiah ...Also Reasons for Becoming a Jew: With a Revision of the Late Lawsuit for Lunacy on that Account*, in 1852, to publicize his victory and in explanation for his conversion. [10]

That year he returned to Palestine and took up various projects for the betterment of the Jews there and their productivization. He attempted to establish a soup house for destitute Jews and a model farm in the Rephaim Valley outside Jerusalem. In a letter on this subject to the *Jewish Chronicle*, Warder Cresson wrote: "Many cases of death might have been avoided,

---

8   Thackeray, *Notes on a Journey*, pp.188-89.

9   Ibid., pp.208-209.

10   Cresson, *The Key of David*; Bar Yosef, "Warder Cresson," pp.11-13; Karp, "The Zionism of Warder Cresson"; Fields, *America in the Mediterranean*, pp.276-77; Kark, "Millenarism," pp.50-53.

especially as only a part of the amount given for the poor might have been laid out...in purchasing or renting a large tract of land upon the rich plains of Jaffa, much more than a reasonable profit might be realized to meet the coming necessities of the Jews in time."[11]

Warder Cresson married Rachel Moleno and together they had two children, Abigail Ruth Israel and David Ben Zion Israel, who died in infancy a few years after their father – the son in 1862, and the daughter in 1865. Cresson himself died on October 27, 1860 and was buried on the Mount of Olives with honors as only given to prominent rabbis.[12]

John Warren Gorham — 1857–1860[13]

The Bostonian physician, John Warren Gorham, was the first American consul to serve in Jerusalem. His appointment came at the request of President Franklin Pierce who asked the secretary of state to nominate Gorham for services rendered.[14]

Having lived in Paris for two years, and nine years in Italy, Gorham spoke French and Italian and was conversant in German and Spanish.[15] He received his appointment on 20 October 1856, and soon thereafter set out for Jerusalem, arriving there on 24 March 1857. During his first month of duty, he set up the consulate in a rented building on Mount Zion near the Jaffa Gate but delayed raising the American flag until the Fourth of July. On that day it happened that the pasha was in Nablus and the garrison commander refused the usual twenty-one gun salute because the United States was governed by a mere president and not a king. On Gorham's threat of complaining directly to Constantinople, the officer capitulated and fired the prescribed salute.[16]

Gorham's activities in Jerusalem were limited in scope. During the period

11   *Jewish Chronicle*, 28 March 1856, p.10a; Bar Yosef, ibid., pp.16-23

12   Victor Beauboucher, U.S. Consul, Jerusalem, to William Seward, Secretary of State, Washington, D.C., 27 March 1866, USNA RG59 T471/2; Bar Yosef, ibid., pp.16-28; Karp, "The Zionism of Warder Cresson," pp.1-20; Fields, *America in the Mediterranean*, pp.276-77; Bartour, "American Consular Aid," pp.16-26. On his estate, see above: Chapter Six, "Management of Estates."

13   Due to an oversight, his name was not sent to the Senate during the 34th Congress, but was submitted on 20 January 1858. See: Mayer, "Records of U.S. Consulate at Jerusalem."

14   Bartour, "American Consular Aid," p.31; Vogel, "Zion as Place," p.314.

15   John Warren Gorham, Boston, to William L. Marcy, Secretary of State, Washington, D.C., 6 November 1856, USNA RG59 T471/1.

16   John Warren Gorham, U.S. Consul, Jerusalem, to Lewis Cass, Secretary of State, Washington, D.C., 30 June 1857, and 12 July 1857, USNA RG59 T471/1.

of his service, there was no commercial intercourse between the district under his jurisdiction and the United States. On only two occasions did American frigates visit harbors in Palestine. Gorham submitted a report to the secretary of state providing information on the district, dated 19 January 1859.[17]

Gorham was relieved of his post in September 1860, the reason being alcoholism exasperated by boredom. He settled in Westerly, Rhode Island in 1861. There he was in contact with the Seventh-Day Baptist Missionary to Palestine, Charles Saunders. Gorham died in Westerly on 19 April 1893.[18]

William R. Page — 1860–1861

William Rufus Page was born in Hallowell, Maine on 17 March 1820. Early in life, Page set out for Constantinople on a ship owned by his father and himself, the twin-screw steamer *Marmora*. Although the vessel was wrecked off the Moroccan coast, he reached his destination and remained there for a number of years. The Gorhams were considered the first to introduce steam navigation to the Dardanelles and the surrounding waters. During his residence at Constantinople, Page became conversant in Turkish, Greek, and Arabic. There he met and married his wife who belonged to a prominent and influential British family in Constantinople, the Churchills.[19]

Page returned to the United States with his family in 1848, established himself at Norfolk, Virginia and lived there for ten years. In Norfolk he conducted a large ship-building business, which however failed for economic reasons. He returned to Constantinople in 1858 and seeking a position in the American consular corps, applied in turn for the post of consul-general in Constantinople and for a consulship in Smyrna.[20]

Page was highly recommended by James Williams of the United States legation at Constantinople who understood his motivation to reside in Constantinople where his familiarity with the habits, customs, laws, and

17 Gorham to Cass, 12 November 1858, 19 January 1859, and 12 October 1859, ibid.

18 Vogel, "Zion as Place," pp.314-15; Manuel, *The Realities,* pp.12-13; Shavit, *U.S. and the Middle East,* p.139.

19 John Hubbard, Washington, D.C., to James Buchanan, President of the United States, Washington, D.C., 1 November 1859, USNA RG59 M650; Charles G. McChesney, Trenton, New Jersey, to James Buchanan, President of the United States, Washington, D.C., 14 November 1859, USNA RG59 M650; Shavit, ibid., p.263.

20 Hubbard to Buchanan, ibid.; Charles G. McChesney to Buchanan, ibid.

commerce of the country would facilitate his consular duties.[21] Nevertheless, to his dismay, Page was appointed to Jerusalem. On his way to Jaffa via Malta, in May 1860, Page met Henry D. Johnson, the newly-appointed consul-general for Constantinople. Shortly afterwards, Johnson took ill and died, and Page requested to be appointed in his stead. He further proposed that John Judson Barclay (the son of the medical missionary, James Turner Barclay) who served as the American consul in Cyprus, be posted to Jerusalem since business on the island was of little importance. Moreover, Page stressed the importance of his placement at Constantinople because ever since the departure of the previous consul-general, the office had fallen into disarray and was run by a vice-consul who was a British subject. But Page was instructed to proceed to Jerusalem just the same.[22]

His appointment from the state of Maine was confirmed on 21 June 1860, and he replaced his predecessor in Jerusalem in September of that year. During his term as consul, he was accused of providing consular protection for payment. Page resigned in a rage as a result of disagreement with the American representative in Constantinople over "promiscuous issuance of letters of protection in Constantinople" to what he called "hordes of spurious Americans" – Jews seeking the protection of an enlightened diplomat. He claimed that the United States had become a shelter for all nations and that there was a corrupt trade of papers and passports in all the region. It may well be that this reaction was an attempt to justify himself in view of the allegations levelled at him. Page later served as the American consul at Port Said, in 1870, but the sources do not detail the date and duration of his appintment.[23]

Franklin Olcott — 1861–1862

Franklin Olcott's claim to the position of consul at Jerusalem was to allow him the pursuit of his Oriental studies. Olcott had attended a German university for two years and spoke several languages. He aimed at making Oriental literature "the leading idea of life." It was suggested that the consul then present at Jerusalem be transferred to Greece so as to facilitate Olcott's

21   James Williams, Legation of the United States, Constantinople, to William R. Page, Constantinople, 3 August 1859, USNA RG59 M650.

22   William R. Page, Constantinople, to Payloe, Washington, D.C., 31 May 1860, USNA RG59 M650.

23   Vogel, "Zion as Place," p.315; Bartour, "American Consular Aid," pp.32-33; Sam M. Wilson, Portsmouth, Virginia, to Lewis Cass, Secretary of State, Washington, D.C., 21 June 1860, USNA RG59 T471/1; Shavit, *U.S. and the Middle East*, p.263.

placement at that post.[24] His sponsor advanced the opinion that if Olcott were to receive the consulship, he would "revel in the dust of ages, literature, vermin, &c &c undisturbed for several years, and at the end, all he could do and have would not buy him a dinner in Albany..."[25]

Olcott was appointed consul at Jerusalem from New York in 1861. He was chosen by Secretary of State William Seward, because of his background in business and in the hope that he would be able to improve American relations in the region. Olcott took over his duties as consul on 28 December 1861 but was confirmed in his appointment only on 12 July 1862.[26] In a report to the State Department, he stated that in the local market American products and funds were not in use. He went on to blame the Ottoman government for not developing the region: "Owing to the imbecility ineption [sic] of the local Government, which has neither the inclination to investigate, nor the ability to correct the abuses of its agents and factors, and the turbulent and warlike disposition of the mixed populations, nominally subject to its control, the resources of the country are being rapidly wasted, whereas under more favorable auspices they might almost indefinitely be increased." [27]

It appears that his disappointment in the potential development of trade between the two nations probably brought about his resignation. He remained at his post until the end of 1862.

Isaac Van Etten — 1863

Isaac Van Etten was appointed consul for Jerusalem for the state of Minnesota on 9 May 1863 but declined the commission on 19 September 1863.[28]

24   Charles Van Benthuysen, Albany, New York, to Thurlow Weed, Washington, 19 August 1861, USNA RG59 M650.

25   Ibid.

26   Bartour, "American Consular Aid," p.33; Vogel, "Zion as Place," p.315; Franklin Olcott, U.S. Consul, Jerusalem, to Georg Rosen, Prussian Consul, Jerusalem, 28 December 1861, ISA RG 67/163; List of U.S. Consular Officers, 1789-1939, Jerusalem, Turkey, USNA RG59 M587/10.

27   Franklin Olcott, U.S. Consul, Jerusalem, Annual Report, to William H. Seward, Secretary of State, Washington, D.C., 30 September 1862, USNA RG59 T471/1.

28   Bartour, "American Consular Aid," p.33; Vogel, "Zion as Place," p.315; List of U.S. Consular Officers, 1789-1939, Jerusalem, Turkey, USNA RG59 M587/10.

Albert Rhodes — 1863–1865

Albert Rhodes, born on 1 February 1840 in Pittsburgh, was a professional diplomat from Pennsylvania. He took office in Jerusalem on 27 January 1864.[29] A few years after having served there, he wrote an article in which he reflected upon his period as consul in the Holy City.

> Uneasy is the head that wears the consular crown. The responsibility of maintaining official dignity is oppressive, incompatible with mirth, and the bearing of such a burden any length of time generally develops a tendency to sadness. This is especially so with the American representative, whose quiet vegetation on Mount Zion is in such contrast to the aggressive life in America. One can fancy with what skepticism this lone American, pacing the house-top of an evening and possessed of homesickness, reads the Bible authority that "Zion is the joy of the whole earth." Days and sometimes weeks pass without incident coming to relieve the general stagnation.[30]

Rhodes was bored by his position in Jerusalem. He noted that other foreign consuls in the city took an interest in scientific research, but took a dim view of their pretensions and ridiculed their fashionable interest in archeology.[31]

Rhodes wrote a book, *Jerusalem As It Is*, based on his experiences, travels, and impressions while serving as consul in Jerusalem. The work expressed his cynicism and was critical of life in Palestine, of the natives, monks, Jews, travelers, and missionaries. "It is a country of idleness and ignorance; monks ignorant of the elementary principles of their faith; Jews living three thousand years ago; natives with minds of children; all sitting, eternally sitting, and none working."[32] He poked fun at those who believed that the land would be restored through practical means by agriculture and commerce; he questioned the practicality of missionary attempts to convert the Jews, seeing it as exorbitant folly. Rhodes also provided vivid descriptions of the country and detailed information on various subjects. He authored another book, *The*

---

29   Shavit, *U.S. and the Middle East,* p.293; Eliav, "An Annotated Listing," p.171; List of U.S. Consular Officers, Jerusalem, Turkey, USNA RG M587/10; Simon S. Murad, U.S. Vice Consul, Jerusalem, to Georg Rosen, Prussian Consul, Jerusalem, 27 January 1864, ISA RG 67/163.

30   Rhodes, "Our Consuls in Jerusalem," p.437.

31   Ibid., p.438.

32   Ibid., p.446.

Dobbs Family in America.[33] Years after his term in Jerusalem, Rhodes wrote a short description of a sentimental trip to the Jordan River – the story of the Bromly family, in particular their daughter Helene, and their travel experiences.[34]

On 31 March 1865, Rhodes submitted his resignation as consul in Jerusalem. He expressed a desire to be retained in the consular service but requested that the government appoint him to some other post than Jerusalem, where his knowledge of French might be of some use. He left Jerusalem for Paris while awaiting a response. He was instructed to report to the United States legation in London for an examination, was found qualified for the diplomatic service, and on 24 August 1865, received an appointment as a consular clerk in Liverpool. On 30 June 1866, Rhodes was appointed consul in Rotterdam, and later became chargé d'affaires in The Hague. He served as consul at Rouen, and at Eberswalde in Germany. After 1885, Rhodes resided in Paris.[35]

After several years in the diplomatic corps, Rhodes publicly expressed his criticism of the American foreign service. In an article, "Our Diplomats and Consuls", he wrote of the declining standard of official honesty and capacity for foreign service. He believed that it had been declining with each succeeding administration since President Jackson, the reason being "the bad elements in politics bred of rotation" which prevailed, with "Companions and friends of demagogues who manipulated elections to secure majorities receiving a large share of foreign appointments." [36] Rhodes advocated legislation for the control of the foreign service and the establishment of a corps of professional diplomats who would not be subject to changes in government. In his article he discussed a number of problems he thought plagued the foreign service and suggested remedies.[37]

Victor Beauboucher — 1865–1870

Victor Beauboucher was born in France. When the American Civil War broke out, he was writing for several liberal journals in Belgium. Determined to fight for his antislavery principles, he volunteered for the Union army and

---

33 Rhodes, *Jerusalem As It Is*, pp.60-62, 459-63; Rhodes, *The Dobbs Family in America.*.

34 Rhodes, "Un voyage," pp.446-56.

35 Albert Rhodes, U.S. Consul, Jerusalem, to William H. Seward, Secretary of State, Washington, D.C., 31 March 1865, USNA RG59 T471/2; Eliav, "An Annotated Listing," p.171; Rhodes, "Our Diplomats," p.175; Shavit, *U.S. and the Middle East*, p.293.

36 Rhodes, ibid., p.170.

37 Ibid., pp.169-76.

was presented to General Stevenson. Beauboucher served in the 28th
Massachusetts Volunteer Regiment under the command of Colonel Bryne.
His foot was shattered when charging a Confederate battery at the Battle of
Coal Harbor on 4 June 1864, and his left leg had to be twice amputated. He
was discharged from service on 6 January 1865, with a governmental pension
and was given work as a clerk in the Subsistence Department on 4 June
1865. On 30 August Beauboucher was appointed consul in Jerusalem for the
District of Columbia at the recommendation of the assistant secretary of war
and former newspaper editor, Charles A. Dana, to Secretary of State Seward.[38]
Although Beauboucher had been wounded in the Civil War, received a
government pension, and served the United States as consul, he had not been
naturalized as a citizen.[39]

Beauboucher took up his position in Jerusalem on 31 January 1866. He
viewed his work as follows:

> It is not a post of much commercial importance, but of great
> interest to the travelling public, of which comparatively little is
> known, while great curiosity exists. It is often in the power of
> Consular officers to be of great service to those who would
> understand its history, geography and political status. The
> performance of such duties generally entails its own reward in
> the appreciation of strangers, who often spend weeks within the
> ancient walls of Jerusalem. If such duties are superfluous and
> unofficial elsewhere, they are not so here...." [40]

During his term as consul, Beauboucher dealt with a number of problematic
matters, among them the Adams colony in Jaffa – an attempt, in 1866, by
157 New Englanders to settle in the vicinity of Jaffa under the leadership of
George W.J. Adams; and the Sarah Steinberg affair – a case of conflicting
claims of the Jewish community of Jerusalem and of missionaries in the city
for guardianship of an orphaned Jewish girl. He was the first American
consul to extend protection to Jews in Palestine.[41]

---

38   Victor Beauboucher, U.S. Consul, Jerusalem, to William H. Seward, Secretary of State, Washington,
     D.C., 12 February 1865, and 21 February 1866, USNA RG59 T471/2; Vogel, "Zion as Place,"
     p.315.

39   Beauboucher to William H. Seward, 21 February 1866, and 25 February 1866, ibid.

40   Beauboucher, Annual Report, to Seward, 30 September 1866, ibid.

41   Vogel, "Zion as Place," p.315,320; Kark, "Millenarism," pp.54-55,57-59; Bartour, "American
     Consular Aid," pp.41-53; Eliav, *The Jews of Palestine*, pp.15-21; Eliav, "The Sarah Steinberg
     Affair," pp.78-88.

Beauboucher's worsening health aggravated his disappointment with his work in Jerusalem. Already in 1866 he requested a transfer to a more suitable post in a more temperate climate, as in Italy. His wound had twice opened during a period of one year, which was seen by the attending physician, Dr. H.D. Mazaraky, as a result of the sudden variations of temperature in Jerusalem.[42] For over seven months, from 27 February 1868 to 1 October 1869, while Beauboucher stayed in Constantinople, he was replaced in his post by the American vice-consul in Jaffa, Lorenzo M. Johnson. With Beauboucher's final departure from Jerusalem following his resignation, Johnson again took charge of the consulate on 1 November 1869.[43]

Richard Beardsley — 1870–1873

Richard Beardsley was born in 1839 and studied international law at the University of Michigan, graduating in 1859. He claimed proficiency in French and a general knowledge of other European languages. During the American Civil War, he served in the Union navy as a paymaster, seeing little action except for the bombardment of several ports below New Orleans. After the war, Beardsley traveled in Africa and Europe. For health reasons he wanted to move to a more suitable climate, preferably in the Mediterranean basin, and as such sought a post in the American foreign service. He wrote that "now without a consulship I cannot live abroad with my family." His application was endorsed by nearly every prominent and influential Republican in Indiana, and in his appeal to Secretary of State Hamilton Fish, he claimed that his physician had warned him that to remain any longer in the United States, would endanger his life. On 13 January 1870 he was appointed United States consul for Jerusalem.[44]

---

42 Certificate of Dr. H.D. Mazaraky, Jerusalem, 30 December 1866, USNA RG59 T471/2; Victor Beauboucher, U.S. Consul, Jerusalem, to William H. Seward, Secretary of State, Washington, D.C., 2 January 1867, USNA RG59 T471/2.

43 Victor Beauboucher, U.S. Consul and Lorenzo M. Johnson, U.S. Vice Consul, Jerusalem, to Dr. Heinrich Julius Petermann, German Consul, Jerusalem, 27 February 1868, 24 September 1868, and 26 September 1868, ISA RG67/163; Victor Beauboucher, U.S. Consul, Jerusalem, to Baron Carl Victor von Alten, German Consul, Jerusalem, 16 October 1869, ISA RG67/163; statement by John B. Hay, Vice and Acting Consul, Jerusalem, 4 November 1869, USNA RG59 T471/2.

44 Richard Beardsley, Elkhart, Indiana, to Hamilton Fish, Secretary of State, Washington, D.C., 23 September 1869, USNA RG59 M650; Richard Beardsley, U.S. Consul, Jerusalem, to Hamilton Fish, Secretary of State, Washington, D.C., 10 February 1872, USNA RG59 M650; Vogel, "Zion as Place," p.320; John B. Hay, U.S. Vice Consul, Jerusalem, to Baron Carl Victor von Alten, German Consul, Jerusalem, 29 April 1870, ISA RG67/163.

Beardsley arrived in Jerusalem on 30 April 1870, His first reports to Washington express an optimistic view of developments in Palestine. "With her climate, soil, and geographic position, Palestine under favourable circumstances would become one of the most prosperous states on the Mediterranean. What she requires is a wise and just government which will protect instead of plunder her people." [45] He also developed an interest in archeology. In a report to the State Department he discussed the discovery of the Moabite Stone and its loss (Plate 20).[46]

A member of the Masonic Order in Elkhart, Indiana, Beardsley worked toward the establishment of the Masonic Order on a legal and permanent basis in Jerusalem, the city of its origin, and pursuing there his activities as a Freemason with great energy. For the first time in centuries, Freemasons – visitors and residents – congregated in the long-abandoned Solomon's Quarries (Zedekiah's Cave), breaking the usual silence there with Masonic utterances.[47]

In his position as consul, Beardsley provided protection for many Jews. He was praised as a gentleman by Simeon Berman, a Jew who attempted to settle in Galilee, and he helped various American travelers in the region. Although in one instance Beardsley was accused of receiving bribes, nothing came of the allegation.[48]

Beardsley desired a better position in another location: his post in Jerusalem offered little challenge and limited financial remuneration. He sought promotion as well as a post where the climate would be healthier, like Alexandria, Marseilles, Lyon, or Bordeaux. He used his political influence to persuade a senator from Indiana to write to the President, stating that Beardsley had been in Egypt for a number of months and that he was familiar with its inhabitants, that he had knowledge of international law and had a respectable past in public office. On 11 September 1873, Beardsley wound up his position in Jerusalem and later served as consul-general at Alexandria, but soon afterwards he left the diplomatic service altogether.[49]

45   Manuel, *The Realities*, p.14.

46   Richard Beardsley, U.S. Consul, Jerusalem, to the Second Secretary of State, Washington, D.C., 28 April 1871, USNA RG59 T471/3.

47   Morris, *Freemasonry in the Holy Land*, pp.418-19,471.

48   Vogel, "Zion as Place," p.324; Bartour, "American Consular Aid," pp.54-57.

49   Vogel, "Zion as Place," pp.324-25; Eliav, "An Annotated Listing," p.170; Bartour, "American Consular Aid," p.55.

Frank S. DeHass — 1873–1877

Frank S. DeHass was a doctor of divinity from New York City. He had served as pastor of the Metropolitan Church in Washington D.C. and had a great interest in biblical archeology. He regarded an appointment as consul in Jerusalem as an opportunity to advance his researches. DeHass wrote to President Grant requesting this position in order to complete a work in his field of interest, and to carry out further research for the American Palestine Exploration Society. Not receiving an immediate reply, DeHass went to Long Branch, New Jersey and brashly handed an application to the President who was vacationing there at the time. He claimed in his request that he needed the post for his wife's health. In further appeals to Secretary of State Hamilton Fish, he stated that he wanted the position for scientific and humanitarian reasons – to keep an eye on the sultan's illicit slave trade – and said that he was giving up a position with an annual salary of $6,000. DeHass also let it be known to the secretary of state that he had sent out ten thousand circulars to American clergymen urging their support for the President in view of the charges of scandal brought against the Grant administration.[50]

In an introduction to his book, *Buried Cities Recovered: Or, Explorations in Bible Lands*, he dwelt upon the reasons for his assuming the consulship in Jerusalem. "The author's object in accepting an appointment under the United States Government, and making his home for several years in Palestine, was not the honor or emoluments of office; but a desire to visit the lands of the Bible, that he might examine and see for himself how far the manners, customs, and traditions of the people and topography of those countries, agreed with the inspired word."[51] DeHass was a member of the American Geographical Society and the American Palestine Exploration Society. He was also associated with the English Palestine Exploration Fund.[52]

He took up his position as American consul for Jerusalem on 17 December 1873. In carrying out his duties he earned both praise and criticism. Rolla Floyd, a well-known American guide and travel agent residing in Jaffa, charged that DeHass was neglecting his responsibilities, that he had visited the United States twice and Europe several times, and that when he left he

---

50 Vogel, "Zion as Place," pp.325-27.

51 DeHass, *Buried Cities*, p.9.

52 Ibid., pp.5,10.

put an Arab in his place – or rather, left him to take charge. Floyd remarked that it was a most shameful thing to put men like DeHass in office.[53]

On the other hand, he was commended for his assistance to American tourists. A traveler named Ridgeway recounted his party's meeting with DeHass on the outskirts of Jerusalem. He came upon them, a lone rider wearing a high beaver hat, a European suit and saddled on an Arabian horse. DeHass warmly shook their hands. Ridgeway related that the consul arranged the entrance of American tourists to the Temple Mount for the lowest possible price, as well as visits to the Western Wall and the Church of the Holy Sepulchre on the Orthodox Easter to witness the ceremony of the Holy Fire (Plate 19).[54]

DeHass's attitude toward the Jewish community in Palestine was regarded by them as most positive. In a case regarding the contested ownership of a courtyard and buildings in Jerusalem between Rabbi Shaul Benjamin Cohen of Radoshkovichi and the Prushim community, the rabbi and his wife had been jailed. DeHass showed compassion and understanding for the imprisoned couple, who were American citizens, and arranged for their release on health grounds. The Jerusalem Hebrew newspaper, *Havatzeleth*, praised the "noble actions" of the American consul and paid him the highest compliment by calling him "one of our Jewish brethren."[55] DeHass also attempted to help Rabbi Haim Zvi Sneersohn carry out his plan of settling in the region of Tiberias.[56]

With the outbreak of hostilities between Russia and Turkey in 1877, many Russian Jews in Palestine were left without protection. DeHass received over a hundred Jews under his protection and informed the State Department while awaiting instructions. Allegations published in the *Jewish Chronicle* that DeHass had received bribes for his actions were apparently unfounded.[57]

53   J. Panayotti, U.S. Dragoman, Jerusalem, to O. Kersten, German Consulate, Jerusalem, 15 December
      1873, and E. Hardegg, U.S. [Acting] Consul, Jerusalem, to O. Kersten, German Consulate, Jerusalem,
      17 December 1873, ISA RG67/163; Rolla Floyd, Jaffa, to Aurilla Floyd Tabbutt, Columbia Falls, 2
      March 1877, in Parsons, *Letters from Palestine*, pp.22-23.

54   Schur, *The Book of Travellers*, pp.247-48.

55   *Havatzeleth* 4, 24 Heshvan 5634 (14 November 1873), p.38 (Hebrew); *HaLevanon* 10, 3 Shevat
      5634 (21 January 1874), p.185 (Hebrew); *Ivri Anokhi* 10, 22 Kislev 5634 (12 December 1873), p.82
      (Hebrew). On the dispute see also the discussion on estates, Chapter Four, below, and Malachi,
      Studies, pp.272-79.

56   Bartour, "American Consular Aid," pp.68-74.

57   *Jewish Chronicle*, 29 June 1877, p.11, 2 November 1877, p.7, 28 December 1877, p.7, 11 January
      1878, p.7; Bartour, "American Consular Aid," pp.77-81

DeHass met with Sir Moses Montefiore during his visit to the Holy Land in 1875. They discussed the improvements which had already taken place in the country and those being introduced.[58] And he used his good offices in providing compensation to the owner of a donkey that was killed in Jaffa by a shore party of drunken sailors from the U.S. sloop of war, *Alaska*.[59]

DeHass resigned his post on 14 July 1877, and the consulate was given to the charge of Vice-Consul Ernst Hardegg on 1 August 1877. DeHass returned to the United States, taking up residence in Ohio.[60]

Joseph G. Willson — 1877–1882

Joseph G. Willson was an Iowa newspaper editor of some political standing. Toward the end of his period of service in Jerusalem, on meeting General Ulysses S. Grant and his party during their visit there in 1882, Willson told him that he had been the first American editor to propose the general for the presidency, and that "He had intended that the entrance of his favorite commander [General Grant] into the Holy City should not be a circus show or a one-horse affair but a pageant."[61]

Willson was appointed consul for Jerusalem and took over the post on 1 October 1877. On taking office, he had to deal with the problem of the protection of the Russian Jews which had occupied Frank DeHass previously. He was involved in attempts to organize the distribution to Jews in Jerusalem of money from America under the auspices of the consulate.[62] In an open letter to the *Jewish Messenger* he wrote:

> I think it proper that the Hebrew people in America should know the condition of their brethren at Jerusalem, who are in distress and need assistance. They are citizens of the United States with naturalization papers and passports. Some of them are Russian and Polish Jews, and since the war, the aid formerly received from their European friends is no longer received...Any money

58   Loewe, *Diaries of Sir Moses Montefiore*, 2:6, entry for July 13, 1875.

59   Frank S. DeHass, U.S. Consul, Jerusalem, to N. Hunter, Second Assistant Secretary of State, Washington, D.C., 6 November 1874, USNA RG59 T471/4.

60   Frank S. DeHass, U.S. Consul, and E. Hardegg, U.S. Vice Consul, Jerusalem, to J.A. Campbell, Third Assistant Secretary of State, Washington, D.C., 14 July 1877 and 1 August 1877, USNA RG59 T471/4; *Jewish Chronicle*, 28 December 1877, p.7.

61   Young, *Around the World*, 1:331.

62   Eliav, "An Annotated Listing," p.172; List of U.S. Consular Officers, Jerusalem, Turkey, USNA RG59 M587/10; Bartour, "American Consular Aid," pp.74-83.

for their relief, sent to me, will be deposited in bank as a relief fund, and distributed by a committee...[63]

But Willson was also seen as incompetent in his role of consul. Rolla Floyd wrote of him as an "old man led by the nose by his Arab Dragoman" and "who by the way is about crazy." In another letter Floyd wrote, "I'm sure you would laugh to hear the old fool of a consul talk. He is certainly the greatest old woman I ever saw and I do not know why our government doesn't send a nurse for such stupid old cows when they put him in office." [64]

Floyd's opinion probably derived from his rivalry with Thomas Cook & Son, and Willson's siding with the latter. Floyd wrote on this matter: "Cook is so well armed with money that he may injure me or any other poor honest American as much as he likes. The consul dare not offend him...What a disgrace to the government." [65]

Willson astutely assessed the profuse literature on Palestine. In one of his annual reports to the State Department he wrote:

> There is no country in the world of equal area of territory of which so much has been written, and of which so little is really known as Palestine. Few persons have remained long enough in the country to make trustworthy observations and reports, or to understand the peculiarities of the people or the relation of the facts as recorded in the different eras....One book writer copies the statements of predecessors and the travellers remaining only a few days, derive their information from native guides who know but little English or French, and who with the fatal infirmity of Oriental mind, know no difference between fact and fiction.[66]

Willson perceived that the attitudes of many foreigners were the result of their theological or political views and not based on fact. "The imagination misleads the judgement, sentiment prevails over the dictates of reason. There

---

63   *Jewish Messenger*, 23 November 1877 in Bartour, ibid., Appendix 20, p.300.

64   Rolla Floyd, Jaffa, to Aurilla Floyd Tabbutt, Columbia Falls, 15 June 1881, 11 August 1881, and 2 February 1882 in Parsons, *Letters from Palestine*, pp.51-52, 58-59.

65   Rolla Floyd, Jaffa, to Aurilla Floyd Tabbutt, Columbia Falls, 16 May 1883, ibid., pp.71-72.

66   Joseph G. Willson, U. S. Consul, Jerusalem, Annual Report, to Robert R. Taft, Assistant Secretary of State, Washington, D.C., 7 October 1881, USNA RG59 T471/5.

is a fervish [sic] state of expectation which attached to events transpiring in Palestine, out of importance to their intrinsic value." [67]

In 1881, Willson requested Secretary of State Addison to allow him to continue serving the United States government abroad and consider transferring him to another post of a higher grade. He pointed to the precedent of one of his predecessors, Richard Beardsley, who had been transferred to the post of consul-general at Alexandria. A year later, on 30 June 1882, Willson left Jerusalem having been appointed to Cairo as consul-general.[68]

Selah Merrill — 1882–1885, 1891–1893, 1898–1907

Selah Merrill was born at Canton Center, Connecticut on 2 May 1837. His education began at Westfield, Massachusetts and continued at the Williston Seminary in Easthampton. He entered Yale with the class of 1863, but left college before graduating to study at the Yale Divinity School.[69]

In 1864 he was ordained as a Congregational minister and was appointed chaplain of a Black regiment, the 49th U.S. Infantry, which served at Vicksburg during 1864–65. After the Civil War, Merrill was a preacher in Le Roy, New York (1866–67), in San Francisco (1867–68), and in Salmon Falls, New Hampshire (1870–72).[70] He was married three times, on 15 March 1866 to Fanny Lucinda Cooke who died the following year, on 16 September 1868 to Phila Wilkins Fargo who died in 1870, and on 27 April 1875 he wed Adelaide Brewster Taylor.[71]

Merrill studied German for two years (1868–70) at the University of Berlin. In 1869 he traveled to Greece, Egypt, Palestine, and Syria with other students of Edward Amasa Park, a teacher at the Andover Theological Seminary. This voyage inspired Merrill to engage in the study of the Holy Land and he returned to the region as archeologist with the American Palestine Exploration Society expedition. During the years 1876–77, Merrill headed three extended trips to Eastern Palestine (Transjordan), collecting archeological,

67   Ibid.

68   Joseph G. Willson, U.S. Consul, Jerusalem, to W.B. Addison, Secretary of State, Washington, D.C., 15 January 1881, USNA, ibid.; List of U.S. Consular Officers, Jerusalem, Turkey, USNA RG59 M587/10; Eliav, "An Annotated Listing," p.172.

69   Albright, "Selah Merrill," p.564-65; *Who was Who in America*, 1:832.

70   Albright, ibid.

71   Ibid.

topographical, and ethnographic information. He published the findings in his book, *East of the Jordan*.[72]

Leading members of the British Palestine Exploration Fund were extremely critical of Merrill's activities. In 1875, Claude Reignier Conder wrote that Merrill's "account of Ruckleh, wrongly spelt Rukleh, is very imperfect". The British consul-general at Beirut, G. Jackson Eldridge, spared no words in criticizing him, in 1876: "Merrill whom I saw a few days ago seems to think he has done a great deal but his opinion was a personal and biased one and I agree with you [George Grove] that nothing will be done East of Jordan by Americans if they continue to organise their expeditions as they do." [73]

His ability as an archeologist was assessed negatively also by W.F. Albright who claimed that Merrill was inadequately trained and that his archeology was therefore not sound.

> Such success as he had was undoubtedly due, in large measure, to his practical ability and his skill in dealing with the natives. He possessed a respectable knowledge of the documentary and philological material, and indeed surpassed his English colleagues of the Palestine Exploration Fund in this respect. Had he been able to follow in the footsteps of Edward Robinson, the founder of the scientific study of Palestinian geography, and to combine a sound European philological and critical training with his New England endurance and practicality, his work might easily have been epoch-making.[74]

Merrill returned to the United States and taught Hebrew at the Andover Theological Seminary for two years. In 1882, he secured the first of his three appointments as American consul at Jerusalem. He occupied this position during the Republican administration, his tenure being interrupted by President Cleveland's two terms.[75]

Merrill's lengthy residence in Jerusalem as American consul allowed for his continued study of the history and archeology of Palestine. He published over fifty articles on these subjects and a comprehensive work, *Ancient*

---

72   Ibid.; Selah Merrill, Andover, Mass., to J.C. Bancroft Davis, Assistant Secretary of State, Washington, D.C., 24 April 1882, USNA RG59 T471/5; Vogel, "Zion as Place," p.111.

73   Claude Reignier Conder, Guilford, to Walter Besant, London, 27 November 1875, and G. Jackson Eldridge, British Consul- General, Beirut, to George Grove, London, 30 November 1876, in Lipman, *Americans and the Holy Land*, pp.175-76.

74   Albright, "Selah Merrill," p.564-65.

75   Ibid.

Jerusalem.[76] George Adam Smith wrote the following of Merrill in a review of that book:

> Dr. Merrill is one of the very oldest workers alive in the field, and, since Dr. Schick's death, has almost no rival among experts on the subject, either in length of residence in Jerusalem, or in the constancy of the vigilance with which he has observed the life of the city and its surroundings, or followed the excavations and discoveries within it. His occasional papers in the *Quarterly Statement* and *The Biblical World*, and the great generosity with which, through many years, he communicated his intimate knowledge, both to specialists and to tourists, have long created an eager anticipation of the time when his manifold official services should allow him to put the stores of his experience into public form.[77]

During Merrill's long period of service in Jerusalem, he formulated very definite opinions regarding the situation in the area under his jurisdiction. And it seems that his personal background and prejudices considerably influenced the objectivity of his decisions and reports.[78] Thus his attitude to Jewish immigration and settlement in Palestine was negative. In his report for 1891 he wrote of the harmful results of aiding Jewish colonies: "...it would seem that the Jews do not have much desire to be colonists." [79] Nor did he have any sympathy for eccentric Christian sects, such as the American Colony in Jerusalem.[80] His blind hatred of these people and what they stood for, and the lengths to which he went in opposing them, may have been a

---

76   See: Röhricht, *Bibliotheca*, pp.580-82. The entry for Merrill which includes the years 1874 to 1890 lists 42 items. *Palestine Exploration Fund Quarterly Statement* index for the years 1869–1892 lists six additional items not mentioned in Röhricht. Merrill's articles were published in other learned journals such as *American Palestine Exploration Society Statement, The Biblical World, Bulletin of the American Geographical Society, Scientific American,* and many others.

77   Smith, "Review of Ancient Jerusalem," p.333.

78   See: Kark, "Annual Reports," pp.146-48 for a discussion of the influence of the consuls' personalities.

79   Selah Merrill, U.S. Consul, Jerusalem, "Jews and Jewish Colonies in Palestine," to William F. Wharton, Assistant Secretary of State, Washington, D.C., 3 October 1891, USNA RG59 T471/7. For the complete report, see: Kark, ibid., pp.133-39.

80   Selah Merrill, U.S. Consul, Jerusalem, "The Condition of Labor and the Laboring Classes in Palestine," to Alvey R. Adee, Third Assistant Secretary of State, Washington, D.C., 5 July 1894, USNA RG59 T471/8.

cause of his dismissal by his superiors.[81] In her book, *Our Jerusalem*, Bertha Spafford-Vester, whose parents had founded the colony, wrote about Selah Merrill's attitude: "In all those years his acrimony against the American Colony never abated, and his official position lent weight to his disapproval and increased his ability to do us harm.... Mr. Merrill had definite ideas as a Congregationalist minister about how philanthropic work should be done, so he would have nothing to do with our Group. His resentment was hidden at first...."[82]

After retiring from his post in Jerusalem, Merrill was appointed consul at Georgetown in British Guyana. He served in this post in 1907–08 and returned to the United States to live out his last years. Selah Merrill died on 22 January 1909, near East Oakland, California.[83]

Nageeb J. Arbeely — 1885–1886

Nageeb J. Arbeely, a physician of Greek origin, was born in Damascus. He was appointed consul for Jerusalem for the state of Tennessee, where he had been naturalized. His appointment resulted from a shift in American politics with the election of Grover Cleveland to the presidency. According to Bertha Spafford-Vester, "his term of office proved a blessing to the American Colony," and Arbeely's appointment was also welcomed by Jerusalem's Muslim population.[84] However, the Turkish government declined to receive him because he was a native of the Ottoman Empire, and he was recalled to Washington on 11 November 1887.[85]

Rolla Floyd characteristically viewed Arbeely's stint in office and departure from his particular angle: "Arbeely ...was appointed U.S. Consul at Jerusalem,

81   Dudman, "American Colony in Jerusalem," pp.168-77; Gustafson, "Records in the National Archives," p.134.

82   Spafford-Vester, *Our Jerusalem*, p.79.

83   Albright, "Selah Merrill."

84   Nageeb J. Arbeely, U.S. Consul, Jerusalem, to James D. Porter, Assistant Secretary of State, Washington, D.C., 19 October 1885, USNA RG59 T471/5; List of U.S. Consular Officers, Jerusalem, Turkey, USNA RG59 M587/10; Spafford-Vester, *Our Jerusalem*, p.159; Rolla Floyd, Jaffa, to Aurilla Floyd Tabbutt, Columbia Falls, 17 December 1885, in Parsons, *Letters from Jerusalem*, p.96.

85   Nageeb J. Arbeely, U.S. Consul, Jerusalem, to James D. Porter, Assistant Secretary of State, Washington, D.C., 19 October 1885, USNA RG59 T471/5; List of U.S. Consular Officers, Jerusalem, Turkey, USNA RG59 M587/10; Spafford-Vester, ibid., p.157.

but because he was a friend of mine and a gentleman, Merrill & the Cooks bribed the Turks to not give him affirmation." [86]

Henry Gillman — 1886–1891

Henry Gillman was born on 16 November 1833, in Kinsale, Ireland. he was educated by private tutors and at Hamilton Academy, Bandon, County Cork, with a view to taking orders in the Established Church. He emigrated with his parents to America in 1850 and settled in Detroit. Gillman became first assistant in the United States Geodetic Survey of the Great Lakes. He married Mary Julia Johnson on 7 December 1858 and they had four children. His wife died in 1878.[87] From 1851 to 1869 he headed topographic and hydrographic teams, his reports being published in scientific journals. During that period Gillman also wrote poetry, and a volume of his poems, *Marked for Life*, appeared in 1863. From 1870 to 1876 he was assistant superintendent of the construction for the 10th and 11th lighthouse districts on the Northern Lakes.[88]

Gillman was elected a fellow of the American Association for the Advancement of Science. The following year he was sent as a member-at-large to attend the International Congress of Americanists at Luxembourg, where he read a paper on the osteological remains of the mound builders. His most important contribution to science was the discovery of certain peculiarities in the bones of mound-building Indians.[89] From April 1880 until the summer of 1885, he was librarian of the Detroit Public Library.

The following year, Gillman, a Democrat supporting Grover Cleveland, accepted a politically motivated appointment as American consul for Jerusalem.[90] As consul he took a stand against the expulsion of Jews from Palestine. He was later backed by several of the European powers in inducing the Ottoman authorities to abrogate these exclusion laws. He aided members

86 Rolla Floyd, Jaffa, to Aurilla Floyd Tabbutt, Columbia Falls, 12 June 1886, in Parsons, *Letters from Jerusalem*, p.105.

87 Henry Gillman, Detroit, to D. Porter, Assistant Secretary of State, Washington, D.C., 28 June 1886, USNA RG59 T471/6; Johnson, *Dictionary of American Biography*, 7:294-95.

88 Johnson, ibid.

89 Ibid.

90 List of U.S. Consular Officers, Jerusalem, Turkey, USNA RG59 M587/10; Bartour, "American Consular Aid," p.98; Spafford-Vester, *Our Jerusalem*, p.159; Johnson, ibid.

of the "New Yishuv" and had reservations with regard to the rabbis who controlled the life of the "Old Yishuv".[91]

In his novel, *Hassan: A Fellah – A Romance of Palestine*, Gillman expressed his attitude toward the Holy Land and its inhabitants, as well as how he perceived himself as consul. He describes the complimentary remarks about the consul made by the local people:

> "He is a good man," said one of the oldest of the natives, venerable with long white flowing beard. "Yea, a good man and just, and one that fears God," was the response of the second, who seemed his duplicate, so much alike were they with their steadfast, unflinching eyes and placid countenances ...A third and younger individual acquiesced with some emotion and even heat;..."Thou speakest truly," he said, with animated gestures. "Verily he makes one love him. He treats us natives like men – the other consuls use us as if we were dogs." [92] (Plate 24)

But Selah Merrill, whose periods of service preceded and followed that of Gillman, thought his colleague's work in carrying out his duties unsatisfactory, inefficient, and tainted with irregularities. In a despatch in 1891, to the secretary of state, Merrill pointed to two problems, the first dealing with upkeep of the consular register. On this subject he wrote that, "During my former term as consul here I had the list of citizens revised every year. It was always attended with special difficulties and sometimes required three or four weeks of labor before the list could be completed. My successor, Mr. Gillman, gave this matter no attention whatever." The second point Merrill raised, had to do with an infraction of the rules, "When any citizen applied for registration, Mr. Gillman recorded his name and always charged a fee for same, clearly in violation of Consular Regulation, paragraph 444, which states that 'No fee will be charged for registration nor for any service connected with it'."[93]

While serving in Jerusalem, Gillman continued his archeological research. He believed that the site of the Holy Sepulchre was not that of the crucifixion. He also continued his work in botany, publishing *Wild Flowers and Gardens*

---

91   Bartour, "American Consular Aid," pp.98-102; Henry Gillman, U.S. Consul, Jerusalem, to Oscar Straus, U.S. Minister, Constantinople, 31 December 1887, in Bartour, ibid., pp.309-12, Appendix 23.

92   Gillman, *Hassan a Fellah*, pp.214-15.

93   Selah Merrill, U.S. Consul, Jerusalem, to William F. Wharton, Assistant Secretary of State, Washington, D.C., 8 September 1891, RG51, [59, R.K.] Consular Dispatches, Jerusalem, USNA in Davis, *With Eyes* I, pp.233-35.

of Palestine. He procured and published photograph facsimiles of early Christian texts. One such document, "The Teaching of the Apostles" in the possession of Nicodemus, the Greek Orthodox patriarch of Jerusalem was photographed in 1877 and sent to the president of Johns Hopkins University.[94]

In 1890, during his term as consul, he took a vacation in Italy and was cordially received by Pope Leo XIII, in recognition of the assistance he had rendered to the first American Catholic pilgrimage to the Holy Land in 1887.[95]

Gillman returned to Detroit in 1891, living with his son. Until his death on 30 July 1915, he occupied his working hours writing scientific and other papers.[96]

Edwin Sherman Wallace — 1893–1898

Edwin Sherman Wallace was born on 3 October 1864, in Butler County, Pennsylvania. He was educated at Washington and Jefferson College and later attended the Princeton Theological Seminary becoming an ordained Presbyterian minister in 1898. He then served in a number of pastorates.[97] While at Aberdeen, South Dakota, he accepted an appointment as consul in Jerusalem by President Grover Cleveland on 17 October 1893.[98]

Wallace was critical of Ottoman rule in Palestine, and in Jerusalem in particular: "Jerusalem has now been practically in undisputed Moslem possession for six hundred years. How long it will continue to be is a question often asked. The weakness of the possessors is very evident." [99] He regarded

94   Johnson, *Dictionary of American Biography*, 7:294-95; Spafford-Vester, Our Jerusalem, p.159; Gillman, *Hassan a Fellah,* p.83; Nicodemus, Greek Patriarch of Jerusalem and Palestine, to Charles R. Hale, Dean of the Cathedral Church of Davenport in the U.S., 20 May 1887, Lambeth Palace Library, E.W. Benson Official Letters, vol.174 (1887), p.510.

95   Johnson, ibid

96   Johnson, ibid. Henry Gillman's son, Dr. Robert Winthrop Gillman, was an assistant surgeon at St. John's Opthalmic Hospital in Jerusalem between the years 1886-1888. Henry Gillman was involved in the public activities of the Order of St. John and its Jerusalem hospital, as seen from the letters of Dr. J.H. Ogilvie, Jerusalem, to Sir Lechmer, London, 3 March 1887 and 16 November 1887, and from minutes of the Council, 19 July 1887, Archives of the Order of St. John, London.

97   Edwin S. Wallace, Aberdeen, South Dakota, to Edward H. Strobel, U.S. State Department, Washington, D.C., 17 October 1893, USNA RG59 T471/8; Handy, *The Holy Land*, p.154; Davis, "American Christian Devotees," p.6.

98   Wallace to Strobel, ibid.

99   Wallace, *Jerusalem the Holy,* p.347

the Jewish population of Palestine with sympathy, writing in his book, *Jerusalem the Holy*:

> My own belief is that the time is not far distant when Palestine will be in the hands of a people who will restore it to its former condition of productiveness. The land is waiting, the people are ready to come and will come as soon as protection to life and property is assured. I am ready to go further and say that the coming inhabitants will be Jews. This must be accepted or numerous prophecies that assert it so positively must be thrown out as worthless. The subject of Israel's restoration I freely admit is not a popular one now; but the unpopular of to-day is the universally accepted of to-morrow.[100]

Wallace's actions reflected his feelings. Notwithstanding the State Department regulations of 1888, he issued new passports to Jews who had claimed that they had lost the documents protecting their rights as Americans.[101]

Wallace became involved in the attempt of Jewish-American citizens to separate from the *"va'ad ha-kelali"* (the general committee of the *kollels*) and to establish an American *kollel*. Wallace offered Rabbi Joshua Diskin the protection of the American consulate in return for assuming the position of rabbi of Kollel America. In 1897, an agreement to this effect was signed in Wallace's presence between the rabbi and Kollel America.[102]

Like his predecessor, Selah Merrill, Wallace was antagonistic to the American Colony people and their "Spaffordism". He continued the dispute over the American graveyard on Mount Zion, which became more acute during his term of office. It had to do with an argument over the ownership of the cemetery and the right of the Colony to bury its members there. At one point, the graves of the American Colony were dug up and desecrated.[103] Bertha Spafford–Vester wrote of Wallace's zeal in gathering derogatory testimony against the Colony: "Mr. Wallace's statements to travelers about us were so gratuitous and uncalled for that they aroused suspicion and a number of people visited the Colony who would not otherwise have done so,

---

100   Ibid., p.355.

101   Bartour, "American Consular Aid," pp.144-45.

102   Fishbane, "Kollel America," pp.121-27

103   Bartour, "American Consular Aid," p.143; Spafford-Vester, *Our Jerusalem*, pp.214-17,220; Ford, "Our American Colony," pp.649-50. For various documents on Wallace and the American Colony, see: Lipman, *Americans and the Holy Land*, pp.150-63.

to find out the truth for themselves. Many wrote back wonderful letters, others were in time to raise powerful voices on our behalf."[104]

In 1898, Edwin Wallace left his post as consul and returned to America, taking up again his former vocation as pastor in a Greensburg, Pennsylvania church. His involvement in the graveyard controversy became known through an article in *Appleton's Magazine* in 1906. He brought action against the publishers but lost. The trial probably cost Wallace several thousand dollars as well as his reputation. In 1910, he went into business in Pittsburgh, but returned to his former vocation of pastor in 1931 to a Blawnox, Pennsylvania congregation. He died in Daytona Beach, Florida on 15 August 1960 aged ninety-six.[105]

Thomas Ross Wallace — 1907–1910

Thomas R. Wallace (no relation to Edwin Wallace) was born in Philadelphia on 20 October 1848. He studied law under a private instructor and worked as a lawyer and teacher. He served for three terms as a clerk of the district and circuit courts of the State of Iowa, was an alderman for a number of years, and later three times mayor of Atlantic, Iowa.[106]

Wallace entered the consular service in 1901, being appointed consul to Krefeld in Germany. He was commissioned consul in Jerusalem on 30 March 1907 and assumed his office in July of that year.[107] It was the first appointment to this position based on merit rather than on political considerations and the spoils system.

Thomas Wallace evinced a positive attitude toward the Jews of Palestine, hoping for their productivization:

> The needs of the Jewish People in the Holy Land are increased opportunities for self support and any industrial enterprise that will furnish them a reasonable return for their labour, deserves encouragement and is far better than charity that takes from their pride and manhood. The economic, social, and sanitary conditions of their lives would be greatly improved if changed from the

---

104 Spafford-Vester, ibid., p.200.

105 Ibid., p.220; Ford, "Our American Colony," pp.643-55.

106 Thomas R. Wallace, U.S. Consul, Jerusalem, to Assistant Secretary of State, Washington, D.C., 26 February 1910, USNA RG59 T471/11.

107 Mayer, "Records of U.S. Consulate at Jerusalem"; Thomas R. Wallace, U.S. Consul, Jerusalem, to Assistant Secretary of State, Washington, D.C., 19 February 1910, USNA RG59 T471/11.

present conditions in which they live to the farm, the gardens, or the orchards.[108]

Wallace acted in favor of the Jews of the country. The new regulations of 1906–07 required the consul to register Jews who deserved protection. He tried to postpone the application of these regulations by forwarding Jewish petitions to Washington.[109]

On 6 June 1910, the State Department transferred Wallace to a post on the island of Martinique. He retired from this position on 24 December 1924, and died in New Orleans on 8 December 1929.[110]

William Coffin — 1910–1913

William Coffin was born in Brooklyn, New York on 8 October 1877. He was educated at St.Paul's School in Concord, New Hampshire. In October 1905 he married Mabel Sands Rees; they had two children, Patricia and Miriam. He worked in the mercantile business in Tennessee and Kentucky between 1894 and 1900, and in New York between 1900 and 1906. Coffin passed examinations for the consular service and received an appointment to Muscat (Oman) in 1906. He was transferred to Tripoli in Libya where he served from 1908 to 1910. On 24 June 1910 he was appointed consul in Jerusalem for Kentucky.[111]

One of the important issues dealt with by Coffin was the status of American citizens and their rights according to the new American law and Ottoman regulations. Coffin acted in accordance with the instructions from the State Department. On 2 March 1912 it was presumed that the expatriation of naturalized American citizens who moved to other countries and resided there for five years would begin. Although he informed those concerned, we do not know of the outcome.[112]

During May and June of 1912, Coffin returned to the United States on special duty in connection with the Twelfth International Congress of Navigation in Philadelphia.[113] He continued his diplomatic career with a number of appointments, serving in Budapest as consul-general in 1913, and

---

108   Thomas R. Wallace, U.S. Consul, Jerusalem, letter of recommendation regarding the activities of Kehillath Jacob Society, in Bartour, "American Consular Aid," p.369, Appendix 51.

109   Bartour, ibid., pp.184-88.

110   Mayer, "Records of U.S. Consulate at Jerusalem."

111   *Who was Who in America*, 1:238; Bartour, "American Consular Aid," pp.189-90.

112   Bartour, ibid.

113   *Who was Who In America*, 1:238; Bartour, ibid., pp.367-68

in Christiania and Stockholm in 1917. He was detailed to the Department of State in 1918 to serve as a representative at the Fifth National Foreign Trade Convention at Cincinnati and the War Reconstruction Congress of the Chamber of Commerce in Atlantic City. In 1919 Coffin took up the position of consul-general in Berlin, remaining in that function until his death from cardiac arrest in Algiers on 13 February 1927.[114]

Otis Allan Glazebrook — 1914–1917

Otis Allan Glazebrook was born in Richmond, Viriginia on 13 October 1845. He studied at Randolph Macon College, at the Virginia Military Institute, and at the Virginia Theological Seminary.[115] His education having led him to church activities, he served for seven years in missionary fields in Virginia, for four years as a rector in Baltimore, and three years in Macon and as rector of St. John's Protestant Episcopal Church in Elizabeth, New Jersey – from 1885 to 1912. Eight times he was clerical deputy from New Jersey to the General Convention of the Protestant Episcopal Church.[116]

Glazebrook also served as chaplain to the Third New Jersey Regiment during the Spanish-American War. He was a Freemason acting as chaplain of the Grand Lodge of Masons of the New Jersey Military Order of Foreign Wars and of similar veterans' organizations. He was decorated with the Masonic degree of Knight of the Holy Sepulchre.[117]

From 1914 until his retirement in 1927, Glazebrook served in the American foreign service. As a personal friend of President Woodrow Wilson, Otis Glazebrook was appointed American consul at Jerusalem for New Jersey under Executive Order of 10 February 1914. Wilson indulged his lifelong wish to live in the Holy Land by sending him to Jerusalem. He was commissioned on 18 February of that year.[118]

In his late sixties when he came to Jerusalem in April 1914, Glazebrook was described as "distinguished and venerable in appearance, young in spirit, full of energy, and always ready to do a friendly service for the Jews."[119] A religious man, "Every morning, before beginning work, Glazebrook would read two chapters of the Bible, which served him with spiritual and moral

114 Ibid. Christiania was renamed Oslo in 1924.

115 *Who was Who In America*, 1:460.

116 Ibid.

117 Ibid

118 Mayer, "Records of U.S. Consulate at Jerusalem."

119 Yaari, *The Goodly Heritage*, p.376.

support for the whole day. He often quoted the words of the prophets he had read that morning when speaking at a Jewish meeting."[120]

With the outbreak of the war on 4 August 1914, Glazebrook's importance increased. He aided the British and other foreign subjects in Palestine whose governments were at war with Turkey after their respective consuls had left Jerusalem. Bertha Spafford-Vester wrote about his activities during the war: "He told us that the most difficult person in power was Hassan Bey, the 'Tyrant of Jaffa,' so called because of his many cruel acts....Dr. Glazebrook said that he 'kept his arm around Hassan Bey's shoulders' until the last British subjects, Canon Hichens and Mr. Reynolds got away. Hassan Bey was determined to hold them as hostages."[121]

Glazebrook also played an important role in aiding the Jewish community in Palestine during the war. Distribution of funds from Europe ceased at this time and relief funds were sent from America. This money was distributed through Glazebrook who showed sympathy and understanding for the suffering Jewish population.[122] His actions won high praise and were considered paramount in saving the Jewish community in Palestine from total ruin. "He was the man who, by means of his intervention and influence, saved several of our most energetic workers from the gallows that awaited them at the beginning of the war. But his main and most consistent activity was concerned with the *yishuv's* economic life. The American consulate in those days became a large financial organization – one of the largest banks – and its clients were almost entirely Jews."[123]

With the entry of the United States into World War I, on 6 April 1917, Glazebrook left Jerusalem, being detailed temporarily to the Department of State as of 8 December 1917. After the end of the war, he was directed to return to Jerusalem on 21 December 1918. He remained there until being assigned to Nice on 20 December 1920. He became U.S. consul in Monaco in 1927. Glazebrook retired in 1929 under the provisions of the Reorganization Act of 1924 and died at sea on 26 April 1931, en route home.[124]

---

120   Ibid., pp.378-79.

121   Spafford-Vester, *Our Jerusalem*, pp.247-48.

122   Shilony, "Changes in the Jewish Leadership," pp.84-85.

123   Yaari, *The Goodly Heritage*, p.377.

124   Mayer, "Records of U.S.Consulate at Jerusalem."

APPENDIX II

LISTS OF STAFF

Appendix II A – Secretaries of State

Name and Origin	Commissioned
Martin Van Buren (New York)	28 March 1829
Edward Livingston (Louisiana)	24 May 1831
Louis McLane (Delaware)	29 May 1833
John Forsyth (Georgia) 1 July 1834	
Jacob L. Martin (North Carolina) ad interim, (Attorney General)	4 March 1841
Daniel Webster (Massachusetts)	6 March 1841
Hugh S. Legare (South Carolina) ad interim, (Attorney General)	9 May 1842
William S. Derrick (Pennsylvania) ad interim, (Chief Clerk)	21 June 1843
Abel P. Upshur (Virginia) ad interim, (Secretary of the Navy)	24 July 1843
Abel P. Upshur (Virginia)	24 July 1843
John Nelson (Maryland) ad interim, (Attorney General)	29 February 1844

John C. Calhoun (South Carolina)	1 April 1844
James Buchanan (Pennsylvania)	10 March 1845
John M. Clayton (Delaware)	8 March 1849
Daniel Webster (Massachusetts)	23 July 1850
Charles M. Conrad (Louisiana) ad interim, (Secretary of War)	25 October 1852
Edward Everett (Massachusetts)	6 November 1852
William Hunter (New York) ad interim, (Chief Clerk)	4 March 1853
William L. Marcy (New York)	8 March 1853
Lewis Cass (Michigan) 6 March 1857	
William Hunter (Rhode Island) ad interim, (Chief Clerk)	15 December 1860
Jeremiah S. Black (Pennsylvania)	17 December 1860
William H. Seward (New York)	6 March 1861
Elihu B. Washburne (Illinois)	5 March 1869
Hamilton Fish (New York)	17 March 1869
William M. Evarts (New York)	12 March 1877
James G. Blaine (Maine)	7 March 1881
Frederick T. Frelinghuysen (New Jersey)	19 December 1881
Thomas F. Bayard (Delaware)	7 March 1885
James G. Blaine (Maine)	7 March 1889

William F. Wharton (Massachusetts)
  ad interim, (Assistant Secretary of State)   4 June 1892

John W. Foster (Indiana)   29 June 1892

William F. Wharton (Massachusetts)
  ad interim, (Assistant Secretary of
  State)   24 February 1893

Walter Q. Gresham (Illinois)   7 March 1893

Edwin F. Uhl (Michigan)
  ad interim, (Assistant Secretary of
  State)   28 May 1895

Richard Olney (Massachusetts)   10 June 1895

John Sherman (Ohio)   6 March 1897

William R. Day (Ohio)   28 April 1898

Alvey A. Adee (District of Columbia)
  ad interim, (Second Assistant
  Secretary of State)   17 September 1898

John Hay (District of Columbia)   30 September 1898

Francis B. Loomis
  ad interim   1 July 1905

Elihu Root (New York)   19 July 1905

Robert Bacon (New York)   27 January 1909

Philander C. Knox (Pennsylvania)   6 March 1909

William Jennings Bryan (Nebraska)   5 March 1913

Robert Lansing
  ad interim   9 June 1915

Robert Lansing   24 June 1915

Source: Malloy, "Treaties."

Appendix II B – U.S. Ministers at Constantinople

David Porter, 1831-1843

Dabney S. Carr, 1843-1849

George P. Marsh, 1849-1853

Carrol Spence, 1855-1858

James Williams, 1858-1861

Edward Joy Morris, 1861-1870

Wane MacVeagh, 1870-1871

George H. Boker, 1871-1875

Horace Maynard, 1875-1880

James Longstreet, 1880-1881

Lewis Wallace, 1881-1885

Samuel S. Cox, 1886-1887

Oscar S. Straus, 1887-1889

Solomon Hirsch, 1889-1892

David P. Thompson, 1892-1893

Alexander W. Terrel, 1893-1897

James B. Angell, 1897-1898

Oscar S. Straus, 1898-1899

William Rockhill, 1899-1906

John Leishman, 1906-1909

Oscar S. Straus, 1909-1910

James Carter, 1910-1911

William Woodville, 1911-1913

Henry Morgenthau, 1913-1916

Source: Manuel, "The Realities," pp. 393-95.

APPENDIX II C – U.S. CONSULAR REPRESENTATIVES
AT CONSTANTINOPLE, 1832-1925[1]

Name	Date Confirmed[2]
Frederick E. Bunker[3]	3 January 1832
John P. Brown	3 March 1835
George A. Porter	10 February 1837
Francis Daines	26 February 1852
A. M. Jackson	6 October 1855
Isaac W. Bowdish	31 July 1856
John P. Brown[4]	19 February 1857
James McDowell	22 December 1858
Marshall M. Smith	10 January 1860
Henry D. Johnson	28 May 1860 (died en route to post)
J. Hosford Smith	7 November 1860
David Porter Heap	24 January 1861
Charles W. Goddard	19 February 1862

1   Based on a card "List of United States Consular Officers by Posts" photostated from a handwritten card list in the Department of State, 21 vols. In Record Group 59, Records of the Department of State.

2   The dates given are generally, but not always, the actual date of confirmation.

3   Bunker did not go to his post. William N. Churchill served in his stead.

4   The first to hold office as consul-general.

Eugene Schuyler   17 January 1876

G. Harris Heap   17 December 1878

G. Harris Heap   18 December 1884

D. Lynch Pringle   16 January 1888

Zachary Sweeny   19 December 1889

William B. Hess   11 January 1892

Luther Short   28 September 1893

Charles M. Dickinson   5 January 1898

Edward H. Ozmun   22 June 1906

Gabriel Bie Ravndal   19 December 1910

Nathaniel B. Stewart   17 August 1925

Source: Stewart, "Preliminary Inventory."

APPENDIX II D – U.S. CONSULAR REPRESENTATIVES AT BEIRUT

Name	Office	Allegiance	Birth Place	Apptd. at	Date Appointed	Remarks
Jasper Chasseaud	Consul		Salonika		3 Mar 1835 conf.	25 Mar - Dec 1840 office suspended
Jasper Chasseaud	-"-		-"-		6 Aug 1842	6 Sep 1843 - Jul 1850
J. Hosford Smith[1]	-"-	U.S.	New York	N.Y.	10 June 1850 conf.	Jul 1850 - 31 Dec 1854
Henry Wood[2]	-"-	-"-	New Hampshire	N.H.	11 Jul 1854 conf.	1 Jan 1855 - 4 Apr 1857 resigned 31 Dec 1856
J. Augustus Johnson	-"-	-"-	Mass.	R.I.	14 Apr 1858	24 Jul 1858
J. Augustus Johnson	Consul -Gen'l	-"-	-"-	-"-	5 Apr 1867	12 Nov 1867 - resignation in U.S. 2 July 1870, died in South Orange, N.J. 28 Jan 1914
Lorenzo M. Johnson	-"-	-"-		Texas	13 July 1870	1 Apr 1870 - 11 Jul 1871, resigned in U.S. 21 Oct 1871
Charles G. Dyer	-"-	-"-		Illinois	17 Nov 1871 recess	Declined by father 27 Nov 1871
John Baldwin Hay	-"-	-"-	Missouri	R.I.	18 Jan 1872	12 Jul 1871 - 30 Apr 1874 to Sivatow 6 May 1874
George S. Fisher	Consul	-"-	Mass.	Georgia	6 May 1874	8 July 1874 - 17 May 1875
John T. Edgar	-"-	-"-	Kentucky	Nebraska	11 Mar 1875 conf.	18 Jun 1875 - 26 Jun 1882 died 26 Jun 1882

Name	Office	Allegiance	Birth Place	Apptd. at	Date Appointed	Remarks
John T. Robeson	- " -	- " -	Tennessee	Tenn	27 Jul 1882 conf.	16 Dec 1882 - 31 Jan 1886
William H. Moffett	- " -	- " -		N.J.	17 May 1885 recess	to Athens 22 Jul 1885
Erhard Bissinger	- " -	- " -	Baden (Ger.)	N.Y.	19 Oct. 1885 recess, 5 May 1885 conf.	12 Feb 1886 - 14 Jun 1892 resigned in Europe 2 Jan 1893
Thomas R. Gibson	- " -	- " -	Georgia	Georgia	28 Sep 1893 conf.	9 Jan 1894 - died 20 Sept 1896
Thomas S. Doyle	- " -	- " -	Illinois	Virginia	25 Nov 1896 recess, 12 Jan 1897 conf.	9 Feb 1897 - 18 Apr 1898
Gabriel Bie Ravndal	- " -	- " -	Norway	So. Dak.	22 Jan 1898 conf.	19 Apr 1898 to apptd. consul Dawson City 5 Jun 1905
Leo Allen Bergholtz	Consul Gen'l.	- " -		N.Y.	5 June 1905 recess 15 Dec 1905 conf.	Apptd. cons.-g'l. Canton 25 May 1906
Gabriel Bie Ravndal	- " -	- " -	Norway	So. Dak.	22 June 1906 conf.	to 31 Dec 1910 apptd. cons. g'l Constantinople 19 Dec 1910
W. Stanley Hollis	- " -	- " -	Mass.	Mass.	19 Dec 1910	Apptd. by act of 2 May 1915
Alexander Weddell	- " -	- " -	Virginia	Virginia	22 Feb 1915 conf.	did not reach Beirut

1   J. Hosford Smith was absent from his post in the United States between December 1850 and January or February 1851, and between July 1852 and 6 January 1853. J. Hosford Smith was in Jerusalem on 29 April 1852 and 11 February 1853.

2   Henry Wood was in Jerusalem between 26 March 1855 and 24 April 1855 with Lord Napier investigating charges against former Consul Smith and the British consul in Jerusalem, James Finn. He spent four more days in Jaffa before returning to Beirut.

Sources: USNA RG59 M587, T367; Blumberg, *A View from Jerusalem*, pp. 105, 123-124, 190-92.

APPENDIX II E – U.S. CONSULS AT JERUSALEM

Name	Date of Confirmation	Date of Appointement	Place of Appointment	Period of Service	Remarks
Warder Cresson	17 May 1844		Penna.	17 May 1844 - 22 Jun 1844	
John Warren Gorham	20 Oct 1856	30 Mar 1858	Mass.	25 Mar 1857 - Sep 1860	
William Rufus Page		21 June 1860	Maine	Sep 1860 - Nov 1861	
Franklin Olcott	7 Sep 1861	12 July 1861	N.Y.	28 Dec 1862 - end of 1862	
Isaac Van Etten		9 May 1863	Minn.		declined 25 May 1863
Albert Rhodes	19 Sep 1863	28 Sept 1863	Penna.	28 Sep - 31 Mar 1865	resigned 31 Mar 1865
Victor Beauboucher	30 Aug 1865	26 Aprt 1866	D.C.	1865 - 1870	
Richard Beardsley		12 Jan 1870	Ind.	30 Apr 1870 - 11 Sep 1873	
Frank S. DeHass		10 Apr 1874	N.Y.	15 Dec 1873 - 1 Aug 1877	
Joseph G. Willson		8 Dec 1877	Iowa	30 Sep 1877 - 30 Jun 1882	retired 30 June 1882
Selah Merrill		31 Mar 1882	Mass.	1882 - 1885	
Nageeb J. Arbeely		15 Oct 1885	Tenn.	1885	
Henry Gillman		7 May 1886	Mich.	1886 - 1891	
Selah Merrill		27 Feb 1891	Mass.	1891 -1893	
Edwin S. Wallace		10 Oct 1893	S. Dak.	1893 -1898	
Selah Merrill		22 Jan 1898	Mass.	1898 -1907	
Thomas Ross Wallace	30 Mar 1907	10 Dec 1907	Iowa	1907 - 14 Jun 1910	
William Coffin		24 June 1910	Ky.	1910 -1914	
Otis A. Glazebrook		18 Feb 1914	N.J.	1914 - 1917	

Sources: USNA M587/10 T471/1-11; Mayer, "Records, Jerusalem."

APPENDIX II F – CONSULAR AGENTS, VICE CONSULS,

AND DEPUTY CONSULS AT JERUSALEM

Name	Position	Date Nominated	Date Approved	Date resigned	Years of Service
David Darmon	C.A				1832-1834
Murad Arutin	C.A.				1835-1842
Jacob S. Murad	D.C.				1842-1858
Simeon S. Murad	C.A.				1857-1865
Lazarus M. Murad	V.C.		13 May 1865	11 Jul 1867	1865-1867
Lorenzo M. Johnson	V.C.		14 Apr 1865	Feb 1868	
Benjamin A. Finkelstein	D.C.		30 Nov 1865		1865-1868
Hermann Friedlander	V.C.		20 Aug 1878		1878
Samuel Bergheim	V.C.		31 Jan 1879		1879-1884
Frank C. Clark	V.C.		16 Jun 1884	23 Jun 1887	1884-1887
Herbert E. Clark	V.C.		30 Jul 1887		1887-1908
John D. Whiting	V.C and D.C.		6 Nov 1908		1908-1910
Lewis Heck	V.C. and D.C.		17 Dec 1910		1910-1912
Samuel Edelman	V.C. and D.C.		26 Aug 1912		1912-1915
Hasser Hutchinson Dick	V.C.		19 July 1915		1915
John D. Whiting	V.C and D.C.		6 Dec 1915		1915-1917

Sources: USNA T471/1-11 and USNA T367/1-3[3]

APPENDIX II G – EMPLOYEES OF THE CONSULATE AT JERUSALEM (PARTIAL LIST)

Name	Position	Nationality	Date Nominated	Date recognized	Years of Service
Simon S. Murad	dragoman				1857-1865
Mustaphe Karesnini	kavass	Turkish	1860	1860	1860-1870
Saäd Bibe	kavass	Turkish			1866-1867
Rahim Bahne	kavass	Turkish	Jun 1866	1866	1866-1870
Vaseri Costa Gargour	dragoman	Turkish	20 June 1866	20 Nov 1866	1866-1871
Mohammed Zwad	kavass	Turkish	1 Jan 1870	1 Jan 1870	1870-1872
Ahmed Zwad	kavass	Turkish	2 Aug 1871	2 Aug 1871	1871-1872
Jacques Panayotti	dragoman	Turkish	29 Aug 1871	3 Oct 1871	1871-1876
Mohammed Tasich	kavass	Turkish	15 Dec 1871	15 June 1872	1871-1874
Yosef Gabriel	interpreter				1877
David Feinstein	clerk				1891-1910
Edwin E. Baldwin	clerk			6 Dec 1909	1909-1910
Antone Gelat	dragoman				1910

Sources: USNA T471/1-9 and Bartour, *"American Consular Aid."*[4]

Appendix II H – U.S Consular Agents and Employees at Jaffa

Jaffa Consular Agents

Name	Posi-tion	Nomina-ted on	Approved	Resigned	Years of Service
David Darmon	C.A.				1832-34
Murad Arutin	C.A.				1836-42
Jacob Serapion Murad	C.A.				1843-58
Charles Saunders	V.C.				1859
Khalil al-Turk[1]	C.A.				1859
J. Hermann Loewenthal	C.A.	3 May 1866	2 June 1866	15 July 1867	1866-67
Lorenzo M. Johnson	V..C.				1868
John B. Hay	C.A.		8 Apr 1869	23 Jul 1870	1869-70
Ernst Hardegg[2]	C.A.	27 Oct 1871	7 Dec 1871	31 Dec 1909	1872-1909
Jacob Hardegg	C.A.		20 Sep 1910	7 Mar 1917	1910-17
Hasser Hutchison Dick	C.A.		7 Mar 1917		1917

Employees of the Consular Agency at Jaffa (partial list)

Name	Position	Date nominated	Date recognized	Nationality	Years of Service
Ismael Baraky	kavass	July 1869	July 1869	Turkish	1869-71
Achmed Chamis Fils	kavass	15 Dec 1871	15 Dec 1871	Turkish	1870-74
Constantine Azar	dragoman	22 Dec 1871	15 June 1872	Turkish	1870-77
Jacob Moussa Shukri	dragoman	15 Dec 1871	15 June 1872	Turkish	1870-95

Sources: USNA M587/9; RG59 T367 and T471; RG84 Jaffa

1   No information is available for the years 1859-1866

2   Between 23 July 1870 and 11 July 1872 business in Jaffa was carried out by the Jerusalem consulate.

Appendix II I - U.S Consular Agants and Employees at Acre-Haifa

Acre-Haifa Consular Agents

Name	Position	Date nominated	Date approved	Date resigned	Years of Service
Gabriel Nasralla	C.A.				1833-72
George Jamal[1]	C.A.				1853-56
Jacob Schumacher[2]	C.A.	18 May 1872		died 7 Sept 1891	1872-91
Gottlieb Schumacher	C.A.	7 Nov 1891	7 Sep 1895	29 Oct 1904	1891-1904
Theodore J. Struve[3]	C.A.		21 Mar 1906		1906-14

Employees of the Consular Agancy in Haifa

Name	Position	Date nominated	Date recognized	Nationality	Years of Service
Mansur Haikal	dragoman		15 Apr 1873	Turkish	1873-76
Friedrich Keller	dragoman		15 Arp 1873	German	1873-76
Mahmud Renno	kavass		15 Apr 1873	Turkish	1873-76
Mahmud Zaidan	kavass		15 Apr 1873	Turkish	1873-76
Yusuf Rizq	interpreter				1876
Abdel Kader	kavass		29 Dec 1877		1877
Ahmad Dik	kavass				1877
Elias Hannah Abiad	dragoman	15 Jan 1880	28 Jun 1880	Turkish	1880-86
Ibrahim Fayad	kavas	1 Sep 1880	1 Nov 1880	Turkish	1880-86
Mahmud Al-Shahadi	kavass	1 Sep 1880	27 Jul 1881	Turkish	1880-86

1   Between the years 1853-1856 Gabriel Nasralla served as C.A. at Haifa

2   In addition to the above list there were two acting consular agents – George Schu. (probably Schumacher) and John G. Scheerer – who served respectively in 1899 for five months and in 1904 for an unknown period.

3   It is probable that Theodore J. Struve served in his post until 1917.

Employees of the Haifa Consular Agency in Akko

Name	Position	Date nominated	Date recognized	Nationality	Years of Service
Bishara Cardahi	dragoman	19 Oct 1872	26 Aug 1875	Turkish	1872-89
Saleh Chani Cablaoni	kavass	6 Feb 1875		Turkish	1875-76

GLOSSARY

Note: Some of the following terms appear as in the original documents quoted in the text, and in the way the writers intended and did not always conform to accepted orthography or meanings. In such cases the correct term is added in parentheses.

ALIYA – Waves of modern Jewish immigration (literally, 'ascent') to Palestine. Tyomkin *aliya* – The wave of Jewish immigration to Palestine at the beginning of the 1890s named after Zev Tyomkin who headed the Palestine Committee of the Hovevei Zion at the time.

ARD – Land.

ASHKENAZI – A member of one of the two great divisions of Jews, comprising the East European, Yiddish-speaking communities.

BAKSHEESH – Gratuity, a present of money.

BALIOS-BEY (BALIO, BALYOS) – Turkish term for the Venetian ambassador to the Sublime Porte, in Italian 'bailo' meaning diplomatic or consular agent.

BASTINADO – A form of punishment consisting of repeated blows on the soles of the feet.

BERAT – A type of order issued by the sultan; a writ for holding an office; formal authorization granting a privilege or conferring a dignity.

BERATLIS – Certain merchants who received a berat and who were protected and exempt from certain taxes.

CAPITULATIONS – An agreement ('chapters') between governments usually granting special privileges such as extraterritorial rights.

CONSULES ELECTI – Consuls who were residents of the country in which they were appointed (literally 'chosen') and were often of a different nationality from the country they served.

CONSULES MISSI – Consuls sent by the state and paid from its treasury.

CONSULUS-BEY – Consul as entitled by Ottoman imperial edict.

DRAGOMAN – Interpreter employed in an official capacity by an embassy or consulate; tour organizer and guide for tourists.

DUNAM – Unit of land of 1,000 square meters, or about a quarter of an acre; Turkish *dunam* 919.3 square meters.

EFFENDI – Master, sir; one of a class of feudal landowners in eastern Mediterranean countries; an official; an educated man of the upper classes.

EXEQUATUR – Written, official recognition and authorization of a consular officer issued by the government to which he is accredited.

FELLAH, FELLAHIN – Peasant(s) in Arabic-speaking countries.

FIRMAN – Decree or mandate, order, license, or grant issued by a ruler of a Muslim country.

GRAND VIZIER – The chief officer of state of a Muslim country such as the Ottoman Empire.

HALUKKAH – Distribution of funds collected in the Diaspora for support of needy Jews in Palestine.

HAWADJA (KHAWADJA) – Mister.

HODJET, HUJJET – Registration certificate from Muslim court.

HOVEVEI ZION – 'Lovers of Zion' movement founded in 1882 in Russia with the aim of promoting and supporting Jewish immigration and settlement in Palestine.

KADI, QADI – Muslim judge who interprets and administers the religious law of Islam (sharia).

KAIMAKAM – Governor of a subdistrict of the Ottoman Empire; deputy-governor.

KAVASS, KAWASS – Armed, uniformed Muslim guard of consulates and officially recognized religious communities.

KHAN – Caravanserai, or resting place for travelers in Muslim countries.

KHATT-I HÜMAYUN – Imperial rescript of reforms issued by the Sublime Porte in 1856.

KHATT-I SHARIF OF GÜLHANE – 'Rescript of the Rose Chamber' issued by the Sublime Porte in 1839.

KOLEL – Community or congregation of Orthodox Jews in Palestine, comprising individuals and families from a particular town or region in the Diaspora who receive financial support from a halukkah fund.

KOLEL AMERIKA – The kolel of American Jews in Palestine founded in 1896.

MAHKAMA, MAHKAMEH – court of justice.

MAHKAMA SHAR'IYA – Muslim (religious) court.

MAJLIS, MECLIS – Council, assembly, or tribunal.
Meclis-i "umumi - Provincial administrative council.

MÂMUR – Title of a consular agent, of a lower official rank than wakil (vekil); plenipotentiary; official.

MÂMUR AL-TABOO (TAPU) – Official of the land registry office.

MAWAT LANDS – Unoccupied ('dead') lands not held by title deed.

MILLET – An officially-recognized non-Muslim group or community in the Ottoman Empire under a religious head of its own who also exercises civilian functions of importance.

MIRI – Land on which the state has ownership rights (raqaba); tax, mainly land tax.

MOSHAVA – Jewish independent, smallholder's agricultural settlement in Palestine.

MUKHTAR – Village headman.

MULK – Real estate; freehold property; full ownership (*raqaba* plus *tasarruf*).

MUTASARRIF – An administrative authority of various sanjaks in the Ottoman Empire.

MUTASARRIFLIK – An administrative district in the Ottoman Empire.

PASHA – Person of high rank in the Ottoman Empire, especially a military commander or provincial governor.

PASHALIK – The jurisdiction of a pasha, or the territory governed by him.

QÂDA, QAZA – A subdistrict in the Ottoman Empire.

PROTÉGÉ – Person under the protection of a foreign government in an extension of extraterritorial rights.

RAQABA, RAKABAH – Ownership of land without usufruct (*nue propriété*).

RAYA, RI'AYA – Non-Muslim Ottoman subject.

SANJAK – A district or subdivision of a vilayet in the Ottoman Empire.

SEPHARDI – A member of Occidental (Spanish and Portuguese) branch of European Jewry in North Africa, the Balkans, and the Ottoman Empire, as well as Holland, England, and the Americas. Compare ASHKENAZI.

SERAI, SARAY (SERAGLIO) – Government building, palace, mansion, large inn.

SHAHBENDER – Consul.

SHARI'A – The corpus of formally established, sacred law in Islam.

SUBLIME PORTE – Official title of the highest instance of the Ottoman government; synonymous with the Ottoman Empire or state.

TABOO, TABU, TAPU – Land registry office; *miri* state lands.

TASARRUF – Right of usufruct; disposal.

TEZKERE, TESKERE, TASCOREY – Travel permit; memorandum; official certificate.

VA'AD HA-KELALI – The general committee of all the kolels (kolelim), founded in Jerusalem in 1866.

VALI, WALI – Governor-general of a vilayet (province).

VERGI – Tax.

VILAYET, WILAYET – A province of the Ottoman Empire.

WAKIL, VEKIL – Title of consular agent; substitute official; agent; deputy; governor; protector.

YISHUV – The Jewish community ('settlement') in Palestine.

Old *yishuv* – The traditional, religious Jewish community in Palestine.

New *yishuv* – The modernizing, Zionist Jewish community in Palestine (from 1882).

BIBLIOGRAPHY

MANUSCRIPT SOURCES

The manuscript sources consulted for this study are listed below. In every case, the complete record group of each set of papers has been listed, rather than the specific files in which relevant material was found. This information is contained in the notes throughout the text.

American Board of Commissioners for Foreign Mission Archives (ABCFM), Houghton Library, Harvard University, Cambridge, Massachusetts, USA.
Record Groups
  RG16 Vols.1-3 The Palestine Mission.
  RG Map and Plan Collection Boxes 1-3.
American Jewish Historical Society Archives (AJHS), Waltham, Massachusetts, USA.
Record Groups
  Adolphus S. Solomons Box 2/P28.
  Jerusalem Model.
Anglo-Jewish Archives (AJ), The University of Southampton, Southampton, England.
  AJ/95/ADD Anglo-Jewish Association Council Minute Books 1871-1918.
Church Missionary Society Archives (CMS), The University of Birmingham, Birmingham, England.
Record Group 3 Vol.6 CM/063/796.
Israel Museum Photographic Archives (IM), Israel Museum, Jerusalem, Israel.
Record Group Merrill's Photographic Collection.
Israel State Archives (ISA), Jerusalem, Israel.
Record Groups
  RG23 District Commissioner's Office, Jerusalem.
  RG67 The German Consulate in Jerusalem.

RG83 Ali Ekrem Bey, Ottoman Governor of the Jerusalem District.

RG123-1 The British Consulate in Jerusalem.

RG690 German Templers.

Jewish National and University Library Archives (JNUL), The Hebrew University of Jerusalem, Jerusalem, Israel.

Record Groups

MS V810 Foreign Relations: Diplomatic Correspondence of the U.S. with Turkey, Having Reference to the Jews, 1840-1901.

Record Group MS V709 Hamizrachi-Lovers of Zion in Russia.

Microfilm of Documents from USNA, Fi2477/10-11, Fi7582/1-4[12-13], Fi8129.

Lambeth Palace Library Archives (LP), Lambeth Palace, London, England.

Record Group E.W. Benson Official Letters, Vol.174 (1887).

Museum of Comparative Zoology (MCZ), Harvard University, Cambridge, Massachusetts, USA.

Record Groups

Selah Merrill.

Collection of Palestine Bird and Animal Specimens.

The Order of St. John Archives (OSJ), London, England.

Record Group St. John's Ophthalmic Hospital, Jerusalem.

Palestine Exploration Fund Archives (PEF), London, England.

Record Group SCHICK/47/3.

Public Record Office (PRO), London, England.

Record Groups

Foreign Office FO78/540,581,626,839,963.

FO195/2287.

N.M. Rothschild Archives (NMR), London, England.

Record Group CAC XI/120/3A (1840).

The Semitic Museum (SM), Harvard University, Cambridge, Massachusetts, USA.

Record Group Selah Merrill and Palestine Collections.

Tel Aviv Municipal Archives (TAMA), Tel Aviv, Israel.

Record Group 1 Box 510-11/14-15.

United States National Archives (USNA), Washington, D.C., USA.

Record Groups

RG45 and T829/438 Lt. Lynch Expedition.

RG59 M453 See T471.

RG59 M587/3,9,10 List of U.S. Consular Officers by Post 1789-1939.
RG59 M650 Letters of Applications and Recommendations.
RG59 T194 Dispatches from United States Consuls in Constantinople,

1820-1906.
RG59 T367 Dispatches from United States Consuls in Beirut, 1836-1906.
RG59 T471 Dispatches from United States Consuls in Jerusalem,

Palestine, 1856-1906.
RG84 Haifa Records of Foreign Service Posts of the Department of
State, Haifa.
RG84 Jaffa Records of the Foreign Service Posts of the Department of

State, Jaffa.
RG84 Jerusalem Records of the Foreign Service Posts of the Department

of State, Jerusalem.
Mayer, Inventory of U.S. Posts in Haifa, Jaffa, Jerusalem in USNA

See Mayer,"Records," below.
Stewart, Inventory of Records of U.S. Consulate General in

Constantinople See Stewart,"Preliminary Inventory," below.

Yad Izhak Ben-Zvi Archives (YIBZ), Jerusalem, Israel.
Record Groups
    RG Finn Archive
    RG4/2/50/01.

PUBLISHED SOURCES

Newspapers

> *Davar*
> *Die Warte des Tempels*
> *Galignani's Messenger*
> *Ha-Poel Ha-Tzair*

Havatzeleth
Ivri Anokhi
The Jerusalem Post
The Jewish Chronicle
The Truth

Congressional Records – Senate Executive Documents

35th Congress, 2nd Session, No.42, 1858-1859, see Cass,"J.S. Murad."
37th Congress, 3rd Session, No.25, 1862-1863, see Goddard, "Consular

Courts in Turkey."
44th Congress, 1st Session, No.170, 1876, see Maynard, "Protection of

American Citizens."
46th Congress, Special Session, No.3, 1881, see Van Dyck, "Report

for 1880."
47th Congress, 1st Session, No.87, 1882, see Van Dyck, "Report on

the Capitulations."
49th Congress, 1st Session, No.234, 17 March 1886.
59th Congress, 2nd Session, No.326, 1907, see Schmavonian,

"Citizenship, Turkey."
61st Congress, 2nd Session, No.357, 1910, see Malloy, "Treaties."
67th Congress, 1st Session, No.34, 1921, see Ravndal, "The Origin of
the Capitulations."

Books, Articles, Dissertations, and Official Publications

Aaronsohn, Ran, and Kark, Ruth. *"Rose of the Jordan." Land and Nature*
24 (1982):55-57 (Hebrew).
Aaronsohn, Ran. "Stages in the Development of Settlements in the First
Aliyah." In *The First Aliya* , edited by Mordechai Eliav. Jerusalem:
Yad Izhak Ben-Zvi, 1981, pp.25-84 (Hebrew).
Adams, Randolph Greenfield. *A History of the Foreign Policy of the United*

States . New York: Macmillan, 1926.

Albright, William Foxwell. "Selah Merrill." *Dictionary of American Biography* 12:564-65.

"Anonymous letter sent to American President." *Galignani's Messenger* . 11 September 1852.

Ariel, Yaakov. "An American Initiative for the Establishment of a Jewish State: William E. Blackstone and the petition of 1891." *Cathedra* 49 (1988):87-102 (Hebrew).

— *On Behalf of Israel, American Fundamentalist Attitudes Toward Jews, Judaism, and Zionism, 1865-1945*. New York: Carlson, 1991.

Avitzur, Shmuel. *The Rise and Decline of the Port of Jaffa, 1865-1965*. Tel Aviv: Milo, 1972 (Hebrew).

Baker, Carlos. "The Place of the Bible in American Fiction." In *Religious Perspectives in American Culture*, edited by James Ward Smith and A. Leland, pp.243-72. Princeton: Princeton University Press, 1961.

Baedeker, Karl. Palestine and Syria, Handbook for Travellers. Leipzig: Baedeker, 1912.

Barker, Theo. "Consular reports: a Rich but Neglected Historical Source." *Business History* 23 (1981):265-66.

— "Consular Reports of the United Kingdom." *Business History* 23 (1981): 266-68.

Barnes, William, and Morgan, John Heath. *The Foreign Service of the United States, Origins, Development, and Functions*. Washington: Department of State, 1961.

Bartour, Ron. "American Consular Aid to Jews in Eretz-Yisrael in the Twilight of the First World War 1856-1914." Ph.D. dissertation, The Hebrew University of Jerusalem, 1985 (Hebrew).

—"Episodes in the Relations of the American Consulate in Jerusalem with the Jewish Community in the 19th Century (1856-1906)." *Cathedra* 5 (1977):109-43 (Hebrew).

Bar Yosef, Naomi. "Warder Cresson: Commitment to Judaism and the Holy Land." Unpublished paper. n.p., n.d.

Ben-Arieh, Yehoshua. "William Lynch's Expedition to the Dead Sea, 1847-48." Prologue (Spring 1973):15-21.

Ben-Zvi, Yitzhak. *Eretz Yisrael under Ottoman Rule*. Jerusalem: Mossad Bialik, 1968 (Hebrew).

Bezanson, Walter E. (ed.). *Clarel, a Poem and a Pilgrimage in the Holy*

Land by Herman Melville. New York: Hendricks House, 1960.

Blancké, W. Wendell. *The Foreign Service of the United States*. New York: Praeger, 1969.

Bliss, Frederick Jones. *The Development of Palestine Exploration*. New York: Arno Press, 1977 (Reprint of 1907 edition).

Bloch, Mark. *The Feudal Society*. Jerusalem: Magnes Press, 1988 (Hebrew).

Blumberg, Arnold. *A View from Jerusalem 1849-1858, the Consular Diary of James and Elizabeth Anne Finn*. London and Toronto: Associated University Presses, 1980.

— "Comments." *In With Eyes Toward Zion*, edited by Moshe Davis. Vol.2, pp.255-58. New York: Praeger, 1968.

— *Zion Before Zionism, 1838-1880*. Syracuse: Syracuse University Press, 1985.

Bovykin, V.I., D.W. Spring and S.J. Thompstone. "Russian Consular Reports up to 1917." Business History 23 (1981):291-93.

Boyce, Richard Fyle. *American Foreign Service Authors: A Bibliography*. Methuen, N.J.: Scarecrow Press, 1973.

Brawer, Avraham Y. "Jewish Enjoyment of the Privileges of the Capitulations in Palestine." *Zion* 5 (1940):161-169 (Hebrew).

Bridge, F.R. *"The Habsburg Monarchy and the Ottoman Empire, 1900-18."* In *The Great Powers at the End of the Ottoman Empire*, edited by Marian Kent, pp.31-49. London: Allen & Unwin, 1984.

Broder, A. "French Consular Reports." 23 (1981):279-82.

Brown, John Ross. *Yusef; or The Journey of the Franji, A Crusade in the East,*. London: Sampson Low, 1853.

Bryson, Thomas A. *Tars, Turks and Tankers: The Role of the U.S. Navy in the Middle East, 1800-1979*. Metuchen, N.J.: Scarecrow Press, 1980.

— *United States/Middle East Diplomatic Relations 1784-1978, An Annotated Bibliography*. Metuchen, N.J.: Scarecrow Press, 1979.

Burnet, David Staats. *The Jerusalem Mission, Under the Direction of the American Christian Missionary Society*. New York: Arno Press, 1977 (Reprint of 1853 edition).

Carmel, Alex. *German Settlement in Eretz-Israel at the End of the Ottoman Period*. Jerusalem: Israel Oriental Society, 1973 (Hebrew).

— "Historical Sources on the History of Eretz Israel During the Ottoman Period in Archives in Austria and Germany." *Cathedra* 1 (1976):148-57 (Hebrew).

— *The History of Haifa Under Turkish Rule*. Haifa: Haifa University College, 1969 (Hebrew).

Carr, Edward Hallett. *What is History?* London: Penguin, 1961.

Carr, Wilbur J. "The American Consular Service." *American Journal of International Law* 1 (1907): 891-913.

Cass, Lewis. "J.S. Murad...Information touching the application for compensation of the late consular agent of the United States at Jaffa." 35th Congress, 2nd Session. Senate Executive Document, No.42. Washington: in USNA RG59 T471/1, 1858-59, pp.1-3.

Cecil, Lamar. *The German Diplomatic Service, 1871-1914*. Princeton: Princeton University Press, 1976.

Chiel, Arthur A. "An Inquisition of Lunacy." *Liberty* 75 (1980):16-20.

Churkowski, Uzi. "The Activity of the Haifa Consular Agency, 1886-1917." Seminar paper, Haifa University, 1980 (Hebrew).

Cox, Samuel S. *Diversions of a Diplomacy in Turkey*. New York: Webster, 1887.

— *Oriental Sunbeams, or From the Porte to the Pyramids by Way of Palestine*. New York and London: Putnam's, 1890.

Cresson, Warder. *Jerusalem the Center and the Joy of the Whole Earth*. Philadelphia: Private printing, 1844.

— *The Key of David the True Messiah...Also Reasons for Becoming a Jew; With a Revision of the Late Lawsuit for Lunacy on That Account*. Philadelphia: Private printing, 1852.

Davis, Moshe. "American Christian Devotees in the Holy Land." *Christian-Jewish Relations* 20 (1987):1-20.

— (ed.) *With Eyes Toward Zion*. Vol. I. New York: Arno Press, 1977.

— (ed.) *With Eyes Toward Zion*. Vol. II. New York: Praeger, 1986.

— and Ben-Aryieh, Yehoshua (eds.). *With Eyes Toward Zion. Western Societies and the Holy Land*. Vol.III. New York: Praeger, 1991.

Davison, Roderic H. "The Advent of the Electric Telegraph in the Ottoman Empire." In *Essays in Ottoman and Turkish History 1774-1923, The Impact of the West*, edited by Roderic H. Davison, pp.133-65. Austin: University of Texas Press, 1990.

— "The Search for Sources." In *With Eyes Toward Zion*, edited by Moshe Davis, Vol. I, pp.88-99. New York: Arno Press, 1977.

DeHass, Frank S. *Buried Cities Recovered or Exploration in Bible Lands*. Philadelphia: Bradley, 1883.

De Leon, Edwin. *Thirty Years of My Life on Three Continents.* 2 vols. London: Ward & Downey, 1890.

De Novo, John D. *American Interests and Policies in the Middle East 1900-1939.* Minneapolis: University of Minnesota Press, 1968.

Department of State. *History of the Department of State of the United States.* Washington: Government Printing Office, 1901.

— *Regulations Prescribed for the Use of the Consular Service of the United States.* Washington: Government Printing Office, 1896.

— *The United States Passport, Past, Present, Future.* Washington: Department of State, 1976.

Dictionary of American Biography. 22 vols. New York: Scribners; see: Johnson and Malone, below.

Dudman, Helga. "The History of the American Colony in Jerusalem." *Keshet* 72 (1976):168-72 (Hebrew).

Edwards Lester, C. "The Consular System of the United States." *Hunt's Merchants' Magazine* 12 (1845):211-23.

Efrati, Nathan. "American Jewry and the Jews of Eretz Israel – Relations at the End of the Nineteenth Century." *Cathedra* 55 (1990):63-88 (Hebrew).

— *The Jewish Community in Eretz-Israel During World War I (1914-1918).* Jerusalem: Yad Izhak Ben-Zvi, 1991 (Hebrew).

Eliav, Mordechai. "An Annotated Listing of Foreign Consuls in Jerusalem." *Cathedra* 28 (1983):161-76 (Hebrew).

— "The Austrian Consulate in Jerusalem and the Jewish Community. " *Cathedra* 18 (1981):73-110 (Hebrew).

— "Diplomatic Intervention Concerning Restrictions on Jewish Immigration and Purchase of Land at the End of the Nineteenth Century." Cathedra 26 (1982):117-32 (Hebrew).

— *Eretz Israel and It's Yishuv in the 19th Century, 1777-1917.* Jerusalem: Keter, 1978 (Hebrew).

— *The Jews of Palestine in German Policy.* Tel Aviv: Hakibutz Hameuchad, 1973 (Hebrew).

— "The Sarah Steinberg Affair." *Sinai* 64 (1969):78-91 (Hebrew).

— (ed.) *Siege and Distress, Eretz Israel During the First World War.* Jerusalem: Yad Izhak Ben-Zvi, 1991 (Hebrew).

— *Under Imperial Austrian Protection, Selected Documents from the Archives of the Austrian Consulate in Jerusalem, 1849-1917.* Jerusalem: Yad Izhak Ben-Zvi, 1985 (Hebrew).

Encyclopaedia Britannica, 15th edition. Chicago: Encyclopaedia Britannica, 1985.

Encyclopaedia Hebraica. Ramat Gan: Encyclopaedia Publishing Co., 1954-1981 (Hebrew).

Evans, Charles. *American Bibliography*. Vol.I, 1639-1729. Chicago: Author & Blakely Press, 1903.

Fawaz, Tarazi Leila. *Merchants and Migrants in Nineteenth Century Beirut.* Cambridge, MA: Harvard University Press, 1983.

Fields, James A. *America and the Mediterranean World 1772-1882*. Princeton: Princeton University Press, 1967.

Fink, Reuben. *America and Palestine*. New York: American Zionist Emergency Council, 1944.

Finn, James. *Stirring Times; or, Record from Jerusalem Consular Chronicles of 1853-1856, by the Late James Finn*. Edited and compiled by his widow. 2 vols. London: Paul, 1878.

Finnie, D.H. Pioneers East: *The Early American Experience in the Middle East*. Cambridge, MA: Harvard University Press, 1967.

Fishbane, Simcha. "The Founding of Kollel America Tifereth Yerus halay im.*" American Jewish Historical Quarterly* 64 (1974):120-36.

Ford, Alexander Hume. "Our American Colony at Jerusalem." *Appleton's Magazine* 7 (1906):643-55.

Freiman, Nahum Dov. *Jerusalem Memory Book*. Vol.I. Jerusalem: Ariel, 1980 (Reprint of 1913 edition).

Friedman, Isaiah. "The System of Capitulations and its Effects on Turco-Jewish Relations in Palestine, 1856-1897." In *Palestine in the Late Ottoman Period*, edited by David Kushner, pp.280-93. Jerusalem and Leiden: Yad Izhak Ben-Zvi and E.J. Brill, 1986.

Frumkin, Israel Dov. "On Working the Land and Handcraft." *Havatzeleth* 5 (20 November 1874):54-55 (Hebrew).

Fulton, Bruce L. "France and the End of the Ottoman Empire." In *The Great Powers and the End of the Ottoman Empire,* edited by Marian Kent, pp.141-71. London: Allen & Unwin, 1984.

Gat, Ben-Zion. *The Jewish Yishuv in Eretz-Israel, 1840-1881*. Jerusalem: Yad Izhak Ben-Zvi, 1974 (Hebrew).

Gaustad, Edwin Scott (ed.). *The Rise of Adventism*. New York: Harper & Row, 1974.

Gehling [Dr.]. "German Consular Reports." *Business History* 23 (1981):283-84.

Gillman, Henry. *Hassan: A Fellah – A Romance of Palestine*. Boston: Brown, 1898.

Glass, Joseph B. and Kark, Ruth. *Sephardi Entrepreneurs in Eretz Israel. The Amzalak Family* 1816-1918. Jerusalem: Magnes Press, 1991.

Goddard, C.W. "Consular Courts in Turkey." 37th Congress, 3rd Session. *Senate Executive Documents*. Vol.1-1149, No.25. Washington: Government Printing Office, 1862-63, pp.1-27.

Goel, Yohai, Demsky, Rivka and Zimmer, Ora. "America and the Holy Land: A Select Bibliography of Publications in English. *The Jerusalem Cathedra* 3 (1983):327-56.

— and Katz-Hyman, Martha B. "Americans in the Holy Land, 1850-1900: A Select Bibliography." In *With Eyes Toward Zion*, edited by Moshe Davis, Vol.I, pp.100-125. New York: Arno Press, 1977.

Gordon, Leland James. *American Relations with Turkey 1830-1930*. Philadelphia: University of Pennsylvania Press, 1932.

Grabill, Joseph L. *Protestant Diplomacy and the Near East: Missionary Influence on American Policy, 1810-1927*. Minneapolis: University of Minnesota Press, 1971.

Greenberg, Gershon. "America-Holy Land and Religious Studies: On Expressing a Sacred Reality." In *With Eyes Toward Zion*, edited by Moshe Davis and Yehoshuah Ben-Arieh, Vol.III, pp.50-62. New York: Praeger, 1991.

— *The Holy Land in American Religious Thought, 1620-1948*. Jerusalem: Institute of Contemporary Jewry, The Hebrew University of Jerusalem and University Press of America, 1993.

Griffin, Appleton Prentice Clark. *List of References on the United States Consular Service*. Washington: Library of Congress, 1905.

Gustafson, Milton O. "Records in the National Archives Relating to America and the Holy Land." In *With Eyes Toward Zion*, edited by Moshe Davis. Vol.I, pp.129-58. New York: Arno Press, 1977.

Haberman, A.M. "The Travel of Rabbi Benjamin Lilienthal to Eretz-Israel One Hundred Years Ago." *Sinai* 24 (1949):236-47 (Hebrew).

Handy, Robert T. (ed.). *The Holy Land in American Protestant Life 1800-1948*. New York: Arno Press, 1981.

— "Studies in the Interrelationships Between America and the Holy Land: A

Fruitful Field for Interdisciplinary and Interfaith Cooperation." *Journal of Church and State* 13 (1971):283-301.

Holmes, Reed M. *The Forerunners*. Independence MO: Herald, 1981.

Hopwood, Derek. *The Russian Presence in Syria and Palestine, 1843-1914*. Oxford: Clarendon Press, 1969.

Horsford, Howard C. (ed.). *Herman Melville's Journal of a Visit to Europe and the Levant, October 11, 1856–May 6, 1857*. Princeton: Princeton University Press, 1955.

Hough, W. "History of the British Consulate in Jerusalem." *Journal of the Middle East Society* 1 (1947):3-14.

Hunt, Gaillard. *The Department of State of the United States, its History and Functions*. Washington: Department of State, 1893.

— *The American Passport, its History and a Digest of Laws, Rulings and Regulations Governing it Issuance by the Department of State*. Washington: Government Printing Office, 1898.

Hunt, Michael H. *Ideology and U.S. Foreign Policy*. New Haven and London: Yale University Press, 1987.

Hurewitz, J.C. *The Middle East and North Africa in World Politics, a Documentary Record*. Vol.I. New Haven and London: Yale University Press, 1975.

Hyamson, Albert M. *The British Consulate in Jerusalem in Relation to the Jews of Palestine, 1838-1914*. 2 vols. London: The Jewish Historical Society of England, 1939 and 1941.

Issawi, Charles. "British Consular Views on Syria's Economy in the 1850's-1860's." In American University of Beirut Festival Book, edited by Fuad Sarrut and Suha Tamim. Beirut: American University of Beirut.

— "British Trade and the Rise of Beirut, 1830-1860." *International Journal of Middle East Studies* 8 (1977):91-101.

Ilan, Zvi. "The Hope Preceding the Hope Neighborhood." *Davar* (19 December 1986) (Hebrew).

Ilchman, Warren Frederick. *Professional Diplomacy in the United States 1779-1939*. Chicago: University of Chicago Press, 1961.

Johnson, Allen and Malone, Dumas (eds.). *Dictionary of American Biography*. 22 vols. New York: Scribner's, 1928-1937.

Jones, Chester Lloyd. *The Consular Service of the United States its History and Activities*. Philadelphia: University of Pennsylvania Press, 1906

Kaganoff, Nathan M. (ed.). *Guide to American Holy Land Studies*. 3 vols.

Vol.1, *American Presence.* Vol. 2, *Political Relations and American Zionism.* Vol.3, *Economic Relations and Philanthropy.* New York: Praeger, 1980-83.

— "Observations on America-Holy Land Relations in the Period Before World War I." In *With Eyes Toward Zion*, edited by Moshe Davis, Vol.I, pp.79-87. New York: Arno Press, 1977.

Kark, Ruth. "Annual Reports of the United States Consuls in the Holy Land as a Source for the Study of 19th-Century Eretz-Israel." In *With Eyes Toward Zion*, edited by Moshe Davis, Vol.II, pp.127-76. New York: Praeger, 1986.

— "Changing Patterns of Landownership in Nineteenth-Century Palestine: The European Influence." *Journal of Historical Geography* 10 (1984):357-84.

— "The Development of the Cities Jerusalem and Jaffa from 1840 up to the First World War." Ph.D. dissertation, The Hebrew University of Jerusalem, 1977 (Hebrew).

— "Historical Sites-Perception and Land Purchase, the Case of Modin, 1882-1931." *Studies in Zionism* 9 (1988):1-17.

— *Jaffa, a City in Evolution 1799-1917.* Jerusalem: Yad Izhak Ben-Zvi, 1990.

— "The Jerusalem Municipality at the End of Ottoman Rule." *Asian and African Studies* 14 (1980):117-41.

— "Land Acquisition and New Agricultural Settlement in Palestine During the 'Tyomkin Period'." In *Zionism*, edited by David Carpi, Vol.9, pp.179-94. Tel Aviv: Hakibutz Hameuchad, 1984 (Hebrew).

— "Millenarism and Agricultural Settlement in the Holy Land in the Nineteenth Century." *Journal of Historical Geography* 9 (1983):47-62.

— "Notes on 'Batei Tura'." *Cathedra* 18 (1981):157-67 (Hebrew).

— "The Rise and Decline of the Coastal Towns in Palestine, 1800-1914." In *Ottoman Palestine 1800-1914 Studies in Economic and Social History*, edited by Gad G. Gilbar, pp.69-89. Leiden: E.J. Brill, 1990.

Karp, Abraham J. "The Zionism of Warder Cresson." In *Early History of Zionism in America*, edited by Isidore S. Meyer, pp.1-20. New York: American Jewish Historical Society, 1958.

Karpat, Kemal H. "Jewish Migration Within the Ottoman Empire in the Late Nineteenth Century." *Cathedra* 51 (1989):78-92 (Hebrew).

— "The Ottoman Immigration to America, 1860-1914." *International Journal of Middle East Studies* 17 (1985):175-209.

— "Ottoman Immigration Policies and Settlement in Palestine. " In *Settlers Regimes in Africa and the Arab World, the Illusion of Endurance*, edited by Ibrahim Abu-Lughod and Baha Abu-Laban , pp.57-72. Wilmette, IL: Medina University Press, 1974.

Kaufman, Menachem and Levine, Mira (eds.). *Guide to America-Holy Land Studies*. Vol.4. New York: Praeger, 1984.

Kennedy, Charles Stuart. *The American Consul, A History of the American Consular Service, 1776-1914*. New York: Greenwood, 1990.

Kenny, Vincent. *Herman Melville's Clarel, A Spiritual Autobiography*. Hamden, CT: Archon Books , 1973.

Kent, Marian (ed.). *The Great Powers and the End of the Ottoman Empire*. London: Allen & Unwin, 1984.

Klatzker, David. "American Christian Travelers to the Holy Land, 1821-1939." Ph.D. dissertation, Temple University, Philadelphia, 1987.

— "Teaching the American Holy Land Experience in the Context of American Culture and Religious Thought." *America-Holy Land Scholars Colloquium*, pp.1-15. Washington: 1983.

Knight, Susan G. *Ned Harwood's Visit to Jerusalem*. Boston: Lothrop, 1888.

Kurgan-Van Hentenryk, G. "Belgian Consular Reports." Business History 23 (1981):286-70.

LaFeber, Walter. *The New Empire, An Interpretation of American Expansion, 1860-1898*. Ithaca: Cornell University Press, 1963.

Landau, Jacob M. and Öke, Mim Kemal. "Ottoman Perspective on American Interests in the Holy Land." In *With Eyes Toward Zion*, edited by Moshe Davis, Vol.II, pp.261-302. New York: Praeger, 1986.

Lay, Tracy Hollingsworth. *The Foreign Service of the United States*. New York: Prentice-Hall, 1928.

Lipman. Vivian D. *Americans and the Holy Land Through British Eyes 1820-1917: A Documentary History*. London: V.D. Lipman, 1989.

Loewe, Louis (ed.). *Diaries of Sir Moses and Lady Montefiore Comprising Their Life and Work as Recorded in Their Diaries from 1812 to 1883*. 2 vols. London: Griffith, Farren, Okden & Welsh, 1890.

Luncz, Avraham Moshe. *Jerusalem Year-Book 1881*. Jerusalem: Carta, 1982. (Reprint of Wien 1882 edition).

Lynch, William F. *Narrative of the United States Expedition to the River Jordan and the Dead Sea*. Philadelphia: Lea & Blanchard, 1849.

MacLeod, Norman. *Eastward.* London & New York: Strahan, 1866.

Madsen, Truman G. "The Mormon Attitude Toward Zionism." *A Haifa University Series of Lectures on Zionism* 5 (1981):1-25.

Malachi, Eliezer Raphael. *Studies in the History of the Old Yishuv.* Tel Aviv: Hakibutz Hameuchad, 1971 (Hebrew).

Malloy, W.M. "Treaties, Conventions, International Acts, Protocols, and Agreements Between the United State s of America and Other Powers 1776-1909. " 61st Congress, 2nd Session, *Senate Document* No.357, pp.13 28-1341. Washington : Government Printing Office, 1910.

Manning, Samuel. *Those Holy Fields. Palestine Illustrated by Pen and Pencil.* London: Religious Tract Society, 1874.

Manuel, Frank E. *The Realities of American-Palestine Relations.* Washington: Public Affairs Press, 1949.

Ma'oz, Moshe. "America and the Holy Land During the Ottoman Period." In *With Eyes Toward Zion*, edited by Moshe Davis, Vol.I, pp.65-78. New York: Praeger, 1977.

Mattox, Henry E. *The Twilight of American Diplomacy, the American Foreign Service and Its Senior Officers in the 1890s.* Kent, OH and London: Kent State University Press, 1989.

Mayer, David Henry. "Records of the United States Consular Agency at Haifa, Syria, Palestine, 1872-1917." Washington: USNA, unpublished paper, 1978.

— "Records of the United States Consular Agency at Jaffa, Palestine, 1872-1917." Washington: USNA, unpublished paper, 1978.

— "Records of the United States Consulate and Consulate General at Jerusalem, Palestine, 1857-1935." Washington: USNA, unpublished paper, 1978.

Maynard, Horace. "Protection of American Citizens in the Ottoman Empire." 44th Congress, 1st Session. *Senate Executive Documents* No.170, pp.1-3. Washington: Government Printing Office, 1876.

Mayo, W.S. "Consular System of the Unites States." *Hunt's Merchants' Magazine* 6 (1842):297-305.

McCamy, James L. *The Administration of American Foreign Affairs.* New York: Knopf, 1950.

McCarthy, Justin. "The Population of Ottoman Syria and Iraq, 1878-1914." *Asian and African Studies* 15 (1981):3-44.

Melville, Herman. *Clarel, a Poem and a Pilgrimage in the Holy Land.* New York: Hendricks House, 1960. (First edition 1876.)

Merrill, Selah. *East of the Jordan*. London: Bentley, 1881.

— The *Galilee in the Time of Christ*. London: Religious Tract Society, 1874.

Middleton, Charles Ronald. The *Administration of British Foreign Policy, 1782-1846*. Durham, NC: Duke University Press, 1977.

Moller, A.M. "Consular Reports: The Danish Monarchy 1797-1904." *Business History* 23 (1981):276-79.

Morris, Robert. *Freemasonry in the Holy Land*. New York: Masonic Publishing Co., 1872.

Naor, Mordechai. "Oscar S. Straus, U.S. Minister to Turkey, Supporter of Aliya to Eretz Yisrael." *Cathedra* 18 (1981):130-56 (Hebrew).

Öke, Mim Kemal. "The Ottoman Empire, Zionism, and the Question of Palestine (1880-1908)." *International Journal of Middle East Studies* 14 (1982):329-41.

Okyar, Osman. "Economic Growth, Technological Change and Investment in the Ottoman Empire, 1800-1914. " International Conference on the Economic History of the Middle East, Haifa , 1980.

Olin, Stephen. *Travels in Egypt, Arabia Petrae, and the Holy Land*. 2 vols. New York: Harper, 1844.

Parfitt, Tudor. "The French Consulate and the Jewish Yishuv in Palestine in the 19th Century." *Cathedra* 5 (1977):144-61.

— The *Jews in Palestine 1800-1882*. Exeter: Boydell Press, 1987.

Parsons, Helen Palmer (ed.). *Letters From Palestine: 1868-1912 Written by Rolla Floyd*. Dexter, ME: private printing, 1981.

Pepper, Charles M. "Report on Trade Conditions in Asiatic Turkey." Washington: Department of Commerce and Labor, Bureau of Manufactures, 1907.

Pinnes, Yehiel M. *Building the Country*. 2 vols. Tel Aviv: Dvir, 1938 (Hebrew).

Pitman, Emma Raymond. *Mission Life in Greece and Palestine as Illustrated in the Missionary Labours of Mary Briscoe Baldwin in Athens and Joppa*. London: Cassell, Petter, Galpin & Co.: n.d. (ca.1877).

Platt, D.C.M. *The Cinderella Service, British Consuls Since 1825*. London: Longman, 1971.

Ravndal, Gabriel Bie. "Capitulations." In *Modern Turkey*, edited by Eliot Grinnell Mears, pp.430-47. New York: Macmillan, 1924.

— "The Origin of the Capitulations and of the Consular Institution." 67th Congress, 1st Session. *Senate Document* No.34, pp.1-112. Washington: Government Printing Office, 1921.

— *Stories of the East Vikings*. Minneapolis: Augsburgh, 1938.

— "Turkey, A Commercial and Industrial Handbook." *Trade Promotion Series* 28 (1926):1-232. Washington: Department of Commerce, Bureau of Foreign and Domestic Commerce.

Rhodes, Albert. *The Dobbs Family in America*. London: [?].

— *Jerusalem As It Is*. London: Maxwell, 1865.

— "Our Consul in Jerusalem." *The Galaxy* 14 (1872):437-47.

— "Our Diplomats and Consuls." *Scribner's Monthly* 13 (1876):169-76.

— "Un voyage sentimental sur le Jourdain." *Revue des Deux Mondes* 31 (15 January 1879):446-56.

Robinson, Edward and Smith, Eli. *Biblical Researches in Palestine, Mount Sinai , and Arabia Petraea in 1838*. Boston: Crocker & Brewster, 1841. (2nd edition 1856) .

Röhricht, Reinhold. *Bibliotheca Geographica Palaestinae*. Jerusalem: Universitas, 1963 (reprint of 1890 edition).

Roth, Yehuda. "The Achievement of Gottlieb Schumacher." In *Zev Vilnay Jubilee Volume*. Vol.2, edited by Eli Schiller, Jerusalem: Ariel, 1987, pp.347-50 (Hebrew).

Rustum, Asad Jibrail. *Material for Corpus of Arabic Documents Relating to the History of Syria Under Mehmet Ali*. 5 vols. Beirut: American Press, 1930-34 (Arabic).

Schick, [Conrad]. "Studien Über Colonisirung des Heiligen Landes." *Oesterreichische Monatschrift für den Orient* 3 (15 March 1881) :37-38, 60.

Schmavonian [Mr.]. "Citizenship of the United States, Expatriation, Etc., Turkey." 59th Congress, 2nd Session. *Senate Executive Documents* No.326, pp.525-32. Washington : Government Printing Office, 1907.

Schmelz, Uziel O. "The Decline in the Population of Palestine During World War I." In *Siege and Distress, Eretz Israel During the First World War*, edited by Mordechai Eliav, pp.17-47. Jerusalem: Yad Izhak Ben-Zvi, 1991 (Hebrew).

Schumacher, Gottlieb. *Across the Jordan: Being an Exploration and Survey of Part of Hauran and Jaulan*. London: Bentley, 1886.

— *The Jaulân, Survey for the German Society for the Exploration of the Holy Land*. London: Bentley, 1888.

Schur, Nathan. *The Book Of Travellers to the Holy Land: the 19th Century*. Jerusalem: Keter, 1988 (Hebrew).

Schuyler, Eugene. *American Diplomacy and the Furtherance of Commerce.* New York: Scribner's, 1885.

Schwarzfuchs, Shimon. "The Jews of Algeria in Northern Eretz-Israel and French Protection." *Shalem* 3 (1981):333-50 (Hebrew).

Seward, Olive Risley (ed.). *William H. Seward's Travels Around the World.* New York: Appleton, 1873.

Shavit, David. *The United States and the Middle East.* New York: Greenwood, 1988.

Shavit, Ya'acov. "'Land in the Deep Shadow of Wings' and the Redemption of Israel – A Millenarian Document from Jerusalem." *Cathedra* 50 (1988):98-110 (Hebrew).

Shepherd, Naomi. The *Zealous Intruders, The Western Rediscovery of Palestine.* London: Collins, 1987.

Shilony, Zvi. "Changes in the Jewish Leadership of Jerusalem During World War I." *Cathedra* 35 (1985):58-90 (Hebrew).

Smith, George Adam. "Review of Ancient Jerusalem." *Palestine Exploration Fund Quarterly Statement* 40 (1908):332-38.

Smout, T.C. "American Consular Reports on Scotland." *Business History* 23 (1981):304-8.

Sousa, Nasim. *The Capitulatory Regime of Turkey. Its History, Origin, and Nature.* Baltimore: Johns Hopkins Press, 1933.

Spafford-Vester, Bertha. *Our Jerusalem, an American Family in the Holy City, 1881-1949.* Garden City, NY: Doubleday, 1950.

Spiegel, Steven L. *The Other Arab-Israeli Conflict; Making America's Middle East Policy, from Truman to Reagan.* Chicago and London: University of Chicago Press, 1985.

Spyridon, S.N. "Annals of Palestine, 1821-1841." *Journal of the Palestine Oriental Society* 18 (1939):63-132.

Steigman, Andrew L. *The Foreign Service of the United States, First Line of Defense.* Boulder and London: Westview, 1985.

Stephens, John Lloyd. *Incidents of Travel in Egypt, Arabia Petraea, and the Holy Land,* edited by Victor Wolfgang von Hagen. Norman: University of Oklahoma Press, 1970 (reprint of 1837 edition).

Stewart, Laddie J. "Preliminary Inventory of the Records of the Consulate General in Constantinople (Istanbul)." Washington: USNA unpublished paper, 1955.

Stowell, Ellery H. *International Law, A Restatement of Principles in*

Conformity with Actual Practice. New York: Holt, 1931.

Straus, Oscar Solomon. *Under Four Administrations, from Cleveland to Taft.* Boston and New York: Houghton Mifflin, 1922.

Stuart, Graham H. *The Department of State, a History of its Organization, Procedure, and Personnel.* New York: Macmillan, 1949.

Tamse, C.A. "The Netherlands Consular Service and the Dutch Consular Reports of the Nineteenth and Twentieth Centuries." *Business History* 23 (1981):271-76.

Tennenbaum, Mark. "The British Consulate in Jerusalem, 1858-1890." *Cathedra* 5 (1977):83-108 (Hebrew).

Thackeray, William Makepeace. *Notes on a Journey from Cornhill to Grand Cairo.* London: Chapman & Hall, 1846.

Thomson, William M. *The Land and the Book; or, Biblical Illustrations Drawn from the Manners and Customs, the Scenes and Scenery of the Holy Land.* Londo n: Nelso n, 1881. (First edition 1859) .

Tibawi, A.L. *American Interests in Syria, 1800-1901.* Oxford: Oxford University Press, 1966.

Tidhar, David. *Encyclopedia of Pioneers and Builders of the Yishuv, Personalities and Pictures.* 19 vols. Tel Aviv: Sefarim Rishonim, 1947-1973 (Hebrew).

Trumpener, Ulrich. "Germany, and the End of the Ottoman Empire." In *The Great Powers and the End of the Ottoman Empire*, edited by Marian Kent, pp.111-40. London: Allen & Unwin, 1984.

Tsunoyama, Sakae. "Japanese Consular Reports." *Business History* 23 (1981):284-91.

Tuchman, Barbara. *Bible and Sword.* London: Macmillan, 1983 (first edition 1956).

Twain, Mark (Samuel L. Clemens). *The Innocents Abroad, or the New Pilgrims' Progress.* Hartford: American Publishing Co., 1869.

Van Dyck, Edward A. "Report for 1880 on the Capitulations of the Ottoman Empire." 46th Congress, Special Session, *Senate Executive Document* No.3, pp.1-134. Washington: Government Printing Office, 1881.

— "Report on the Capitulations of the Ottoman Empire." 47th Congress, 1st Session, *Senate Executive Document* No.87, pp.1-50. Washington: Government Printing Office, 1882.

Vereté, Mayir. "Why was a British Consulate Established in Jerusalem?" *English Historical Review* 85 (1970):316-45.

Vilnay, Zev. "America's Part in the Study of the Land of Israel." *American Jewry Year Book, 1939*, pp.405-19 (Hebrew).

— "Biblical Names Given to Places in the United States." *Ariel* 13 (1991):65-69 (Hebrew).

Vogel, Lester I. "Zion as Place and Past: An American Myth: Ottoman Palestine in the American Mind Perceived Through Protestant Consciousness and Experience." Ph.D. dissertation, The George Washington University, 1984.

Wallace, Edwin S. *Jerusalem the Holy*. Edinburgh and London: Oliphant, Anderson & Ferrier, 1898.

Wallace, Lewis. *Ben Hur, a Tale of Christ*. New York: Harper, [ca. 1880].

Wallace, Susan E. *Along the Bosphorus and Other Sketches*. Chicago and New York: Rand McNally, 1898.

Weiss, Mordechai Y. *Lilienthal's Family in Jerusalem*. Jerusalem: Weiss, 1947 (Hebrew).

Werking, Richard Hume. *The Master Architects, Building the United States Foreign Service, 1890-1913*. Lexington: University Press of Kentucky, 1977.

— "United States Consular Reports: Evolution and Present Possibilities." *Business History* 23 (1981):300-304.

Who Was Who in America. Chicago: Marquis, 1943.

Wisch, Judy. "Shimon Berman and Mordechai Lubowsky, Experiments of Agricultural Settlement by Individuals in Nineteenth Century Palestine." Seminar paper, The Hebrew University of Jerusalem, 1980 (Hebrew).

Wright, Walter Livingston. "American Relations with Turkey to 1831." Ph.D. dissertation, Princeton University, 1928.

Yaari, Avraham. *The Goodly Heritage*. Jerusalem: Youth and Hechalutz Department of the Zionist Organization, 1958.

Young, John Russell. *Around the World with General Grant: A Narrative of the Visit of General U.S. Grant, Ex-President of the United States, to Various Countries in Europe, Asia and Africa, in 1877, 1878, 1879*. Vol.I. New York: American News Co., 1879.

INDEX